D0221037

Secrets and Leaks

. . . .

Secrets and Leaks

The Dilemma of State Secrecy

Rahul Sagar

PRINCETON UNIVERSITY PRESS *Princeton and Oxford*

Copyright © 2013 by Princeton University Press

Published by Princeton University Press, 41 William Street,

Princeton, New Jersey 08540

In the United Kingdom: Princeton University Press, 6 Oxford Street,

Woodstock, Oxfordshire OX20 1TW

press.princeton.edu

Library of Congress Cataloging-in-Publication Data

Sagar, Rahul.

Secrets and leaks : the dilemma of state secrecy / Rahul Sagar.

pages   cm

Includes bibliographical references and index.

ISBN 978-0-691-14987-5 (hardback)

1. Official secrets. 2. Leaks (Disclosure of information) 3. Whistle blowing—Political aspects.

I. Title.

JF1525.S4S48 2013

352.3'79—dc23

2013007163

British Library Cataloging-in-Publication Data is available

This book has been composed in Minion and Glypha

Printed on acid-free paper. ∞

Printed in the United States of America

10 9 8 7 6 5 4 3 2 1

To these great and glorious United States

For in the order of things it is found that one never seeks to avoid one inconvenience without running into another; but prudence consists in knowing how to recognize the qualities of inconveniences, and in picking the less bad as good.

—MACHIAVELLI, *The Prince*, chap. 21

Contents

· ·

Acknowledgments

· ·

To write a book is to undertake an arduous trek through a beautiful wilderness; the expedition is exhilarating and excruciating in turns. At the end, one is left with a sense of deep gratitude toward the individuals and institutions that have made the enterprise possible.

In this regard the deepest thanks are owed to my teachers: to Veena Sondhi at Mount St. Mary's, who helped me break free; to Stephen Winkley, Martin Priestley, J. D. Shipton, and Peter Cannings who taught me at Uppingham; to James Forder, Sudhir Hazareesingh, David Vines, Andrew Graham, Nandini Gooptu, Stewart Wood, and W.P.S. Sidhu who trained me at Oxford; and to Dennis Thompson, Richard Tuck, Nancy Rosenblum, Pratap Bhanu Mehta, and Devesh Kapur, who guided me at Harvard.

It is no exaggeration to say that studying under Richard and Dennis, who supervised my doctoral education, changed the course of my life. Like so many, I was instantly mesmerized by Richard's boundless knowledge and gentle manner. To him I owe a lasting love for history and the constant feeling that I ought to read more. More immediately, I am deeply grateful for his guidance on the research that prompted this book. I was already indebted to Dennis's scholarship before I arrived at Harvard. Since then the debts have only multiplied. But I am grateful above all else for his professionalism as an adviser and mentor. I share with Dennis's many students the conviction that we have been truly fortunate to work with the model scholar-teacher.

This book is the product of many years of reflection. This reflection could not have been undertaken without support from a number of organizations. At the very top of the list is the Michael and Louisa Von

Clemm Foundation, the product of two remarkable lives. The foundation provided the scholarship that took me to Harvard. Once there, I was fortunate enough to receive fellowships from the C. Douglas Dillon Fund, the Edmond J. Safra Center for the Ethics and Professions, the Program on Justice, Welfare, and Economics, and the Institute for Humane Studies. More recently, I received support from the Mamdouha S. Bobst Center for Peace and Justice and the Tuck Research Fund at Princeton University. In every one of these instances, I was left with a sense of awe at the workings of the philanthropic spirit in America. Truly, a society that gives is owed in turn, and I shall never forget how much I owe this extraordinary country.

The ideas contained in this book were presented at a number of venues, including the Political Theory Workshop, the Edmond J. Safra Center for Ethics and Professions, and the Project on Justice and Welfare (all at Harvard), the Department of Political Science at the National University of Singapore, the School of Social Sciences at Singapore Management University, the Department of Politics at Princeton University, the Department of Government and Politics at the University of Maryland at College Park, the University of Texas at Austin School of Law, and the Political Theory Workshop at Columbia University. At these venues I benefited from questions raised by Andrew Sabl, Eric Beerbohm, Michael Frazer, Arthur Applbaum, Frances Kamm, Vlad Perju, Jane Mansbridge, David Grewal, Daniela Cammack, Terry Nardin, John Donaldson, Steven Ney, Tobias Rettig, Alex Zakaras, Leif Wenar, Stephen Elkin, Sanford Levinson, Nomi Lazar, Benjamin Kleinerman, Eric Posner, Heidi Kitrosser, Robert Chesney, Clement Fatovic, Nadia Urbinati, Turkuler Isiksel, Melissa Schwartzberg, Kevin Elliot, and Douglas Chalmers. I was also very fortunate to have the chance to discuss the ideas contained in this book with Corey Brettschneider, Jeffrey Tulis, Pratap Bhanu Mehta, David Lefkowitz, Diane Snyder, Nannerl Keohane, Matthew Baggetta, Sonali Chakravarti, Dorota Mokrosinska, Sunil Khilnani, Eduard Jordaan, Prasenjit Duara, Kanti Bajpai, and Kim Lane Schepple.

A significant amount of research went into the writing of this book. In this context I received valuable assistance from Chan Ying Xian, Melissa Loewinger, Rhiannon Thomas, Abigail Weiss, Joe Gotoff, Jessie Ye, Grace Ma, and Shirley Wu. I am particularly grateful to Ledina Gocaj, Brian Lipshutz, and Jessica Blake, who proofread countless drafts and offered helpful feedback. I am also deeply indebted to the staff at Firestone Library, who helped locate important research materials.

I know how incredibly fortunate I am to be at Princeton, and to have colleagues who are at once learned and amiable: Stephen Macedo, Charles Beitz, Anna Stilz, Jan-Werner Mueller, Alan Patten, Philip Pettit, Melissa Lane, Maurizio Viroli, Alan Ryan, and George Kateb. Though all of these colleagues have in one way or another helped me think more clearly about the ideas discussed in this book, I want to specially thank Steve, Melissa, Chuck, Jan, and Annie for carefully reading through lengthy drafts. I also owe thanks to Helen Milner and Nolan McCarty for being supportive department chairs.

I am well aware of my good fortune in having this book published by Princeton University Press. I am indebted to Chuck for introducing me to Rob Tempio, and I am deeply grateful to Rob for supporting this project from our first meeting. He has been the ideal editor: patient, warm, supportive, and a source of wise counsel. Thanks are also due to Lauren Lepow for her prompt and expert editorial guidance, and to the anonymous reviewers for their helpful advice and constructive criticism. Needless to say, I am solely responsible for the shortcomings of this book.

I am also deeply grateful to friends and family who brought warmth and cheer into my life over the many months of writing: Matthew Baggetta and Jennifer Brass, Annie Stilz and Hillel Soifer, Joe Perkins, Pramit Chaudhuri and Ayelet Lushkov, Karthik Muralidharan, David Grewal and Daniela Cammack, Siddharth Mohandas, Arunabha Ghosh and Meghana Narayan, Abhishek and Devika Rao, Arjun and Anjali Purkayastha, Kapil and Tamanna Kapoor, Eduard Jordaan and Margaret Dunn, John Donaldson and Qu Li, Janak Nabar and Shirin Wadia, Rahul and Anjali Mukherji, Satish and Anjhula Selvanathan, Shreya Mukherjee, Jake and Roshni Sacks, Nikhil Thakur, Priyanka Dasgupta and Chad Marshall, Karna Basu and Shabnam Faruki, Neeti Nair, Prerna and Bhrigu Singh, Emi Nakamura and Jon Steinsson, Ritu and Dilip Chopra, Adarsh and Sat Dev Sharma, Serena Chopra, Rudrajit Sabhaney, Vidyun Sabhaney, Dominic Twyford, and Isabella Twyford.

My greatest debts are to my family—Una, Prema, Jyoti, Simran, Kitty, Ranjit, Trudi, and Idan—whose love and support have nourished and strengthened me. Above all I am grateful to God for my parents, Jyoti and Prema, and for my wife, Una, who have time and again made sacrifices so that I may study and write in peace. No words can come close to expressing what they mean to me.

Rahul Sagar
Princeton, NJ

Secrets and Leaks

. . . .

Introduction

· ·

Who Watches the Watchers?

Does state secrecy threaten democracy? Although this question has been at the forefront of public debate for more than half a century now, the debate has become especially heated in recent years. The principal factor behind the heightened feelings has been the sense that state secrecy has made it especially difficult for citizens and lawmakers to oversee and bring the president to account for the vigorous exercise of executive power since 9/11. For instance, over the past decade, state secrecy has served to limit public debate on questions such as whether the United States ought to undertake preventive war and utilize practices like extraordinary rendition and targeted killing. It has also hindered members of Congress from knowing about, much less overseeing, the use of secret prisons, extralegal surveillance, and so-called enhanced interrogation techniques. And it has prevented the courts from proceeding with cases brought by citizens and foreigners who have been subjected to warrantless wiretaps, incarceration, and torture by the United States or its allies.

This is not, however, the only reason why state secrecy has been the subject of public debate. There has also been growing concern about violations of state secrecy in the form of unauthorized disclosures of classified information. Perhaps the best-known example is the publication on the WikiLeaks website of a quarter million American diplomatic cables. It has been argued, not unreasonably, that disclosures of this variety threaten the United States' diplomatic capabilities because, if repeated often enough, they will lessen the willingness of local sources to share sensitive information with American diplomats (and also make American diplomats reluctant to share with each other what they have learned through their carefully cultivated networks of informants). No less controversial have been the disclosures that have appeared in leading newspapers such as the *New York Times* and the *Washington Post*, which have revealed details about various covert measures utilized in the so-called war on terror—for example, the surveillance of banking transactions and the monitoring of communications. These disclosures have been condemned on the grounds that they allow the United States' adversaries to understand, and thereby defeat, the sources and methods the U.S. government uses to obtain intelligence about their activities. Such disclosures, it has been argued, spring from a failure to recognize that state secrecy actually furthers the interests of citizens.

What are we to make of these contending claims? Does state secrecy threaten the interests of citizens or does it actually further them? Some might argue that there is no conflict here at all. They might claim that in modern democracies citizens choose representatives rather than policies, and that public sources of information are sufficient to judge policies and performance. But this argument fails to recognize that officials can use secrecy to conceal wrongdoing and to justify policies by claiming to have information that validates their decisions but which cannot be shared with citizens. Consider, for instance, Attorney General Alberto Gonzales's defense of the NSA's warrantless surveillance program:

> Gonzales said the warrantless surveillance has "been extremely helpful in protecting America" from terrorist attacks. However, because the program is highly classified, he said he could not make public examples of how terrorist attacks were actually disrupted by the eavesdropping.[1]

It might be proposed that claims of this kind should always be discounted. But given that there will inevitably be information whose disclosure would in fact harm national security, such skepticism has its limits. Consequently, if secrecy is not to undermine public deliberation and government accountability—practices that are central to most conceptions of democracy—then secrecy must be minimized or citizens must have some reason to believe that information will not be withheld in order to conceal wrongdoing or to manipulate public opinion. A few scholars emphasize the former requirement: democracy they insist requires publicity or transparency. John Dunn, for example, writes that "government seclusion is the most direct and also the deepest subversion of the democratic claim" because the "more governments control what their fellow citizens know the less they can claim the authority of those citizens for how they rule."[2] But claims of this kind have rightly been challenged. As Dennis Thompson has pointed out, democracy does not require "unconditional publicity," because citizens may themselves prefer secrecy when it leads to the execution of worthy policies that cannot otherwise be carried out.[3]

If it is widely accepted in theory and practice that secrecy is desirable so long as it is used to protect national security and not to conceal the abuse of power, then what explains the controversies cited earlier? These controversies might appear to be disagreements over whether secrecy is *really* necessary to protect national security in a given instance (for instance, whether the cables published by WikiLeaks really need to be kept secret in the interests of national security). But the fact that such controversies are so frequent and so heated indicates a deeper problem. Arguably, it speaks to a fundamental disagreement about *who* should ensure that secrecy is being used only for the purposes of furthering national security. That is, should we rely on self-discipline, legislative oversight, judicial arbitration, or media investigations to ensure that information is not being withheld for the wrong reasons? In other words, the question at the heart of the contemporary debate on state secrecy is not about whether or not there should be state secrecy; rather, it is about what sort of regulatory framework will ensure that state secrecy will be used to protect national security and not to conceal the abuse of power. This debate has arisen because many commentators believe that the existing regulatory framework is so deficient that it has allowed practice to diverge far and wide from the norm. Arthur Schlesinger has penned the most widely cited such condemnation. "No one questions the state's right to keep certain things secret," he writes, but the "real function of the secrecy system *in practice* is to protect the executive branch from accountability for its incompetence and its venality, its follies, errors and crimes."[4]

Given that the contemporary debate on state secrecy is not about the legitimacy of state secrecy per se, but rather about ensuring that state secrecy is used only to further national security, it is tempting to conclude that whether state secrecy furthers or threatens our interests ultimately depends on whether we design the corresponding regulatory framework well. If we design the framework well, then there will be no reason to worry that state secrecy poses a threat to democracy, since it will then be used only to further national security. The current scholarship on state secrecy certainly encourages us to think this way. Few, if any, scholars argue that the regulatory framework required to prevent the misuse of state secrecy poses anything like a major normative challenge. I believe this picture is misleading. The error stems from a failure to fully comprehend how difficult it is to design an effective regulatory framework—one that could inspire confidence that state secrecy will not be used to systematically conceal the abuse of power. As I show below, the only credible regulatory mechanism that we have to monitor the use of state secrecy does *not* sit easily with our moral and political values, especially not with key democratic norms.

To see why this is the case, consider the challenge we face when we try to ensure that state secrecy is being used only to further national security. It is widely asserted that we can be confident that the president will not be able to misuse state secrecy only if he is not allowed to have the final say on whether a given piece of classified information should be made public or shared with the other branches of government. Otherwise, there would be little to prevent him from using state secrecy to conceal information that has the potential to embarrass his administration. But to whom, then, should we give the final say? There are powerful institutional reasons to doubt that this responsibility should be vested in the hands of the obvious candidates—namely, Congress or the courts. As far as Congress is concerned, its structure and composition, particularly the fact that it is made up of adversarial parties, make it prone to indisciplined disclosures of classified information, that is, to disclosures contrary to Congress's own rules and orders. The partisan character of congressional politics is the reason why many scholars recommend turning to the courts or to an independent tribunal, either of which, they argue, could supervise the use of state secrecy more impartially than could the president or Congress. But this advice glosses over the fact that judges are not trained, and courts are not equipped, to make politically charged decisions about what uses of state secrecy are appropriate. This is not some trumped-up charge of judicial incompetence; these are the institutional reasons that judges themselves have offered in defense of their long-standing record of deferring to the executive branch's estimation of the harm that might be caused by the disclosure of classified information.

Suppose we are not convinced by these institutional reasons. Perhaps we feel that Congress could overcome the problem of indiscipline, or that the courts or an independent tribunal could master the business of judging national security harm. Even so, there remains another reason to doubt whether vesting the final say in any of these bodies can make us any more confident that state secrecy will not be used to hide wrongdoing. The concern is this: since the decisions of a committee or a bench that supervises the use of state secrecy will not be any more amenable to external scrutiny than the president's decisions are, what is to prevent the members of this committee or bench from behaving in a decidedly narrow fashion—permitting the use of state secrecy to conceal the abuse of power by their copartisans?

One might argue that the decisions of an independent panel or tribunal are likely to be more disinterested than those of Congress. But if a panel or a tribunal were to be routinely involved in the regulation of state secrecy, then could the politicization of appointments be far behind, and with it the loss of the disinterestedness that makes this panel or tribunal such an appealing venue? More to the point, is there such a thing as a nonpartisan view of whether, for example, the use of warrantless surveillance constitutes an abuse of executive power (and that therefore classified documents evidencing the use of such surveillance ought to be made public)? Remarkably, the liberal scholars who champion using the courts, or an "independent" tribunal, to rein in presidents do not seem to consider that the members of such a body could have more in common with Justice Antonin Scalia than with Justice William Brennan. This is not to say that the members of an independent panel or tribunal are bound to act in a narrowly partisan manner. They may very well act disinterestedly or objectively (as far as this is possible). But how are we to know if and when this is the case, that is, whether and when they have been able to resist being swayed by their political affiliations, when their deliberations must be in camera and ex parte? In short, the conceptual problem associated with transferring the final say on the employment of state secrecy from the president to a "secrecy regulator" is that it leaves us with no way of knowing whether this regulator's behavior is any different from the president's. It is therefore not clear why turning to Congress or the courts, or indeed to an "independent" tribunal, should inspire great confidence that state secrecy will not be misused.

So is the goal of this book to argue that there is no way to part the veil of state secrecy, that we can never really know whether state secrecy is being used only to protect national security and not to conceal the abuse of power? To the contrary, the purpose of this book is to focus attention on a remarkable means by which citizens and lawmakers can be—and indeed are—alerted to wrongdoing. I refer here to unauthorized disclosures of classified information, which have become an increasingly common feature of our public life, having grown almost in lockstep with the dramatic transformation in the scope and scale of the president's national security powers. The possibility of unauthorized disclosures provides the most effective and credible guarantee that those who have the formal authority over state secrecy cannot systematically use it to their own advantage. This practice effectively *disperses* rather than *centralizes* the power to disclose classified information. By doing so, it eliminates the problem of "regulatory capture" accompanying any scheme that entrusts the responsibility for supervising state secrecy to a single authority, such as a committee in Congress or a panel or tribunal.

What diminishes the appeal of unauthorized disclosures, though, is the fact that they are not always used to further the interests and values of citizens. At least since Daniel Ellsberg's disclosure of the Pentagon Papers to the *New York Times* in 1971, there has been a sense that, if all else fails, citizens and lawmakers can rely on "insiders" to blow the whistle on wrongdoing that has been shrouded in state secrecy. The reality, though, is that very few officials have an incentive to blow the whistle, because doing so exposes them to bruising professional and social sanctions from managers, supervisors, and colleagues, whose reputations and careers are threatened, directly or indirectly, by their disclosures. As we shall see, there is little that we can do to protect would-be whistleblowers from such sanctions. Though the law does try to prevent supervisors and managers from retaliating against whistleblowers, it cannot easily prevent them from withholding career-enhancing plum positions or choice assignments. Nor indeed can the law compel a whistleblower's colleagues to behave in anything more than a tolerable fashion. It cannot, for instance, prevent them from shunning the whistleblower in social settings.

It should come as no surprise, then, that officials usually make unauthorized disclosures by *leaking* classified information: that is, by divulging it anonymously. This is where the complications begin to arise. There is a tendency for scholars to view the practice of leaking as a form of civil disobedience, a morally justified act of resistance to the wrongful use of political power. But this claim is highly problematic. When an official discloses classified information anonymously, citizens and lawmakers have little ability to discern his motives, much less to punish a harmful or misguided disclosure. Of course it is possible for an anonymous disclosure to reveal such severe wrongdoing that the identity and motives of the discloser are rendered irrelevant. In practice, though, relatively few leaks reveal activities that are so wrongful as to invite widespread condemnation. Consequently, anonymity allows an official to disclose classified information and then leave the public to pick up the pieces in the event that his disclosure eventually proves to be unwarranted. Worse yet, anonymity allows officials to make unauthorized disclosures that are actually intended to further narrow or partisan interests. These practices are at odds with the theory of civil disobedience, not to mention the democratic norms of publicity and accountability.

The realization that the practice of leaking is itself prone to grave abuse puts us in a difficult position. If we prohibit the publication of leaks of classified information, we stand to lose the most effective and credible means by which we can be alerted to wrongdoing that occurs under cover of secrecy. But if we permit the publication of such leaks, then we risk contaminating our public life with conspiracy and covert warfare, as not only good men and women but also partisans and zealots take advantage of anonymity to disclose information that suits their narrow purposes. Remarkably, the advocates of the press generally fail to acknowledge the existence of this dilemma. On the contrary, they claim that the press can be trusted to act in the public interest, and that it should therefore be allowed to decide what classified information ought to be made public. But this is a remarkable conceit. Why should we believe that the press will always act in the public interest, especially when its role as information broker is shrouded in secrecy, thus preventing the public from ascertaining the motives and the precise actions of reporters, editors, and publishers, not to mention their sources? It is not clear why champions of the First Amendment, who refuse to believe that the president or Congress ought to be trusted to use state secrecy in the public interest, are so willing to trust reporters, editors, and publishers to use anonymity in the public interest. This blind faith appears to be a legacy of the fierce political battles of the 1970s, a time when reporters and publishers determined, albeit not without some hesitation, that they best served their own interests by playing the watchdog role cast for them by the First Amendment.[5] This experience seems to have left many scholars and commentators with a lasting impression of the press as a heroic institution, perennially on the hunt for the abuse of power, in the fashion of *All the President's Men*. Whatever the precise reason for this one-sided view of the press, it is increasingly undermined by the facts. In recent decades, it has become ever more apparent that not only insiders, but also reporters, editors, and publishers, have learned to exploit leaks of classified information to their own advantage, whether to pursue vendettas, manipulate public opinion, obtain prizes, or earn profits.

The fact that leaks of classified information can be used both for good (to sound the alarm) and for ill (to pursue a narrow or partisan agenda) has a serious implication for democracy. It implies that our collective fate depends in no small measure on the outcome of battles fought out of public sight: it is the contest of morals and interests under the cloak of anonymity that determines whether state secrecy is used to protect or to manipulate the public. If so, the existence of state secrecy poses a great quandary for the American people, and indeed for all peoples that wish to live according to the norms of democracy. The quandary is this: we cannot do without state secrecy, as it is essential for national security, but so long as there is state secrecy, our ability to guard against its misuse depends not so much on the checks and balances established by the Constitution as on the virtues and vices of those men and women who secretly take the law into their own hands in order to either open our eyes or close our minds.

Clarifications

Before I outline the forthcoming chapters, a few clarifications are in order. The first concerns the scope of the study. Its focus is state secrecy: secrecy motivated by a concern for national security. It will not address civil forms of secrecy. This latter form of secrecy, which is utilized by a range of public and private institutions including Congress, the Supreme Court, and the Federal Reserve, involves concealing deliberations or decisions in order to promote objectives such as fairness, candor, and efficiency.[6] This form of secrecy raises fascinating moral and political questions of its own, but I will not be examining it here.[7]

Let me also preempt concerns about the scope of the conclusions drawn here. The evidence cited in this book is drawn almost entirely from the United States. I have focused on the United States because its extensive military and diplomatic commitments sharply elevate the demand for state secrecy—and hence the challenge of regulation. This focus might lead to the charge that the prognosis offered here is not generalizable, because it is based on an extreme case. In other words, it might be argued that state secrecy is an American problem rather than a problem in political theory more generally. I reject this charge. Although citizens and lawmakers in other democracies, especially in Europe, may be relatively less troubled by state secrecy, this difference should not be attributed to cultural or institutional variation but to the relatively modest role these countries currently play in world affairs. I have no doubt that if and when these democracies find themselves in a context that stimulates the vigorous use of executive power, they will be forced to confront the very same questions we shall be examining, namely, how best to regulate state secrecy.

The validity of the conclusions drawn here might also be challenged on the grounds that the remarkable growth in state secrecy since 9/11, and the press's role in monitoring it, are mere aberrations. These developments, it may be argued, are the product of the personalities and circumstances that have dominated American politics over the past decade, specifically President George W. Bush and his colleagues Vice President Richard Cheney and Defense Secretary Donald Rumsfeld, who, it is alleged, had a unique proclivity for secrecy.[8] But this claim is not borne out by the evidence. If President Bush and his colleagues were indeed unique in this respect, then public anxiety about state secrecy ought to have died down following their departure. But that is not has what happened. Though candidate Barack Obama roundly criticized the "excessive" secrecy of the Bush administration, the Obama administration has itself been strongly condemned for its use of the "state secrets privilege," for expanding the use of covert drone strikes, and for clamping down harder than ever before on the unauthorized disclosure of classified information.[9] This record suggests that public anxiety about state secrecy cannot be attributed solely (or even substantially) to the proclivities of a particular administration.

It is also tempting to take the view that the weakening of Al-Qaeda and the United States' impending withdrawal from Iraq and Afghanistan will lessen the need for secretive executive action, and thereby ease the burden of regulating state secrecy. But this view seems shortsighted. Arguably, the need for boldness and discretion is linked to the United States' involvement in world affairs. So long as the United States continues to play a leading role in the international system, it will undoubtedly continue to encounter the sorts of tensions and crises that will compel or allow presidents to act energetically under cover of secrecy. Indeed, even before the ink has dried on the order to wind down in Iraq and Afghanistan, the Obama administration has announced that it will refocus the military on the Asia-Pacific region, a move that portends prolonged tensions with China.[10] Meanwhile, there are, at the time of writing, news reports about the possibility of preemptive strikes on Iran, based on secret intelligence about its nuclear weapons program.[11] Other developments along the same lines, including continuing instability in the Middle East, suggest that the need for state secrecy and corresponding concerns about the abuse of this power are not likely to die down anytime soon.

Finally, it may be objected that the conclusions reached here are unimportant because the underlying arguments are applicable only in rare cases. For example, the claim that judges ought not to conduct penetrating review of state secrecy owing to their limited expertise in the field of national security is likeliest to hold true when courts are asked to make complex prudential judgments—for instance, whether disclosing an outdated nuclear blueprint will help a foreign country build a more refined nuclear weapon. This claim is less likely to hold true when an inventor seeks the court's help to obtain access to blueprints of a military weapon that he himself has designed. In the latter case, one might think, it would be entirely fitting for a judge to seriously question whether secrecy is warranted.

No doubt the conclusion reached here—that it is very difficult to design a regulatory scheme that is effective, credible, and legitimate—holds truer in cases of the former variety. As we shall see in chapters 4–6, there can be little objection to judges (or lawmakers and editors) countermanding patently abusive or foolish classification orders. But it is far from clear that most controversies concerning the exercise of state secrecy are of this kind. Certainly, the leading controversies—such as Iran-Contra or the Iraq War—have not been open-and-shut cases. Besides, given how high the stakes have been in these cases, improving our understanding of the pitfalls associated with regulating state secrecy seems important even if complex cases turn out to be rarer than we realize.

The Plan

Having outlined the broad argument, and preempted some common objections, I want to sketch out the contributions of the individual chapters. Our point of departure in chapter 1 is the observation that many commentators believe that state secrecy is commonly abused in contemporary America. This observation raises the question of how the Constitution, otherwise revered for establishing checks and balances, could have allowed the president a free hand when it comes to state secrecy. As we shall see, a number of scholars argue that the Framers never intended this outcome. The president, they claim, has come to exercise state secrecy as he alone sees fit, because war and conflict have prompted deference from lawmakers and judges and unquestioning loyalty from citizens. The real and apparent abuses of state secrecy are due, they argue, not to flaws in the Constitution but rather to a lack of courage and wisdom on the part of representatives and citizens.

Chapter 1 challenges this explanation. It argues that the Framers viewed state secrecy as an essential element of statecraft, and that they vested the authority to keep secrets in the executive because they saw it as best suited to exercise this power. Of course the Framers were not oblivious to the possibility that this authority could be abused. They identified three means of countering its abuse: elections, the separation of powers, and unauthorized disclosures. The problem, however, is that the Framers did not elaborate how these checks and balances can operate when the president has the right to keep secrets (and the ability to enforce this right). This silence, as we shall see, means that the Framers bequeathed future generations three puzzles: First, how can citizens hold the president accountable for the use of secrecy, since the president gets to decide when, if ever, to disclose secret information to the public? Second, how can lawmakers oversee the use of state secrecy, since the executive gets to decide when, if ever, to disclose secret information to Congress? Third, under what circumstances, if any, are subordinate officials entitled to disclose secret information that reveals wrongdoing?

The Framers' silence, as we will see, did not produce lasting crises of confidence in the nineteenth century because the dearth of foreign entanglements afforded presidents little reason or opportunity to employ state secrecy extensively. However, once the United States immersed itself in international politics after the turn of the twentieth century, the concomitant increase in the scope and scale of state secrecy made the Framers' silence impossible to ignore. Following real and perceived abuses of state secrecy, concerted efforts were made to counter the president's stranglehold over the flow of secret information. But these efforts, we will see, have now arrived at an impasse. The regulatory mechanisms that have been championed in recent decades—the judicial enforcement of the Freedom of Information Act and the establishment of congressional oversight committees in particular—have proven ineffective at exposing wrongdoing. Meanwhile, the regulatory mechanisms that have proven effective at exposing wrongdoing—the practices of whistleblowing and leaking—are condemned as unlawful or undemocratic and therefore illegitimate. In sum, the regulatory mechanisms that are being used to counter the president's stranglehold over secret information are widely seen as either ineffectual or undesirable.

This impasse, I conclude in chapter 1, suggests that the president's continuing monopoly of state secrecy cannot be attributed to the docility of lawmakers and judges, and the gullibility of citizens. It should be attributed instead to the intractability of the puzzles we have inherited from the Framers: the difficulty of constructing a regulatory authority to oversee state secrecy that is at once effective, credible, and legitimate. If we wish to subject the exercise of state secrecy to checks and balances, then we must examine whether it is possible to bolster the effectiveness of judicial review and legislative oversight, and to defend the legitimacy of whistleblowing and leaking.

Chapter 2 takes up the first part of the challenge laid down in chapter 1. It examines whether the judicial review of state secrecy has in fact been deferential, and, if so, whether such deference can be justified. After surveying the evidence, I conclude that the courts have indeed adopted a deferential posture toward the executive's claims about the harm likely to be caused by the disclosure of classified information, even in instances where the classified information appears innocuous. The question then becomes whether the judiciary ought to shed this posture. As we shall see, some scholars argue that judicial review of classification decisions ought to be expanded so that citizens can be confident that information is not being wrongly concealed from them. I challenge this view on two grounds. First, I make the case that judges are not qualified to challenge the executive's claims about the harm likely to be caused by the disclosure of secret information. Second, I contend that requiring judges to make what are effectively subjective judgments about the costs and benefits of disclosure will merely encourage the politicization of the relevant benches and thereby defeat the whole purpose of turning to the courts, which is to have an impartial regulator.

Given these objections, I devote the latter part of chapter 2 to evaluating whether judges can instead make state secrecy less opaque by requiring executive officers to justify why the information in their possession cannot be made public. I argue that while this strategy appears to ease the epistemic burden placed on judges, it is conceivable that offering reasons as to why a secret ought to remain a secret can itself harm national security. It is not surprising, then, that judges prefer to treat secrecy claims as justified so long as they satisfy narrow procedural guidelines.

In spite of rejecting the idea that we can—or should—expect judges to take the lead in overseeing state secrecy, I conclude chapter 2 on a somewhat positive note. I note that judicial deference can be—and often is—set aside once unauthorized disclosures of classified information give judges reason to challenge executive branch claims about the harm likely to be caused by disclosure. The question that remains to be resolved, though, is whether we ought to condone such disclosures, seeing as the law vests control over classified information in the hands of the president.

In chapter 3 I examine why Congress typically struggles to stay abreast of the president's covert actions and policies. The principal challenge that Congress faces in its endeavor to oversee the exercise of state secrecy, I note, is that the executive does not believe that it is obliged to comply with Congress's requests for information. A number of scholars have argued that such invocations of an "executive privilege" to withhold information do not pose a serious obstacle to oversight because Congress can use its wide-ranging constitutional powers to compel the president to part with the information needed to perform oversight. But this claim, I argue, is problematic because absent some initial hint of wrongdoing, Congress will be hard-pressed to know whether and when it ought to enter into combat with the president. Hence, if we wish to bolster the effectiveness of oversight, we must strip the president of his privilege to withhold information so that Congress can have independent and timely access to classified information. But such a drastic move, I contend, is unwise for two reasons. First, it is sensible to vest control over national security information in the hands of the president because Congress's structure and composition mean that its members are more prone to making indisciplined disclosures. Second, transferring the final say over the disclosure of classified information to a special committee in Congress or to an independent panel ultimately provides little comfort, because citizens have no way of ascertaining whether the members of this bench or panel have been "captured" by vested or partisan interests, since their decisions to withhold or to selectively reveal information will not be open to external review.

In spite of rejecting the idea that we can—or should—expect lawmakers to take the lead in overseeing state secrecy, chapter 3 concludes in a hopeful vein. I note that while executive privilege would appear to make it difficult for Congress to oversee the president, Congress is actually able to obtain crucial hints of wrongdoing quite easily, owing to unauthorized disclosures from the executive branch. What remains to be seen, though, is whether Congress's dependence on such disclosures is acceptable, since these disclosures violate criminal and civil laws enacted by Congress itself.

Having seen the complications that arise when we try to invigorate judicial review and legislative oversight, as well as the extent to which judges and lawmakers depend on unauthorized disclosures to alert them to potential wrongdoing, I then turn in chapter 4 to examine whether the law ought to condone unauthorized disclosures. I begin by clarifying what the law has to say about unauthorized disclosures of classified information. I show that, contrary to common belief, the law is not favorably disposed toward the most important link in the transmission chain, namely, the official responsible for making the unauthorized disclosure. Following this, I ask whether the law ought to be revised to take account of the fact that unauthorized disclosures can allow lawmakers and citizens to become aware of misconduct that would otherwise be shielded by state secrecy. I argue that, for two reasons, the law should *not* be revised: first, because neither officials nor the reporters, editors, and publishers who transmit their disclosures can reliably know the extent to which an unauthorized disclosure will harm national security; and second, because neither officials nor reporters, editors, and publishers can readily claim to be acting on behalf of citizens, since they are unelected and also cannot be easily held accountable for irresponsible disclosures. At the same time, however, I point out that even though the law is right to forbid unauthorized disclosures, this does not rule out the possibility that officials could be morally justified in disobeying the law in order to bring incriminating information to the attention of citizens and lawmakers.

Chapter 5 then considers the circumstances under which an official will be justified in violating laws that prohibit unauthorized disclosures. Here I argue that an official may "blow the whistle" if he encounters classified information that clearly reveals wrongdoing posing an immediate and serious threat to the public interest, and if he makes a good faith effort to minimize the harm that the publication of this information may cause national security. I also argue that the official must identify himself so that we can examine whether his view of what constitutes a wrongful exercise of executive power is a disinterested one. Unfortunately, the last requirement, as we shall see, gravely complicates matters. A would-be whistleblower has little incentive to disclose her identity, because doing so makes her vulnerable to retaliation from her managers and colleagues, who are likely to take a dim view of the negative publicity resulting from her disclosures. There is, I will argue, little we can do to ameliorate this situation, for even if we were to enact a law to shield whistleblowers from outright harassment, we will not be able to protect them against subtler forms of administrative and social retaliation. Nor, I will argue, can we hope that officials will routinely blow the whistle in spite of the threat of retaliation, because the uncompromising attitude required to spur such defiant behavior is hard to instill, and can easily shade into an imprudent moral absolutism.

Having established that we cannot rely on the practice of whistleblowing to counter the misuse of state secrecy, I then turn to examine whether there is a more practical means by which officials could alert citizens and lawmakers to wrongdoing. Chapter 6 argues that the practice of leaking meets this requirement. In particular, I show that officials are able to disclose classified information anonymously, because they recognize that presidents are often hard-pressed to identify the responsible party. But I also draw attention to the fact that officials can—and do—make anonymous disclosures to advance narrow or partisan agendas by revealing classified information that casts their actions (or those of their adversaries) in a favorable (or unfavorable) light. In light of this danger, the latter half of chapter 6 considers whether we might be able to utilize reporters, editors, and publishers—who are the likeliest to know the identity, and thereby the motives, of their sources—to help us detect when anonymity is being used to advance narrow or partisan interests. I conclude that reporters, editors, and publishers cannot be relied upon to act as filters in the public interest, and that the means by which we can compel them to take up this responsibility are severely limited by a variety of constitutional and practical factors, including the First Amendment's constraints on press regulation, and our inability to regulate foreign media outlets.

The arguments outlined above lead to a bittersweet conclusion. Since officials can disclose classified information without being detected, and reporters, editors, and publishers can publicize such information without being regulated, there will inevitably be leaks of classified information. This outcome is to be welcomed, I argue, insofar as it means that it is very difficult for any president to use state secrecy to systematically conceal the abuse of power. However, this outcome is to be bemoaned insofar as unwarranted or malicious leaks of classified information undermine energetic leadership as well as public deliberation and democratic accountability. There is, in other words, no neat answer to the puzzles we have inherited from the Framers. It really is very difficult to construct a regulatory framework that is efficient, credible, and legitimate.

Given this less than ideal outcome, I devote the concluding chapter to outlining some of the means by which we might minimize the downsides of our dependence on unauthorized disclosures. The president, I note, can try to stem unauthorized disclosures by acting in ways that will encourage his subordinates to defer to his decisions about what to keep secret, and media critics can try to foster responsible journalism by subjecting anonymously sourced reports to critical review. But these measures, I warn, can go only so far. The president will not always be able to take everyone along when morally or politically controversial decisions need to be made, and even the threat of public censure will not always deter officials, reporters, editors, and publishers from making selective disclosures in order to promote their own agendas. This in turn means that the "unruly contest" between the president and the press, which causes so much heartburn in our day, is here to stay. The wisest course, I conclude, is to reconcile ourselves to the attendant disadvantages, because there is, at present, no better way to regulate the exercise of state secrecy.

Chapter 1

· ·

The Problem

How to Regulate State Secrecy?

In the introduction we noted that there is broad agreement that state secrecy is justified so long as it is used to protect national security and not to conceal wrongdoing. However, there is also broad agreement that in practice state secrecy has become the "all-purpose means" by which the presidency has "sought to dissemble its purposes, bury its mistakes, manipulate its citizens and maximize its power."[1] Assuming this complaint is at least partially correct, it raises the question of why it has proven so difficult to regulate the employment of state secrecy. Why, in other words, has practice been able to diverge so far from principle?

The leading explanation places the blame on fairly recent developments. The presidency, Arthur Schlesinger argues, is responsible for transforming the "legitimate system of restriction" established by the Framers "into an extravagant and indefensible system of denial." Because those who receive "prestige and protection" from secrecy control the classification system, he writes, concealment has "overridden its legitimate objectives."[2] There is, however, something puzzling about this claim. How can the Constitution, otherwise revered for establishing checks and balances, have allowed the president a free hand when it comes to state secrecy? The culprits, according to Schlesinger, have been war and conflict, which have prompted deference from lawmakers and judges, and "unquestioning" loyalty from citizens, thereby ensuring that "the only control over the secrecy system" has come to be "exercised by the executive branch itself."[3]

But this explanation only deepens the mystery. Did the Framers not foresee that war and conflict might open the door to extensive government secrecy? A number of scholars believe not. The Framers, they maintain, intended to construct a political system where secrecy would be a rare and short-lived exception rather than an enduring presence. This claim was first pressed by an earlier generation of scholars, including Schlesinger, Henry Steele Commager, Raoul Berger, and Daniel Hoffman, who took the view that the Framers supported the "principle of disclosure."[4] And it has since been reiterated by, among others, Geoffrey Stone, Robert Pallitto and William Weaver, David Pozen, and Heidi Kitrosser, who have declared that the Constitution is premised on a "philosophy of openness."[5]

The claim that the Framers expected state secrecy to be the exception rather than the norm in American government has rightly been challenged in recent years.[6] Abraham Sofaer, Mark Rozell, Stephen Knott, and Gabriel Schoenfeld, among others, have marshaled evidence showing that early administrations, which were led by prominent Framers, readily utilized covert action and withheld information from citizens and lawmakers. Even so, because these scholars have not examined in detail the examples and ideas that influenced the Framers, they have somewhat understated the case that can be made against the prevailing view. I cannot address this lacuna at length here, but even a brief overview of the broader intellectual and historical context will show that the Framers cannot be understood to have supported "the principle of disclosure" or "a philosophy of openness."

There are, then, at least three reasons to be skeptical about the view that the Framers were leery of state secrecy. In the first place, we should bear in mind that the Framers undoubtedly knew that prior republics had readily employed secrecy. Though neither Athens nor Rome developed an infrastructure or corps dedicated to the collection and protection of secret intelligence, the Framers would have learned from the classical sources they knew well that the Athenians and Romans had utilized an array of sources and methods to obtain intelligence on an ad hoc basis, and that their leaders had made frequent, if often private, efforts to obtain secret intelligence when this was necessary and feasible.[7]

The Framers' consideration of the history of modern republics would only have sharpened this understanding. The experience of the English Commonwealth would have been especially telling in this regard. In the century preceding the English Civil War, the business of intelligence in England had been transformed by the emergence of a new breed of officials who came to occupy the office of principal secretary.[8] The men who filled this office—Thomas Cromwell, William Cecil, and Francis Walsingham—were renowned for their "peculiar knowledge" of "dangers both abroad and at home," which they obtained by building an effective, far-reaching, and secretive "intelligence system" consisting of clerks, translators, archivists, code-breakers, forgers, and messengers, through whom the principal secretaries controlled a "shifting legion of freelancers" and dozens of foreign "correspondents."[9] Did a sense of republican propriety lead the officers of the English Commonwealth to spurn the methods and practices utilized by the principal secretaries? Far from it. These officials readily followed their Tudor and Stuart forerunners in cultivating a far-flung network of spies and correspondents.[10] Indeed, they went further, secretly coordinating the publication of propaganda and institutionalizing the covert interception of mail.[11] The same holds true after the Glorious Revolution. Over the course of the eighteenth century, the executive in England (increasingly the prime minister rather than the monarch) immersed itself ever deeper in the business of intelligence, as can be discerned from the steady growth of public funding on this front. Under James I and Charles I, the funds made available to the secretaries of state under this head had been seven hundred pounds each; by 1786, the budget for intelligence was twenty-five thousand pounds.[12] These resources were used to cement the precedents established in the sixteenth and seventeenth centuries—as the Framers experienced firsthand during the Revolutionary War.[13]

A second reason to be skeptical about the claim that the Framers were wary of state secrecy is that many of the republican theorists they were familiar with endorsed it as valuable.[14] Recall that the first major step toward the institutionalization of secret intelligence had actually been taken in the republican city-states of Renaissance Italy. Having discerned the value of information in navigating the treacherous world they inhabited, these city-states were among the first to post ambassadors abroad.[15] As the primary mission of an ambassador was to communicate back to the chancery whatever intelligence he could obtain, the emergent enterprise of modern diplomacy naturally prompted calls for discretion, most notably in Francesco Guicciardini's *Dialogue on the Government of Florence*; there it is asserted that informants are more likely to cooperate with a "closed regime" than an "open regime," because no one "wants to reveal a hidden secret" in a place where "it will no sooner be said than publicized."[16]

Even more striking are the claims put forward in the aftermath of the English Civil War. Confronted with the charge that representative assemblies (such as Parliament) were prone to indiscretion, the defenders of the English Commonwealth replied that these bodies could—and indeed should—maintain secrecy by delegating sensitive business to smaller bodies appointed by the people's representatives. Thus we find James Harrington recommending in *The Commonwealth of Oceana* that those affairs that must be conducted in secrecy "for the good of the commonwealth" should be entrusted to a "Council of War."[17] Similarly, Marchamont Nedham argues in *The Excellencie of a Free State* that the "prudence, time, and experience" required to manage "secrets of state" are best obtained by entrusting such matters to an executive council.[18] John Milton, too, recommends in *The Ready and Easy Way to Establish a Free Commonwealth* the establishment of a "Council of State" for the purposes of "carrying on some particular affairs with more secrecy and expedition."[19]

The utility of state secrecy is appreciated in eighteenth-century republican literature as well. For instance, in *A Short Introduction to Moral Philosophy* Francis Hutcheson describes "secret and speedy execution" as one of the four points "to be aimed at" in constituting an ideal polity.[20] Meanwhile, David Hume argues in his "Idea of a Perfect Commonwealth" that the executive ought to be made "absolute" in the sphere of foreign affairs because "otherwise there could be no secrecy or refined policy."[21] Richard Price, that influential friend of the American revolutionaries, writes in his *Additional Observations on the Nature and Value of Civil Liberty* that what distinguished a free government from an ideal one was that the latter joined to the liberty enjoyed by the former the "dispatch, secrecy, and vigour" required to successfully execute the "will of the community."[22] And citing "the disclosure of public counsels and designs" as one of the "evils" of democracy, William Paley warns in *The Principles of Moral and Political Philosophy* that a well-ordered regime ought to guard against the sort of "officious and inquisitive interference with the executive functions" that would lead to the disclosure of "what it is expedient to conceal."[23]

Now, to be sure, there were, from the sixteenth century onward, a number of republican theorists who were troubled by state secrecy, especially after the Renaissance had shown it to be one of the foremost elements of *arcana imperii* (mysteries of state)—that body of stratagems by which rulers could maintain their rule over their unwitting subjects.[24] This was a point that one of the Commonwealth's fiercest critics, Clement Walker, stressed when he charged that Charles I had been replaced not by a republican regime, but by "forty tyrants" (the number of members in the Commonwealth's Council of State), who were "dispatching all affairs privately and in the dark, whereas Justice delights in the light, and ought to be as public as the common air."[25] But the defenders of the English Commonwealth had a simple answer to this objection: secrecy, they argued, was necessary, and had been seen as such in Greece, Rome, and Florence too.[26] Note also that later republican critiques of state secrecy, such as Algernon Sidney's famous riposte against *arcana imperii* in his *Discourses Concerning Government*, written just prior to the Glorious Revolution, were directed at the exercise of secrecy by absolute monarchs rather than republican magistrates. Indeed it would be strange if Sidney thought a republic ought to eschew secrecy, since in his view "the best Government" is that "which best provides for War."[27]

Certainly, not everyone was convinced by the argument from necessity. Over the long eighteenth century—a time of intricate diplomatic maneuvering and incessant war—the notion that state secrecy posed a standing threat to the public interest found subscribers. The most striking critique in this vein is Jeremy Bentham's "A Plan for an Universal and Perpetual Peace," wherein Bentham depicts the elimination of state secrecy as a prerequisite to the achievement of peace. "Between the interests of nations," he writes, "there is nowhere any real conflict," and where such conflicts appear, he argues, they can be traced to deliberate or inadvertent misunderstandings fostered by state secrecy.[28] Therefore, "if we think peace better than war," he writes, then secrecy "can not be too soon abolished."[29] Bentham was not the only one to think this way; this was a view shared by a diverse set of theorists, including the abbé de Saint-Pierre, Pierre-André Gargaz, the marquis de Condorcet, Immanuel Kant, and Jean-Jacques Rousseau. Though these writers did not discuss state secrecy at length, their various "peace plans," which sought to replace diplomacy and intrigue with orderly international confederations, favored openness. Note, however, that prominent Framers explicitly rejected such proposals as impractical.[30]

The third reason to doubt that the Framers were leery of state secrecy is that there is evidence to show that they viewed it as an essential element of statecraft.[31] Certainly, a number of important texts from the Revolutionary period underscored the importance of state secrecy. John Adams's "Thoughts on Government," for instance, described secrecy as one of the properties "essential" to the exercise of executive power.[32] In "The Genuine Principles of the Ancient Saxon or English Constitution," a radical Whig writing under the name Demophilus observed that even the best government would be short-lived unless it provided for its self-defense that "dangerous, but necessary engine of state, a standing army, whose operations must be conducted with all possible secrecy and dispatch."[33] And Theophilus Parsons's remarkable report, "The Essex Result," warned that "want of secrecy may prevent the successful execution of any measures, however excellently formed and digested."[34]

That the leaders of the Revolution appreciated state secrecy is evidenced most clearly, though, by the measures they introduced to preserve the confidentiality of proceedings in the Second Continental Congress, and by their use of covert action under the auspices of the Committee of Secret Correspondence, which was made responsible for an array of intelligence functions, including espionage, covert operations, and postal interception—activities that, in the words of the participants, called for "great circumspection and impenetrable secrecy."[35] Notably, these measures remained in place even after the Revolutionary War had drawn to a close.[36] Another important piece of evidence in favor of a wider political consensus on the value of secrecy is provided by the adoption of Article IX of the Articles of Confederation, authorizing Congress to withhold from publication those proceedings "relating to treaties, alliances or military operations, as in their judgement require secrecy."[37] Though the states proposed a number of changes to the Articles of Confederation prior to the document's eventual ratification, they did not challenge this provision. Nor, for that matter, did they try to amend this provision once their delegates to Congress pleaded an inability to share information that Congress had recorded in its Secret Journal.

That the Framers appreciated the value of state secrecy becomes only clearer as we consider the period leading up to the Constitutional Convention. Far from viewing Congress's extensive use of secrecy with alarm, the Framers appear to have drawn from the Revolution and its aftermath the lesson that the country needed a political system capable of ensuring rather than reducing secrecy. This is evident in George Washington's correspondence with James Madison in March 1787. Welcoming the decision to meet in Philadelphia, Washington averred that "a thorough reform of the present system is indispensable" because it lacked, among other things, the "secrecy and dispatch . . . characteristic of good government."[38] This was not the first time Washington had expressed such a view. In a letter to Henry Knox, written a month earlier, he emphasized that a central failing of the Continental Congress was that it was "defective in that secrecy, which, for the accomplishment of many of the most important national objects, is indispensably necessary."[39]

Why did the men who were to draft the Constitution consider secrecy "characteristic of good government"? One must appreciate that these men saw international politics as a ruthless business. They accepted, as John Jay would write in *The Federalist* No. 4, that "nations in general will make war whenever they have a prospect of getting anything by it."[40] At the same time, they were unwilling to rely on leagues or alliances as a principal means of securing peace. The fragility of the "triple and quadruple alliances" that had recently been formed in Europe had taught them, Alexander Hamilton would write in *The Federalist* No. 15, "how little dependence is to be placed on treaties which have no other sanction than the obligations of good faith."[41] This belief was one of the principal reasons why the leading men of the day were votaries of a powerful national government. "If a federal constitution could chain the ambition, or set the bounds to the exertions of all other nations," Madison would argue in *The Federalist* No. 41, "then indeed might it prudently chain the discretion of its own government, and set bounds to the exertions for its own safety." But, in the absence of such sureties, said Madison, "with what color of propriety could the force necessary for defence, be limited by those who cannot limit the force of offence?"[42] At the same time, the Framers noted that power, though necessary, was not sufficient for the end that they had in mind. The security and stability of the nation, they observed, depended in no small measure on *how* power was exercised. In particular, they agreed that a government ought to display "energy"—that is, "decision, activity, secrecy, and dispatch."[43]

None of what has been said so far should be seen as implying that late eighteenth-century Americans were unquestioning proponents of state secrecy. On the contrary, they were well aware of the accompanying danger. For example, having acknowledged that the preservation of society required an executive capable of "secrecy and expedition" and that "expedition, secrecy, and dispatch" are present only when execution is undertaken by "one or a small number of persons," Parsons warned in "The Essex Result" that "from a single person, or very small number, we are not to expect that political honesty, and upright regard to the interest of the body of the people, and the civil rights of each individual, which are essential to a good and free constitution."[44] "For these properties," he wrote, "we are to go to the body of the people," who "have always a disposition to promote their own happiness."[45]

Consider as well what Zabdiel Adams, cousin to both John Adams and Samuel Adams, had to say in his "Election Sermon" before the General Court of Massachusetts in May 1782. Speaking in the wake of controversy over Congress's recommendation that the states impose a 5 percent duty on imports in order to rescue the finances of the United States, Adams observed that "there is a maxim often mentioned of late, that there should be no mysteries in government." But this maxim, Adams pointed out, could not always be followed because "necessities of the state sometimes require great secrecy"; "the most important expedition or negotiation might otherwise fail." Nonetheless, "where secrecy is not essential," he continued, "there the authority ought to make known the necessity of their measures." For "if taxes are heavy, and people know not to what uses they are applied," Adams warned, then "they conclude that they are swallowed up in a manner not beneficial to the public."[46]

The concern that secrecy could obscure abuses of power was voiced most clearly, though, during the debates over the Constitution, particularly with respect to Article I, Section 5, Clause 3, which permits Congress to withhold the publication of those parts of their journals of proceedings that "may in their Judgment require Secrecy."[47] Every time such objections were raised, however, the supporters of the Constitution firmly responded that decisions about what information should be concealed ought to be left to officials. In Pennsylvania, for example, James Wilson acknowledged that "some gentlemen" were worried that the Senate and the president might commit the United States to treaties enacted in secret. Confessing that he, too, was "not an advocate for secrecy in transactions relating to the public; not generally even in forming treaties," Wilson declared that upon reflection he had been compelled to accept that it would "be extremely improper" to publish treaties when "secrecy may be necessary."[48] A month later the same concern was voiced in North Carolina. John Steele admitted there that "he had heard objections" to the provision allowing Congress to exercise secrecy, but he joined with William Davie and James Iredell in emphasizing that "every principle of prudence and good policy pointed out the necessity of not publishing such transactions as related to military arrangements and war."[49] In Massachusetts, William Widgery, a county lawyer who had declared earlier in the proceedings that rulers "ought never to have a power they could abuse," informed his fellow delegates that the words "excepting such parts as may in their judgment require secrecy" implied that "Congress might withhold the whole journals under this pretence, and thereby the people be kept in ignorance of their doings." This assertion provoked a curt response from Nathaniel Gorham, who informed Widgery that "many things in great bodies are to be kept secret, and records must be brought to maturity before [being] published." "Would it be policy," he asked, "to inform the world of the extent of the powers to be vested in our ambassador, and thus give our enemies [an] opportunity to defeat our negotiations?"[50]

The most revealing debate of all occurred in Virginia, where Patrick Henry informed his fellow delegates that his "greatest objection" to the Constitution was that it undermined "true responsibility" because it allowed Congress "not to publish what parts they think require secrecy."[51] This opening salvo was easily deflected by Edmund Randolph, who reminded his audience that "without secrecy, no government can carry on its operations on great occasions."[52] Randolph's reply prompted Henry to refine his position. "Such transactions as relate to military operations or affairs of great consequence, the immediate promulgation of which might defeat the interests of the community," he declared, "I would not wish to be published, till the end which required their secrecy should have been effected." But the impact of this more refined argument was blunted when Henry characteristically veered off course and urged Americans to imitate the "manly boldness" of the British, who "divulged to all the world their political disquisitions and operations," a fanciful claim that attracted John Marshall's ire.[53] Do the British, Marshall asked, "deliberate in the open fields" when they determine "the propriety of declaring war, or on military arrangements?" "No," he continued, "the British government affords secrecy when necessary, and so ought every government."[54]

Henry responded to this challenge by retracing his steps. Though Marshall had indicated that "war was the case wherein secrecy was most necessary," said Henry, the Constitution also permitted the Senate to withhold information in other contexts as well, most notably the formation of treaties. This meant, he argued, that "the federal veil of secrecy" would prevent citizens from "knowing or being able to punish" those responsible for the passage of unfavorable treaties. Henry challenged this "destruction of responsibility" by revisiting the nuanced position that he had carved out earlier. "I did not wish that transactions relative to treaties should, when unfinished, be exposed," he argued, "but it should be known, after they were concluded, who had advised them to be made, in order to secure some degree of certainty that the public interest shall be consulted in their formation."[55] But his final opponent, Madison, was not convinced by the wisdom of this demand either. Henry, said Madison, desired that once a treaty had been made, "the public ought to be made acquainted with every circumstance relative to it." But "the policy of not divulging the most important transactions and negotiations of nations," Madison argued, "is universally admitted."[56]

Constitutional Puzzles

I have suggested that the Framers did not subscribe to a "philosophy of openness" or promote the "principle of disclosure." On the contrary, they anticipated and defended the use of state secrecy as an essential element of statecraft. This raises an obvious question: did they not worry about the possible misuse of secrecy? The Anti-Federalists, as we have seen, certainly did. Henry charged that the president and Congress could find it in their mutual interests to keep instances of maladministration out of the public's sight. Hence he stressed the need for what we might today term "compulsory declassification." Madison, as we have seen, rejected this idea on the grounds that the delicate nature of international affairs militated against compelled or scheduled disclosure. But Madison was not content simply to say that state secrecy was necessary. He also emphasized that the Constitution's provisions would combat the abuse of secrecy—"there can be no real danger," Madison said to Henry, "as long as the government is constructed on such principles."[57] What did Madison mean by this?

Recall that in the period leading up to the Constitutional Convention, the Framers had become increasingly vocal about the idea that energy was a vital prerequisite of national security and stability, and that the Continental Congress was incapable of exhibiting the requisite degree of energy. A major factor was Congress's inability to maintain that "secrecy which

is the life of execution and despatch."[58] According to those most familiar with the problem, the very "nature and construction" of Congress—its
size and varied membership in particular—militated against the maintenance of internal discipline.[59] As a result, no one at the convention appears
to have doubted that one of the president's key functions would be to employ secrecy in a more effective manner. According to Rufus King, when
Wilson moved on June 1, 1787, that the "executive consist of a single person," he explicitly stated that an executive "ought to possess the powers of
secrecy, vigour and dispatch."[60] In the debate that followed, few, if any, of
the delegates questioned this claim.[61] Instead, they focused on what form
the executive should take so as to strike an appropriate balance between
energy and safety. The most notable objection came from George Mason.
Mason observed that "unity in the executive" promised "the secrecy, the
dispatch, the vigour and energy" that not only he but also "the ablest and
most candid defenders of republican government" acknowledged as "great
advantages."[62] But allowing the executive to consist "only of one person,"
he argued, raised the specter of usurpation. Far better then, he concluded,
to create an executive council, an arrangement that would sacrifice a degree of energy in return for greater security against the misuse of executive power.[63]

Mason was not alone in taking this view. Randolph and Elbridge
Gerry offered much the same diagnosis and prescription.[64] But these
views did not find sufficient support in the convention, which ultimately
rejected both Randolph's proposal for an executive council and Mason's
subsequent call for an advisory council.[65] The delegates, Oliver Ellsworth
and David Ramsay later recounted, decided that not only secrecy, but also
responsibility, and thereby accountability, were best served by vesting executive power in one person.[66] The reasoning behind this view was made
clearer in the state conventions and in *The Federalist* No. 70. In North
Carolina, Davie explained that while "the superior energy and secrecy
wherewith one person can act, was one of the principles on which the
Convention went . . . a more predominant principle was the more obvious responsibility of one person." "It was observed" by delegates, he said,
"that if there were a plurality of persons, and a crime should be committed, when their conduct came to be examined, it would be impossible to
fix the fact on any one of them, but that the public were never at a loss
when there was but one man."[67] Similarly, having observed that the presidency was best designed to take the lead on national security matters,
Hamilton reassured his audience in *The Federalist* No. 70 that the elective
nature of the office and the singularity of the occupant provided citizens
with the "two greatest securities" possible against the misuse of delegated
power—namely, "the restraints of public opinion" and "the opportunity

of discovering with facility and clearness the misconduct of the persons they trust."[68]

But how credible are these claims? How can citizens "fix the facts" or ascertain misconduct with "facility and clearness" when the president has the authority to conceal the relevant information (or to disclose only selected bits)? Indeed, how might citizens even discover wrongdoing in the first place? This, as we have seen, was the concern that led Henry to demand the timely disclosure of military and diplomatic secrets. And Madison, as we have also seen, responded—completely reasonably—that the delicate nature of international affairs made it inadvisable to compel prompt disclosure. But, then again, if citizens can scrutinize the secret conduct of their representatives only after their representatives have judged that the relevant information can be safely shared with them, then what security do they have that their representatives will not simply decline to share incriminating or embarrassing information?

A reply might be sought in what Madison described as the "auxiliary precautions" contained in the Constitution, most notably the separation of powers, which, he argued, would oblige the government "to control itself."[69] But how precisely would this mechanism constrain the misuse of state secrecy? In particular, how could it overcome the objection voiced by a host of Anti-Federalists, including Henry, that the president and a cabal in Congress could jointly conceal wrongdoing? *The Federalist* No. 26 provided an answer. Hamilton wrote there that those who feared that Congress and the president might build up "vast augmentations of military force" had failed to appreciate that the Constitution required Congress to annually approve military appropriations. "Can it be supposed," Hamilton asks, that when debates on these appropriations took place, "there would not be found one man, discerning enough to detect so atrocious a conspiracy, or bold or honest enough to apprise his constituents of the danger?" "If such presumptions can fairly be made," Hamilton argues, "there ought at once to be an end of all delegated authority."[70] In other words, Hamilton's argument was that the separation of powers provides a simple but effective safeguard against secret machinations—since any member of Congress can sound the alarm, ambition would have every chance to counteract ambition. The Anti-Federalists' fears of cabals and combinations were unrealistic, he implied, because in practice it would be extremely difficult for conspirators to quietly secure the collective agreement required to cheat the public.

There are, however, some wrinkles in this story. The first is that neither Madison nor Hamilton seems to have thought that officials entrusted with state secrets have a right to disclose such information as they see fit. Consider, for example, Madison's commentary on the events of

December 1782 when David Howell, Rhode Island's delegate to Congress, was found to have leaked to the *Providence Gazette* news of a friendly overture from the Swedish court.[71] Howell had leaked the news, which had been recorded in the Secret Journal, because he believed it vindicated his stance that the United States would be able to raise new loans in Europe, and that Congress therefore did not have to impose a 5 percent import duty that Rhode Islanders opposed. Claiming to have informed his constituents of "such things as they have a right to know," Howell subsequently defended his action as an exercise of "the freedom of speech."[72] But his colleagues were thoroughly unimpressed by this claim. Howell's response, Madison observed in his *Notes on Debates*, provoked "universal indignation" in Congress, because Howell's colleagues viewed his actions as having betrayed the Swedish court and presented the public with a distorted picture of the United States' financial dealings that they could not correct without revealing "many delicate transactions."[73] Not surprisingly, Howell's defense of his action was firmly repudiated—on Hamilton's motion—as "highly derogatory to the honor and dignity of the United States in Congress."[74]

This episode does not of course rule out the possibility that Madison and Hamilton believed that officials have a moral right to disclose secret information as and when this reveals a conspiracy against the people, and that Howell deserved to be castigated only because he had exposed secret information without due cause. But this quite plausible interpretation is complicated by the fact that neither Madison nor Hamilton elaborated on what might constitute due cause for making an unauthorized disclosure. When was a conspiracy truly a conspiracy (as opposed to the fevered imagination or self-serving claim of a partisan)? Howell, for his part, certainly seems to have thought his disclosure had defeated a conspiracy.[75]

The other wrinkle in the claim that the separation of powers would counter the misuse of state secrecy is that the Framers left Congress dependent on the president for access to secret information. This becomes evident when we contrast *The Federalist* No. 53 and No. 75. In the former, Madison discusses what a legislator must do to gain competence. "No man can be a competent legislator," he writes, "who does not add to an upright intention and a sound judgement, a certain degree of knowledge of the subjects on which he is to legislate." One such "branch of knowledge which belongs to the acquirements of a federal representative," Madison says, "is that of foreign affairs"—a subject that will "sometimes demand particular legislative sanction and cooperation." While "some portion" of this knowledge can be acquired from "a man's closet" and some of it "can only be derived from the public sources of information," Madison concludes that "all of it will be acquired to the best effect by a practical attention to the subject during the period of actual service in the legislature."[76] But how could legislators attain such familiarity with foreign affairs when, as Hamilton noted in *The Federalist* No. 75, the degree of secrecy required to safeguard intelligence was "incompatible with the genius of a body so variable and numerous" as the House?[77]

The conflict between *The Federalist* No. 53 and No. 75 was not unprecedented. The proceedings of the Constitutional Convention reveal that the confusion ran deep. On August 11, 1787, the delegates agreed to incorporate language that would allow the House and the Senate to withhold publication of such of their records "as may in their judgment require secrecy."[78] But consider what happened when, on September 7, the delegates turned to discuss Article II, Section 2, Clause 2, which authorized the president to make treaties "by and with the advice and consent of the Senate." At this point, Wilson moved that the House be included in this clause alongside the Senate on the grounds that since "treaties are to have the operation of laws, they ought to have the sanction of laws." The "only objection" to including the House, Wilson said, was the "circumstance of secrecy in the business of treaties."[79] This was a remarkable argument because, as we have seen, less than a month earlier, the delegates had authorized the House to exercise secrecy. Why grant the House the authority to exercise secrecy if it could not be trusted to maintain secrets? This question was not raised at the time. Instead, Roger Sherman challenged Wilson's motion by reemphasizing the importance of secrecy, arguing that "the necessity of secrecy in the case of treaties forbade a reference of them to the whole Legislature."[80] His colleagues appear to have been persuaded, for they rejected Wilson's motion by a margin of 10–1.

This was not to be the end of the story. On September 14, Gerry joined with Mason to propose that only the Senate be allowed to exercise secrecy. Their proposal was rejected 7–3, Madison reports, after the delegates were informed that "cases might arise where secrecy might be necessary in both Houses," for instance with respect to "measures preparatory to a declaration of war."[81] Why did the delegates believe that the House would be able to keep preparations for war secret, but that it would not be able to keep diplomatic proceedings secret? Had the delegates changed their minds? This seems unlikely given what advocates of the Constitution had to say in the various state conventions. In Virginia, for instance, Francis Corbin affirmed—in Madison's presence—that the House had been "excluded from interposing in making treaties, because large popular assemblies are very improper to transact such business, from the impossibility of their acting with sufficient secrecy, despatch, and decision, which can only be found in small bodies."[82] In South Carolina, Charles Cotesworth Pinckney put the point more directly still. "Can secrecy," he asked, "be expected in sixty-five members?" "The idea," he said, "is absurd."[83]

What about the Senate? A number of the Constitution's defenders seem to have believed that the Senate's role in foreign affairs would help combat the abuse of secrecy. In Pennsylvania, for example, Wilson argued that since "neither the President nor the Senate, solely, can complete a treaty; they are checks upon each other, and are so balanced as to produce security to the people."[84] Similarly in South Carolina, Pinckney, having ridiculed the indiscreetness of the House, went on to argue that "the Senate, from the smallness of its numbers . . . joined with the President, who is the federal head of the United States, form together a body in whom can be best and most safely vested the diplomatic power of the Union."[85] But consider what Jay has to say in *The Federalist* No. 64. "There are cases," he writes, "where the most useful intelligence may be obtained, if the persons possessing it can be relieved from apprehensions of discovery." Such persons, he claims, "would rely on the secrecy of the President, but would not confide in that of the Senate, and still less in that of a large popular Assembly," which is why the convention did well to require the president to act by the advice and consent of the Senate, but simultaneously vesting in him alone the management of the "business of intelligence in such a manner as prudence may suggest."[86] In other words, according to *The Federalist* No. 64, even the Senate would not have independent or unmediated access to secret intelligence.

Strikingly, Jay does not discuss here the possibility that the president's monopoly of secret intelligence could make it harder for the Senate to exercise its coordinate powers in opposition to the president. On the contrary, he focuses solely on the advantage of this division of functions, saying that it shows how "the Constitution provides that our negotiations for treaties shall have every advantage which can be derived from talents, information, integrity, and deliberate investigations, on the one hand, and from secrecy and despatch on the other."[87] But there is something puzzling about this claim. If the president is *required* to share secret intelligence with the Senate, then this defeats the purpose of vesting control over the "business of intelligence" in his hands, namely, to take advantage of his greater capacity to maintain discretion. But if the president is *not* required to share secret intelligence, then what is to prevent him from sharing only information advantageous to his own cause? It is tempting to assume that the Framers expected the Senate to extract information by withholding cooperation on funds, appointments, and the approval of treaties. But then again, if the point of creating the office of president is to maintain discretion, then how can it be sensible for the Senate to compel the disclosure of information that the president judges ought to be kept secret? And if the reply is that the Senate should utilize compulsion only when this is truly necessary, then one must ask how Senators can ascertain when to utilize compulsion, since they will not know in advance whether or not the information held by the president is genuinely sensitive.

Insulated Circumstances

I have been arguing that though the Framers did not expect the executive to maintain only a few, short-lived secrets, the checks and balances they devised feature a number of silences about how to counter the abuse of state secrecy. I have identified three such silences. First, how can citizens hold the president and Congress accountable for the use of secrecy, since the president and Congress get to decide when, if ever, to disclose secret information to the public? Second, how can lawmakers check the executive's use of state secrecy, since the president gets to decide when, if ever, to disclose secret information to Congress? And third, under what circumstances, if any, are officials entitled to disclose secret information that reveals wrongdoing? Since these lacunae are not insignificant, it is only reasonable to assume that succeeding generations ought to have noticed and then sought to fill these silences. As we shall now see, the effects of these lacunae certainly were felt in the nineteenth century, but not acutely enough or often enough to compel the fashioning of a remedy.

In the nineteenth century there appear to have been few challenges at the level of principle to the notion that the president and Congress were entitled to maintain secrecy in the national interest. Certainly, presidents did not display any sense of anxiety when they requested Congress to join with them in concealing information, be it in the matter of ransoms paid to Algeria, diplomatic initiatives with European powers, or negotiations with Mexico.[88] This principle was also readily defended by the leading commentators of the day. In *A View of the Constitution*, for instance, William Rawle observes that calls for the president to disclose information relating to foreign affairs had been justified on the ground that "in republics there ought to be few or no secrets." But this is, Rawle writes, "an illusory opinion, founded on ideal conceptions, and at variance with the useful practice of mankind," since exposing the transactions of a cabinet to "the public eye" would merely serve to impede its operations and allow "improper advantages" to be taken.[89] This point is reiterated in Justice Joseph Story's *Commentaries on the Constitution*, which stresses the need for secrecy in foreign relations, especially with regard to the formation of treaties, on the grounds that "no man at all acquainted with diplomacy" could have failed to realize that "the success of negotiations as often depends upon their being unknown by the public, as upon their justice or their policy."[90]

This is not to imply that no criticism of state secrecy was voiced during this time. Certainly there were members of Congress who spoke up quite strongly on behalf of publicity.[91] But even these members typically conceded that the final say on how far this ideal could be realized lay with the president. For instance, during the epic debate on the Jay Treaty in 1796, Representative Abraham Baldwin argued that "the importance of having many Government secrets was diminishing," since experience had shown that "the greater the publicity of measures the greater the success." Moreover, in a "free Government," said Baldwin, the "arguments for and against measures [ought] to be known to the people." Nevertheless, he ultimately affirmed that the president was entitled to exercise secrecy if there was "any temporary impropriety" associated with making the relevant information public.[92] Similarly, Article I, Section 5, Clause 3 of the Constitution continued to attract scattered criticism in the decades immediately after Ratification, most notably in St. George Tucker's *View of the Constitution*.[93] But such views were evidently in the minority, as the Senate and the House faced little opposition when they established rules formalizing the secrecy of their executive sessions.[94]

More controversial, though, were the attempts of presidents to withhold military and diplomatic information from Congress. This was a domain over which presidents asserted their control quite early on, as the Senate learned when it asked President Washington in 1794 for details pertaining to the ongoing negotiation of the Jay Treaty. President Washington agreed to share some information, but he withheld "those particulars, which in my judgment, for public considerations, ought not to be communicated."[95] The House soon learned that it was even more disadvantaged on this front. In 1796, it demanded access to all the materials relating to formulation of the (now completed) Jay Treaty before it would make the relevant appropriations. But President Washington declined to share the information, arguing that "even when brought to a conclusion a full disclosure of all the measures, demands, or eventual concessions which may have been proposed or contemplated would be extremely impolitic."[96] The evidence indicates that these precedents hardened over the course of the nineteenth century. Sofaer and Rozell have very ably documented the relevant instances.[97] I would add only that the leading commentaries of the day evidently did not view this practice as a travesty. James Kent, for instance, in his *Commentaries on American Law* notes forthrightly that though in republics "determinations respecting peace, as well as war" had hitherto been made in assemblies, the Constitution had been influenced by the realization that "secrecy and despatch" rendered it "expedient to place this power in the hands of the executive department."[98]

Why did these claims not provoke a more sustained critique from Congress? It was not as if lawmakers were unaware of what this arrangement boded. On the contrary, they stood up at regular intervals to voice concern that the president's control over the flow of secret information threatened to hollow out Congress's coordinate powers. For instance, in 1796 (now Representative) Madison observed that the president's claim that he had the right to withhold information relating to foreign relations (in the context of the Jay Treaty) could make it difficult for the House to deliberate "on the subjects submitted to them by the Constitution."[99] In 1826 when President John Quincy Adams proposed to send ministers to the Panama Congress, his critics in Congress, alarmed by what this implied for America's policy of abstaining from foreign entanglements, demanded that he share further information about the mission. When he declined to comply in full, Senator Robert Hayne complained that while the president "leaves us free to act as we think proper, he refuses to furnish us with the information on which alone we could act, and for which we had respectfully called."[100] Then again in 1843 when the Senate was confronted with reports indicating that President John Tyler was secretly negotiating with the British on the future of Oregon, Senator William Allen complained that "the hitherto tolerated practice" of "concluding the most important treaties" without "even informing this body that negotiations are pending" was a "practical and dangerous departure from the letter and spirit of the constitution."[101] The problem, his colleague Senator Thomas Benton explained, was that the secret formulation of treaties "deprived the Senate of their free action upon the ratification of treaties" because it left them facing a stark choice: either "to confirm what was done, or to embarrass the President."[102]

In the end, though, these complaints had no lasting effect because leading members of Congress also admitted the weight of the argument on the other side. As we have seen, one of the central justifications for creating the presidency was that the size and structure of the Continental Congress had made it difficult to maintain secrecy. Given this history, it should come as no surprise that when Madison stood up to respond to the Washington administration's refusal to share documents relating to the Jay Treaty, he could not help but admit that while the House "must have a right, in all cases, to ask for information which might assist in their deliberations," the president also "had a right" and "a due responsibility" to withhold information that was of a nature "that did not permit a disclosure of it at the time."[103] This posture soon crystallized into precedent as Congress began to qualify its requests for secret information with a fateful formula—that the executive should share relevant information "unless in the opinion of the President it is contrary to the public interest" to do so.[104]

Needless to say, this formula did little to resolve the question of how Congress might safeguard the independent exercise of its coordinate powers. In the absence of clarity, members of Congress occasionally attempted to force the issue. More often than not, though, these attempts failed to obtain the support of Congress itself, as was the case in 1826 when Representative Samuel Ingham tried to persuade his colleagues that the gravity of the question before them (whether to fund delegates to the Panama Congress) provided sufficient reason to demand information from the president "without limitation of any kind." Shall we tell our constituents, said Ingham, that we voted for the measure because "the President knew all about it?" This would be to admit, he said, "that we, the Representatives of the People . . . had agreed to become a mere registering assembly for Executive edicts."[105] Quite a few of Ingham's colleagues agreed with this characterization of the problem. Representative James Hamilton argued, for instance, that to fail to inquire deeply would be to assume that "the President can do no wrong."[106] However, the majority still sided with Representatives Daniel Cook and Daniel Webster, who outlined a much more modest role for Congress when they argued that, in the absence of clear evidence of wrongdoing, there was no reason to doubt that "the President may have the best reasons" for withholding information.[107]

Other lawmakers were more blunt in their assessment of Congress's claims. In 1831 a bloc of senators charged President Andrew Jackson with having violated the Constitution by secretly dispatching ministers to negotiate a treaty with the Ottoman Empire. Led by Senator Littleton Tazewell, the chairman of the Senate Committee on Foreign Relations, they argued that the Senate ought to decline the president's request for appropriations to reimburse these ministers since the Senate had not confirmed their appointments. But Senator John Forsyth, the future secretary of state, pushed back, arguing that prior indiscretions, such as Senator Stevens Mason's 1795 disclosure of the Jay Treaty, had taught the executive that senators could not be counted upon to live up to the "sacred obligation" to preserve the secrecy required to conduct foreign relations.[108] And more recent experience, he added, had served only to make it apparent that "if a desire was felt that any subject should . . . become a topic of universal conversation, nothing more was necessary than to close the doors of the Senate Chamber, and make it the object of a secret, confidential deliberation."[109]

Not every attempt to rouse Congress failed, though. In 1848, for instance, the House asked President James Polk to communicate information about the activities of John Slidell, the United States' minister in Mexico. The request, Polk noted in his reply to the House, was "unconditional," as it omitted the "customary and usual reservation contained in calls of either House of Congress upon the Executive for information relating to our intercourse with foreign nations." However, Polk was not to be cowed. Arguing that he could not "violate an important principle, always heretofore held sacred by my predecessors," he transmitted only information that he believed could be communicated "without serious injury to the public interest."[110] Unwilling to push the matter further, Congress reverted to the old formula. By the late nineteenth century, this formula was so well rehearsed that Hermann von Holst could state in *The Constitutional and Political History of the United States* that control over the flow of information allowed the president to judge "when the constitutional cooperation of the Senate shall begin."[111]

I have been arguing that the absence in the nineteenth century of a sustained challenge to the executive's monopoly of secret information can be attributed to continuing faith in the idea that the president had the right to determine when secret information should be made available to the public, and to Congress's deference to the claim that the president was entitled to determine when it could have access to secret information. This account may lead one to wonder why citizens and lawmakers did not chafe more at the fact that the executive's control over information made it harder for them to enforce accountability. Arguably, the significance of this monopoly was obscured by the United States' insulated circumstances, which limited the scope and scale of state secrecy, and correspondingly limited the points of conflict between lawmakers and citizens on one side and the president on the other.[112] As Francis Lieber observes in *On Civil Liberty and Self Government*, while the secrecy associated with diplomacy militates against the publicity required for self-government, "a great change has been wrought in modern times, and comparatively a great degree of publicity now prevails in the foreign intercourse of nations."[113] As evidence Lieber cites "one of our first statesmen," who had privately written to him that "I would not give a dime for all the secrets that people may imagine to be locked up in the United States' archives."[114]

It might be objected that the first half of the nineteenth century witnessed more than a few presidents who made extensive use of secrecy, particularly in the cause of expansion. This is of course true—the acquisitions of Louisiana, Florida, Texas, Oregon, and California were furtive. Note, however, that the furtiveness in these cases was bounded in key respects: the objective of the secrecy was tightly defined, its duration was limited, and the outcome was unavoidably public. In other words, covert activities during this period did not emerge from or stay within the recesses of a security apparatus shrouded in deep secrecy. Indeed the United States had an emaciated security apparatus during this period.[115] The principal vehicles for intelligence initiatives were "executive agents" who acted as "pathfinders for American foreign policy."[116] These agents were primarily amateurs who "worked alone and without the support of any far-flung intelligence organization."[117] The "highly sporadic and individualistic" nature of these activities in turn helped limit conflict between the president and Congress.[118] For instance, presidents were able to avoid confrontations with Congress by obfuscating the precise role played by these executive agents, often communicating with them via private letters, a practice that allowed presidents to unhesitatingly comply with Congress's requests for official correspondence.[119] The transient nature of these activities also helped calm Congress's fears. Consider, for example, President Polk's message to Congress in 1846 where, having declined to share the certificates (or secret payments) drawn up by his predecessor, he diplomatically added, "[F]or my own part . . . I have had no occasion rendering it necessary in my judgment to make such a certificate, and it would be an extreme case which would ever induce me to exercise this authority."[120]

The other reason the executive's monopoly of secret information did not arouse prolonged concern is that even when the president did undertake covert activity, unauthorized disclosures ensured that lawmakers and citizens were "seldom left . . . ignorant of executive aims."[121] At times the disclosures came from Congress. Perhaps the best-known example dates to April 1844 when, in the face of political divisions over the wisdom of acquiring Texas, President John Tyler sought to have the treaty of annexation ratified in closed session. As part of the ratification process, the Tyler administration submitted documents pertaining to the negotiations. These documents included diplomatic correspondence suggesting that one of the annexation's purposes was to bolster the institution of slavery. Senator Benjamin Tappan, an abolitionist opposed to the treaty, secretly disclosed this correspondence, thereby sparking public debate that contributed to the Senate's rejection of the treaty.[122]

More often, though, unauthorized disclosures came from within the executive branch. Consequently, throughout the nineteenth century, presidents struggled to keep covert activities out of the press, especially during times of war.[123] A prominent episode from the end of the century nicely summarizes the challenge they faced. During the Philippine War, President William McKinley's administration sought to censor American correspondents posted in Manila. The experiment backfired after the press corps eventually cabled home a widely publicized statement deploring the censorship as a means of preventing Americans from knowing about the military's excesses and failures. Reflecting on the episode, the *Nation* warned the president that "if there is one thing which no system of military discipline or official terrorism can long force American officers to do, it is to suppress facts to conceal blunders." "Leakages," it said," are sure to occur," and so, "the harder the President squats on the safety valve, the higher will he be blown when the explosion takes place."[124]

It is not a new observation that unauthorized disclosures helped nineteenth-century citizens and lawmakers challenge secretive executive action. Schlesinger was one of the first to discern this "recurrent pattern" in American history—namely, that "when the republic faced a hard decision in foreign policy and the executive branch had not revealed facts that would enable the people to reach their own judgment, aggrieved citizens felt themselves morally warranted in violating a system of secrecy exploited (as they earnestly believed) by government against the national interest."[125] What Schlesinger glosses over, though, is that these disclosures were highly controversial. Tappan, for instance, was censured by the Senate and only narrowly escaped expulsion.[126] At other points, Congress subpoenaed, interrogated, and even imprisoned journalists in an effort to discover their sources.[127] In 1890, for example, the Senate created a so-called smelling committee that spent more than five months investigating reporters, staffers, and even senators, in an effort to trace the source of a recent spate of leaks.[128] These episodes might well be seen as a manifestation of one of the aforementioned silences in the Framers' theory. The Framers had implied that secrecy might legitimately be breached in the public interest, but then did not properly explain what constituted good cause. The consequence was controversy: like Rhode Island's Howell, Tappan believed himself to be justified in disclosing secret information, while Congress evidently thought otherwise. Which side was in the right? The question was not posed frequently or acutely enough in the nineteenth century to provoke a search for a systematic answer.

Turning Points

I have argued that though the Framers did not fully explain how citizens or lawmakers would be able to bring the president to account for the employment of state secrecy, the limited scope and scale of state secrecy in the nineteenth century meant that their silence did not attract sustained attention at the time. This picture, as we shall now see, began to alter once America immersed itself in international politics.

In *The American Commonwealth*, published toward the close of the nineteenth century, James Bryce observed that republics usually struggled to "define the respective spheres of the legislature and executive in foreign affairs, for while publicity and parliamentary control are needed to protect the people, promptitude and secrecy are the conditions of diplomatic success"; America, however, had been fortunate enough to sidestep the problem because "happy America" stood "apart in a world of her own."[129] A little more than a decade after Bryce wrote these words, America's long-standing aversion to foreign entanglements began to fade. Woodrow Wilson was one of the first to discern what this meant for the nation. Writing after the Spanish-American War of 1898, Wilson observed that from a constitutional perspective, "interesting things" might come out of the country's "plunge into international politics and the administration of distant dependencies" such as Hawaii and the Philippines.[130] For "when foreign affairs play a prominent part in the politics and policy of a nation," he wrote, "its Executive must of necessity be its guide: it must utter every initial judgment, take every first step of action, supply the information upon which it is to act, suggest and in large measure control its conduct."[131]

Congress soon made the same discovery. The point was brought home in 1906 by a famous debate between Senators John Spooner and Augustus Bacon as to whether Congress was entitled to request from President Theodore Roosevelt information about his decision to send delegates to the Algeciras Conference, which had been called to settle a dispute between France and Germany over control of Morocco. Bacon, fearing that the United States' decision to attend indicated that "the whole policy of noninterference and nonentanglement is being given away and abandoned," demanded to know "the limitations of the instructions" given to the American delegates.[132] When Spooner questioned the propriety of Bacon's demand on the grounds that Congress ought not to interfere in the conduct of negotiations, the latter responded that since the Constitution had authorized the president to make treaties "by and with the Advice and Consent of the Senate," how can "it be proper for the Senate to offer advice or counsel to the President as to the policy or impolicy of a proposed treaty, and at the same time improper to ask for information upon which to base such advice or counsel?"[133] Nonetheless, when pressed by Spooner to clarify whether the president was *obliged* to comply with Congress's request, Bacon conceded that it was for the president to judge whether such a disclosure was "compatible with the public interest."[134] And so the senators ultimately concluded by reiterating what Madison had stated more than a century earlier: they agreed that "the President has the same right to refuse to share the information as the Senate has to request it."[135]

Although the exchange between Bacon and Spooner offered the clearest indication yet that the precedents established in the nineteenth century would make it difficult for Congress to rein in a secretive executive, the scale of the challenge was not immediately evident. This is because as

America entered the world stage, the statesmen of the day calmed fears by appealing to liberal-democratic ideals that had taken shape in nineteenth-century Europe, where revolutionaries like Giuseppe Mazzini and Lajos Kossuth, and liberals like Benjamin Constant and François Guizot, had argued that democracies ought to eschew state secrecy, which they associated with the old monarchies of Europe.[136] In short order it became commonplace to assert, as former Secretary of State Elihu Root did in 1917, that a democracy was "incapable" of pursuing "sinister policies of ambition," since the "open and public avowal and discussion which must precede their adoption by a democracy is destructive of them."[137] Following the United States' entry into World War I, this view took center stage. The belief that the use of "secret counsels" had been responsible for allowing "so stupendous a contest" to be unleashed "without warning to the world," led (now President) Wilson to urge that the lesson to be learned from the experience was that "the peace of the world must henceforth depend upon a new and more wholesome diplomacy" that would "proceed always frankly and in the public view."[138] Soon, however, the realization dawned that state secrecy had actually increased rather than decreased since Wilson's famous "Fourteen Points" speech. As the political scientist and former envoy to China Paul Reinsch lamented in 1922, whereas "it was substantially true that the United States had no diplomatic secrets" immediately prior to World War I, now "even in the American government, particularly during and since the war, foreign affairs have been handled with what would ordinarily seem insufficient information to the public."[139]

To the scholars who reflected on these developments, it was quite clear that the path ahead lay not in eschewing state secrecy but rather in ensuring that it was used responsibly. "It is all very well to say that an open and straightforward policy best befits a free and high-minded people," Bryce wrote in *Modern Democracies*, "but if such a people should stand alone in a naughty world, it will have to suffer for its virtues."[140] At the same time, Bryce acknowledged that, as recent experience had shown, there was a need to address the possibility that state secrecy could obscure "unwise action" and the use of "dishonorable methods."[141] His response to this conundrum presaged future developments. "The risk that secrecy and discretion will be abused will be gradually lessened," Bryce wrote, "the more public opinion becomes better instructed on foreign affairs, and the more that legislatures learn to give unremitting attention to foreign policy."[142]

Bryce's proposal that Congress involve itself more thoroughly in foreign affairs was echoed by other influential commentators including Edward Corwin, Quincy Wright, DeWitt Poole, Carl Friedrich, and Harold Laski.[143] But how could Congress take on this responsibility when it relied on the president for information, as the debate between Senators

Bacon and Spooner had underscored? The leading observers of the day were aware of the problem. "Parliamentary action is becoming notoriously ineffective," Walter Lippmann wrote in *Liberty and the News*, because Congress's "sources of information are hardly better than that of any other reader of the newspaper," whereas the president has "an elaborate hierarchy reaching to every part of the nation and to all parts of the world."[144] This divergence, he noted, was steadily weakening the checks and balances established by the Framers because when the "legislature is haphazardly informed . . . the people themselves prefer to trust the executive which knows, rather than the Congress which is vainly trying to know."[145]

The scholars who counseled faith in the separation of powers accepted that Congress was becoming ever more dependent on the president for information, but they had little to offer by way of concrete solutions. Wright's suggestion that the president and Congress alleviate conflict over information sharing by cultivating informal "constitutional understandings" was typical of the period.[146] But what if such "comity" were to break down? There would still be no cause for concern, Poole argued, because Congress could obtain whatever it needed through the judicious use of the powers at its disposal, including its control over finances, appointments, and the approval of treaties.[147] What Poole did not address, though, was the question that Spooner had used to checkmate Bacon—that is, *ought* Congress to force the president to divulge information when the Framers had created the latter to keep secrets that they thought the former could not?

Bryce's other proposal—the instruction of public opinion— accommodated the demand for great public oversight. But this proposal raised the question of who was to do the instructing. It was Lippmann, once again, who discerned the problem. If the task of instructing the public was left to officials, he warned, then propaganda would win the day. At a time when individual opinion relied more than ever on public opinion, there could be, he wrote, "no liberty for a community which lacks the information by which to detect lies."[148] Consequently, the need of the hour, Lippmann argued, was to increase the participation of disinterested experts, who could investigate policy questions without fear or favor and then guide public opinion in the appropriate direction.[149] But how could such experts form "more comprehensive and distant views" when the relevant information might be secreted within the recesses of the state? "It is difficult to see," Lippmann wrote, why, save for "a few diplomatic and military secrets," all the information at the disposal of the State Department "should not be open to the scholars of the country."[150] The problem with this line of reasoning, though, was that, as Reinsch had correctly discerned, diplomatic and military secrets were not so few any more.

Few felt the expansion of secrecy more keenly than the press. Confronted with the Wilson administration's concerted effort to introduce formal censorship during World War I, the press defended its freedom to cast the "pitiless light of publicity" on "every scandal" and "every blunder," including those in the diplomatic arena, by arguing that in view of the propensity of state secrecy to foster misunderstanding and incompetence, "even reckless speech may be a moderating influence, whereas drastic censorship chokes the safety valve."[151] However, Congress's debate on the Wilson administration's proposal shows only limited support for this point of view. Certainly, a whole host of congressmen, led by Senator William Borah, objected to censorship on the grounds that a vigilant press was needed more than ever during war, a time "when sordidness and greed are always active," thus emphasizing what Vincent Blasi would later term the "checking value" of the First Amendment.[152] But the slender majority in Congress who supported this view conceded that the executive was entitled to prevent the disclosure of secret information in the first place, and that Congress retained the right to penalize the publication of information harmful to national security.[153]

If the questions raised by the proposals put forward in the wake of World War I were initially left unexplored, this was because even though state secrecy had now officially appeared on the scene—in the form of classification guidelines and the passage of the Espionage Act in 1917—the scope and scale of the United States' national security apparatus was still limited at this point.[154] Indeed, even as late as the onset of World War II, President Franklin Roosevelt was still relying on executive agents, who were, as one important observer noted, "amateurs without special qualifications and without training," who lacked "special means of communication or other facilities," and thus constituted a "small and uncoordinated force."[155] By the end of World War II, though, the picture was very different: whereas in 1916 the Department of State had had only four officials officially charged with managing intelligence matters, by 1945 upwards of fifteen thousand had worked for the Office of Strategic Service (OSS), which was only one of a plethora of intelligence organizations created during the war.[156] Soon a new threshold was breached. With Pearl Harbor still fresh in the minds of decision-makers, and with the Soviet Union looming large on the horizon, support grew for the notion that America required a permanent peacetime intelligence establishment, and, in short order, a host of powerful new organizations including the Central Intelligence Agency (CIA) and the National Security Agency (NSA) had been established.[157]

Accompanying these institutional advances were constitutional developments formalizing the president's right to control the flow of information relating to this emergent national security apparatus. The first such development came in the form of Executive Order 10290, which cited the president's "implied powers" as the basis for establishing, in 1951, a thoroughgoing "system for the safeguarding of official information the unauthorized disclosure of which would or could harm, tend to impair, or otherwise threaten the security of the nation."[158] Another was the formal enunciation in 1954 of an "executive privilege" to withhold information from Congress. Drawing on new research detailing the instances in which presidents had previously withheld information from Congress, Attorney General Herbert Brownell now argued that the president had a right to withhold information from Congress. These precedents showed, he wrote, that "throughout our history the President has withheld information whenever he found that what was sought was confidential or its disclosure would be incompatible with the public interest or jeopardize the safety of the Nation."[159]

A third development was the recognition in *United States v. Reynolds* (1953) of what has since come to be termed the "state secrets privilege"— that is, the right of the state to refuse to produce evidence sought by plaintiffs on the grounds that its disclosure would gravely harm national security. Although this privilege had already been recognized in the nineteenth century, it had rarely been invoked. However, once the United States began to undertake covert activities, the courts encountered plaintiffs seeking access to secret information to prove violation of their rights.[160] *Reynolds* revealed that the judicial process could do little to lift the veil on such activities because "even the most compelling necessity," the Supreme Court ruled, "cannot overcome the claim of privilege if the court is ultimately satisfied that military secrets are at stake."[161]

As these events unfolded, observers now began to recognize for the first time how the checks and balances inherited from the Framers could be short-circuited by state secrecy. The heightened use of secrecy, Harold Lasswell warned, meant that "the member of Congress who takes up a critical attitude toward the executive on national defense issues will find himself in a less and less tenable position," because he will not be able to share with the public information that challenges the president's statements and policies.[162] Wallace Parks pushed further. Congress, he noted, typically relies on experts from the "non-governmental community" for the information needed to check the executive. How can Congress receive such guidance in military and diplomatic matters, he asked, when "the necessary information and communications have been severely restricted?"[163] Robert Dahl and Lewis Coser drew attention to the problem of democratic control in the face of increasing state secrecy. "Given a monopoly on knowledge," Coser observed, "power holders can exert dominion over all those who are incapable of acting rationally because they do not know the real situation." "Hence an increase in the secrecy of governmental action," he concluded, "may be taken as an index of the drift toward the garrison state in America."[164] Meanwhile, Zechariah Chafee fretted that the "enormous recent expansion of the subjects which officials are seeking to hide from publication" meant that "official encroachments on the freedom of the press will be probable unless the boundary line between secrecy and publicity is very carefully demarcated."[165]

These grim pronouncements prompted calls for a "proper balance" to be struck "between secrecy and disclosure."[166] But could officials be trusted to strike the right balance? Chafee sounded an early note of skepticism, warning that "officials must not do the demarcating" because they would be tempted to use this power to "hoist public safety as an umbrella to cover their own mistakes."[167] In a little over a decade, such skepticism became mainstream. One reason for the change was the U-2 incident of May 1960, when Americans discovered that President Eisenhower had misled them about provocative surveillance flights over the Soviet Union. The incident, Francis Rourke observed at the time, provided "a clear indication of the power that has come to rest in the hands of government officials to influence public attitudes in foreign affairs through their control over the release of information."[168] President Eisenhower's subsequent claim that the administration had lied in order to deceive the Soviets only made matters worse, Rourke pointed out, not only because the explanation seemed implausible (as the Soviets already knew about the surveillance flights), but also because it implied that officials might deceive the American public again, if they deemed it necessary to do so.

The other reason for growing public skepticism was newfound public awareness of officials' tendency to classify information whose disclosure could not realistically be said to threaten national security. This problem of "overclassification" was brought to the public's attention by high-profile congressional hearings and news reports citing instances where the classification stamp had been used to conceal information ranging from the mundane to the embarrassing. As they searched for a theoretical explanation for this phenomenon, commentators latched on to Max Weber's essay "Bureaucracy," which had recently been translated into English. From Weber they took the idea that bureaucracies had self-interested reasons to extend secrecy "far beyond those areas where purely functional interests make for secrecy." In particular, they became convinced that Weber was right to argue that "every bureaucracy seeks to increase the superiority of the professionally informed by keeping their knowledge and intentions secret."[169]

If the bureaucracy could not be trusted to deal fairly, then how was secrecy to be checked? Crucially, prominent bipartisan investigations emphasized that unauthorized disclosures were *not* the answer. In 1956 the

Defense Department Committee on Classified Information (the Coolidge Committee) declared that though "reasonable men may differ" over national security decisions, it was a "deplorable thing" for officials to "carry their ardor to the point of undermining the system on which the nation relies for the protection of its defense secrets." Such action, the committee concluded, ought to be checked by punishment—"however high the motives of an individual might seem to himself, he is guilty of a serious offense and should be dealt with accordingly." And should it prove difficult to identify the source, the committee added, the reporter ought to "be summoned to testify in a grand jury investigation in order to discover the source of the leak."[170] The Commission on Government Security (the Wright Commission), which reported in 1957, was even more blunt, calling for the "unequivocal prohibition" of unauthorized disclosures and the "vigorous prosecution of every offender." "The final responsibility for the difficult decisions of what shall be secret," Chairman Lloyd Wright declared, "must be confided in those loyal and devoted public servants who are qualified to make the judgment." "No citizen," he emphasized, "is entitled to take the law, and the safety of the nation, into his own hands."[171]

The recommendations of the Coolidge Committee and the Wright Commission were not adopted. But the skepticism these recommendations embodied did reflect wider political concern about uncontrolled disclosures. Chafee, for instance, cautioned that allowing secret information to slip out in the form of gossip "is more dangerous than frank discussion in the general press." It would be far preferable, he concluded, for Congress to determine what matters should be kept secret, thereby allowing for "frank official disclosures."[172] Rourke made much the same point. "As the situation now stands," he observed in 1961, "the leak often serves as something of a safety valve." But there was the distinct chance, he added, that the officials responsible for disclosing information could make erroneous judgments about the need for secrecy, thereby keeping secret either too much or too little.[173]

It was in this context that proposals to legislate a "right to know" gained traction. A series of publications by members of the American Society of Newspaper Editors, most prominently, Harold Cross's *The People's Right to Know* and James Wiggins's *Freedom or Secrecy*, struck some of the first blows.[174] Crucially, these writers did not oppose state secrecy itself. Rather, they warned that the unchecked use of the classification stamp meant that citizens were increasingly being deprived of the knowledge required to determine the "adequacy of policy and the fidelity of individual public servants."[175] Hence they proposed that classification decisions take due account of the public's interest in the availability of information—and that the courts play the role of arbiters.

This argument found a receptive audience in Congress, where Representative John Moss and Senator Thomas Hennings championed it to great effect. "No one denies the necessity for true security measures in the interest of national defense," Moss argued, but in recent years secrecy claims had been "so broadly stated as to constitute a real and present danger to our system of representative government."[176] The need of the hour, his colleague Hennings argued, was for guidelines ensuring that information would be withheld "only to the extent that the effective and proper exercise of the President's power to conduct the foreign affairs of the nation requires it."[177] Such guidelines were soon put in place. In 1966 Congress passed the Freedom of Information Act (FOIA), which placed on the executive the burden of proving that the imposition of secrecy in a given case was "specifically authorized under criteria established by an Executive Order to be kept secret in the interest of national defense or foreign policy."[178] As the conference report accompanying the legislation explained, the objective of FOIA was to establish "a general philosophy of full agency disclosure unless information is exempted under clearly delineated statutory language and to provide a court procedure by which citizens and the press may obtain information wrongly withheld."[179]

Around this time Congress also began attending to its own needs by contesting the president's claim that he had a right to withhold information from it. Initially, it collated a rival set of precedents that evidenced "the power of Congress and its committees to obtain information deemed necessary to the legislative process."[180] Subsequently, it took on Attorney General Rogers's claim that the executive privilege was founded on the separation of powers by making the case that the very same doctrine also supported its right to information, since "a legislative body cannot legislate wisely or effectively in the absence of information respecting the conditions which the legislation is intended to affect or change."[181] For the most part, though, both of these challenges were directed at invocations of an executive privilege to withhold unclassified materials pertaining to internal deliberations. As far as classified information was concerned, Congress continued to show deference. During this period the subcommittees responsible for overseeing the intelligence community were composed of a few senior members who, according to Frank Smist, "chose not to be involved and preferred to be uninformed."[182] This deferential attitude was soon to be cast aside, though.

The turning point came in the first half of the 1970s when a sequence of events exposed the extent to which state secrecy could be used to conceal questionable, and in some cases blatantly illegal, activities. In June 1971, the *New York Times* published the Pentagon Papers, a classified study of decision making leading up to and during the Vietnam War. The study revealed that successive administrations had "systematically lied, not only to the public but also to Congress" about the reasons for, and prospects of, the war.[183] Then in July 1973, a whistleblower, Major Hal Knight, informed Congress that the Nixon administration had secretly ordered the bombing of Cambodia, even as it publicly claimed to be respecting that country's neutrality.[184] The ensuing investigation revealed that the administration had been systematically falsifying records, including those submitted to the Senate Armed Services Committee, in order to hide the secret bombing missions from public view. Not long after this revelation came Watergate. Though this scandal did not directly involve national security matters, the Supreme Court–ordered disclosure in July 1974 of tape recordings from the White House revealed that President Richard Nixon and his aides had attempted to ward off FBI investigators by hinting that the Watergate break-in was part of a secret national security operation.[185] Finally, in December 1974 Seymour Hersh of the *New York Times* published the so-called Family Jewels, an internal CIA document listing the activities that the organization had undertaken in contravention of domestic and international law, including assassination plots against foreign leaders, the overthrow of foreign regimes, the infiltration of domestic political groups, and warrantless domestic surveillance.[186]

These revelations sparked outrage and transformed what had previously been a general uneasiness about state secrecy into outright hostility. It now began to be argued, most prominently in Schlesinger's *The Imperial Presidency*, that Americans needed to combat "the rise of the religion of secrecy" by depriving the executive of its monopoly of the classification system.[187] But how was this to be done? First Amendment scholars argued that recent events provided a clue. The seminal contribution came from Alexander Bickel. In Bickel's view, the Pentagon Papers episode had demonstrated that the press provided *the* "countervailing power" against undue secrecy, because the First Amendment's disapproval of prior restraint meant that while the government was allowed to "guard mightily" against leaks, it had little choice but to "suffer them if they occur." Though the resulting cat-and-mouse "game" might be "disorderly," Bickel observed, it was nonetheless "effective."[188]

But this argument received a lukewarm reception. Louis Henkin, for instance, argued that "trial by battle and cleverness between the three estates and the fourth hardly seems the way best to further the various aims of a democratic society." This "unhappy game," he argued, "does not ensure that what should be concealed will not be uncovered," and "the rare, haphazard, fortuitous, journalistic uncovering will hardly achieve effective public knowledge of all that should be known."[189] It would be far better, he concluded, for Congress and president to tackle the problem of overclassification. This point was echoed by Schlesinger, who also expressed hesitation about the wisdom of relying on a "rebellious collaboration between anonymous and disgusted officials and the press." Since the rightness or wrongness of an unauthorized disclosure could be worked out only *after* such an action had already been undertaken, there was the danger, he warned, of too little or too much disclosure, depending on the proclivities of the officials and reporters involved. "Might it not be better," he asked, "to maintain the balance between secrecy and disclosure in a less nerve-racking way?"[190] To this end, he proposed two paths along which reform could proceed. The first was to establish "some form of appellate procedure" to help ensure that "classification decisions met standards of reason."[191] The second was to compel the president to "supply Congress the information necessary to responsible debate," for instance, by establishing "as a matter of law that CIA intelligence analyses be made available to the relevant committees."[192]

Schlesinger's analysis proved prescient. Emboldened by the widespread distrust of the presidency, Congress enacted two major changes in the institutional framework regulating the employment of state secrecy. In 1974, it amended FOIA to authorize the courts to examine classified records in camera in order to determine whether they legitimately qualified to be withheld under various national security exemptions. These amendments, adopted over President Gerald Ford's veto, effectively invited the courts to oversee the classification system. The other change was the creation of an intelligence oversight system in the form of the House Permanent Select Committee on Intelligence in 1977 and the Senate Select Committee on Intelligence in 1976.[193] Congress also passed the Hughes-Ryan Act in 1974 and the Intelligence Oversight Act in 1980, making it compulsory for the president to keep select members of Congress "fully and currently informed" of "significant anticipated intelligence activity," including covert operations.[194] Congress did not, however, bolster protection for the officials, reporters, and publishers responsible for transmitting unauthorized disclosures, declining, for instance, to establish a reporter's privilege to protect the identity of confidential sources or to revise the Espionage Act, which had been used to prosecute Daniel Ellsberg in the Pentagon Papers case.

In short order, however, it became clear that the enacted reforms had failed to challenge the president's control over the flow of secret information. During President Ronald Reagan's second term, citizens and lawmakers learned—once again via unauthorized disclosures—that the administration had secretly facilitated the sale of arms to Iran, covertly provided support to the Contras in Nicaragua in violation of the law, and utilized American media outlets to undertake a disinformation campaign targeted at Libya. Representative Norman Mineta, a member of the House intelligence committee during this period, described Congress's position in memorable terms: "we are like mushrooms. They keep us in the dark and feed us a lot of manure."[195] Meanwhile, civil society activists discovered that judicial deference to the executive's claims about the harm likely to be caused by the disclosure of classified information meant that FOIA could not help them obtain access to seemingly basic information about the executive's activities—for example, the size of the intelligence budget. As Robert Deyling glumly reported in 1992 after surveying the empirical evidence, since the enactment of FOIA the courts had "ruled on hundreds of cases involving classified information, affirming the government's decision to withhold the requested information in nearly every case."[196]

These setbacks prompted further calls for reform. For instance, Harold Koh argued that Congress ought to delegate the oversight of national security matters to a "core group of members" comprising a handful of its highest-ranked officials: limiting the number of overseers would, he felt, make it harder for the president to refuse to share information on the grounds that Congress was prone to indiscretion.[197] Sissela Bok, meanwhile, argued that the level of concealment in American government had become "pathological" owing to a deficiency at the heart of FOIA, whose proponents had failed to see that allowing information to be withheld on national security grounds would enable conniving officials to defeat the realization of publicity. Citing Weber, Bok warned that laws such as FOIA "can serve the public well only if the exceptions to them are kept to a minimum and are prevented from expanding."[198] This point was reiterated by the Commission on Protecting and Reducing Government Secrecy (the Moynihan Commission), which concluded in 1997 that there was a pressing need for "some check on the unrestrained discretion to create secrets" and for an "effective mode of declassification." To this end, the commission recommended the establishment of an independent National Declassification Center to oversee "systematic declassification."[199] What the commission explicitly rejected, though, was the idea that unauthorized disclosures might serve as a means of countering overclassification. "There must be," Senator Daniel Moynihan declared, "zero tolerance for permitting such information to be released through unauthorized means."[200]

Barely had the ink dried on the Moynihan Commission's report than the onset of the so-called war on terror prompted the administrations of Presidents George Bush and Barack Obama to employ an array of covert capabilities. As events unfolded, it quickly became clear that the executive continued to maintain a stranglehold over the flow of information relating to the use of these capabilities. For instance, in 2002 Congress authorized the use of military force in the wake of assertions by officials that secret intelligence revealed Iraq to be developing weapons of mass destruction and aiding terrorist organizations hostile to the United States. When these assertions eventually proved to be unfounded, members of Congress drew the conclusion that there had been "an exaggeration" of the threat.[201] According to Senator Dianne Feinstein, the episode underscored how vital it is for Congress to have "fairly presented, timely and accurate intelligence when they consider whether to invest in the President the authority as Commander-in-Chief to put American lives, as well as those of innocent civilians, at risk."[202] However, in spite of promises of closer oversight in the future, in 2006 a majority of the Senate intelligence committee found out about the NSA's warrantless wiretapping program only after the *New York Times* published a story on the program. Peeved, Senator Ron Wyden, a committee member, complained that he and his fellow senators had been forced to hire a news-clipping service to bring such reports to their notice. "My line," he is reported to have said, is "What do I know? I'm only on the Intelligence Committee."[203]

Congress is not the only branch to have struggled to oversee the president's secret activities during the war on terror. Over the past decade, the courts too have been hard-pressed to help citizens and lawmakers lift the veil on covert operations that have apparently violated the dignity and rights of individuals targeted in counterterrorism operations. For instance, FOIA has proven ineffective as a means of compelling the disclosure of documents detailing the treatment of suspected terrorists because judges continue to defer to the executive's assessment of the harm likely to be caused by disclosure of such information. This record has led critics such as Pallitto and Weaver to declare that judges have "abdicated" the role that FOIA intended for them to play—namely, to serve as independent assessors of classification decisions.[204] The courts have also proven unwilling to closely scrutinize the government's invocations of the state secrets privilege. As a result, complainants who have been subjected to extraordinary rendition and warrantless wiretapping have found themselves denied a forum in which to establish their claims and seek judicial remedy—a "harsh result" that has also attracted criticism from legal scholars.[205]

Not every regulatory mechanism has proven ineffective, though. To the extent that citizens and lawmakers have become aware of potential wrongdoing in the past decade—the establishment of secret prisons, the practice of extraordinary rendition, and the existence of warrantless surveillance programs—this has been due to unauthorized disclosures. The executive's response to this development has been unambiguous: the Bush and Obama administrations have together prosecuted more officials than all their predecessors combined.[206] Notably, neither Congress nor the courts have intervened strongly on behalf of either officials or the press. On the contrary, lawmakers have routinely condemned such disclosures, while the courts have permitted legal action against officials and reporters to proceed. Not surprisingly, these developments have drawn strong criticism from First Amendment scholars such as Stone and Kitrosser, who have called for enhanced protection for officials and reporters on the grounds that the law currently "gives inordinate weight to secrecy at the expense of informed public opinion."[207] However, proposals of this variety have been fiercely opposed, most recently by Lillian BeVier and Schoenfeld, who argue that unauthorized disclosures are unacceptable because of the "injury to democratic rule when unelected individuals act to override the public will" as expressed by elected representatives.[208]

The Dilemma

To recapitulate: I began by asking why state secrecy is approved in principle and censured in practice. The prevailing explanation, as we have seen, blames the presidency for having exploited "popular fear" and "popular faith" during the Cold War to establish a secrecy system that it has since used to its advantage. The problem with this explanation, I have argued, is that the Framers clearly expected the executive to employ state secrecy. Hence the executive's real and imagined transgressions cannot simply be a product of war hysteria; they must derive from something more deep-seated than that. The real cause, we have seen, is a silence in the Framers' theory. The Framers authorized the president to employ secrecy in the public interest, but did not fully explain how citizens and lawmakers could know whether the president is in fact exercising this power responsibly. This silence did not produce lasting crises of confidence in the nineteenth century because the dearth of foreign entanglements afforded presidents little reason or opportunity to employ state secrecy extensively. However, once the United States immersed itself in international politics at the turn of the twentieth century, the concomitant increase in the scope and scale of secrecy magnified the impact of the Framers' silence.

This conclusion raises an obvious question. For more than half a century now, scholars have addressed the Framers' silence by pushing for reforms intended to loosen the president's stranglehold over the flow of secret information. Why, then, does American public life continue to be roiled by controversies over the employment of state secrecy? The problem, as we have seen, is that it is not easy to fill the Framers' silence. Contemporary efforts have arrived at an impasse. The regulatory mechanisms that have been championed in recent decades—the Freedom of

Information Act and the establishment of congressional oversight committees in particular—have proven ineffective at exposing wrongdoing. Meanwhile, the regulatory mechanisms that have proven effective at exposing wrongdoing—the practices of whistleblowing and leaking—are condemned as unlawful and therefore illegitimate. It turns out, in other words, that the available safeguards are either ineffective or undesirable.

Can this dilemma be solved? That is, is it possible to transform legislative oversight and judicial review into more *effective* checks on the employment of state secrecy? And if not, are there conditions under which the making of unauthorized disclosures by officials, reporters, and publishers can be defended as *legitimate*? These are the questions we shall examine going forward. What we shall find is that this dilemma is far harder to solve than commentators have hitherto recognized.

Chapter 2

· ·

Should We Rely on Judges?

Transparency and the Problem of Judicial Deference

The difficulty in regulating state secrecy, we have seen, is that there is a mismatch between *who should* and *who does* serve as regulator. One reason for the mismatch is judicial deference toward the executive's claims about the harm likely to be caused by the disclosure of classified information—a posture, critics argue, that encourages and justifies unauthorized disclosures. Hence, if we want secrecy to be regulated by more orderly and lawful means, they argue, then judicial review must be expanded.

Why Do We Need Judges?

There are a variety of means that citizens can use to pressure the president to share the information they need to conduct oversight and enforce accountability: they can threaten to vote him out of office, they can signal suspicion through protests and demonstrations, and they can ask him to justify continuing secrecy. But citizens are hard-pressed to make use of these checks—elections, public opinion, and public deliberation—unless they have some prior indication of wrongdoing, since they will not want to call for the unwarranted disclosure of state secrets. In other words, before citizens can demand that the curtain be raised, they need to know at least something about what has been going on behind the curtain. This is what makes the idea of qualified transparency appealing. This conception of the norm of transparency calls on officials to disclose information unless secrecy is genuinely required to protect national security. But *who* can be trusted to enforce this norm? The challenge we confront when we ask officials to abide by this norm is that we have no way to tell whether their claims about the costs of making a particular piece of information public are reasonable. Indeed, there is something paradoxical about relying on officials to enforce the norm of qualified transparency: it places citizens in the position of a detective who expects the suspect to surrender the evidence of wrongdoing.

A number of commentators have argued that attending to the framework within which declassification decisions are made can lessen this regulatory challenge. The idea here is not to divest the executive of the final say over classification. Rather, it is to subject the classification decisions made by officials at the CIA or NSA—who may be tempted to use their classification power to shield their organizations from critical scrutiny—to *internal review* by peers from other intelligence agencies or legal officers such as the attorney general. If a classification decision survives such scrutiny, these commentators argue, then we have reason to be more confident about its merit, since the reviewers are not likely to share the parochial interests of the original classifier.[1] As David Pozen has put it, "admitting a mere handful" of lawyers into the classification process "may dramatically change" how secrecy is employed, because their "distinctive skill-sets and socialization" and "institutional responsibilities" will bring "a different perspective to the contemplated policy."[2] Or as Christina Wells has claimed, requiring officials to justify secrecy claims to lawyers from the Justice Department "could alleviate a number of cognitive biases," including "the tendency to rely only on confirmatory evidence while ignoring disconfirmatory evidence" about the harm likely to be caused by disclosure.[3] We could build on these insights by requiring government attorneys to publish sworn statements affirming that the classification decisions they have reviewed are justified and would survive public scrutiny. This requirement would raise the stakes for the internal reviewer: should subsequent disclosures reveal activity that the public deems unacceptable, her concurrence in the concealment of those activities would expose her to professional and legal sanction.

The idea of internal review is appealing because it promises to allow executive officers who have expertise in intelligence matters to balance the costs and benefits of disclosure. But can widening the circle of reviewers really improve the credibility of internal review in hard cases? It may well be the case that the officials responsible for reviewing classification decisions will not have exactly the same incentives as the officials responsible for the original classification decisions—but this does not mean that the former *will* have an incentive to promote transparency. Broader administration-wide objectives could lead internal reviewers to play along with the original classifiers, especially when the stakes are high. An embarrassing disclosure may not be an embarrassment exclusively to the parent organization of a particular classifier—it may embarrass or even weaken the administration as a whole and thus prompt a loyal silence from internal reviewers. Consider, for example, Kathleen Clark's complaint that the Bush administration's refusal to provide security clearances to investigators from the Office of Professional Responsibility—on the advice of Attorney General Alberto Gonzales—blocked an investigation into whether Justice Department lawyers acted inappropriately in approving the NSA's warrantless surveillance program.[4]

Furthermore, even if broader interests and loyalties do not influence internal reviewers, how can we be confident that their understanding of the appropriate balance between secrecy and accountability is in fact reasonable? As Dennis Thompson has pointed out, the justifiability of covert actions depends "on judgments about the value of the ends they promote." But these judgments are usually "too contestable to be resolved through assumptions about human nature, shared beliefs and interests under hypothetical conditions."[5] In practice this means that a government attorney may not know what might be a reasonable standard against which to compare the classification decision under review. A likely outcome under the circumstances is that, convinced of the righteousness of her employer's cause, she will consider the classification of a controversial policy well justified (if not, she may well find herself replaced with a more like-minded lawyer, who does).[6]

Are there other ways to bind the hands of those charged with reviewing classification decisions? One answer that many observers fall back upon is to impose limits on the duration of secrecy, principally in the form of "automatic" disclosure rules.[7] A rule of this kind effectively establishes a "shelf life" for a classification stamp. For example, a rule might require records stamped "confidential" to be treated as such for one year from the date of classification, following which the need to maintain confidentiality is presumed to have expired and the record is deemed declassified. The utility of such disclosure rules is that they seem to lessen the discretionary power that officials enjoy over declassification decisions, thus increasing the likelihood that citizens and lawmakers will obtain access to records that might otherwise have been withheld by officials wishing to cover up wrongdoing. However, such rules have two obvious shortcomings. The first is that they tend to have long fuses. That is, they tend to be premised on the idea that the harm likely to be caused by the disclosure of secret information diminishes only with the passage of a substantial period of time, typically between twenty to thirty years. Needless to say, requiring citizens and lawmakers to wait this long before they can examine how decision-makers have acted greatly constrains their ability to enforce accountability. Indeed, a long delay could mean that decision-makers will not face moral censure or legal penalties during their lifetimes. Conversely, the knowledge that declassification is likely to take place after a decision-maker's death, or at least well after the completion of his tenure in office, may well serve to undermine one of the key reasons to pursue accountability: to deter wrongdoing in the future. Then there is the problem of irretrievability: the greater the delay before declassification, the harder it becomes to remedy in any meaningful sense the harm caused by poor decision making.[8]

A further problem with automatic disclosure rules is that we cannot demand that they be followed absolutely, as we cannot be certain of the length of time after which the disclosure of a secret will prove harmless. Consider *Aftergood v. CIA* (2005), a case brought under the Freedom of Information Act (FOIA) by Steven Aftergood of the Federation of American Scientists, who had sought from the CIA information about the size of its Cold War–era intelligence budgets. In its declaration before Judge Ricardo Urbina of the District Court for the District of Columbia, the CIA argued that it was entitled to withhold the information in question in order to "protect the classified intelligence methods used to transfer funds to and between intelligence agencies." Aftergood challenged this claim, arguing that he had previously published the intelligence budgets for 1953, 1954, 1955, and 1972 that the historian David Barrett had discovered in the personal archives of former congressmen. The publication of these documents, Aftergood claimed, had "had no identifiable" negative consequences for the United States.[9] Hence the court, he argued, ought to order the CIA to disclose the requested information. However, Judge Urbina concluded otherwise. "The plaintiff invites the court to conclude that the plaintiff is more knowledgeable than the ADCI [assistant director of central intelligence] about what disclosure of information would harm intelligence sources and methods," he observed. "The court declines the plaintiff's invitation."[10]

If the passage of time cannot eliminate the discretion officials enjoy to withhold information, then officials will have the opportunity to stall the disclosure of classified information if they so wish. Can we prevent an abuse of this discretionary power by rotating decision-makers or by utilizing term limits? This proposal certainly has one benefit—a change of administration may well terminate the ongoing misuse of secrecy. Bear in mind, though, that this step will not prevent new misuses of state secrecy. Nor should we assume that an incoming administration will have the opportunity or the incentive to disclose the wrongful conduct of its predecessors. It may lack the opportunity since prior incumbents will have a strong incentive to avoid leaving a paper trail or else to destroy incriminating documents before departing—as they did during Iran-Contra.[11]

Moreover, any incentive that incoming officials may have to disclose wrongdoing by their predecessors will surely be counterbalanced by the desire not to establish a precedent that could be used against them when they leave office. Indeed, a new administration will have an incentive to actively conceal past wrongdoing because such revelations are likely to lead to calls for oversight (thereby making it harder for the new administration to employ state secrecy as *it* sees fit) and to embarrass the United States on the world stage (thereby making it harder for the new administration to pursue its own policies). It is also possible that party affiliations will align the interests of administrations. An example of this is provided by Executive Order 13233, which authorized President Bush to withhold the papers of his predecessors. Though the order was justified on grounds of national security, archivists and historians have pointed out that the order was passed shortly before President Reagan's papers were due to be made public.[12] The papers are believed to contain information relating to the Iran-Contra affair and its protagonists, which include some prominent personalities in the Republican establishment.

The Problem of Judicial Deference

For the reasons outlined above, internal review mechanisms and automatic disclosure rules do not provide much assurance that embarrassing or incriminating information will be made public, especially when the political stakes are high. Scholars therefore argue that we ought to transfer the final say on classification to an institution that will have a less immediate incentive to misuse this authority. Given the partisan character of Congress's membership, many scholars favor vesting this authority in the courts. But is this a wise choice? Can judges, far removed from the cut and thrust of diplomacy and international intrigue, really challenge the president's contentions as to what information should not be made public? The evidence, as we shall now see, is not promising.

As we saw in chapter 1, in 1966 Congress passed the Freedom of Information Act (FOIA) in order to provide the public with "access to official information" and to "create a judicially enforceable public right to secure such information from possibly unwilling official hands."[13] Congress acknowledged, however, that unconditional transparency or publicity would not be in the public interest. Hence FOIA exempts nine specific categories of information from disclosure. From our perspective, the relevant provisions are §552(b)(1) and §552(b)(3), commonly referred to as Exemptions 1 and 3. The former allows officials to withhold records that are "specifically authorized under criteria established by an Executive order to be kept secret in the interest of national defense or foreign policy"; the latter allows officials to withhold records "specifically exempted from disclosure by statute."[14] Though the latter provision may seem innocuous, it actually creates a substantial exception to FOIA because the statutes that can be invoked—such as the Central Intelligence Agency Act and the National Security Agency Act—allow intelligence agencies to withhold vast swathes of information about sources and methods, operations and personnel, and organizational features and functions.[15]

It is not difficult to see that officials who have something to hide may try to take advantage of these provisions. How far have the courts been willing to go to ensure that invocations of these exemptions are justified? The Supreme Court first tackled this issue in *EPA v. Mink* (1973), a case that arose after Congresswoman Patsy Mink sought access to a National Security Council (NSC) report addressing a dispute within the Nixon administration over whether to conduct an underground nuclear test in Alaska. Having been turned down by the administration, Mink appealed to the Supreme Court, asking it to examine in camera whether the report really needed to be kept secret in the interest of national defense. A number of the justices expressed sympathy for Mink's cause. As Justice Potter Stewart observed, "One would suppose that a nuclear test that engendered fierce controversy within the Executive Branch of our Government would be precisely the kind of event that should be opened to the fullest possible disclosure consistent with legitimate interests of national defense" because, in the absence of such information, "the people and their representatives [are] reduced to a state of ignorance, [and] the democratic process is paralyzed." Nonetheless, the court came down on the administration's side on the grounds that FOIA limited the courts to ascertaining only whether an exempted document was in fact classified. As Justice Stewart underscored, FOIA provided "no means to question an Executive decision to stamp a document 'secret,' however cynical, myopic, or even corrupt that decision might have been."[16]

In 1974 Congress responded to *Mink*, and to growing public outrage over real and apparent abuses of secrecy, by amending FOIA to authorize the courts to conduct in camera reviews of documents that officials claimed were exempt from disclosure. But Congress also constrained in camera review in two key respects. The conference report accompanying the legislation advised that "before the court orders *in camera* inspection, the Government should be given the opportunity to establish by means of testimony or detailed affidavits that the documents are clearly exempt from disclosure." Furthermore, the report emphasized Congress's expectation that, when evaluating the validity of an exemption claim, the courts "will accord *substantial weight* to an agency's affidavit concerning the details of the classification status of the disputed record," since "the Executive departments responsible for national defense and foreign policy matters have *unique insights* into what adverse effects might occur as a result of public disclosure of a particular classified record."[17]

Congress's instructions did not go unheeded. Shortly after the 1974 amendments had passed into law, the courts were confronted in *Weissman v. CIA* (1977) with a plaintiff who, having learned through news reports that the CIA had been spying on political activists within the United States, requested the CIA to disclose any files it might have on him. The CIA admitted to having files on the plaintiff, but argued that it was entitled to withhold them as they revealed intelligence sources and methods. After the district court found in favor of the CIA, the plaintiff approached the D.C. Circuit, asking it to conduct an in camera review to "check the truthfulness of Agency claims." But Judge Gerhard Gesell rejected this appeal, arguing that since "few judges have the skill or experience to weigh the repercussions of disclosure of intelligence information," once the court was satisfied "that proper procedures have been followed, and that by its sufficient description the contested document logically falls into the category of the exemption indicated," then "it need not go further to test the expertise of the agency, or to question its veracity when nothing appears to raise the issue of good faith."[18]

But what if there were doubts about the sufficiency of the government's explanation? In *Halperin v. CIA* (1980) an appellant sought the names of private attorneys retained by the CIA as well as the fees paid to them. The CIA responded to this request by arguing that disclosing the identity of an attorney who is an agent of the CIA in intelligence activities "might expose him to adverse action from hostile powers" and thereby create "a strong disincentive to those who are considering future employment or continued affiliation with the CIA." The appellant, Morton Halperin, a former assistant secretary of state, retorted that this "projection of potential harm" was "pure speculation." But the D.C. Circuit disagreed, observing that "any affidavit or other agency statement of threatened harm to national security will always be speculative to some extent, in the sense that it describes a potential future harm rather than an actual past harm." Under the circumstances, the only question before the court, Judge Malcolm Wilkey wrote, was whether "the predicted danger is a reasonable expectation," and on this front, he noted, "a court, lacking expertise in the substantive matters at hand, must give substantial weight to agency statements."[19]

But how far ought such judicial deference to extend? Could a judge challenge officials' claims that they needed to withhold even seemingly innocuous information on national security grounds? *Halperin* was instructive on this count too. The CIA argued that it was entitled to conceal even the total fees paid to the unnamed private attorneys because disclosing this figure "could give leads to information about covert activities that constitute intelligence methods." "If a large legal bill is incurred in a covert operation," it explained, then "a trained intelligence analyst could reason from the size of the legal bill to the size and nature of the operation." Though Judge Wilkey averred that the showing of the harm in this case was "not so great," he still upheld the CIA's claim, citing what has now come to be termed "mosaic theory." "We must take into account," he wrote, "that each individual piece of intelligence information, much like a piece of jigsaw puzzle, may aid in piecing together other bits of information even when the individual piece is not of obvious importance in itself."[20]

The cautious stance adopted in *Halperin* was subsequently affirmed in the landmark case *CIA v. Sims* (1985). As in other important FOIA cases, *Sims* involved a plaintiff who had been alerted to potential wrongdoing via a leak of classified information—in this case about the CIA's MKULTRA project, which involved research into brainwashing. Here the plaintiff sought from the CIA "the names of the institutions and individuals that had performed research" as part of MKULTRA. The CIA declined to comply with this request, citing the 1947 National Security Act, which states that "the Director of Central Intelligence shall be responsible for protecting intelligence sources and methods from unauthorized disclosure." After the district court and the D.C. Circuit disagreed over whether the institutions and individuals that participated in MKULTRA constituted the kind of "intelligence sources" that the CIA was authorized to protect under the act, the matter reached the Supreme Court, which unanimously concluded that the CIA ought to have wide latitude in defining what constitutes an intelligence source. Chief Justice Warren Burger invoked "the realities of intelligence work, which often involves seemingly innocuous sources as well as unsuspecting individuals who provide valuable intelligence information." Hence the CIA was entitled to withhold even "superficially innocuous information" because "a foreign government can learn a great deal about the Agency's activities by knowing the public sources of information that interest the Agency." In this domain, the court instructed, "the decisions of the Director, who must of course be familiar with 'the whole picture,' as judges are not, are worthy of *great deference* given the magnitude of the national security interests and potential risks at stake."[21]

The effect that *Sims* has had on subsequent FOIA litigation can be seen most clearly in *Fitzgibbon v. CIA* (1990). In this case, historian Alan Fitzgibbon had sought from the CIA information relating to the disappearance in the United States of a critic of the Dominican Rafael Trujillo regime. After the CIA released a limited number of documents featuring heavy deletions, Fitzgibbon sought relief from the District Court for the District of Columbia in 1979. As in other FOIA cases, the CIA filed a classified affidavit justifying its decision to withhold information. But unlike in prior FOIA cases, District Judge Harold Greene subjected the CIA's claim to careful scrutiny. Having examined the original documents in camera, Judge Greene determined that some of the deletions that the CIA had made were "unexplained" or "unrelated" to the justification offered, and hence ordered the disclosure of the deleted matter.[22]

Taken aback, the CIA appealed, but with *Sims* having been decided in the interim, the case was remanded to the district court. On remand, Judge Greene now reversed his previous order in light of *Sims*. He persisted, however, in ordering the disclosure of a document identifying the location of a CIA station that had already been disclosed in a congressional committee report. Now *both* Fitzgibbon and the CIA appealed. Before the D.C. Circuit, Fitzgibbon argued that the CIA ought not to be allowed to withhold information that Judge Greene had previously described as "so basic and innocent that its release could not harm the national security or betray a CIA method."[23] The CIA, on the other hand, sought reversal of the order to disclose the document identifying the location of its station. The D.C. Circuit rejected Fitzgibbon's appeal outright, noting that *Sims*'s endorsement of mosaic theory had "vaporized" the merits of his case. In addition, it rapped the district court on the knuckles for having "performed its own calculus as to whether or not harm to the national security or to intelligence sources and methods would result from disclosure" of the location of the CIA station. "The assessment of harm to intelligence sources, methods and operations," Judge David Sentelle emphasized, "is entrusted to the Director of Central Intelligence, not to the courts."[24]

It is not necessary to trace FOIA case history further than this, as the standard of review developed over the course of *Weissman*, *Halperin*, *Sims*, and *Fitzgibbon* has been consistently reaffirmed in recent decades.[25] However, lest this deferential standard be viewed as a consequence of the guidance that Congress issued alongside FOIA in 1974, let us briefly examine how the courts have reacted to invocations of the state secrets privilege. As we shall see, in this domain the courts *themselves* have fashioned a highly deferential standard of review.

The state secrets privilege is an evidentiary privilege that allows the United States to "block discovery in a lawsuit of any information that, if disclosed, would adversely affect national security."[26] The foundational case here is *United States v. Reynolds* (1953), which involved a lawsuit brought by the widows of individuals who were on board a military aircraft that crashed during a flight to test secret electronic equipment. In order to assess whether the Air Force had been negligent, the plaintiffs requested access to the accident investigation report. After the Air Force failed to comply, citing a right to withhold documents in the public interest, the district court treated the claim of negligence as justified and awarded damages. The United States then appealed this decision all the way to the Supreme Court, which concluded in a 6–3 decision that the United States did enjoy an evidentiary privilege, and that "even the most compelling necessity cannot overcome the claim of privilege *if* the court is ultimately satisfied that military secrets are at stake."[27]

So what would it take to satisfy a court that state secrets are in fact at stake? Here the *Reynolds* court discerned a "real difficulty"—namely, that "too much judicial inquiry into the claim of privilege would force disclosure of the thing the privilege was meant to protect, while a complete abandonment of judicial control would lead to intolerable abuses."[28] Not surprisingly, the court then went on to formulate a compromise. Crucially, it rejected the contention that it was for the executive to decide whether the requested evidence could be produced: "judicial control over the evidence in a case," Chief Justice Fred Vinson wrote, "cannot be abdicated to the caprice of executive officers." "Yet we will not go so far as to say," he added, "that the court may automatically require a complete disclosure to the judge before the claim of privilege will be accepted in any case."[29]

So when would it be appropriate for a judge to subject a claim of privilege to close analysis? "It may be possible to satisfy the court, from all the circumstances of the case," the chief justice observed, "that there is a reasonable danger that compulsion of the evidence will expose military matters which, in the interest of national security, should not be divulged." "When this is the case, the occasion for the privilege is appropriate," he instructed, "and the court should not jeopardize the security which the privilege is meant to protect by insisting upon an examination of the evidence, *even by the judge alone, in chambers*."[30] The italicized portion of this passage is important because the outcome in *Reynolds* ended up hinging upon it. The *Reynolds* court ruled—without the benefit of an in camera examination—that the accident investigation report was privileged because "there was a reasonable danger" that it "would contain references to the secret electronic equipment" undergoing testing on the Air Force plane.[31]

This passage in *Reynolds* has been criticized by scholars who have argued that the Supreme Court made an inexplicable error here—it examined whether there was a reasonable danger that the crash report *contained* secret information, instead of examining whether there was a reasonable danger that the *disclosure* of this information to the plaintiffs would harm national security.[32] According to these critics, the *Reynolds* court failed to do what it said a court ought to do—which is to determine whether the claim of privilege was actually justified. But this criticism misapprehends the court's reasoning. Arguably, the *Reynolds* court believed that there are *two* risks that a court needs to account for when handling a state secrets privilege claim. First, there is the risk that national security could be harmed by the *unauthorized* or *inadvertent* disclosure of evidence during in camera proceedings; and second, there is the risk that national security could be harmed by the *authorized* disclosure of evidence to litigants. Though Robert Chesney and Louis Fisher, among others, assert that the court was unduly deferential because it failed to investigate the latter risk by examining the report in camera, another way to understand *Reynolds* is to see the court as having ceased its investigation after completing the first of the two steps outlined above. That is, the court reasoned that since even an in camera, ex parte examination of privileged evidence comes with a risk of inadvertent or unauthorized disclosure, a court is not obliged to undertake such an examination unless the plaintiff can prove that she has no way of proceeding without the evidence in question. The court believed that this necessity was lacking in *Reynolds*, because the plaintiffs could have established negligence on the Air Force's part via depositions. Hence, it concluded, it was not obliged to take on the risk of examining the report in camera.

Since the Court in *Reynolds* had not seen the need to closely examine whether the Air Force's invocation of the state secrets privilege was justified, its opinion shed little light on how far judges ought to defer to the executive's claims in the event of uncertainty about whether the privilege had been invoked correctly. The first real opportunity to develop a standard of review came in *Jabara v. Kelley* (1977), a case brought by an individual seeking damages for having been subjected to warrantless wiretapping. Frustrated by the refusal of officials to respond to queries about the presumptive wiretaps, the plaintiff sought the assistance of the District Court of the Eastern District of Michigan, in turn prompting the Defense Department to invoke the state secrets privilege. Since there was a clear showing of need in this case—the plaintiff's action could not proceed without the requested information—Judge Ralph Freeman agreed to examine the Defense Department's affidavits in camera in order to ascertain whether the claim of privilege was justified. Following this examination Judge Freeman upheld the claim of privilege with respect to all information "that would reasonably tend to reveal foreign intelligence sources and capabilities."[33] But he also ruled that the privilege could not be invoked to shield information that did not relate to the conduct of foreign intelligence, citing in particular the Pentagon's refusal to disclose the name of the "federal agency" that had helped the FBI wiretap the plaintiff.[34] Noting that the name of this federal agency (the NSA) had already been revealed in a recent congressional report, Judge Freeman opined that "it would be a farce to conclude that the name of this other federal agency remains a military or state secret."[35]

The *Jabara* court's willingness to challenge the executive's claim about what constitutes a state secret was striking. But barely had *Jabara* been decided than the D.C. Circuit fashioned a rather different, and ultimately more influential, standard of review in *Halkin v. Helms* (1978). This was a case brought by antiwar protesters who believed that they had been subjected to warrantless surveillance by the NSA. In order to prove that their rights had in fact been violated, the plaintiffs requested the NSA to disclose the presumed intercepts of their communications. The NSA, however, declined to comply on the grounds that "identification of the individuals or organizations whose communications have or have not been acquired presents a reasonable danger that state secrets would be revealed" because it "would enable foreign governments or organizations to extrapolate the focus and concerns of our nation's intelligence agencies."[36] Following an in camera review of classified affidavits, the district court concluded that the plaintiffs' requests for information about intercepts from one NSA operation (MINARET) could not be compelled "because the ultimate issue, the fact of acquisition, could neither be admitted nor denied."[37] However, the district court also ruled that the NSA was obliged to respond to the plaintiffs' requests for information about intercepts from another operation (SHAMROCK), because congressional investigations had already revealed so much about this operation that national security would not be endangered if the NSA were to admit its existence.

Both the protesters and the NSA appealed from this decision. The former challenged the district court's deference to the executive's claims about the harm caused by the disclosure of intercepts from MINARET, whereas the latter challenged the order to disclose intercepts from SHAMROCK. Upon review, the D.C. Circuit rejected the protesters' appeal on the grounds that the standard of review for a state secrets privilege claim must be "a narrow one." Judges, the court instructed, must be cautious in challenging claims about the need to withhold information that might seem trivial or unimportant to ordinary observers. As Judge Roger Robb explained, "the business of foreign intelligence gathering in this age of computer technology is more akin to the construction of a mosaic" because "bits and pieces of seemingly innocuous information can be analyzed and fitted into place to reveal with startling clarity how the unseen whole must operate."[38] Hence the courts must "accord the *utmost deference* to executive assertions of privilege upon grounds of military or diplomatic secrets."[39] Accordingly, the D.C. Circuit concluded by affirming the order to protect intercepts from MINARET and overturned the order to disclose intercepts from SHAMROCK.

Clearly, if the courts must show utmost deference to the executive's claim about the harm likely to be caused by discovery—even when "seemingly innocuous information" is involved—then there is little to prevent officials from shielding potentially incriminating information by claiming that practically *any* discovery threatens national security. This is evidenced in *Kasza v. Browner* (1998), a case in which the Ninth Circuit was confronted with an appellant who sought to compel the Air Force to disclose details about allegedly unlawful handling of hazardous waste at a secret facility in Nevada. The Air Force responded to this action by invoking the state secrets privilege and refusing to share "any evidence tending to confirm or disprove that any hazardous waste had been generated, stored, or disposed of at the operating location."[40] The appellant then challenged this use of the privilege as "overbroad," arguing that the Air Force's claim that "the existence or nonexistence of hazardous waste is a state secret is absurd."[41] However, following an in camera review of affidavits that explained how the disclosure of unclassified information about the facility could serve to expose "security sensitive environmental data," the Ninth Circuit ruled that "if seemingly innocuous information is part of a classified mosaic, the state secrets privilege may be invoked to bar its disclosure and the court cannot order the government to disentangle this information from other classified information."[42] Since the appellant could not move forward without requiring the disclosure of classified information, the Ninth Circuit dismissed the entire action.[43]

There have now been a number of suits akin to *Kasza*, where entire cases have been dismissed because officials have claimed that discovery cannot proceed *at all* without revealing state secrets. The moral and political implications of deference to such broad privilege claims have been made starkly clear by the recent series of cases brought by individuals seeking redress for the practice of extraordinary rendition. The most revealing of these cases are *Mohamed v. Jeppesen Dataplan Inc.* (2009) (*Jeppesen I*) and *Mohamed v. Jeppesen Dataplan Inc.* (2010) (*Jeppesen II*). Both of these rulings emerged out of a complaint against Jeppesen Dataplan, a subsidiary of Boeing Corporation, which had provided the CIA with the logistical support required to transport suspected terrorists to secret detention facilities overseas where these detainees were subjected to torture. Before the original complaint reached the trial stage, the CIA intervened and sought dismissal on the grounds that the "core" of the plaintiffs' complaint involved covert CIA operations—"clearly a subject matter which is a state secret."[44] After the District Court of the North District of California agreed with the CIA, the plaintiffs appealed to the Ninth Circuit.

In *Jeppesen I*, the Ninth Circuit drew a line. The notion that a lawsuit should be dismissed "any time a complaint contains allegations, the truth or falsity of which has been classified as secret by a government official," Judge Michael Hawkins observed, implies that "the Judiciary should effectively cordon off all secret government actions from judicial scrutiny, immunizing the CIA and its partners from the demands and limits of the law."[45] This theory, he argued, threatened "the principles of the separation of powers and judicial review," which called for a careful "item-by-item" analysis to determine whether the privileged evidence was genuinely "indispensable" to the maintenance of the suit or whether the plaintiffs could make their case by reference to nonprivileged evidence.[46] Of course such close analysis would serve little purpose if judges simply deferred to the executive's claims about what counts as a state secret since, as *Halkin* and *Kasza* show, even information that has already been made public by Congress (the SHAMROCK operation) or is unclassified (the presence of hazardous waste) can be part of a classified "mosaic." Hence, not surprisingly, Judge Hawkins also pushed back on the question of *who* was to judge what counted as a state secret. "A rule that categorically equated 'classified' matters with 'secret' matters," he wrote, "would perversely encourage the President to classify politically embarrassing information simply to place it beyond the reach of judicial process." Hence, "while classification may be a strong indication of secrecy as a practical matter," he instructed, "courts must undertake an independent evaluation of any evidence sought to be excluded to determine whether its contents are secret within the meaning of the privilege."[47] Having said this, Judge Hawkins went on to offer an evaluation of his own—classified information about the extraordinary rendition program that had made its way into the public domain could not, he contended, be considered a state secret. "The government could not seriously argue," he wrote, "that the Pentagon Papers remained 'secret' and therefore subject to the state secrets privilege even after having been published in the *New York Times*, simply because the government itself refused to declassify or otherwise 'officially disclose' the content of the papers."[48]

The decision in *Jeppesen I* was soon reversed, though. Given the "exceptional importance" of the subject, the Ninth Circuit voted to rehear the case en banc and subsequently affirmed the district court's decision by a margin of 6–5. Writing for the majority, Judge Raymond Fisher conceded that the existence of the extraordinary rendition program could no longer be considered a state secret—*not* because leaks had revealed "alleged" details of the program, but rather because its existence had been "publicly acknowledged" by "numerous government officials."[49] But the "partial disclosure of the existence and even some aspects of the extraordinary rendition program," he emphasized, did not "preclude other details from remaining state secrets if their disclosure would risk grave harm to national security."[50] The existence of these valid state secrets, Judge Fisher argued, posed a quandary for the courts. "Because the facts underlying plaintiffs' claims are so infused with these secrets," he claimed, "any plausible effort by Jeppesen to defend against them would create an unjustifiable risk of revealing state secrets."[51] But what about *Reynolds*'s instruction that the greater the showing of necessity on the part of the plaintiff, the greater the obligation of the court to take on the risk of examining whether the claim of privilege was appropriate? Here Judge Fisher begged off, noting that even though "district courts are well equipped to wall off isolated secrets from disclosure, the challenge is exponentially greater in exceptional cases like this one, where the relevant secrets are difficult or impossible to isolate and even efforts to define a boundary between privileged and unprivileged evidence would risk disclosure by implication."[52]

Is Judicial Deference Justified?

So far we have seen that the courts have displayed "great deference" and "utmost deference" to the executive's claims about the harm likely to be caused by disclosure, even where "seemingly innocuous information" is concerned. This record has attracted criticism from commentators who have argued that such sweeping deference is unjustified, especially when civil liberties are at stake. Fisher, for instance, asserts that for judges "to defer to agency claims about privileged documents and state secrets is to abandon the independence that the Constitution vests in the courts and place in jeopardy the individual liberties that depend on institutional and public checks."[53] It has also been argued that judicial deference tends to be premised on faulty grounds. In a pathbreaking essay, Chesney warns that officials and judges alike have a tendency to "oversimplify" the reasons why deference is owed to the executive in the national security context.[54] A closer inspection, he argues, would reveal that judges have reason to scrutinize the executive's claims more carefully than they do at present.

These are weighty charges. However, before we advise judges to subject the executive's claims to close scrutiny, we ought to be clear about the reasons that the courts themselves have offered in defense of deference. The first reason in favor of judicial deference is the prudential concern we touched upon during the discussion of *Reynolds* and *Jeppesen II*—namely, the worry that the examination of classified materials even in camera could lead to unauthorized or inadvertent disclosures. Importantly, the concern here is *not* that judges and their clerks cannot be *personally* trusted with state secrets. Claims along these lines have been made in the past, and they have rightly been rejected by the Supreme Court in *United States v. United States Dist. Court* (1972) (also known as the *Keith* case) where Justice Lewis Powell underscored that "judges may be counted upon to be especially conscious of security requirements in national security cases."[55] The concern we have, by contrast, is about the limited *institutional capacity* of the courts, which, judges themselves have argued, are ill-equipped to handle large volumes of classified materials on an ongoing basis. As the D.C. Circuit explained in *Ellsberg v. Mitchell* (1983), to assert that an examination in camera "is not entirely safe" is not meant to "slight judges, lawyers or anyone else." Rather, the problem is that "in our own chambers, we are ill equipped to provide the kind of security highly sensitive information should have."[56]

Notably, the passage of time and prolonged experience with cases involving classified information have not altered this view. For instance, in *Sterling v. Tenet* (2005), a high-profile racial discrimination case brought by an employee of the CIA, the Fourth Circuit recited *Reynolds*'s injunction against conducting in camera review of highly secret materials as the key reason to refrain from calling for the CIA's personnel files, a necessary step to evaluating the charge of discrimination. The courts, the Fourth Circuit warned, "are not required to play with fire and chance further disclosure—inadvertent, mistaken, or even intentional—that would defeat the very purpose for which the privilege exists."[57] The Fourth Circuit has been far from alone in taking this view. As noted above, the Ninth Circuit reversed *Jeppesen I* precisely because it was convinced that "the risk of disclosure that further proceedings would create cannot be averted through the use of devices such as protective orders or restrictions on testimony."[58]

We have also already touched on the second reason in favor of judicial deference—namely, the concern for expertise as highlighted in *Halkin* and *Sims*. As the Fourth Circuit has recently summarized in *El-Masri v. United States* (2007), "deference is appropriate not only for constitutional reasons, but also practical ones: the Executive and the intelligence agencies under his control occupy a position superior to that of the courts in evaluating the consequences of a release of sensitive information."[59] Once again, it is not the intellectual competence of judges that is in doubt. To question the expertise of judges is not to "see the judiciary as a hapless incompetent."[60] Rather, the concern is about specialization or *comparative advantage* in making judgments about the harm likely to be caused by the disclosure of information. As the Fourth Circuit explained in *El-Masri*, deference in the areas of military and foreign affairs and secret intelligence is founded on the assumption that executive officers who are continuously immersed in these domains are likely to make *more* refined or accurate predictive judgments.[61] The federal judiciary, by contrast, "is a generalist institution composed of generalist judges," as John Yoo has emphasized. "Very few judges," he points out, "have significant foreign affairs experience before their appointment to the federal bench," and the organization of courts along geographic lines "not only prevents specialization, but also retards the accumulation of experience."[62]

To be sure, a few courts have tried to circumvent the question of expertise by allowing cases to proceed on the basis of evidence that is already in the public domain. In two such widely cited cases, *Hepting v. AT&T* (2006) and *ACLU v. NSA* (2006), courts were confronted with invocations of the state secrets privilege that prevented the plaintiffs from proving that they had in fact been subject to warrantless wiretaps. Rather than compelling the disclosure of the relevant information, which would have required dismissing the NSA's concerns about harm to national security, the courts decided that official acknowledgment of the existence of a warrantless surveillance program was sufficient to grant the plaintiffs standing.[63] This is an interesting precedent, but its utility over the long term seems questionable, because it creates a strong incentive for officials to say as little as possible in public. Moreover, legal action based on public statements remains vulnerable to the problem that even secrets that have been publicly acknowledged will usually be too closely tied up with undisclosed secrets to permit the sort of evidentiary disclosures required to allow plaintiffs to actually proceed with their case. This is precisely what prevented *Jeppesen II* from proceeding in spite of extensive public discussion about the extraordinary rendition program.

So why have these arguments in favor of deference been rejected? Briefly put, critics have argued that the prudential and epistemic concerns cited above can be addressed via "procedural innovations"—either by modifying trial procedures by, for example, calling upon outside experts, or by establishing special courts staffed by judges and clerks deeply versed in intelligence matters and able to conduct trials in camera and ex parte where necessary.[64] Meredith Fuchs, for instance, has argued that the appointment of "a neutral and experienced [special] master with the appropriate security clearances could . . . relieve the court of its expertise and burden concerns," while Pozen has submitted that "extrajudicial assistants" could help judges "evaluate the plausibility" of claims based on mosaic theory, which tend to be "highly speculative."[65] More radically, Chesney has suggested that Congress could create "a classified judicial forum" where Article III judges could hear cases involving state secrets "*in camera* on a permanently sealed, bench-trial basis," where plaintiffs could be represented by a *guardian ad litem* "selected from among a cadre of, for example, federal public defenders with the requisite clearances."[66]

There are, however, reasons to be skeptical about these proposals. As Fuchs admits, the use of outside experts raises concerns about the "improper delegation" of judicial authority and consequently about the integrity of the judicial process. Her response to the problem is twofold. First, she instructs that an outside expert must be "truly autonomous, lacking any current or known future relationship with either the government or plaintiffs." Second, she advises that "experts should be used primarily as case administrators" tasked with "winnowing down voluminous records."[67] Both these instructions are problematic, though. An expert who is familiar with the challenges associated with national security will presumably have worked extensively for the government and will therefore likely have ties to serving officials.[68] Furthermore, since a security clearance can be taken away, one must also question the disinterestedness of an outside expert who wants to retain her clearance. And if the outside expert has long since retired or has no intention of being employed in the near future, then one must wonder how knowledgeable she can be about contemporary security concerns. Finally, if the purpose of an outside expert is to be limited to merely winnowing records, and "judges must still make the hard decisions over what information is rightfully released," as Fuchs puts it, then how does the appointment of such an expert actually help the judge overcome his lack of expertise?[69]

Chesney's proposal too is problematic. Most immediately, it relies upon public defenders armed with the requisite security clearances to uphold the interests of plaintiffs. Presumably, these lawyers will want to retain their clearances, especially if they have spent their careers developing expertise in the area of national security law. No doubt the termination of the military career of Charles Swift, the navy lawyer assigned to represent Salim Hamdan, will give them some pause.[70] More fundamentally, once we move to a system where entire trials are conducted in camera, the distinction between an independent court and an internal executive branch review process begins to fade. It may be objected that the accoutrements of national security will not interfere with the independence of an Article III judge. But consider the likely outcome once a judge goes from occasionally dipping his toes into the world of secret intelligence to embracing it on a permanent basis. It is not unreasonable to expect that a court that routinely handles classified information will become a target of espionage. Nor is it unreasonable to expect the occasional leak from a headstrong clerk or public defender. Additionally, there is the near certainty that these judicial officers will come under increased scrutiny when the protagonists in a national security emergency belong to the same ethnic or racial or religious group as they do. As a result, we should be prepared for the eventuality that judges, clerks, and public defenders will be subject to counter-intelligence surveillance and may be liable to prosecution for disclosing classified information. How will the resulting intrusions into the private lives of these actors affect their decisions? What sorts of actions will count as troubling enough to justify the loss of a security clearance? What security will there be against "dirty tricks," especially those aimed at subduing zealous public defenders? Scholars tend not to discuss these scenarios, but they should, because these are precisely the sorts of threats that employees in the intelligence world must contend with when they expose or challenge perceived wrongdoing.

Suppose the prudential and epistemic concerns outlined above are rejected as overblown. There is still one more reason to support judicial deference—namely, a concern for accountability. The starting point for this argument lies in recognizing the fragility of the idea of expertise. There is a tendency on the part of the critics of judicial deference to assume that there is something akin to a science of intelligence. That is, they seem to believe that there are objective answers to questions about the harm likely to be caused by the disclosure of a given piece of information. However, if intelligence professionals are to be believed, it is not uncommon for intelligence assessments to diverge sharply. This is because, as the Supreme Court observed in *Department of Navy v. Egan* (1988), the business of intelligence "is an inexact science at best"—one that frequently involves making judgment calls about the consequences of particular choices under conditions of highly incomplete information.[71] There is no better example of how such calls can turn out badly than *Weatherhead v. United States* (1998), one of the very few FOIA cases in which an appellate court has ruled against the executive branch.

Weatherhead emerged out of a FOIA request for a copy of the correspondence between the British Foreign Office and the U.S. government about the extradition and impending trial of a British national. After the British government deemed the correspondence to be confidential in nature, the State Department withheld it, prompting the plaintiff to seek review by the District Court for the Eastern District of Washington. Upon review, the district court ordered that the letter be disclosed because the State Department's affidavits justifying the withholding had "failed to provide a particularized explanation of how disclosure of the letter would damage the relations between the United States and the United Kingdom."[72] However, following an appeal for reconsideration, Judge Frederick Van Sickle conducted an in camera review and then proceeded to reverse his earlier decision. Now, having read the letter in question, he declared that he "knew without hesitation or reservation that the letter could not be released," adding that "there is no portion of it which could be disclosed without simultaneously disclosing injurious materials." The plaintiff, Judge Van Sickle concluded, "would have to be satisfied with the solace of knowing that not only do two high ranking [Department of State] officers believe disclosure of the subject material injurious to the national interest, but so does an independent federal judge."[73]

Unimpressed, the plaintiff appealed to the Ninth Circuit, which also examined the document in camera—and reached precisely the *opposite* conclusion. Writing for the majority, Chief Judge Procter Hug observed that having reviewed the letter, "we fail to comprehend how disclosing the letter at this time could cause harm to the national defense or foreign relations of the United States." The letter, he added, is "innocuous."[74] The embarrassing contrast between the language used by the district court and the Ninth Circuit did not pass unnoticed. In a sharply worded dissent, Judge Barry Silverman of the Ninth Circuit asserted that the contrast showed that "we judges are outside of our area of expertise here." "It's one thing to examine a document *in camera* for the existence of facts," he argued, but "it's a whole different kettle of fish to do what the majority has presumed to do here, to make its own evaluation of both the sensitivity of a classified document and the damage to national security that might be caused by disclosure."[75] For his part, Judge Silverman concluded by siding with Judge Van Sickle on the grounds that the Ninth Circuit should not have treated the "sobering assessment" provided in the government's affidavits "with so little regard."[76]

If only this were the end of the story. Following the Ninth Circuit's decision, the United States appealed to the Supreme Court. However, as the court prepared to hear oral arguments, the litigants discovered that the British consul in Seattle had long ago transmitted a "significant portion of the contents of the supposedly confidential letter" to the plaintiff.[77] Following this embarrassing discovery, the case was deemed moot and the decisions of the lower courts were vacated.

Arguably, what *Weatherhead* makes clear is that there often is a strongly *subjective* aspect to the business of predicting the harm likely to be caused by the disclosure of classified information. Before we can strike a balance between the costs and benefits of disclosure, we must take the vital first step of deciding what the costs and benefits *are*, and here much depends on one's moral intuitions, political awareness, and common sense—in other words, on one's political judgment. The classic explanation as to why the courts ought to steer clear of making such judgment calls comes in *Chicago & Southern Air Lines, Inc. v. Waterman SS Corp* (1948), where Justice Robert Jackson observed that such decisions should be made "only by those directly responsible to the people whose welfare they advance or imperil."[78] This warning may seem overblown in the context of *Weatherhead*, which was more a farce than a national security emergency, but it does loom large when we consider cases involving extraordinary rendition and secret imprisonment, practices that appear necessary to some but frightful to others.

Here it may be objected that even if decisions about whether and when to release classified information are indeed political in nature, it is still preferable to have this decision made by judges rather than executive officers, as the latter have an obvious conflict of interest. In other words, it can be claimed that the subjective but disinterested decision of a judge is preferable to the subjective and likely self-interested decision of an executive officer, especially since the presence of secrecy means that citizens may not actually be able to hold the latter any more accountable than the former. But is it prudent to assume that judges will remain disinterested for long once they are drawn into the business of substantively evaluating whether secret information ought to be disclosed to the public? On the contrary, it is likely that vesting such politically significant authority in the courts will make appointments to the relevant benches a point of strong contention. And since the appointed judges will need to keep the grounds for their decisions secret, it will be difficult for the public to ascertain that they have *not* been influenced by partisan or ideological considerations.

An illustration of this difficulty is provided by questions that have been asked about the record of the Foreign Intelligence Surveillance Court (FISC). For obvious reasons, this court examines warrants in camera and ex parte. Should we be disturbed by the fact that this court has reportedly ruled against the United States only a handful of times in the more than twenty thousand cases brought before it?[79] Or, on the contrary, should we take the court's track record as evidence of the government's unwillingness to bring weak cases before it? And if the latter interpretation seems the more reasonable one, then how do we make sense of reports that the FISC has retrospectively accused the government of misleading it in at least seventy-five instances since 2001?[80] We have no informed basis on which to answer any of these questions. Equally, should we be troubled by the decision of the chief judge of the FISC to cooperate with the NSA's warrantless surveillance program? A number of scholars seem convinced that the NSA program was unconstitutional. Should we be worried then about what other potentially unconstitutional activities the FISC may have permitted? How would we even know if such decisions have been made?

The point, in short, is that compelling judges to take on the responsibility of assessing the harm likely to be caused by the disclosure of classified information is not likely to further our confidence that the norm of transparency is being observed. On the contrary, this step is likely to merely shift the locus of fear—away from officials and toward judges. This is not to suggest that judicial intervention *will* replicate the conflict of interest that arises when the final say over classification is left in the hands of the executive. Rather, the point is that under conditions of secrecy citizens will lack a reason to be confident that judges are behaving disinterestedly, since the public will not have access to the information necessary for rational trust. This problem would persist, moreover, even if we were to appoint an "independent" Declassification Commission, as scholars and lawmakers have proposed.[81] Indeed, the extensive regulatory capture at bodies such as the Securities and Exchange Commission and the Federal Communications Commission, which operate in public sight, suggests that establishing an opaque and unelected "secrecy regulator" ought to actually *deepen* fears about the misuse of secrecy, seeing as the financial, political, and ideological interests at stake in important national security decisions would give the affected parties a powerful motive to try to "capture" the regulator.

The concern about unaccountable judicial intervention may be challenged in two ways. First, it may be argued that judges are in fact accountable—even when they judge in secret—because unlike those of executive officers, their judgments may be appealed to higher courts. But, as the prognostication of the harm likely to be caused by the disclosure of state secrets depends heavily on political judgment, what exactly can a higher court hold a lower court accountable for? Certainly, a lower court might be sanctioned for outright bias or gross negligence. But how can it be penalized for a difference of opinion over the harm likely to be caused by the disclosure of a piece of classified information? And is the Supreme Court even likely to be able to hold lower courts accountable for "mistaken interferences with regard to foreign and national security policies set by the political branches"?[82] There are, as Yoo has reminded proponents of judicial review, hundreds of federal judges, dozens of district courts, and thirteen appellate courts. If the Supreme Court, which currently hears fewer than a hundred cases each year, cannot devote more time to resolving differences between these decentralized actors, then it is reasonable to conclude that "judicial involvement in foreign and national security policy will create disharmony where uniformity is crucial."[83]

Second, it may be argued that concerns about unaccountable decision making can be tempered by having members of the intelligence committees in Congress serve in an "advisory capacity," principally by offering judges their views about whether a request to withhold information is well founded.[84] But this proposal is not attractive either. It is widely recognized that Congress tends to defer to the president in the domain of national security. Indeed, this is precisely why proponents of transparency criticize judicial deference—they see the courts as the only safeguard against undue secrecy, especially during emergencies. In their view, judges are insulated from everyday political pressures precisely so that *they* will ask the hard questions that Congress will not.[85] Moreover, presidents have long reserved the right to keep national security information from Congress on the grounds that a lawmaker from a rival party might disclose such information with an eye to gaining political advantage.[86] This claim, as we shall see in chapter 3, is not without foundation. Consequently, even if involving Congress lessens the fears that judges are making arbitrary decisions about what information should be disclosed to the public, this may well turn out to be a pyrrhic victory, since it will actually make it harder for the courts to maintain the secrecy they are supposed to protect.

Can Judges Moderate Secrecy?

So far I have been making the case that judges are not well positioned to promote transparency because they are not qualified to challenge the executive's claims about the harm likely to be caused by the disclosure of secret information. I have also argued that judges should not be asked to make what are effectively subjective judgments about the costs and benefits of disclosure, as this will merely encourage the politicization of the relevant benches and thereby defeat the whole point of turning to the courts, which is to obtain an impartial adjudicator. This is not the end of the road, though. There is another way in which judges may be able to help promote transparency: by policing norms about *how* officials ought to employ secrecy rather than about *what* precisely ought to be made public. In particular, by requiring officials to offer reasons in defense of secrecy, judges may be able to moderate the scope and scale of state secrecy—that is, they may be able to help make secrecy *shallower*.

The concept of shallow state secrecy emerges from Amy Gutmann and Dennis Thompson's observation that when secrecy prevents the content of policies from being exposed to public scrutiny, it becomes especially important to make sure that citizens "have a chance to decide in advance whether the policy is justified and to review the details of the policy after it is implemented."[87] Of course citizens can have such a chance only if they know that something has in fact been kept secret. Hence Gutmann and Thompson argue that the exercise of secrecy must abide by two conditions: only "the details" of the relevant policy, and not the existence of the policy, must be kept secret; and "the fact that the details of the policy are secret should itself not be a secret."[88] Thus, for example, if the government wishes to establish a spy satellite program, then the norm of shallow secrecy would require it to inform the public or Congress and obtain approval for the policy of having spy satellites even if it does not disclose the details of the program. Only if the government acts in this way, Gutmann and Thompson argue, will citizens have the "opportunity to challenge the keepers of secrets and ultimately to decide whether the secret should be kept."[89]

But must officials always keep secrets shallow? That is, are they obliged to declare the existence of every state secret? It is not difficult to imagine cases where announcing the existence of a state secret can *itself* have undesirable consequences—for example, merely acknowledging the existence of a spy satellite program could prompt terrorist organizations to take countermeasures like moving their training facilities underground. Gutmann and Thompson acknowledge this possibility when they discuss "deep secrets"—secrets whose very existence is kept secret from citizens and lawmakers out of a concern for national security. They argue that such deep secrets can be "justified only if they can be shown to be necessary to safeguard the democratic values of basic liberty, opportunity, and deliberation, and only if this showing can meet the test of accountability."[90] But to whom should this showing be made? It cannot be made publicly, as this would lead to the disclosure of the very information the government wants to protect. Yet if officials are not required to make a public showing, then how can we know whether they are exercising deep secrecy for the right reasons?

It may be objected that it is unlikely that officials will need to maintain many deep secrets. But even if this were true, it remains the case that even an "ordinary" state secret can be maintained at varying depths. For instance, the United States could *either* declare that it has a spy satellite program *or* it could declare that it has a dozen spy satellites that cost X and feature Y and Z groundbreaking capabilities. Before we can determine whether officials are obliged to make the latter, more informative declaration, we need to know something about the harm this declaration may engender (such as whether it will in fact prompt terrorist organizations or rival states to move their training facilities or weapons factories underground). It seems reasonable to assume that the executive alone can supply this estimate. But in that case what is to prevent officials from overstating the cost of the latter declaration, leading us to conclude that they are obliged to make only the former, less informative declaration? Needless to say, if we cannot prevent such "threat inflation," then demands for shallow secrecy will not greatly increase the extent of information available to the public.

So how can we enforce the norm of shallow secrecy—that is, how can we make sure that officials will say all that can safely be said about the secrets in their possession? Are the courts any more likely to be able to help on this front? At first glance the evidence seems promising, especially in the FOIA context where the courts have demanded that officials submit "a detailed public justification for any claimed right to withhold a document."[91] The purpose of this requirement, as the D.C. Circuit explained in the landmark case *Vaughn v. Rosen* (1973), is that it allows judges to determine whether the records that officials wish to withhold are in fact related to the exemption being claimed, and it also provides plaintiffs an "opportunity to contest the withholding of the documents," and to identify and seek the disclosure of those records that are less likely to be exempt from disclosure.[92] To this end, *Vaughn* obliges officials to submit a detailed and itemized affidavit (now referred to as a "Vaughn index") that "must describe the material being withheld, state the justification for nondisclosure, and cite each exemption asserted."[93] This requirement nicely parallels the idea of shallow secrecy. However, the picture is complicated by the fact that *Vaughn* also allows affidavits to exclude "factual descriptions that if made public would compromise the secret nature of the information."[94] This concession—that an explanation as to why a secret ought to remain a secret could itself harm national security—has given rise to an array of cases in which officials have been excused from having to even acknowledge the existence of secrets, much less to justify keeping the secret itself.

The foundational case here is *Phillippi v. CIA* (1975), one of a series of cases in which plaintiffs sought records pertaining to the *Glomar Explorer*, a ship that had reportedly been employed in a covert operation aimed at recovering a sunken Soviet submarine. In the case at hand, a journalist, Harriet Phillippi, requested from the CIA information about its contacts with reporters covering the *Glomar Explorer* story. The CIA responded that it could not fulfill Phillippi's request as the information sought involved an activity that "in the interest of national security" could "neither be confirmed nor denied" (a response that has since been named a "Glomar response").[95] Phillippi then approached the district court, asking it to compel the CIA "to provide a detailed justification for each document claimed to be exempt from disclosure." The CIA responded by submitting classified affidavits, which the district court then examined in camera. After the district court subsequently issued a summary judgment in favor of the CIA, Phillippi approached the D.C. Circuit, arguing that courts were entitled to examine only the withheld documents in camera, not the affidavits themselves. However, the D.C. Circuit rejected this claim. It concluded that courts were entitled "to examine classified affidavits in camera and without participation by plaintiff's counsel" because "when the Agency's position is that it can neither confirm nor deny the existence of the requested records, there are no relevant documents for the court to examine other than the affidavits which explain the Agency's refusal."[96]

I have been arguing that efforts to enforce the norm of shallowness—that is, to compel government officials to declare the existence, if not the content, of state secrets—can be frustrated by the fact that officials can claim (1) that acknowledging the existence of a state secret could harm national security, and (2) that explaining why acknowledging the existence of a state secret could harm national security could itself harm national security. The courts, to their credit, have pushed back against the latter of these claims. Although the *Phillippi* court allowed officials to submit classified affidavits explaining why they could not confirm or deny the *Glomar Explorer* operation, it instructed the CIA to "provide a public affidavit explaining in as much detail as is possible the basis for its claim that it can be required neither to confirm nor to deny the existence of the requested records." The purpose of doing so, the *Phillippi* court said, was to "create as complete a public record as is possible."[97]

But how detailed can such a public record be? Can it reliably procure the shallow secrecy that Gutmann and Thompson recommend? The prospects appear dim. As the D.C. Circuit acknowledged in *Hayden v. NSA* (1979), when "itemization and justification are themselves sensitive . . . to place them on public record could damage security in precisely the way that FOIA Exemption 1 is intended to prevent."[98] In other words, *Hayden* confirms that in some cases officials may legitimately refuse to offer *any* public explanation whatsoever for their decision to withhold information from a FOIA requester. Of course not every FOIA case involves the supersecret NSA as *Hayden* did. In two well-known cases, *Gardels v. CIA* (1982) and *Miller v. Casey* (1984), officials refused to confirm or deny the existence of the requested records, but they *did* offer public affidavits explaining why confirming or denying the existence of the state secret in question could harm national security. In *Gardels*, which involved a request for information about covert CIA contacts with members of the University of California, the CIA explained that it could not confirm or deny such contacts because if it "were required to indicate those schools with which it had had no covert contact," then foreign intelligence organizations "could and would concentrate their efforts on the remaining American colleges and universities" in order to "discover what the CIA is up to" on those campuses.[99] Arguably, this explanation satisfies the norm of shallowness—it offers the public a plausible reason as to why the CIA cannot confirm or deny the existence of a secret activity. However, at this degree of abstraction we have no way of knowing whether campus contacts are being used in ways we might consider improper (for instance, to entrap foreign students). At the same time, there is little we can do to obtain more detail. So long as we defer to the CIA's factual claim that "foreign intelligence agencies are zealous ferrets," we have little basis on which to demand greater specificity in the public affidavits filed by officials, lest this alert foreign observers and thereby endanger national security.[100]

The justifications for secrecy tend to be even more vague in cases where the state secrets privilege has been invoked. The first significant effort to extend the *Vaughn* standard to this domain came with *Halkin v. Helms* (1982) where the plaintiffs, who were seeking to discover whether they had been subjected to unlawful surveillance, argued that the public affidavit submitted by the CIA justifying its invocation of the state secrets privilege "was too vague to establish the privilege."[101] The D.C. Circuit disagreed. The CIA's public affidavit, it argued, "while *necessarily unspecific*, set forth the grounds requiring secrecy in this context."[102] The grounds were twofold: first, that "revelation of particular instances in which foreign governments assisted the CIA in conducting surveillance of dissidents could strain diplomatic relations," and second, that information that allowed the plaintiffs to know they have been the subjects of surveillance, might "when combined with knowledge of the individual's other activities," allow foreign intelligence agencies "to identify CIA operatives."[103] As in *Gardels*, the FOIA case examined above, these justifications for invoking the state secrets privilege are pitched at such an abstract level that they shed little light on the CIA's conduct. Indeed, these justifications could theoretically support *any* invocation of the state secrets privilege by the CIA, since the revelation of almost any of its covert activities could "strain diplomatic relations" in one way or another.

So ought the courts to demand the submission of a more detailed public justification for the invocation of the state secrets privilege? This question was addressed frontally in *Ellsberg v. Mitchell* (1983), a case in which the protagonists in the Pentagon Papers episode sought damages after learning that they had been subjected to warrantless surveillance. After the District Court for the District of Columbia sided with the attorney general on the basis of in camera submissions justifying the invocation of the state secrets privilege, the plaintiffs approached the D.C. Circuit, challenging the "meager public justifications" offered by the government. The public affidavits, the plaintiffs argued, alleged "that the national interest would be prejudiced by release of the requested materials," but did not specify "what that 'interest' consists of and how it might be damaged." Hence the government should be compelled to "provide a fuller public account of why disclosure of the information would harm national security" or, alternatively, to explain "why a more specific description of the anticipated adverse consequences would itself damage national security."[104]

Judge Harry Edwards expressed sympathy with the plaintiff's complaint, observing that "the more specific the public explanation, the greater the ability of the opposing party to contest it." Yet there could not be, he argued, "a strict rule that the trial judge must compel the government to defend its claim publicly before submitting materials *in camera*," because it is "imperative that the procedure used to evaluate the legitimacy of a state secrets privilege claim not force disclosure of the very thing the privilege is designed to protect." The most that could reasonably be demanded, he wrote, was that "the government's public statement need be no more (and no less) specific than is practicable under the circumstances."[105] And who is to decide what is "practicable"? Though there could be "no abdication of a judicial role in connection with proposed applications of the state secrets doctrine," Judge Edwards declared, the courts "should accord considerable deference to recommendations from the executive department."[106]

What Is the Alternative?

There are, as we have seen, good reasons why judges will not—and indeed should not—take the lead in compelling the revelation of secret information. Consequently, we should expect judges to set only a low procedural hurdle rather than a high substantive barrier before the executive's pleas for secrecy on national security grounds. This does *not* mean that judges can make no valuable contribution whatsoever in combating the abuse of secrecy. As Chesney has underscored, procedural requirements ought to be an important "precondition" for judicial deference, because they allow judges to verify that harm-claims have not been made carelessly.[107] And as Pozen has rightly emphasized, deference is not the same thing as abdication; a deferential standard of review does not preclude "demanding plausible arguments tailored to specific documents withheld."[108] There is no reason to believe that the courts are unqualified to conduct close scrutiny in this more limited sense. As Justice Powell dryly stated in *Keith*, if a purported threat "is too subtle or complex for our senior law enforcement officers to convey its significance to a court," then one must wonder whether it really exists.[109]

Happily, there is evidence that procedural requirements have had a sobering effect on officials from the executive branch. In the FOIA context, for instance, the Justice Department has warned government lawyers that judges will not grant summary judgments when affidavits contain "boilerplate explanations" that are not "tailored" to justify the "particular information" that officials want to withhold.[110] Meanwhile, a remarkable recent case, *Horn v. Huddle* (2009), has reminded officials that procedural requirements associated with the invocation of the state secrets privilege are not to be taken lightly either. In this case District Judge Royce Lamberth of the District of Columbia moved to penalize government lawyers and senior CIA officials after discovering that the state secrets privilege had been invoked fraudulently: one of the litigants was not in fact a covert operative at the time of the trial (as the CIA had claimed).[111] Shaken, the CIA reached a three-million-dollar settlement with the plaintiff in short order so as to preempt further legal proceedings.

Though *Horn* certainly sends out a clear signal that federal judges are not to be trifled with, it is important to recognize the limits of procedural requirements. Arguably, *Horn* indicates that such requirements will allow judges to guard against only ham-handed uses of secrecy. Indeed, had a government lawyer not voluntarily informed Judge Lamberth of the CIA's fraudulent claim, *Horn* might have turned out very differently.[112] Much the same lesson holds as far as FOIA is concerned. That is, there is no denying that *once* embarrassing or incriminating information has been made public, FOIA has had a powerful countervailing effect, as Seth Kreimer has detailed in two excellent essays on the subject.[113] For example, though the American Civil Liberties Union (ACLU) has not prevailed in FOIA cases where it has requested the disclosure of highly classified documents pertaining to the United States' controversial detention policies, it has nevertheless been able to use FOIA to shake loose reams of associated documents—cumulatively upwards of a hundred thousand pages—that have helped shed light on a controversial practice. Still, we must not lose sight of the fact that the ACLU was able to make good use of FOIA only *after* leaks brought reports of potential wrongdoing to its notice. The "ecology of transparency," as Kreimer has nicely put it, is that "leaks provide the basis of FOIA requests, and FOIA requests in turn provide an occasion for courts to address the justifiability of continued secrecy."[114] But the worry here, as noted in chapter 1, is that the practice of leaking violates the law and is therefore prone to suppression. There is, to stay with Kreimer's metaphor, a standing threat to the sustainability of the "ecology of transparency." We will address this vulnerability in chapters 4–6. But let us first examine whether it is possible to bolster the effectiveness and credibility of congressional oversight.

Chapter 3

. . . .

Should We Rely on Congress?

Oversight and the Problem of Executive Privilege

We have now seen why we should be cautious about relying upon judges to determine whether the executive is employing secrecy responsibly. Does it make sense to rely on Congress instead? As we noted in chapter 1, Congress's record on this count is less than promising. Though the Framers claimed that the separation of powers would allow Congress to oversee the executive's conduct of war and diplomacy, in practice lawmakers have invariably found themselves in the dark in precisely those instances where they ought to have been best informed—that is, in cases where presidents have made far-reaching national security decisions under the veil of secrecy.

Why has Congress struggled to stay abreast of the president's secret actions and policies? The blame is usually placed on the fact that Congress relies on the executive to keep it properly informed.[1] Congress "remains at the forbearance of the executive in terms of the intelligence it is given," Britt Snider has written, because it "cannot request information it does not know exists."[2] To be sure, the establishment of intelligence oversight committees in Congress has led to expanded oversight of *routine* intelligence community activity.[3] For instance, the numbers of briefings and testimonies provided by the intelligence community have escalated sharply since the mid-1970s.[4] "Congress now receives nearly every intelligence item the executive does," according to Gregory Treverton.[5] But these developments notwithstanding, the record shows that Congress tends to become aware of far-reaching national security initiatives rather late in the day, the best-known examples being the Iran-Contra affair and, more recently, the politicization of intelligence on Iraq's weapons program, the establishment of secret prisons, and the use of "enhanced" interrogation techniques and warrantless surveillance.[6]

This record may seem puzzling. Why, one might wonder, does Congress not demand fuller access to national security information, especially about operations that have the potential to violate domestic and international law? There are a number of explanations on offer. One focuses on the overseers themselves, a great many of whom, Loch Johnson has argued, have acted not as watchful "guardians" of the public trust, but rather as uncritical "cheerleaders" for the intelligence community.[7] Another explanation draws attention to the high turnover and large memberships of the intelligence oversight committees, which, according to two recent congressional reports, gives members little chance or incentive to develop expertise in intelligence affairs.[8] A third explanation emphasizes the relative obscurity of intelligence matters, which, Frank Smist has argued, offer little opportunity for patronage or grandstanding and therefore do not generate much interest among members of Congress.[9]

These accounts undoubtedly help us understand why Congress sometimes makes little or no effort to conduct oversight. But is a lack of will the only problem? The explanations cited above assume that Congress can have access to national security information—so long as it *really* wants it. Is the story really that simple? At least some scholars seem to think so. Mark Rozell, Gary Schmitt, David Crockett, and Neal Devins, among others, have suggested that we need "do nothing" about the fact that Congress depends on the president for information, because Congress can use its wide-ranging powers to compel the president to part with the information it needs to perform oversight.[10] If Congress "wants something badly enough," Crockett has argued, "it will use its political resources to full effect."[11]

Consider, then, the powers that Congress enjoys. Foremost among these is the power to legislate. In principle, Congress can use this power to limit the kinds of activities that an unforthcoming president can undertake in secret. This approach draws on the concept of "generalization": the idea that "if a particular decision cannot be disclosed in advance, the general type of decision can be discussed publicly, its justifiability in various hypothetical circumstances considered, and guidelines for making it in those circumstances formulated."[12] The appeal of a generalized restriction lies in the fact that it appears to eliminate the sorts of moral and legal ambiguities that officials often utilize to justify questionable behavior that is shrouded in secrecy. Because it leaves no doubt about the sorts of covert actions or secret policies that lawmakers are willing to condone, a statutory restriction or prohibition affords officials little "wiggle room" (and little excuse once violations are discovered).

However, the closer we come to practice, the less useful a generalized restriction becomes. The problem, as Dennis Thompson has noted, is that the complex and unpredictable nature of political life can make it difficult for lawmakers to specify restrictions in advance. Consider, for example, the recent controversy surrounding the NSA's warrantless surveillance program. When critics charged that the program violated the law, the Bush administration defended the program by pointing to Congress's Joint Resolution on the Authorization for Use of Military Force Against Terrorists, which called on the president to "use all necessary and appropriate force against those nations, organizations, or persons he determines planned, authorized, committed, or aided the terrorist attacks" on September 11, 2001, in order to prevent "any future acts of international terrorism against the United States."[13] The lesson one might draw from this controversy is that Congress ought to be more careful in drafting resolutions. But better lawyering can go only so far because, as the well-worn phrase "necessity knows no law" reminds us, even the most precisely worded restrictions can legitimately be overridden during emergencies. In such cases lawmakers are typically confronted with the question of whether necessity *genuinely* warrants a drastic response. And, as Thompson has pointed out, the executive's control over national security information usually provides the president with a significant advantage in determining whether the circumstances are ripe for a dismissal of previously mandated guidelines.[14]

So what can Congress do to obtain the information it needs to tailor laws, monitor potential violations, and enforce accountability? It has two powers that it can call upon. It can use its subpoena power to compel officials and agency heads to disclose pertinent information, and it can withhold cooperation by dragging its heels on the confirmation of appointments, the ratification of treaties, and the passage of appropriations until the president complies with requests for information. In practice, though, Congress is usually hard-pressed to employ these powers to the fullest extent. Its subpoena power is hobbled by the problem of nonenforcement because the Justice Department, which is responsible for prosecuting cases involving contempt of Congress, has traditionally refused to press charges against officials who decline to share information with Congress on the orders of the president.[15] In theory, Congress could attempt to enforce these subpoenas on its own steam but, as Joseph Bishop has dryly noted, "it has never in the past been willing to push matters to the point of dispatching the Sergeant at Arms to cleave a path through the Secret Service cordon and seize the person of the President, or even one of his subordinates."[16] Congress's ability to withhold cooperation from the executive is also far from certain. This course of action is vulnerable to swings in public opinion and subject to the usual challenges associated with undertaking collective action.[17] It often takes only a little maneuvering by the president to make it painful for Congress to stymie national security initiatives—a point made best by Senator George Aiken's memorable observation in the heyday of the Cold War: "We all know that when the appropriations bill is pending the Russians in particular become extremely powerful."[18]

We have so far been examining the practical obstacles that Congress faces when it tries to compel the president to share information. Suppose, however, that Congress is able to overcome these obstacles and gather the will to challenge the president. Is this the end of the problem? Not quite. Congress faces yet another challenge: since compelling the president to disclose national security information could lead to the release of information that ought to be kept secret in the interests of national security, it would be irresponsible of Congress to utilize compulsion unless it is confident that the president is actually withholding evidence of wrongdoing. But how is Congress to know *when* this is the case, since it can ascertain whether the withholding was justified only *after* it sees the information in question?

To appreciate the seriousness of this conundrum, consider William C. Banks and Peter Raven-Hansen's recommendation that Congress ought to use its power of the purse to obtain some degree of control over national security policy-making. Wishing to encourage congressional oversight, but cognizant of the danger that fiscal restrictions could interfere with the president's duty to maintain national security, Banks and Raven-Hansen argue that Congress can determine the acceptability of a restrictive appropriation by "weighing the extent to which the restrictions prevent Presidents from accomplishing their constitutionally assigned functions against the need for restriction to promote objectives within the authority of Congress."[19] What Banks and Raven-Hansen do not explain, though, is how Congress might employ this formula when the president alone knows how far such a restriction would hinder the realization of an important national security objective. Unable to verify the president's claim about the harm likely to be caused by a restrictive appropriation, Congress would be hard-pressed to issue a rebuttal. Congress could try ignoring the president's claim—a tactic that might help it test the president's resolve. But to persist in this course of action once the president refuses to submit could have highly undesirable consequences. For example, imagine that the president concludes a nuclear stockpile reduction agreement that favors the United States. Not wishing to embarrass the other side, and to thereby imperil the agreement, the president publicly represents the deal as having achieved a modest outcome that imposes significant burdens on both sides. Unaware of this gambit, a bloc of hawkish senators declares that they will not fund the stockpile reduction program unless they are granted access to the details of the agreement. The president, however, refuses to cooperate because he fears that should the senators leak the details of the agreement—which he thinks they are likely to do in order to prove to *their* constituents that they are not backing a burdensome agreement—the counterparty would be greatly embarrassed before *its* constituents and thereby compelled to renege on the agreement. In this case, does it not seem that Congress would be barking up the wrong tree by refusing to fund the stockpile reduction program unless the president shares the information they want?

The conundrum outlined above implies that if Congress wants to compel the disclosure of information without jeopardizing national security, then it ought to use subpoenas or refuse to cooperate only *after* it has obtained some knowledge of the nature of the information being withheld by the president. But how can Congress obtain such knowledge when the president controls the flow of information? A common response to this predicament is that Congress ought to strike an information-sharing agreement with the president. Consider the proposal that Antonin Scalia, then an assistant attorney general in President Gerald Ford's administration, floated before Congress in 1975. Scalia proposed that in return for a promise of nondisclosure, the president could informally transfer to Congress the information that he deemed privileged so as to allow Congress to assess the merit of his decision. In the event that Congress determined that the president's decision lacked merit, it would be obliged to return the documents and to formally seek access to them by using the constitutional powers at its disposal.

So why did Congress not take advantage of this offer? The catch was that under Scalia's scheme the president could take the view that "even conditional transmittal to Congress might result in irreparable harm."[20] In other words, Scalia's proposal left the president's control over the flow of national security information intact. His proposal was not unusual in this regard—by their very nature, information-sharing agreements cannot be enforced by the courts; they rely on comity between the branches. This in turn explains the lack of enthusiasm in Congress for this device. For if the president can stall even a conditional transmittal to Congress, then lawmakers have little reason to expect that a president who has something to hide will hold up his end of an information-sharing agreement. A case in point is the outcome of the so-called Casey Accord of 1986, an informal agreement reached between William Casey, the director of central intelligence, and Robert McFarlane, the national security adviser, on the one side, and Senators Barry Goldwater and Daniel Moynihan of the Senate Intelligence Committee, on the other. Under this agreement, which followed in the wake of uproar in Congress over the previously undisclosed mining of harbors in Nicaragua, Casey and McFarlane promised to keep the intelligence committees in Congress fully informed of covert activities. Yet, as Harold Koh has observed, "within days after accepting these voluntary reporting requirements, the Reagan administration began planning its secret arms sales to Iran."[21]

If the analysis presented above is correct, then we must conclude, contrary to Rozell, Devins, Schmitt, and Crockett, that Congress is *not* well positioned to compel the president to share national security information. This conclusion may seem implausible since Congress has conducted a number of high-profile national security investigations in recent decades, including those by the Church and Pike Committees in 1975, the Iran-Contra Committee in 1986, and the 9/11 Commission in 2004. But, significantly, Congress undertook these investigations only *after* the press brought potential wrongdoing to public attention, thus allowing lawmakers to feel justified in compelling the president to disclose privileged information.[22] In the absence of such assistance, Congress's powers would arguably have proven far less useful than they otherwise seem. To take just one example, the 9/11 Commission successfully used the threat of subpoenas to obtain access to the President's Daily Briefing (PDB), which the Bush administration had previously refused to share.[23] Yet, as the leaders of the commission have acknowledged, their focus on the PDBs owed substantially to the unauthorized disclosure of the title of the infamous PDB "Bin Laden Determined to Strike in US," a disclosure that had raised the initial question about the competence of decision-makers in the White House.[24]

As noted in chapter 1, Congress's tendency to ride to the rescue on the back of leaks of classified information is troubling for a number of reasons. It has long been recognized that news reports constitute one of the most important means by which Congress keeps track of what the president is doing.[25] But news reports based on leaks of classified information are a different matter because such unauthorized disclosures violate laws enacted by Congress itself. To be sure, under certain conditions executive officers may well be justified in disobeying these laws (as we shall see in chapter 5). However, the scope of the cases where such disobedience is justified becomes significantly narrower when secret information is disclosed to the world at large (rather than to overseers in Congress alone, who could address the problem discreetly). As a result, oversight provided by a Congress that relies on leaks will tend to be underinclusive—that is, it will overlook wrongdoing that is not leaked or published out of concern for collateral damage to national security. Furthermore, since leaks typically occur quite some time after wrongdoing has taken place, they often leave Congress with little opportunity to take remedial measures. For example, important disclosures about the politicization of secret intelligence pertaining to Iraq's weapons program came only after the decision to invade had already been made. And, perhaps most troublingly of all, since unauthorized disclosures are typically made anonymously, Congress may find itself unable to ascertain the motives of the source, leaving it vulnerable to being manipulated by disgruntled or partisan officials. As such, Congress's dependence on leaks seems to be in some tension with the democratic norm that decisions on vital matters of public concern must be made by individuals who are directly or at least indirectly accountable to the public. Given these concerns, we cannot conclude that Congress is currently well positioned to oversee the employment of state secrecy. Instead, we ought to examine whether Congress can have *timely* and *independent* access to the national security information it needs to conduct oversight on its own steam.

The Problem of Executive Privilege

The principal challenge that Congress faces in its endeavor to obtain national security information is that the executive does not believe itself to be obliged to comply with Congress's requests. As Snider has observed, though Congress routinely passes laws reserving the right to examine intelligence materials as it sees fit, none of these statutes has "been interpreted by the executive to require that *all* intelligence be turned over to Congress."[26] Is this state of affairs defensible? Should the president be allowed to withhold national security information from Congress?[27]

So far the subject of executive privilege has primarily been addressed at the level of constitutional doctrine: scholars have focused on whether precedent or original intent or the doctrine of inherent or implied powers *entitles* the president to withhold information from Congress.[28] This scholarship must not be overlooked, because if the president is clearly entitled to control the flow of information to Congress, then we could still ask whether the president *ought* to have such authority, but there would be, realistically speaking, little hope of wresting this authority away from him. As it turns out, though, the president's constitutional right to control the flow of information is heavily contested. Moreover, the courts, which usually resolve such interpretive disputes through authoritative rulings, have declined to offer relief in this instance, citing the need, in *United States v. AT&T* (1977), to "avoid a resolution that might disturb the balance of power between the two branches and inaccurately reflect their true needs."[29]

Given the absence of clarity at the constitutional level, let us consider whether there are *general* reasons in favor of executive privilege. Arguably, there are two justifications to consider here. The first is that the executive privilege provides a means to uphold the independence of the executive branch and to thereby maintain the separation of powers. This claim can be traced back to Attorney General William Rogers, whose testimony before Congress in 1958 drew attention to a well-known passage from *Kilbourne v. Thompson* (1880) to the effect that separation of powers theory requires "that the persons entrusted with power in any one of the branches shall not be permitted to encroach upon the powers confided to the others."[30] The import of this passage, Rogers argued, was that Congress could not, for instance, pry into judicial deliberations, as this would "be utterly destructive of a free judiciary." "The same considerations," he continued, "may be said to operate with respect to an investigation of confidential advice within the executive branch."[31]

This argument is not entirely convincing, though. In cases where the information subject to a claim of privilege relates to matters that lie *exclusively* within the ambit of the executive (e.g., the conduct of a secret military operation), the president's interest in protecting confidentiality ought to trump Congress's more general interest in accessing such information. But when the information in question bears on matters that call for Congress to use *its* constitutional powers—for instance, by funding covert action or authorizing war—then it seems that the president's interest in protecting confidentiality cannot be conclusive; we must also account for Congress's interest in having access to the information it needs to ascertain what laws should be passed under the circumstances.[32]

The second justification for executive privilege is based on the notion that the separation of powers theory vests responsibility for the "stability and security of the nation" in the executive because this branch is best suited to acting with "secrecy and speed."[33] This responsibility in turn, the argument goes, authorizes the president to withhold national security information from Congress whenever this is necessary to protect national security.[34] But this argument does not seem entirely convincing either—at least not as it has been presented thus far. In particular, its advocates have not clearly explained why we should believe that Congress is less capable of maintaining due secrecy. Usually the explanation offered cites Hamilton's claim in *The Federalist* No. 70 that "decision, activity, secrecy and dispatch will generally characterize the proceedings of one man, in a much more eminent degree, than the proceedings of any greater number; and in proportion as the number is increased, these qualities will be destroyed."[35] To support this observation Congress's critics often cite the famous letter that Benjamin Franklin and Robert Morris wrote on October 1, 1776, in their capacity as members of the Committee of Secret Correspondence. After informing their fellow committee members of recently arrived intelligence about the willingness of the French to provide military aid, Franklin and Morris argued that it was their "indispensable duty to keep it a secret, even from Congress," because "we find, by fatal experience, the Congress consists of too many members to keep secrets."[36]

Now, to be sure, Hamilton's theory and Franklin and Morris's observation are far from trivial. We know that in order to prevent unauthorized disclosures, decisions on matters of state are often made by a few leading officers, with their subordinates having only "compartmentalized" access to information.[37] But if the claim at hand is just about the *number* of decision-makers, then we are hard-pressed to explain why a committee of Congress should not be provided unrestricted access to national security information, because a committee will comprise only a handful of members. This is why when Eric Posner and Adrian Vermeule argue that executive privilege is justified by the concern that "Congress leaks like a sieve," David Pozen retorts that no one has explained why "the odds of public disclosure increase not linearly but geometrically" when the "circle of secret-keepers is widened to include authorities from another branch."[38]

As it happens, there is an explanation as to why the odds of public disclosure increase exponentially when we provide even a few members of Congress with unrestricted access to national security information. The key factor is not the size of the groups that have access to information, but rather how their memberships are *composed* and *structured*. In the executive branch, officials owe their position to the president. This makes it less likely that they will have an incentive to reveal information contrary to the decision-maker's wishes. A committee of Congress, by contrast, invariably comprises adversarial parties, who will usually have a greater incentive to disclose sensitive information in a bid to gain political advantage. The Framer James Wilson makes this point best in his *Lectures on Law*: "Can secrecy," he writes, be expected from a body in which "to every enterprise, and to every step in the progress of every enterprise, mutual communication, mutual consultation, and mutual agreement amongst men, perhaps of discordant views, of discordant tempers and of discordant interests, are indispensably necessary?"[39]

There is a predictable response to Wilson's charge. It is that Congress can prevent partisanship from having undesirable consequences by strengthening internal safeguards on the handling of classified information and establishing penalties for unauthorized disclosure.[40] But this response lacks credibility for at least three reasons. First, lawmakers can find refuge in the Speech and Debate Clause, which shields them from criminal and civil action. This is the provision that Senator Mike Gravel took advantage of in 1971 when he placed the Pentagon Papers on the *Congressional Record* before the Supreme Court had reached its verdict in that case.[41] Second, lawmakers can be subject to disciplinary action only if they are found guilty of having made an unauthorized disclosure. Yet the evidence required to prove guilt is usually hard to come by because lawmakers who make unauthorized disclosures outside the safety of the floor of the House or the Senate tend to do so under cover of anonymity, safe in the knowledge that the president will be hard-pressed to order a penetrating investigation lest he be accused of criminalizing political differences or violating Congress's dignity and independence. Consider in this respect the events surrounding the House Intelligence Committee's investigation in 1975 of claims that the CIA and FBI had violated domestic and international laws. The committee produced a final report that the House voted 264 to 124 to withhold from the public. The report was nevertheless disclosed to Daniel Schorr, a reporter for *CBS News*, who in turn passed it on to the *Village Voice*, which published it in full. Though the House conducted an inquiry into the source of the disclosure, the culprit was never identified.[42] Finally, even when the source is identified, the adversarial nature of congressional politics raises questions about the impartiality of the judges—members of Congress themselves—who are invariably more forgiving of unauthorized disclosures made by members of their own party. Indeed, it is notably the case that congressional resolutions on whether to inquire into unauthorized disclosures invariably proceed along party lines.[43] This is what happened in 1992, for example, when Republican lawmakers called for Representative Henry Gonzalez, chairman of the House Committee on Banking, Finance, and Urban Affairs, to be subject to an ethics inquiry after he placed on the *Congressional Record* classified documents that his committee had obtained during an investigation into the United States' support for Iraq prior to 1991.[44]

Contrast the foregoing with the position of officials in the executive branch. These individuals *are* vulnerable to criminal, civil, and administrative action should they be found responsible for unauthorized disclosures (and, as we shall see in chapters 4–6, such punishments are far from rare). Moreover, as these officials serve at the pleasure of the president, they can be dismissed or transferred or demoted upon the slightest suspicion, making the maintenance of internal discipline that much easier—a point starkly evidenced by President Eisenhower's well-known announcement at a cabinet meeting that any official who violated the confidentiality he wanted to protect wouldn't be working for him the following day.[45]

I have been arguing that executive privilege can be justified on the grounds that the executive branch is better designed to maintain secrecy. At this point it may be objected that, in practice, Congress is actually *not* prone to making unauthorized disclosures. Heidi Kitrosser has claimed that "Congress is considered to have a reliable track record for non-leakage," while Pozen has asserted that no one has "marshaled any evidence, even anecdotal evidence," showing that Congress "leaks like a sieve."[46] Indeed, it may even be objected that when it comes to keeping secrets, Congress is in fact the more reliable institution. For example, Koh has stated that "the executive branch, not Congress, has been responsible for the vast bulk of recent national security leaks," while Fisher has averred that "there should be little doubt that congressional leaks, as compared to executive leaks, are infrequent and small in number."[47]

But claims of this variety are not well founded. As one lawmaker has pointed out, since "only a handful of leaks have ever been traced through investigation to the culpable individual," the lack of proof of leaks from Congress "hardly establishes that Congress has a good record."[48] Furthermore, claims that the executive branch leaks more than Congress fail to distinguish between two kinds of disclosures: authorized disclosures and unauthorized disclosures. The former are disclosures that are condoned and may even be ordered by the leadership of the branch, because they are intended to "enhance the implementation of a policy."[49] Since control over national security information is presently vested in the executive branch, it might well be responsible for the majority of authorized disclosures . But this fact tells us very little about the relative merits of either of the branches in terms of their ability to keep secrets, since there is no reason to believe that Congress would desist from making equal use of authorized disclosures were *it* granted unrestricted access to national security information. Hence the argument actually hinges on the question of which branch is better at preventing *un*authorized disclosures: disclosures of information that the leadership of the branch has determined *ought* to be kept secret.

Before we address this question, though, a further distinction is needed. It is no doubt true, as Johnson has noted, that the "most egregious" unauthorized disclosures have come from "officials in the executive branch who sold America's top secrets to foreign intelligence agents."[50] But such unauthorized disclosures—effectively acts of espionage—are part and parcel of the business of intelligence, a managerial hazard that would exist regardless of who is responsible for managing the intelligence services. Therefore, we should not count this sort of unauthorized disclosure against the executive branch per se. By contrast, the kind of unauthorized disclosure that is relevant to our argument is that which occurs when, to paraphrase Stephen Knott, political actors deliberately reveal information with a view to crippling a policy that they could not defeat through the normal processes of decision making.[51] This problem of *indiscipline* arises from the tendency of individuals to disregard the rules of the institution in the midst of political conflict.[52] Since the executive branch manages the national security apparatus, it would not be surprising if the bulk of such unauthorized disclosures could be traced back to its officers. But if we are to fairly compare the ability of the branches to prevent unauthorized disclosures, then we need to know how Congress would perform if *its* access to national security information were unrestricted.

Now, for obvious reasons, we are unlikely to be able to resolve this question empirically. However, two observations are worth making. First, given that the Continental Congress *did* have wide access to national security information, we should not overlook the Framers' dim view of that body's capacity to maintain discretion. Furthermore, though the modern Congress has limited access to national security information, its inability to punish even blatant violations of its own rules suggests that granting it wider access to national security information could cause grave harm. Consider, for example, the actions of Senator Burton Wheeler, a staunch isolationist opposed to the United States' entry into World War II, who in 1941 revealed the United States' plan to ship troops to Iceland.[53] Wheeler defended his decision to reveal news of troop movements, made at a time when German submarines were aggressively patrolling the North Atlantic, as an exercise of his "right to free speech."[54] Another widely cited example comes from 1974, when Representative Michael Harrington disclosed to the press secret testimony given to an intelligence subcommittee by William Colby, the director of central intelligence, about the United States' efforts to overthrow Salvador Allende of Chile. Though Harrington had initially agreed to keep Colby's testimony confidential, he later claimed that "he felt he had a greater duty to release the information."[55] Consider as well the case of Representative Clement Zablocki, the chairman of the House Foreign Affairs Committee, who in 1981 leaked to *Newsweek* information about a planned covert operation against Libya.[56] Zablocki suffered no disciplinary action because, in the words of Edward Boland, then chairman of the House intelligence committee, "leaks were epidemic."[57] Then there is the case of Representative Les Aspin, the chairman of the House Armed Services Committee, who in 1987 disclosed to the press information gleaned from a briefing on planned military maneuvers in the Persian Gulf.[58] Aspin defended this disclosure with the argument that he had not been informed that the information was classified.[59]

These examples of reckless behavior by lawmakers in the face of disagreement with the president, and with their colleagues in Congress, shed light on why observers have argued that releasing information to Congress is "tantamount to setting a ship afloat at sea without benefit of motor, rudder, or sails."[60] To be sure, the executive branch is by no means immune to the problem of indiscipline. On the contrary, as we shall see in chapters 4–6, the executive branch faces disciplinary challenges of its own. But the president's power over his subordinates—and his willingness to use it—allow us to believe that the executive branch can punish (or at least seriously try to punish) those responsible for making unauthorized disclosures. By contrast, Congress's structure and composition give little reason to believe that its leadership could do likewise. Indeed, what is most striking about the examples cited above is how often lawmakers have *openly* defied Congress's norms and regulations concerning secrecy, a practice suggesting that they do not greatly fear the penalties associated with indiscipline (indeed, *none* of the individuals mentioned in these examples suffered any meaningful sanctions). Contrast this with the preference that disgruntled officials in the executive branch have for anonymity, and the heavy hand of the president comes into sharp relief. To put it differently, even though both branches suffer unauthorized disclosures, one seems more willing and able to patch the holes. Herein lies the justification for the executive privilege.

Should We Abolish Executive Privilege?

We have now established that the executive's greater capacity for discretion warrants granting the president the right to withhold national security information from Congress. This conclusion may give rise to the objection that we ought to allow Congress unrestricted access to national security information *even if* lawmakers are more prone to making unauthorized disclosures. This is because under certain circumstances—for example, when the country is faced with a decision to wage war—the benefit of allowing lawmakers unrestricted access could outweigh the harm that might be caused if they disclosed such information. If we fail to provide Congress with unrestricted access in such cases, the objection goes, we will be guilty of treating national security as a "trump" rather than as only one of a number of important interests that need to be taken into account, including, critically, the Framers' desire to prevent the concentration of power.

This objection is ill-conceived. The justification offered above on behalf of executive privilege does *not* preclude a balancing of the public's interest in national security on one hand and oversight on the other. It implies only that the responsibility for balancing these interests ought to be vested in the hands of the president. To see the logic behind this arrangement, consider the following: while we can agree that the benefit of allowing lawmakers unrestricted access to national security information *could* outweigh the risk that they may disclose this information at great cost to the nation, how are we to know *when* this is the case? Obviously, this question cannot be answered without first ascertaining the value of the information in question. Needless to say, we cannot ask Congress to judge the value of this information, since this would prematurely expose the information to the higher risk of disclosure associated with congressional access, thereby defeating our attempt to balance interests. What we need, then, is an intermediary. And this is precisely what an executive privilege accomplishes: it allows the president to withhold information in instances where he judges that the public's interest in preventing unauthorized disclosure outweighs its interest in allowing Congress access to that information. A good example is the so-called Canadian Caper, a CIA covert operation that led to the rescue of American hostages hiding in the Canadian embassy in Tehran in 1979. In this case, President Jimmy Carter notified Congress about the covert operation only after the three-month-long operation was complete—even though the law required more timely notification—because the Canadian government premised its cooperation on Congress's being kept out of the loop, as it feared that a brash or unguarded lawmaker might expose the operation.[61] In this instance, the existence of a discreet intermediary—namely, the president—made it possible to strike a measured balance between secrecy and oversight.

Nonetheless, we cannot ignore the fact that permitting the president to serve as an intermediary comes with a substantial risk. The president could use his control over the flow of secret information to disarm opposition from Congress by sharing with it only those pieces of secret intelligence that support his preferred policy choices.[62] In such cases, Congress may well exercise its powers by, for example, issuing declarations of war or appropriating funds, but its actions will not be informed—its situation will be akin to that of a president granted the power to veto a bill, but not to examine its contents. Under the circumstances, we would be justified in curtailing executive privilege should we determine that this privilege is likely to engender abuses of power that will ultimately prove more harmful than the unauthorized disclosures it is meant to prevent.

Although it is hard to prove that the balance of risk actually works out this way, let us assume for the sake of argument that allowing the president to withhold information from Congress is in fact more dangerous than allowing Congress to have unrestricted access to it. Even so, would curtailing executive privilege greatly reduce the chance that secrecy may be employed to conceal wrongdoing? I have been arguing that lawmakers cannot be counted upon to oversee the president so long as the executive controls the flow of information. Presumably, then, once Congress is provided unrestricted access to national security information, the problem of ascertaining whether secrecy has been employed responsibly should be eliminated. Upon closer inspection, though, this turns out not to be the case.

To see why providing Congress with independent access to national security information will not eliminate fears about the misuse of secrecy, we must account for the steps that Congress would need to take in order to merit such access. Given its structural disposition toward indiscipline, it would arguably be irresponsible for Congress to seek independent access without first attempting to reduce the risk of unauthorized disclosure. How might this be achieved? The recommendation offered by scholars such as Koh and Kitrosser is that Congress should delegate the oversight of national security matters to a "core group of members" comprising a handful of its highest-ranked officials.[63] Given our previous discussion, we know that this recommendation misses the point; it fails to recognize that the risk of unauthorized disclosure is less a function of the number of people who have access to a given secret and more a function of the degree of partisan conflict. Needless to say, there is not much we can do to address the issue of partisanship, since we cannot eliminate members who belong to political parties opposed to the president without also undermining the credibility of the oversight provided by this core group. Therefore, our hope must be that members will be deterred from making unauthorized disclosures by the threat of severe legal and political sanctions. The credibility of this deterrent is rendered somewhat doubtful, though, by the fact that unauthorized disclosures can be made anonymously. Indeed, there is the possibility that members of the core group who belong to the president's party could make anonymous disclosures in order to discredit lawmakers from the rival party. This possibility is less far-fetched than it sounds. For instance, in 2002 an unauthorized disclosure by a member of Congress's joint inquiry into the events leading up to the 9/11 terrorist attacks prompted the Bush administration to threaten to cease to cooperate. A prolonged investigation by the FBI eventually revealed the source of the disclosure to be a Republican, Senator Richard Shelby.[64] This turn of events led Senator Bob Graham, the cochair of the joint inquiry, to publicly wonder whether the unauthorized disclosure had been intended to sabotage the joint inquiry (presumably by giving the Bush administration a pretext to end its cooperation with an unwelcome investigation).[65]

Let us nonetheless assume, for the sake of argument, that restricting the membership of this core group will increase the probability that "cheaters" will be caught to a level high enough to bring unauthorized disclosures under control. The question to ponder, then, is this—how effective is such a core group likely to be at preventing the misuse of secrecy? Presumably, the group's members will now have the information needed to determine whether Congress ought to support or oppose the president's policies. But can we be confident that they will act dutifully when their *own* conduct as overseers is shielded from public view?

One problem is that the secrecy accompanying the activities of this core group may leave its members unable to explain to the public why they wish to block or investigate the president's policies or decisions. Hobbled in their ability to rally public opposition to policies that they view as harmful or unwise, the group members may be rendered little more than mute spectators—as Senator Jay Rockefeller discovered in 2003 after being briefed, in his capacity as vice chairman of the Senate Select Committee on Intelligence, about the NSA's warrantless wiretapping program. According to Senator Rockefeller, because he was not allowed to discuss the program with his staff, outside experts, or colleagues, the only way he could voice his concern about the propriety of the program was to complain privately to Vice President Cheney.[66] This sort of predicament is far from unprecedented—indeed similar complaints can be traced back to the 1970s, when intelligence oversight procedures were first put in place.[67]

The prospect that the core group may be bulldozed by the president may lead to the demand that it be allowed to overrule the president and to share its views with Congress or even the public.[68] However, before we accede to this demand, we ought to ask what will prevent the group from misusing such a prerogative? This question will of course be posed most acutely when a majority of the members of the core group come from the same political party as the president, an arrangement that naturally raises fears of collusion. These fears do not seem misplaced when we consider, for instance, the criticism of the Republican-dominated intelligence committees for their willingness to turn a blind eye to the Bush administration's more controversial national security initiatives.[69]

Some scholars have responded to the prospect of ineffectual oversight by calling for oversight committees to be chaired by members of the rival party. Bruce Ackerman, for instance, recommends that during an emergency the president ought to be allowed to exercise extraordinary powers subject to close and continuing oversight by Congress. Noting that Congress cannot provide the requisite degree of oversight "if it is at the mercy of the Executive for information," Ackerman instructs that during an emergency "members of opposition political parties should be guaranteed a majority of seats on oversight committees," and that the president should be required "to provide the committees with complete and immediate access to all documents."[70] This arrangement "puts the government on notice," Ackerman writes, "that it cannot keep secrets from key members of the opposition and serves, without more, as an important check on the abuse of power."[71] This proposal has been backed even more strongly by Kim Scheppele, who has argued that adversarial oversight ought to become a permanent feature of the American institutional landscape (rather than being confined merely to emergency settings). In particular, she has urged the United States to consider following the example set by Germany, where the system of oversight is premised on the idea "that the opposition parties must be able to check that majority parties are not using the intelligence services for their own political purposes."[72] The German political system creates such a "political check," Scheppele reports, by requiring the government to "report all intelligence activities" to the Parliamentary Control Commission, which is chaired by the majority and minority parties on a rotating basis.[73]

Upon closer inspection, though, these proposals turn out to be problematic in a number of respects. First, both Ackerman and Scheppele assume that lawmakers will have the expertise and political capital available to enter into bruising contests over intelligence matters with the executive, especially during times of crisis. However, as Martha Minnow has pointed out, the evidence suggests that congressional deference to the executive branch actually increases during times of crisis.[74] Moreover, even if oversight committees are stocked with experienced and unflappable lawmakers, can officials be trusted to divulge incriminating information to lawmakers, especially when they are appointed by, and likely owe loyalty to, the president?[75] It is worth recalling how often Congress has been misled by executive officers. In 1977, for example, Congress discovered that Richard Helms, then the director of central intelligence, had misled it during his testimony over the CIA's activities in Chile.[76] In 1986 Congress discovered that Colonel Oliver North had misled it with regard to the Iran-Contra affair.[77] Congress's testy relationship with William Casey, the director of the CIA during the Reagan administration, is legendary. As Representative Mineta once said in exasperation, "[I]f you were talking to Casey, and your coat caught fire, he wouldn't tell you unless you asked about it."[78] This pattern does not seem to have faded with the passage of time. Over the past decade both George Tenet and General Michael Hayden have been accused of misleading Congress during their tenures as directors of the CIA and the NSA, respectively.[79] Nor does the problem of noncooperation seem unique to the United States. In 2011–12 German investigators discovered that members of the intelligence services had hidden documents from overseers and utilized espionage and surveillance techniques beyond those approved by the Federal Constitutional Court.[80]

These practical concerns are not, however, the primary reason to be doubtful about Ackerman's and Scheppele's proposals, because these issues could conceivably be addressed by Congress's vigilance in approving appointments to senior positions in the intelligence community. Let us focus therefore on a deeper problem: namely, that concerns about the quality of oversight do not fade away *even when* a majority of the members of the core group come from the party opposed to the president. This is because the majority could exploit *its* position for partisan purposes—for example, by selectively revealing national security information that furthers its own agenda or by taking one position in a closed session and then another in public when the political winds turn unfavorable.[81] In this setting, the shoe will simply be on the other foot, as it will now be the president who is left unable to fully explain why the released information should be discounted. An illustration of this problem is provided by controversy surrounding the findings of the Rumsfeld Commission, which was created in 1998 after Republicans in Congress, who wished to see the United States pursue national missile defense, accused the Clinton administration of forcing the CIA to downplay the ballistic missile threat posed by rogue states like Iran and North Korea.[82] The Rumsfeld Commission, which demanded and was subsequently given unrestricted access to classified information, concluded that the available intelligence analysis was faulty, and that the United States faced a far greater threat than the Clinton administration was willing to admit.[83] The Clinton administration responded by challenging this "alarmist" interpretation of the available intelligence. But since external observers could not verify the claims made by either side, the entire dispute quickly turned into little more than a public relations battle. And though the Clinton administration quickly lost this battle, the passage of time has shown that its measured claims were well founded.[84]

The quality of oversight provided by a core group is also brought into question by the fact that the secrecy surrounding their operations makes it unlikely that they will be held accountable for regulatory failures. Consider, for example, the aforementioned case involving Senator Rockefeller. Did the secrecy demanded by the Gang of Eight (the leaders of the parties in both chambers and the ranking members of the intelligence committees) provide Senator Rockefeller with the opportunity to turn a blind eye to a policy that would have deeply upset his constituents, or was he, as he later claimed, an unhappy but silent observer of the Bush administration's policy? What we do know is that at the time, Senator Rockefeller placed a copy of his letter to the vice president in his personal safe as a testament to his unhappiness with the Bush administration's policy. But a skeptic might argue that this move merely ensured that Senator Rockefeller would have political cover no matter which way the political winds blew: had the warrantless wiretapping program produced a stunning success in the war on terror, he would have avoided the awkwardness of having publicly opposed the program; conversely, if it proved deeply controversial (as it eventually did), then he would have a get-out-of-jail-free card at hand. The point of this example is not to impugn Senator Rockefeller's motives. Rather, its purpose is to show that when we rely on a core group like the Gang of Eight to oversee national security matters in secret, we are invariably left with more questions than answers about the conduct of its members.

Contrary to what Ackerman and Scheppele assume, then, the use of secretive oversight committees is unlikely to greatly improve our confidence in the quality of oversight on offer. There is a deeper point here that is not always recognized in discussions on the subject of oversight: to the extent that *someone* must decide what information is to be shared or concealed, it is always possible that such a person or committee will abuse this authority. It is often assumed that a committee will be less vulnerable to committing such abuse. But why should this be so? A committee will have to make decisions via a decision-making rule such as majority or supermajority voting. What is to prevent a factional or corporate interest from emerging dominant within the committee? It is not possible to cancel out the effect of factions by expanding the size of the committee. Nor should we expect or encourage individuals or minorities to violate the rules of the committee and make ad hoc unilateral disclosures to Congress or the public—were this to happen, the whole purpose of entrusting the decision to a group would be defeated.

It appears, then, that taking the final say over information sharing away from the president and vesting it in a congressional committee serves only to re-create the opportunity for the abuse of state secrecy. This realization may well prompt proponents of checks and balances to argue that the problem of destructive partisanship can be countered by entrusting the final say on information sharing to a court or an independent panel composed of "nonpartisan experts," who would decide when the president should be allowed to withhold national security information from Congress. For example, John Orman has proposed that Congress should legislate categories of information that the president can legitimately withhold from it, and that in the event of conflict over what is to count as a legitimate secret, "the courts should act as the final arbitrators over all uncategorized information as well as all disputes about the proper categorization of information."[85] Similarly, William Weaver and Robert Pallitto have called for the judicial arbitration of executive privilege claims on the grounds that the "courts must help establish what the separation of powers is, rather than using the phrase itself as a justification for staying out of the fray altogether."[86]

This line of thought finds some support in *United States v. AT&T* (1977), a case involving a dispute between Congress and the Department of Justice over access to classified documents concerning the FBI's use of warrantless wiretaps. Although the Court of Appeals for the District of Columbia declined to address the constitutional aspect of this "portentous clash" between "the executive branch asserting its authority to maintain tight control over information related to our national security, and the legislative branch asserting its authority to gather information," it did volunteer to fashion a compromise on the grounds that judicial abstention would not encourage an "orderly resolution of the dispute."[87] The compromise it forged was to allow select congressional staffers to review a random sample of the relevant documents on the condition that the FBI could, subject to an in camera review by the court, substitute the randomly chosen documents with others, should any of the original choices be too sensitive to expose to the higher risk of disclosure associated with congressional involvement.[88] Although the proceedings in *AT&T* did not exactly vindicate the utility of judicial involvement—it eventually took three cases, two courts, and more than eighteen months before the two sides could be coaxed into reaching a contentious settlement—it is still worth considering whether this precedent ought to become more the norm.

The first question we ought to ask here is what reason is there to believe that judges or independent experts are likely to prove reliable arbitrators? The answer, presumably, is that we expect these actors to make decisions based on reasons rather than interests. But what are the relevant sorts of reasons in the present context? Arguably, disputes about information sharing turn on the question of which branch has the most reasonable claim to the information *under the circumstances*. That is to say, the appropriate answer in a particular case would presumably change if the court believed that a congressional committee seeking highly sensitive national security information contained an alcoholic prone to indiscretions, or if it believed that a president refusing to share information was actually shielding evidence of criminal actions.[89] If so, then, as Schmitt has observed, to require the courts to act as arbitrators is to ask them to exercise "political wisdom *par excellence*," even though they are usually not in a position to "assess adequately the political conditions and nuances which may infect a dispute."[90] This point shines through in *AT&T* where the D.C. Circuit Court initially asserted that witnessing negotiations between the two parties had helped it ascertain the "relative magnitude" of the relevant considerations—Congress's need for information, the likelihood of an unauthorized disclosure, and the magnitude of resultant harm to national security—but then later concluded that briefs on the sensitivity of the material in question may still be of "significant help."[91]

Furthermore, even if the courts or an independent panel of experts are willing and able to take on the role of arbitrators, the notion that decisions concerning the distribution of national security information can be made apolitically is itself highly problematic.[92] The difficulty lies in the nature and the import of the decisions this court or panel will have to make. Consider, for example, a case where an independent panel of experts has to decide whether to release information pertaining to nuclear proliferation by another country. In making its decision, the panel will want to take into account the potential costs (e.g., the harm that would be caused by the revelation of sources and methods of intelligence gathering) as well as the potential benefits (most notably, an informed Congress). It is hard to imagine that such costs and benefits can be estimated or indeed compared objectively. On the contrary, a great deal will depend on the political beliefs of the adjudicators. Now if the matter at stake were politically unimportant, the beliefs of these adjudicators would also be relatively unimportant. But when the decision in question significantly affects the ability of the political branches to justify controversial policies and to become aware of potential violations of law, the beliefs of these adjudicators will matter enormously. Consequently, it will surely not be long before political parties begin to take interest in the sorts of individuals appointed to such positions, the end result being a less-than-disinterested bench or panel.

This is not all. If a court or panel is to prevent unauthorized disclosures as effectively as the executive branch does, then it will likely have to create special forums where one or very few judges or experts will examine the relevant materials in camera and ex parte. But if we take away the opportunity for external observers to study the basis of the decision reached by these judges or experts, how can we ascertain their disinterestedness? Put another way, what reason will we have to believe that a panel of judges or experts acting in secret will exercise their discretionary powers any differently from their counterparts in the political branches?[93] For instance, what are the chances that an "independent" panel would have disagreed with President Bush's decision to keep information about the warrantless surveillance program from Congress if Presidents Reagan or George H. W. Bush had previously nominated to such a panel individuals who shared the worldview of Chief Justice William Rehnquist or Justice Antonin Scalia? In the end, then, one might expect to see Congress granted or denied access to national security information depending on shifts in the ideological composition of this court or panel.

The arguments made above bring us back to the conclusion reached earlier concerning the advisability of creating a core group. That is, it makes sense to disturb the president's control over national security information only if the proposed alternative—be it a committee, a court, or a panel—is more certain to serve the public interest. This is *not* to argue that entrusting the final say over information sharing to a body other than the executive branch is certain to have no positive effect whatsoever. Such a body may well have a less immediate incentive to misuse its control over national security information, since it cannot hope to use this authority to "unlock" additional powers—for example, by manipulating Congress into declaring war. But the problem is that we will not know if and when this is the case, that is, whether the members of this bench or panel have been able to resist being swayed by their partisan affiliations. This is especially troubling given that the political significance of the subject—the distribution of national security information—makes it difficult to imagine that there could even *be* such a thing as a disinterested intermediary. In other words, under conditions of state secrecy, we will invariably lack a good and sufficient reason to trust any "secrecy regulator," since we will not have access to the information necessary for rational trust.[94] This may be contrasted with the case of a regulator of an industry, where the availability of information allows the regulator's disinterestedness to be critically evaluated rather than assumed.

What Is the Alternative?

I began by making the case that Congress is not well positioned to oversee the employment of state secrecy because even when it has the willpower to challenge the president, it cannot easily obtain the information it needs to conduct oversight. This does *not* mean that the current system of congressional oversight is pointless. As Minnow has rightly argued, even limited briefings to lawmakers can serve as a "black box" that can keep a "record of all that is done" so that there are "subsequent occasions for evaluation and review."[95] For this reason it makes sense to take the small but important steps that will incentivize overseers to take their roles more seriously. For instance, we can agree with Kitrosser that requiring members of the Gang of Eight to offer written responses to secret briefings will lessen their ability to pass the buck at a later date and may therefore incentivize them to push officials for explanations at the appropriate time.[96] Similarly, we can agree with Kathleen Clark that Congress ought to ensure that lawmakers are able to have their lawyers and staff members present at closed-door briefings; otherwise lawmakers will be hard-pressed to evaluate what information is shared with them.[97]

Nonetheless, we ought to be realistic about what congressional oversight can achieve even if these small steps are taken. Given the president's stranglehold over the flow of national security information, there is little reason to believe that lawmakers will be able to *take the lead* in uncovering policies and actions that the president has decided to conceal. It is now clear why it would be unhelpful to respond to this obstacle by calling for the abolition of executive privilege. Such a step would demand a sacrifice of either secrecy (if the authority to decide what information is shared with Congress is transferred to a committee composed of adversarial parties) or expertise (if this authority is transferred to an ad hoc bench). Furthermore, because it would concentrate regulatory authority in a different but still inscrutable institution—such as a secretive bench or congressional committee—such a step would beg the question of how we can ascertain whether the new regulators of state secrecy are in fact behaving responsibly. Thus abolishing executive privilege would likely hurt national security without really bolstering regulatory credibility.

It is important to recognize that leaving executive privilege intact does *not* render Congress helpless as an overseer. Though the president can utilize his control over the flow of secret information to thwart Congress's "police patrols," we have seen that he cannot easily prevent his subordinates from sounding "fire alarms" (to use the terminology coined by Mathew McCubbins and Thomas Schwartz).[98] Therefore, Congress *will* often be able to rein in the presidency. The question is—at what cost? To answer this question, we must examine whether we can regulate unauthorized disclosures: the more we can minimize the risk that such disclosures will violate key democratic norms, the less uncomfortable we will have to feel about Congress's dependence upon them.

Chapter 4

· ·

Should the Law Condone
Unauthorized Disclosures?

Fire Alarms and the Problem of Legitimacy

Now that we have seen the complications that arise when we try to invigorate legislative oversight and judicial review, let us turn our attention to the second part of the dilemma outlined in chapter 1. As noted there, the features that make the unauthorized disclosure of classified information an effective and credible regulatory mechanism are the very same ones that raise concerns about its lawfulness and legitimacy. Because this regulatory mechanism disperses regulatory power (in that any official who is aware of troubling secrets can sound the alarm), it is less prone to failure than a committee or bench (where the concentration of regulatory power invites capture). At the same time, because such disclosures override the classification decisions made by officials responsible for national security, our reliance on them seems to conflict with our commitment to the rule of law and the norms of democracy. Should we, then, revise the laws to condone unauthorized disclosures?

What Does the Law Say?

It is widely believed that the First Amendment protects the officials, reporters, and publishers responsible for the transmission and publication of unauthorized disclosures of classified information. This belief is not entirely without foundation, as can be seen in the Pentagon Papers case, where the Supreme Court refused to restrain the *New York Times* from publishing a secret history of the Vietnam War. The reality, though, is that those who disclose classified information are subject to administrative, civil, and criminal action. Therefore, in order to remove any misconceptions, let me start by clarifying what the law actually says about unauthorized disclosures.

At present unauthorized disclosures are prohibited via a mosaic of contracts and statutes. The most immediate of these controls comes in the form of a nondisclosure agreement that officials are required to sign before they are granted access to classified information. This agreement obliges signatories to refrain from disclosing classified information to unauthorized persons and serves as an acknowledgment that doing so constitutes grounds for dismissal.[1] The constitutionality of such "secrecy agreements" was challenged in *National Federation of Federal Employees v. United States* (1988), where it was argued that such agreements constitute an unacceptable condition on employment because they restrict the First Amendment rights of government employees. However, the D.C. District Court observed that it was widely accepted that "First Amendment protections may be tempered by governmental interests," and that the government has an "undeniably substantial" interest in safeguarding national security information.[2] Hence, even though "all governmental employees enjoy First Amendment rights," Judge Oliver Gasch ruled, "those with access to classified information must accept a different application of free speech protection."[3]

A second contractual prohibition against the unauthorized disclosure of classified information comes in the form of a prepublication review agreement that officials must sign before they are granted access to highly classified information. The constitutionality of such prepublication review agreements is also well established.[4] A central precedent here is *United States v. Marchetti* (1972), which involved an injunction against the publication of a book claiming to expose the CIA's involvement in unlawful activities.[5] In his appeal to the Fourth Circuit, the author, Victor Marchetti, a former employee of the CIA, argued that the CIA's prepublication review agreement amounted to prior restraint and therefore should be struck down. However, the Fourth Circuit concluded otherwise: it held that the need for secrecy in the conduct of foreign affairs "lends justification to a system of prior restraint against disclosure by employees and former employees of classified information obtained during the course of employment."[6] Indeed, the need for confidentiality in this arena was so pressing, the Fourth Circuit observed, that "the law would probably imply a secrecy agreement had there been no formally expressed agreement."[7]

The ruling in *Marchetti* was subsequently affirmed in *Snepp v. United States* (1980). This case involved Frank Snepp, a former CIA employee, who had been stationed in Saigon toward the end of the Vietnam War. Following his return to the United States, Snepp published a book describing the harm that the CIA's "treacherous withdrawal" had caused the South Vietnamese.[8] The government filed suit, asking that Snepp be held in breach of the prepublication review requirement and forced to turn over profits from the publication. The case eventually reached the Supreme Court, which rejected Snepp's claim that the prepublication review requirement violated the First Amendment. The agreement, the court observed, constitutes a "reasonable means" for safeguarding the government's "compelling interest in protecting both the secrecy of information important to our national security and the appearance of confidentiality so essential to the effective operation of our foreign intelligence service."[9]

In addition to the administrative and civil sanctions outlined above, officials who make unauthorized disclosures can be charged under two kinds of criminal statutes. There are statutes prohibiting the unauthorized disclosure of *specific* categories of classified information, including communications intelligence, the identities of covert agents, and nuclear weapons data.[10] Then there are statutes such as the antitheft statute and the Espionage Act that have been employed against unauthorized disclosures more generally.[11] The latter set of statutes were first employed in *United States v. Russo* (1973), which addressed the activities of Daniel Ellsberg and Anthony Russo, the protagonists in the Pentagon Papers case. The applicability of these statutes was left undetermined though, as *Russo* was dismissed on grounds of prosecutorial misconduct. These statutes were subsequently employed in *United States v. Morison* (1988), a case involving an employee of the navy, Samuel Morison, who delivered to *Jane's Defence Weekly* documents he had pilfered from the desk of a fellow employee. But this precedent has limited value because even though Morison claimed to have sent the documents to *Jane's* "for public dissemination and information," the evidence indicates that his actual motive was to convince *Jane's* to employ him.[12] So even though the Fourth Circuit rejected Morison's claim that his prosecution under the Espionage Act violated the First Amendment, it is not clear that it would have responded in the same way had Morison actually disclosed information that revealed unlawful activity.[13]

So far I have outlined the laws that prohibit the unauthorized disclosure of classified information by officials. What about others in the transmission chain? As far as reporters are concerned, their role in the transmission of unauthorized disclosures exposes them to two kinds of legal action: they may face criminal charges, and they may be compelled to reveal the identities of their sources. At present, it is unclear whether there is in fact a statutory basis for prosecuting reporters themselves. Conceivably, reporters could be prosecuted for "conspiring" with officials to violate the Espionage Act.[14] They could also be prosecuted under the Espionage Act for transmitting "information relating to the national defense" to "any person not entitled to receive it" when they have "reason to believe" that such information "could be used to the injury of the United

States."[15] However, no reporter has ever been prosecuted for either soliciting or transmitting classified information—an outcome due in no small part to the convoluted language of the Espionage Act. As a result, it remains unclear whether the prosecution of a reporter under the Espionage Act would fall foul of the First Amendment.[16]

It is reasonably clear, though, that reporters can lawfully be compelled to reveal the identities of those who have disclosed classified information to them, especially when such information is vital to the prosecution's case. The governing precedent here is *Branzburg v. Hayes* (1972), a case in which reporters faced contempt charges because they refused to disclose to grand juries information obtained from or related to their confidential sources. Faced with the question of whether the First Amendment affords reporters a privilege against testifying before grand juries, the Supreme Court concluded that "we cannot seriously entertain the notion that the First Amendment protects a newsman's agreement to conceal the criminal conduct of his source, or evidence thereof, on the theory that it is better to write about crime than to do something about it."[17]

Branzburg implies that news reporters subpoenaed in grand jury investigations into criminal leaks of classified information can maintain the confidentiality of their sources only if they are willing to brave punishment for contempt of court. It is hardly surprising, then, that First Amendment activists have repeatedly called for a federal "shield law" that would accord reporters a privilege against compelled disclosure. However, despite some sixty attempts over the past century, Congress has yet to enact such a law.[18] The absence of such a shield law has not been greatly felt, though, because the Justice Department's internal guidelines caution prosecutors against compelling the disclosure of the identity of a reporter's sources (an exercise of self-restraint motivated no doubt by the realization that prosecuting reporters is a "messy," politically inexpedient, exercise).[19] Nonetheless, a recent flurry of cases have underscored that these internal guidelines are not fixed in stone.

The most prominent of these cases arose after news organizations reported that two officials in the White House had disclosed to reporters that Valerie Plame, the wife of Joseph Wilson, a critic of President Bush's foreign policy, worked for the CIA. As these disclosures potentially violated the Intelligence Identities Protection Act, a special prosecutor, Patrick Fitzgerald, was appointed to investigate the matter. Unfettered by the Justice Department's usual guidelines, Fitzgerald subpoenaed the reporters contacted by the White House officials in question. When the D.C. District Court held in *In re Special Counsel Investigation* (2004) that *Branzburg* required the reporters to obey the subpoenas, two of the reporters, Judith Miller of the *New York Times* and Matthew Cooper of

Time, appealed to the D.C. Circuit.[20] The resulting case, *In re Grand Jury Subpoena* (2005), reiterated the message of *Branzburg*.[21] In a unanimous decision, the D.C. Circuit reaffirmed that the First Amendment does not protect reporters from having to testify "before a grand jury or otherwise providing evidence to a grand jury regardless of any confidence promised by the reporter to any source."[22]

Finally, publishers issuing news reports that contain unauthorized disclosures are exposed to two kinds of legal action: their publications may be enjoined, and they may face criminal charges subsequent to publication. The former course of action has rarely been adopted owing to the demanding standard established in *Near v. Minnesota* (1931), where the court held that prior restraint is allowed "only in exceptional cases," for example, "the publication of the sailing dates of transports or the number and location of troops."[23] This standard was first discussed in the national security context in *New York Times v. United States* (1971), which addressed the legality of an injunction granted against the *New York Times*'s publication of the Pentagon Papers. Here the court concluded that the United States had not met the "heavy burden" of justification required to impose prior restraint.[24] Crucially, this language implied that the court rejected Justices Hugo Black and William Douglas's view that the First Amendment disallows prior restraint altogether.[25] Instead, the court's opinion indicated that it would grant an injunction when, in the words of Justice Potter Stewart, publication would "surely result in direct, immediate, and irreparable damage to our Nation or its people."[26]

This prudential logic was subsequently affirmed in *United States v. Progressive* (1979). This case arose when a magazine sought to publish an article containing technical information about the design and manufacture of the hydrogen bomb (albeit from publicly available sources, including two documents that were subsequently deemed to have been incorrectly declassified).[27] When the magazine refused to desist, the United States sought to bar publication.[28] This time around, the United States prevailed. In his opinion, Judge Robert Warren cited the statutory support offered by the Atomic Energy Act as a factor in his decision, but he ultimately relied on the standard established by *Near*.[29] The fact that the publication of the article "could materially reduce the time required by certain countries to achieve a thermonuclear weapon capability," Judge Warren wrote, meant that "a preliminary injunction would be warranted even in the absence of statutory authorization because of the existence of the likelihood of direct, immediate and irreparable injury to our nation and its people."[30]

In addition to injunctions, publishers can face criminal charges subsequent to the publication of unauthorized disclosures. The criminal code features statutes that explicitly prohibit the publication of certain kinds of information, including that relating to wartime security measures, communications intelligence, and visual representations of sensitive military installations.[31] There is also the possibility—highlighted by Justice White's opinion in the Pentagon Papers case—that publishers might be liable under the Espionage Act for communicating classified documents relating to national defense to persons "not entitled to receive it."[32] Though Justice White's reading of the Espionage Act was endorsed by a majority of his colleagues, some disagreed sharply.[33] Justice Douglas's counterblast asserted that the plain language of the Espionage Act does not forbid publication per se, and that its legislative history suggests that Congress did not intend for it to apply to publishers.[34] The court has not had an opportunity to resolve this dispute, but the broader point to take away is that post-publication sanctions have not been deemed incompatible with the First Amendment.[35] Hence there seems to be, for now at least, no explicit bar against the introduction of additional criminal penalties.

Should Unauthorized Disclosures Be Condoned?

We have now established that officials, reporters, and publishers who participate in the unauthorized disclosure of classified information are confronted with the prospect of administrative, civil, and criminal action. Admittedly, the reach of the law in these cases is not always apparent, most notably with respect to the criminal liability of reporters and publishers under the Espionage Act. But it is quite clear that the law is not favorably disposed toward the most important link in the transmission chain—namely, the officials who make the initial disclosure of classified information. Given this, let us now examine whether the law ought to be revised to condone unauthorized disclosures.

There are typically two justifications offered in favor of prohibiting unauthorized disclosures. The first is that such disclosures can hurt the United States' national security interests.[36] This damage can take a number of forms. Most visibly, unauthorized disclosures can expose sensitive policies and decisions, thereby making it harder for the United States to realize its strategic objectives. In addition, disclosures can reveal the sources and methods used to obtain secret intelligence, making it easier for foreign actors to take measures that hinder the United States' ability to collect intelligence in the future. There can be some subtle costs, too. For instance, unauthorized disclosures can undermine the United States' ability to secure the cooperation of other countries in undertaking activities that are morally troubling or politically embarrassing, but are nevertheless vital for national security. These countries may decline to cooperate, fearing that they will be subject to criticism or retaliation should their cooperation be disclosed. Finally, unauthorized disclosures can have spill-over effects. For example, a disclosure that comes in the midst of international negotiations could lead to the collapse of a valuable international agreement or weaken the United States' bargaining position, leading to an adverse outcome that has an enduring effect on national security.

Few would deny that these reasons are weighty. It can, however, often prove a challenge to identify exactly how weighty they are, because claims about the harm caused by unauthorized disclosures are rarely accompanied by hard evidence. This is because law enforcement officials invariably take the view that discussing the harm caused by unauthorized disclosures can itself be harmful, as it can provide rival states with further information about the activities that have been revealed. Consequently, official statements about the harm caused by unauthorized disclosures tend to verge on the banal (as in the assertion by James Bruce, the vice chairman of the CIA's Foreign Denial and Deception Committee, that "it is impossible to measure the damage done to U.S. intelligence through leaks, but knowledgeable specialists assess the cumulative impact as truly significant") or the mysterious (as in a prominent bipartisan congressional report claiming that "hundreds of serious press leaks have significantly impaired U.S. capabilities against our hardest targets," adding that "we cannot, however, discuss them in an unclassified format").[37]

The evidentiary challenge created by such reticence is frustrating, but it does not undermine the case for prohibiting unauthorized disclosures. In part, this is because our knowledge of close calls in the past can help us appreciate the threat posed by unauthorized disclosures. One such example dates to June 1942 when the *Chicago Tribune* published an article revealing that the United States had managed to break Japanese ciphers prior to the Battle of Midway.[38] Although the Japanese apparently failed to notice the article, the harm it could have caused is instructive (indeed this episode motivated the passage of 18 USC §798(a), which prohibits the publication of classified information relating to communications intelligence).[39] Furthermore, there are some, albeit few, cases where the harm caused by unauthorized disclosures has become public knowledge. One example is Jack Anderson's decision to reveal that the NSA was intercepting telephonic communications from limousines ferrying members of the Soviet Politburo around Moscow. Almost immediately after Anderson's article was published in September 1971, Christopher Andrew and Matthew Aid have reported, the Russians enacted measures to prevent further interception.[40] Another example dates to April 1983 when, following a bomb attack on the U.S. embassy in Beirut, news reports disclosed that communication intercepts had revealed the involvement of Syria and

Iran. According to Katherine Graham, this disclosure prompted the terrorists to cease using the compromised communications channel, making it harder for the United States to monitor their activities. This intelligence loss may in turn have made it easier for the same terrorists to carry out a bomb attack on the marine barracks in Beirut five months later, causing the deaths of 241 personnel.[41]

The second reason to prohibit unauthorized disclosures of classified information is that they can hurt the efficient functioning of the government, which, like any other collective enterprise, cannot achieve its aims in the absence of loyalty and faithfulness on the part of its members.[42] The anonymity that typically accompanies unauthorized disclosures is particularly worrisome in this respect, because it can foster distrust and discord among decision-makers. Consider, for example, the consequences of navy stenographer Charles Radford's decision to pass on to Jack Anderson the minutes of a meeting that evidenced President Nixon's and National Security Advisor Henry Kissinger's "tilt" toward Pakistan during the India-Pakistan War of 1971. This disclosure greatly embarrassed both Nixon and Kissinger, because it ran counter to their public announcements that the United States would adopt an evenhanded approach. Not surprisingly, this disclosure led to a well-documented bout of finger-pointing within the administration that exacerbated rifts between key decision-makers, including Nixon and Kissinger.[43] It also led to an intense internal investigation that distracted staff and decision-makers for a prolonged period of time.

This is not to argue that unauthorized disclosures are the sole or even the leading cause of discord and distrust within the executive branch. The internal divisions fostered by Radford's disclosure may ultimately have contributed only a little to the strife that had already been generated by the turf wars and personality clashes that plagued the Nixon administration. But the fact that administrations experience internal bickering even in the absence of unauthorized disclosures cannot be taken to mean that unauthorized disclosures cause no harm. To reason this way is akin to arguing that throwing gasoline on a burning building does no harm since the fire is already underway. In other words, even if internal bickering is to be expected, it is not unreasonable to want to restrain unauthorized disclosures with a view to preventing a bad situation from becoming worse, an outcome that would only make it harder for political leaders to pursue the policies they have been elected to carry out.

The view that unauthorized disclosures should be prohibited because they endanger national security and undermine efficiency has been challenged in two ways. The first challenge comes from scholars who question whether every unauthorized disclosure of classified information can be said to threaten national security. The premise of this challenge is that the classification system tends to produce "rampant overclassification," because the officials and bureaucrats who operate this system use it to hide embarrassing information.[44] Given this, it is argued, we should not prohibit all unauthorized disclosures, since at least some disclosures will reveal information that is only tangentially related to national security— well-known examples here being the Pentagon Papers disclosed by Daniel Ellsberg and, more recently, the diplomatic cables disclosed by Bradley Manning via the WikiLeaks website.

A second challenge comes from scholars who question whether we ought to prohibit every unauthorized disclosure that threatens national security. This challenge is also premised on dissatisfaction with the prevailing classification system, though here the problem of overclassification is attributed not to officials and bureaucrats exaggerating the need for secrecy, but rather to their failure to account for the public's legitimate need for information concerning matters of national security. The issue is not *whether* unauthorized disclosures threaten national security; rather it is about *when* such disclosures should be condoned *in spite of* the threat they pose to national security. In these scholars' view, officials and bureaucrats will refuse to make public information that poses even the slightest threat to national security, lest "the enemy" profit from such information. As such a conservative stance threatens to leave citizens entirely in the dark on matters of deep moral and political significance (e.g., the use of torture in counterterrorism operations), unauthorized disclosures should be condoned, the argument goes, when the public's interest in the information revealed by such disclosures outweighs the prospective harm to national security.[45]

I would argue that these justifications for condoning unauthorized disclosures are faulty in two respects. First, unauthorized disclosures are not a costless remedy to the problem of overclassification. States must be able to retain information whose disclosure would genuinely harm national security. In order to guide the handling of such information, states need to rely on a system of classification markings. It is not difficult to see that the deterrent effect of such classification markings will be weaker when the threat of punishment for violating the relevant guidelines is conditional rather than assured. This is simply a matter of incentives: the more certain an individual is that disobedience will be met with punishment, the more likely he is to respect the relevant classification guidelines. Furthermore, if the threat of punishment is conditional rather than assured, then the deterrent effect of classification markings will ultimately depend on an official's willingness to take his chances before a jury. This arrangement invites disgruntled or scheming officials to disclose classified information, since proving that the information they have disclosed was appropriately classified will likely put prosecutors in the unhappy position of having to disclose additional classified information to a jury. Consequently, making punishment conditional rather than assured will ultimately make it harder for the government to deter the unauthorized disclosure of information that has been *appropriately* classified.

This argument implies that the more suitable response to the problem of overclassification is to reform the classification system. But this argument is likely to be met with the objection that it is fruitless to combat overclassification through statutory reform, because even the strictest classification statute must leave the executive branch broad discretion to withhold information under the heading of national security.[46] Hence, as overclassification seems "inevitable" under any classification system, critics such as Heidi Kitrosser argue, it becomes important to prohibit only those unauthorized disclosures that are highly likely to harm national security.[47] This is all the more necessary, the criticism goes, in light of the systemic weaknesses associated with judicial review and legislative oversight discussed in chapters 2–3.

Suppose we accept this claim. Even so, can we be confident that the ensuing unauthorized disclosures of classified information will not harm national security? Presumably, we will have to lay our faith in the judgment of the officials, reporters, and publishers responsible for making such disclosures. But is it sensible to assume that they will always have a grasp of the repercussions of *every* disclosure they make? This seems implausible; on the contrary, it is reasonable to assume that they will often be unaware of the bigger picture; they will not always know how the disclosure of a given piece of information might affect plans or activities that *have* remained secret, such as back-channel diplomacy or counterintelligence operations. Certainly, there will be cases where the bigger picture will hardly matter. The official who disclosed the Iraqi high school science exam reportedly classified as secret by overzealous American weapons inspectors will clearly not be putting national security at risk.[48] But can we assume that officials, reporters, and publishers will always know whether a given piece of information is an instance of overclassification? Consider, for example, the *Los Angeles Times*'s decision to run an article revealing that the CIA had been recruiting Iranian-American businessmen to act as informants. The paper published the article over the objections of the CIA because, in the words of its then-managing editor Dean Baquet, what the CIA "were doing in the [Iranian expatriate] community was well known and they were kidding themselves if they thought it wouldn't get out."[49] It is not facetious to suggest that if we are persuaded by Baquet's claim, then we should favor disestablishing the CIA, since we would then believe that the staff of the *Los Angeles Times* is better equipped than the

CIA is to judge the harm an article is likely to cause intelligence-related activities. (For the record, the CIA maintains that the story did have an adverse impact. According to a spokesperson, "the plan to use the Iranian-Americans to bring back intelligence had worked quite well, but not since the *Times* story. It was a one-day story in the *Times*, but got much bigger play in Iran. . . . Now, an Iranian expatriate going to Iran is going to find he is under much greater scrutiny.")[50]

If we allow private actors to ignore classification markings, then we ought to ask ourselves why we have established a classification system in the first place. The point is not that officials do not engage in overclassification. Rather, it is that if we do not want private actors to undermine the public authority that we have created through law and armed with expertise and information, then we must accept, warts and all, the decisions produced by a classification system designed, authorized, and funded by publicly elected officials.[51] Conversely, to the extent the prevailing system is flawed, the appropriate remedy must be public reform directed by our chosen representatives, not subversion by under-informed private actors.

So far I have been arguing that overclassification cannot be accepted as a reason for allowing officials, reporters, and publishers to make unauthorized disclosures, as they are not well placed to estimate the harm likely to be caused by such disclosures. Now consider a second flaw in the argument that overclassification justifies allowing unauthorized disclosures. Why should we believe that officials, reporters, and publishers have the legitimacy to decide that the public interest is better served by the revelation of a given piece of classified information? These actors typically justify their actions on two grounds. First, it is argued that unauthorized disclosures further democratic accountability when they draw attention to potential violations of the public's trust and provide citizens with the (otherwise classified) information they need to ascertain responsibility.[52] Second, it is asserted that unauthorized disclosures protect civil liberties when they expose government policies that violate individual rights.

These justifications are founded on a premise that few could disagree with, namely, that a polity will typically want to balance its interests in national security and efficiency against its interests in securing accountability and protecting civil liberties. But what these justifications do not address is whether unauthorized disclosures by officials, reporters, and publishers constitute a legitimate means by which to balance these interests when they come into conflict. There are at least two reasons to doubt that this is the case. The first is that whatever their shortcomings, the decision-makers who supervise the classification system can genuinely claim to have been authorized by citizens to strike a suitable balance between competing interests and priorities. By contrast, the parties involved in disclosing, reporting, and publishing classified information are neither elected by the people nor appointed by their representatives. Thus when unauthorized disclosures occur, vital decisions on matters of national security are effectively being made by private actors, an outcome that violates the democratic ideal that such decisions should be made by persons or institutions that have been directly or indirectly endorsed by citizens. In the case of such disclosures, we have a powerful reason to disapprove of the activities of officials, reporters, and publishers—namely, that they constitute a form of usurpation.

Here it may be objected that officials, reporters, and publishers are individual and corporate members of civil society whose actions merely promote or uphold shared interests. Hence they cannot be charged with usurping political power when they make unauthorized disclosures, any more than the American Civil Liberties Union (ACLU) can be charged with usurping political power when it seeks to influence public policy on behalf of the public. But is this analogy valid? Arguably, the behavior of officials, reporters, and publishers who disclose classified information is akin to the ACLU spiriting out and publishing minutes of the Supreme Court's closed-door deliberations under the pretext of furthering the public interest. To be sure, under certain circumstances, the ACLU may be justified in *disobeying* the court's rules. For example, if it obtains minutes that show the court's decision making to be predicated on some sort of racial theory, then exposing the court's deliberations would be defensible on a variety of grounds. But do we want to grant the ACLU—and, by extension, other organizations in civil society—the *right* to expose the court's deliberations whenever they believe this would further the public interest? Wouldn't the ensuing violations of the court's confidentiality by various groups—each believing that its disclosures further the public interest—ultimately serve to impair the court's deliberative capacity? The point, in short, is that we establish procedures and authorities—such as elections and courts—in order to balance and arbitrate between conflicting interests. These authorities and procedures allow us to collectively determine what is in the public interest. Consequently, to permit these authorities and procedures to be undermined on the basis of private judgments about what constitutes the public interest plainly seems a recipe for disorder. (This does not, as we shall see in chapter 5, rule out *disobedience* when there is a clear evidence of serious wrongdoing.)[53]

The second reason to doubt whether unauthorized disclosures constitute a legitimate means for balancing potentially conflicting interests is that it is difficult for citizens to hold officials, reporters, and publishers accountable for rash or malicious disclosures. Although reporters, editors, and publishers claim that they are held accountable by their readers and advertisers, this claim, as Lillian BeVier has argued, cannot be taken seriously because the marketplace is not a suitable analogue for the electoral system.[54] And even if it were, the usually anonymous and fragmentary character of unauthorized disclosures makes it hard for the public to ascertain the motives and judgments of the officials, reporters, and publishers involved, which in turn makes it a challenge to identify and punish those responsible for publishing rash or malicious disclosures. To feel the weight of this problem, consider the following example. In the mid-1990s the *New York Times* ran a story about how the CIA was using "unsavory characters" as informers to help fight terrorism. Although the CIA was able to persuade the *New York Times* to delete the name of one such informant, the article still described him in some detail. The outcome, according to the CIA, was that "the asset disappeared shortly thereafter and his family believed terrorists killed him."[55]

How should we react to this example? Our first impulse might be to feel outrage at the *New York Times*'s apparently irresponsible behavior. But there are a number of possibilities that we ought to consider. To begin, we will want to know whether the details contained in the published article actually proved decisive in revealing the identity of the informer (after all, the terrorists may have already considered the informant a likely CIA source). Equally, we will want to be sure that the informant's reported "disappearance" is not actually part of an elaborate cover story conceived to ensure his safety. And to ascertain whether it was appropriate for the *New York Times* to expose the CIA's dealings with "unsavory characters," we will need to know whether there were alternative, less troubling, means that the CIA could have used to apprehend wanted terrorists. But how are we to obtain such information? It is safe to assume that neither the CIA nor the informant's former associates will volunteer to fill in the blanks. And so we are unable to say much about whether this disclosure actually served the public interest. And yet it seems essential that we be able to say something in cases such as this. We cannot simply assume that officials, reporters and editors, and publishers are more public-spirited than the representatives and senior officials they undercut—after all, subordinate officials can have axes to grind, reporters and editors have careers to make, and publishers have advertising space to sell. As a result, our inability to hold these actors accountable should be seen as reviving, rather than redressing, our fear of the abuse of regulatory power.

The charge that it is difficult to hold officials, reporters, and publishers accountable can be countered in two ways. In the first place, it may be argued that unauthorized disclosures tend to be made anonymously precisely because they are illegal. If the laws were revised to allow unauthorized disclosures to be made in the public interest, then the use of anonymity would diminish, which in turn would allow the officials responsible to be held accountable. But this argument seems implausible, as a host of factors make anonymity appealing, not the least of which is the desire of officials to maintain their privacy and to avoid suffering embarrassment and hostility in the workplace (as we shall see in chapter 5). Besides, even if officials responsible for unauthorized disclosures are attracted to anonymity solely because they fear the law, how far could the law be changed to address their fear of being prosecuted? Since a law permitting unauthorized disclosures will condone only disclosures that are in the public interest, we should expect officials who make controversial disclosures—disclosures that both inform the public and endanger national security—to still take shelter behind anonymity, lest they end up on the wrong side of the law. Yet it is precisely such controversial disclosures that we will most want to scrutinize in order to preserve accountability (as we shall see in chaper 6).

The other way in which the charge can be countered is to argue that the anonymity that typically accompanies unauthorized disclosures can at worst be used to cover up bureaucratic infighting, whereas state secrecy can be used to shield violations of the law. Hence, from the point of view of accountability, it might be claimed, the costs associated with tolerating anonymous disclosures are a small price to pay in return for the security that grave crimes will not go unnoticed. But this claim does not seem credible in light of recent experience.[56] Over the past decade, anonymous disclosures have been used to falsely accuse Wen Ho Lee and Steven Hatfill of engaging in espionage and bioterrorism, respectively, and to maliciously reveal the identity of a covert CIA officer, Valerie Plame.[57] Crucially, in each of these cases, reporters and publishers refused to obey court orders to disclose the names of their sources, preferring, in the words of one critic, to show "loyalty to sources with an axe to grind."[58] More troublingly still, anonymous disclosures have been used to manipulate the public. In the run-up to the war on Iraq, for instance, reports based on sources with "knowledge" of Iraq's weapons of mass destruction program played a significant role in making the case for war.[59] Yet it is now widely believed that these reports presented a one-sided view, and indeed may have been part of a concerted effort to influence public opinion.[60] As a result, we cannot claim with confidence that in terms of accountability the harm likely to be caused by state secrecy will typically outweigh the harm likely to be caused by anonymous disclosures.

Can Unauthorized Disclosures Be Adjudicated?

I have argued that the law should not condone unauthorized disclosures because the officials, reporters, and publishers responsible have neither expertise nor legitimacy on their side since they are not authorized to balance the public's competing interests in secrecy and knowledge, and cannot be reliably held accountable for their decisions. Are there means by which these deficiencies might be remedied? For example, could Congress intercede on behalf of citizens? A number of scholars, most notably Harold Edgar and Benno Schmidt, argue that lawmakers have already spoken through their actions. Congress's unwillingness to explicitly criminalize *all* unauthorized disclosures, they claim, indicates that lawmakers endorse the role played by officials, reporters, and publishers (save in a few, narrowly drawn areas such as reporting on wartime measures and communications intelligence, where Congress has explicitly prohibited *all* unauthorized disclosures). But this claim is not supported by the evidence, as we can see from the House's decision in June 2006 to formally condemn the *New York Times* for revealing the existence of the Terrorist Financing Tracking Program, a counterterrorism initiative conducted by the Department of the Treasury.[61] Such inconsistencies in the public record make claims about congressional support for unauthorized disclosures more an assumption than a fact. Hence if we are to believe that lawmakers do in fact approve of unauthorized disclosures as a means of regulating the employment of state secrecy, then we need an explicit signal of their approval.

What form could this signal take? It should be evident that lawmakers cannot simply authorize officials, reporters, and publishers to disclose classified information as they see fit: to do so would create a contradiction in the structure of public authority, with one bearer of public authority (officials, reporters, and publishers) allowed to disclose what another bearer of public authority (the executive) has been allowed to conceal. Consequently, lawmakers will need to appoint an arbitrator to evaluate whether a given unauthorized disclosure is actually in the public interest. In whom should this authority be vested?

Congress could take on this role by requiring unauthorized disclosures to be routed via itself so that lawmakers can decide which disclosures serve the public interest.[62] But is it advisable, not to mention feasible, for Congress to undertake such screening? There are at least two reasons to think otherwise. The first is constitutional in nature. As we saw in chapter 3, the executive branch takes the view that Article II entitles the president to control the behavior of his subordinates, especially with respect to the maintenance of secrecy, a claim that finds some support in *Department of the Navy v. Egan* (1988), where the court ruled that the president's authority to control information bearing on national security flows primarily from his role as commander-in-chief, "and exists quite apart from any explicit congressional grant."[63] On this view, then, a statutory scheme authorizing officials in the executive branch to make disclosures to Congress in violation of the president's orders would be unconstitutional. Note that its protests to the contrary notwithstanding, Congress has thus far acceded to this point of view. For instance, the Intelligence Community Whistle-blower Protection Act authorizes officials who wish to "engage in whis-tleblowing activity relating to intelligence matters" to approach Congress, but only after they first raise the issue with the relevant inspector general, who is to "advise" the official on the procedures for making a complaint to Congress.[64] As one might imagine, this procedural requirement has meant that Congress has received few disclosures via this channel, since few offi-cials have wanted to risk incurring the wrath of their colleagues and man-agers by announcing their desire to approach Congress.[65]

Suppose we decide that the president's Article II claims are un-founded. There remains another reason to be skeptical about the util-ity of having lawmakers screen unauthorized disclosures. As I argued in chapter 3, the structure and composition of Congress hinder its ability to prevent its members from making unauthorized disclosures. In the pres-ent context, the same argument gives us reason to doubt whether Con-gress will be able to restrain its members from *retransmitting* unautho-rized disclosures to the press. There is evidence to support this fear. One example dates back to 1941 when an army captain passed on a copy of the United States' highly secret plans for World War II to Senator Wheeler (whom we met in chapter 3). Wheeler, an isolationist avidly opposed to American involvement in the war, chose to pass the plans on to the *Wash-ington Herald Tribune* rather than to the Senate leadership because "he believed the [Foreign Relations] Committee would not want to publi-cize them."[66] Another example dates to 1995 when Richard Nuncio, then an official in the Department of State, informed Representative Robert Torricelli, a member of the House Intelligence Committee, that the CIA had on its payroll in Guatemala an informant potentially involved in the murder of an American citizen.[67] Rather than bring the information to the attention of the House Intelligence Committee or the leadership of Congress, Torricelli chose to disclose what he had learned, including the identity of the informant, to the *New York Times*.[68] Torricelli defended his decision not to alert the president on the grounds that "the President might have shared classified information that would have placed me in an ethical bind."[69]

Now, in both the examples cited above, the unauthorized disclosures in question were made to individual congressmen rather than to the rel-evant congressional committees. This fact may prompt the suggestion that the risk of retransmission would be lower if we were to establish a formal procedure by which unauthorized disclosures could be made di-rectly to the relevant committees of Congress. But it is not at all clear why

congressional committees will be more disciplined in handling unauthorized disclosures than they are in handling classified information more
generally. On the contrary, one ought to fear that lawmakers will evaluate
such disclosures with an eye to the partisan rewards to be gained from
their publication or suppression. Besides, there is reason to doubt that
officials who wish to make unauthorized disclosures will be willing to approach Congress. The fundamental problem here, as Alan Katz has noted,
is that officials recognize that lawmakers do not have a strong incentive to
maintain the confidentiality of their sources.[70] In contrast to reporters and
publishers, who stand to pay a heavy price professionally if they disclose
the identity of an anonymous source, congressmen have little to lose and
much to gain by striking a deal with the administration or by selectively
retransmitting disclosures in order to settle scores or to attract favorable
publicity. Given this, we should not be surprised to find that officials who
want to make unauthorized disclosures generally prefer to approach the
press rather than Congress. Consider the following exchange, recorded in
the report of the Senate Select Committee on Intelligence on the potential
misuse of secret intelligence in the run-up to the Iraq War. The committee
asked Mr. Richard Kerr, a former member of the intelligence community,
whether intelligence analysts felt they had faced political pressure to skew
secret intelligence:

> *Mr. Kerr:* "There's always people who are going to feel pressured in
> these situations and feel they were pushed upon."
> *Committee Interviewer:* "That's what we've heard. We can't find any
> of them, though."
> *Mr. Kerr:* "Maybe they are wiser than to come talk to you."[71]

The drawbacks associated with having Congress determine whether
unauthorized disclosures are in the public interest inevitably throw into
sharp relief the institutional characteristics of the judicial branch, most
notably its proven ability to maintain secrecy and its insulation from the
imperatives of electoral politics. Should Congress call upon the courts to
determine when an unauthorized disclosure is in the public interest? This
is what some scholars believe. Cass Sunstein, for instance, has argued that
since there is "no reason to believe" that allowing officials, reporters, and
publishers to decide whether and when to disclose classified information
"will ensure a workable accommodation of the interests in disclosure and
secrecy," we should call upon judges to balance the interests that might be
served or hindered by an unauthorized disclosure.[72] Before we can take
refuge in the courts, though, we ought to account for three challenges to
the courts' ability to determine which unauthorized disclosures are in the
public interest.

The first challenge concerns the incommensurability of interests. As Louis Henkin has asked, even though the principle of balancing interests is unobjectionable, can courts "meaningfully weigh the Government's 'need' to conceal, the Press' 'need' to publish, and the people's 'need' to know?"[73] The objection is not that courts cannot come to *some* conclusion about the public interest in every case, but that there appears to be no firm basis on which to compare costs and benefits, especially when a given disclosure is *both* harmful to national security and valuable to citizens and lawmakers.[74] For instance, suppose a newspaper reveals that the president, who has been elected on a "no compromise" platform, has been secretly pursuing a peace deal with a terrorist group. The newspaper claims that the public has a clear interest in knowing that the president has acted contrary to his electoral platform. Meanwhile, the president claims that he has not violated any laws, and that the disclosure has led to a demonstrable loss of diplomatic credibility. How should the court go about weighing the benefit of greater public knowledge against the loss of diplomatic credibility? Suppose an election is due. Does this make public knowledge more valuable than diplomatic credibility? What if the polls show that the president is tied with his opponent? Does this make it more important for the public to know that the president is more moderate than he claims to be? Suppose the loss of diplomatic credibility is likely to make antiterrorism operations less effective. Does this make diplomatic credibility more valuable? What if a key ally announces that the unauthorized disclosure will not be allowed to derail antiterror cooperation? Should the court now discount the harm caused to the United States? Or should the court assume that this ally will extract its pound of flesh at a later date—perhaps by demanding valuable intelligence as compensation—and that the harm to national security is therefore indirect but still quite real? The answers to these questions will ultimately depend on political judgment—that is, on the capacity to comprehend interests, to discern what compromises might be feasible, and to then make a decision in the midst of constantly evolving circumstances and highly incomplete information. Unfortunately, calls for "interest balancing" obscure this messy reality and do not explain why we should believe that judges' decisions will be qualitatively better than those made by the president. It might be objected that in the hypothetical case outlined above, the court's judgment will be less impaired by the upcoming election than the president's might be. Perhaps so, but are we to assume that judges have no parochial concerns of their own? Certainly they will be free from electoral pressures, but will they be immune to the wrath of the press, which has the power to besmirch their reputations, devalue their legacies, and generally undermine their prospects for elevation to higher courts?

The second challenge the courts face is that of estimation. This challenge arises when the courts are called upon to decide whether an impending unauthorized disclosure is contrary to the public interest. In order to provide a reasoned answer, the courts will need to estimate the degree of harm likely to be caused by the unauthorized disclosure in question. The courts have not shied away from making such an estimate in the two prior restraint cases discussed earlier—*New York Times* and *Progressive*. This may seem surprising given that the courts have otherwise been hesitant to second-guess the executive's judgment of the harm likely to be caused by the disclosure of classified information (as we saw in chapter 2). Part of the explanation must be that prior restraint cases are less demanding to adjudicate. In cases adjudicated under FOIA, judges must evaluate whether a given disclosure will harm national security more generally, an evaluation that calls for familiarity with the ins and outs of national security. By contrast, prior restraint cases require judges to agree upon whether the publication of an unauthorized disclosure is likely to cause "direct, immediate, and irreparable" harm, a criterion that, presumably, even an inexpert observer ought to be able to apply.[75]

Or so it would seem. A closer examination of *New York Times* and *Progressive* reveals just how difficult it is for judges to agree upon the harm likely to be caused by an unauthorized disclosure. Consider the discrepancies in the justices' estimates as to the harm likely to be caused by the publication of the Pentagon Papers. Whereas Justice Douglas emphasized that the Pentagon Papers contained "history, not future events," Justice White claimed that he was "confident" that their publication would do "substantial damage to public interests," while Justice Blackmun supported the proposition that publication "could clearly result in great harm to the nation."[76] To be sure, such variances are not unusual—as noted in chapter 2, intelligence analysts consider such variances an inevitable part of the business of estimation. But are such variances acceptable in the context of legal adjudication? We ought to be concerned that such variances will make it difficult for the courts to fashion consistent answers to the question of whether a particular kind of unauthorized disclosure is likely to serve the public interest. Consequently, there is a significant chance that broadly similar unauthorized disclosures will be judged differently by different courts depending on the viewpoint of the judges involved—an outcome that confounds our effort to establish the legitimacy of such disclosures.

We may be tempted to take the view that such variances in estimates of harm can be eliminated or at least narrowed if the courts are provided with sufficient information and the advice of experts. Kitrosser, for example, has argued that if judges can deal with complicated financial and scientific cases as well as incitement cases in the vein of *Brandenburg v. Ohio* (1969), then they should have no trouble dealing with cases involving unauthorized disclosures.[77] But this view is mistaken for at least two reasons. First, as discussed below, the relevant evidence is far harder to come by in cases involving unauthorized disclosures, as opposed to scientific and financial disputes. Second, even when the evidence is available, the probabilities that need to be calculated in national security cases are far more complex than in an incitement case, because of uncertainties about who might exploit an unauthorized disclosure and how they might exploit it. As a consequence, objective answers tend to be few and far between, as we can see from the *Progressive* case, where after confronting a battery of affidavits arguing for and against the publication of the article about how to build a hydrogen bomb, Judge Warren was led to observe that "if there is any one inescapable conclusion that one arrives at after wading through all these experts' affidavits, it is that many wise, intelligent, patriotic individuals can hold diametrically opposite opinions on the issues before us."[78] Of course Judge Warren was required to reach a conclusion and so he did: he concluded that the publication of the article "would irreparably harm the national security of the United States."[79] And when no such harm materialized after another periodical in Wisconsin published a letter detailing much of the information contained in the enjoined article (an event that led the United States to drop its case against the *Progressive*), the brickbats quickly followed, with one leading nuclear scientist telling *Time* that the article should have been ignored rather than enjoined "because so much of it is wrong anyway."[80]

So far I have offered two reasons why courts will find it difficult to determine whether unauthorized disclosures are in the public interest. Now consider a further challenge—that of marshaling and managing evidence. This challenge arises when the courts are asked to ascertain whether an unauthorized disclosure that has already occurred has harmed the public interest. To answer this question the court will obviously need to know the facts surrounding the unauthorized disclosure, particularly the harm caused to national security. However, there will inevitably be cases where law enforcement officials will be unwilling to pursue legal action against unauthorized disclosures, much less to confirm or deny that harm has been caused, because this may signal to rival states the truth or falsity of the information revealed by the disclosure in question. Clearly, it is hard to be sure how many unauthorized disclosures are likely to be of this nature, but it is worth bearing in mind that the bipartisan congressional report cited earlier identified "hundreds of serious press leaks" that could not be discussed in a public setting.[81]

Furthermore, there will inevitably be cases where law enforcement officials will refrain from taking legal action because of the likelihood that the defendant will taking access to classified information in order to mount a defense. To see just how penetrating such demands can prove, consider what would likely have happened had the Justice Department tried to prosecute an unauthorized disclosure widely cited as evidencing the harm that leaks can cause. I refer here to the *Glomar Explorer* saga, which began in February 1975 when the *Los Angeles Times* and the *New York Times* reported that the CIA had been partially successful in covertly salvaging a sunken Russian submarine using a specially designed ship, the *Glomar Explorer*.[82] Following this revelation, director of central intelligence William Colby attempted to persuade reporters and publishers not to further publicize the story, lest it alert the Russians and thereby undermine the CIA's effort to salvage the remainder of the submarine's contents. However, Jack Anderson refused to cooperate and revealed the operation in a radio broadcast, attacking it as an expensive "boondoggle."[83] The consequence, according to Colby, was that the Russians began patrolling the area around the sunken submarine, forcing the CIA to cancel its planned second attempt to recover what promised to be a treasure trove of intelligence. Or so it would seem. A closer examination of the episode reveals just how difficult it is to know what exactly was at stake when Anderson disclosed the *Glomar Explorer*'s mission.[84] There are at least four plausible claims in circulation. The first is that Colby exaggerated the harm caused by Anderson's disclosure in order to turn public opinion against him.[85] The second is that Colby only pretended to be troubled by the disclosure in order to conceal the fact that he actually wanted to draw attention to the operation so that the CIA would receive credit for "the single greatest intelligence coup in history."[86] The third claim is that the *Glomar Explorer* actually succeeded in recovering the contents of the submarine on the first attempt, and that Colby had only pretended to be distressed by Anderson's disclosure in an effort to hide the success from the Russians.[87] Then there is of course the possibility that Colby was telling the truth.[88]

Now suppose the CIA had attempted to prosecute Anderson, and that there had then existed a law permitting unauthorized disclosures in the public interest. It is not hard to imagine how Anderson's lawyers would have reacted. They would have demanded access to the CIA's files in order to vindicate Anderson's claim that the operation was a wasteful exercise and not an intelligence coup. It is also not hard to envision what the outcome of this scenario would have been. The Justice Department would undoubtedly have chosen to drop the prosecution rather than expose the inner workings of the CIA to Anderson's lawyers. Such an outcome would serve the cause of due process, but it would hardly constitute a vindication of the public interest.[89]

There is a further kind of evidentiary problem that the courts will have to confront when they try to adjudicate whether unauthorized disclosures are in the public interest. In at least some cases where an unauthorized disclosure is blamed for having harmed national security, substantiating the charge will likely require testimony from foreign officials or from members of foreign organizations, who alone will know whether they genuinely benefited from the disclosure in question. But the courts will obviously be in no position to compel such testimony. The consequence will be an evidentiary paralysis of the sort that has gripped another case that is widely cited as demonstrating the harm caused by unauthorized disclosures.[90] I refer here to the publication in August 1998 of an article in the *Washington Times* stating that Osama bin Laden "keeps in touch with the world via computers and satellite phones."[91] Following the attacks of September 11, 2001, Daniel Benjamin, a former National Security Council official claimed that after the publication of this report "bin Laden stopped using the satellite phone instantly," adding that "when bin Laden stopped using his phone and let his aides do the calling, the United States lost its best chance to find him."[92] In July 2004, the 9/11 Commission echoed the allegation, noting in its report that "Al-Qaeda's senior leadership had stopped using a particular means of communication almost immediately after a leak to the *Washington Times*. This made it much more difficult for the National Security Agency to intercept his conversations."[93] The accusation was reiterated in February 2005 by Michael Sheuer, the former chief of the Bin Laden Issue Station at the CIA; Sheuer reportedly said of the *Washington Times* article that "a direct causal line can be drawn between the publication of that story and the events of September 11."[94] In September 2005, Representative Pete Hoekstra, then the chairman of the House Intelligence Committee, repeated the accusation, and in December 2005 President Bush referenced the *Washington Times* article when castigating the *New York Times* for revealing that the NSA had undertaken warrantless wiretapping.[95]

With so many public officials making the same claim, one might assume that the evidence of the *Washington Times*'s culpability must have been incontrovertible. But shortly after President Bush spoke, the story began to unravel. Jack Shafer of *Slate* promptly pointed out that Bin Laden's use of a satellite phone had actually first been reported by *Time* in December 1996, nearly two years prior to the article in the *Washington Times*.[96] Then Glenn Kessler of the *Washington Post* added that Bin Laden's satellite phone had been mentioned on *CNN* and *CBS* one day prior to the article published in the *Washington Times* and in *USA Today* on the very day the article was published.[97] Subsequently, Peter Bergen, one of the few Western reporters to have met Bin Laden, added that "bin Laden had been careful not to use satellite phones or cell phones long before the 9/11 attacks."[98] Meanwhile, Bill Gertz of the *Washington Times* offered a simpler explanation as to why Bin Laden may have stopped using the satellite phone: on August 21, 1998, the day before the *Washington Times* ran the article in question, the United States had tried to kill Bin Laden with a missile strike. "For a terrorist," Gertz dryly observed, "those kinds of near-death experiences can prompt a change in operating procedures."[99] This was not to be the last twist in the tale. When the *Washington Post's* Kessler sought a reaction from Lee Hamilton, the vice chairman of the 9/11 Commission, Hamilton replied that the commission had "relied on the testimony of three 'very responsible, very senior intelligence officers,' who had 'linked the Times story to the cessation of the use of the phone,' describing it as a 'very serious leak.'" Kessler then approached the CIA, but it declined to comment because the matter concerned "intelligence sources and methods." The White House, meanwhile, reasserted that it "was confident that press reports changed bin Laden's behavior."[100]

Imagine, then, the plight of a judge faced with having to determine whether the article in the *Washington Times* has in fact damaged national security. Should he believe Gertz, who has speculated that the "very responsible, very senior intelligence officers" described by Hamilton were in fact merely parroting the "flawed theory" first publicized by Benjamin?[101] Or should he believe Porter Goss, the former director of central intelligence, who has stated in no uncertain terms that although reporters depict the claim that the *Washington Times* article hurt national security as an "urban myth," the reality is that "the revelation of the phone tracking was, without question, one of the most egregious examples of an unauthorized criminal disclosure of classified national defense information in recent years."[102] And what if the judge were able to compel Goss to substantiate this charge, and the evidence turned out to be—as is often the case in intelligence analysis—well-informed conjecture? The judge would be left wishing for the testimony of the persons most likely to know why Bin Laden stopped using a satellite phone after August 1998, namely, Bin Laden's aides.

How to Sound the Alarm?

The objections presented immediately above imply that the case for revising the laws to condone unauthorized disclosures of classified information is not compelling. If we cannot be confident that officials, reporters, and publishers will know which unauthorized disclosures are in the public interest, and if they cannot be reliably brought to account for making rash or malicious disclosures, then allowing them to make disclosures whenever they think this is in the public interest will endanger national security and undermine democratic accountability.

It is important to note, however, that these objections militate only against granting officials, reporters, and publishers the legal right to make unauthorized disclosures. The implication is not that such actors can *never* be justified in making an unauthorized disclosure. Arguably, our concern—that officials, reporters, and publishers do not have the knowledge or the legitimacy to decide whether unauthorized disclosures are in the public interest—fades away whenever such disclosures reveal grave wrongdoing. Thus the objections presented above do not preclude officials, reporters, and publishers from sounding the alarm; they only imply that these actors should make such disclosures by disobeying laws prohibiting unauthorized disclosures when it is appropriate to do so.

This conclusion will no doubt displease officials, reporters, and publishers, who will as a consequence have to put their necks on the line. But the alternative—granting underinformed and unaccountable private actors the right to make unauthorized disclosures whenever they think this serves the public interest—is certainly not attractive. With this thought in mind, let us now examine *when* officials, reporters, and publishers would be justified in disobeying the laws prohibiting unauthorized disclosures, and *whether* they are likely to do so in spite of the threat of retaliation.

Chapter 5

. . . .

Should We Rely on Whistleblowers?

Disobedience and the Problem of Retaliation

In chapter 4 I argued that the law should not condone unauthorized disclosures of classified information because officials will not always know
which disclosures are in the public interest, and cannot be easily held
to account when they act rashly or maliciously. But this does not mean
that officials can never be justified in making unauthorized disclosures
of classified information. If an official possesses classified information
that reveals wrongdoing, then she may well be justified in disobeying laws
that prohibit the disclosure of classified information. But what counts as
wrongdoing? And when does wrongdoing justify disclosing classified information to reporters and publishers? These are the questions we must
examine next.

When to Blow the Whistle?

There are five conditions that must be met before an official can be justified
in disobeying laws prohibiting the unauthorized disclosure of classified
information. The first is that the disclosure must reveal wrongdoing. But
what counts as wrongdoing? There are two reasons why an official must
not evaluate wrongdoing in terms of her own moral, religious, or political
views. First, unlike the unhappy conscript contemplating her conscience,
the official in question will presumably have volunteered to be entrusted
with classified information (and likely on the explicit condition that she
will not disclose it without authorization). Consequently, if the president's
secret activities and policies run counter to the dictates of her conscience,

she ought to resign from her post rather than publicize the president's actions and policies. To her employer she owes loyalty—and she may disregard this obligation only if she is confronted with a greater obligation that even her employer could recognize as legitimate.[1] Second, the potentially adverse consequences of her disobedience will be borne not by her alone, but by other citizens as well, whose safety she endangers. An unauthorized disclosure, as Alexander Bickel has written, is an "impositional," morally coercive act.[2] Because she imposes a burden on her fellow citizens, an official who makes an unauthorized disclosure must evaluate wrongdoing in terms of the violation of *shared* interests.

Yet shared interests will often conflict. For instance, a secret surveillance program may violate the privacy of citizens but also uphold public safety. So how, then, is an official involved in such a program to ascertain whether wrongdoing has occurred? The official cannot decide that the president has violated shared interests simply because *she* believes that her fellow citizens consider privacy more important than safety. To think this way would be to ignore the fact that there tends to be disagreement over how to balance shared interests, especially under conditions of uncertainty. For example, there might be disagreement not only over how much we ought to value safety as opposed to privacy, but also over how far the surveillance program actually contributes to safety. The pervasiveness of disagreement is precisely why we value and utilize voting and representation—these procedures allow us to draw conclusions as to what we collectively see as being in the public interest.

Arguably, as an official cannot rely on her own interpretation as to how shared but conflicting interests should be balanced—because we have granted the president and not her the authority to make that decision on our behalf—she can claim that wrongdoing has occurred only when the president exceeds the authority that we have allocated to him.[3] Thus, for example, if our hypothetical official comes across evidence showing that the secret surveillance program is being used to monitor political rivals rather than security threats (and the law authorizes the latter and not the former), then she might well be justified in concluding that the president has exceeded his authority.

But are the bounds of public authority always clear? In some instances they are. Suppose an official discovers that the president has covered up the fact that he has recruited individuals to burgle the offices of his political rivals. This official will have little reason to doubt that she is witnessing a gross abuse of public authority. But the picture becomes murkier when we consider the sorts of measures that a president might order in the midst of war and conflict—for example, the use of enhanced interrogation techniques or the use of deception against citizens. Should such unlawful or extralegal conduct *always* count as wrongdoing sufficient to warrant an unauthorized disclosure?

Some scholars argue in the affirmative. Geoffrey Stone, for example, has claimed that when a policy or program "is in fact unlawful, the public's need to know outweighs the government's interest in secrecy."[4] But this seems hasty. It is possible to envision cases where presidents might engage in conduct that lawmakers have not authorized, or have even prohibited, but *would* authorize if they were aware of the circumstances. For example, imagine that the FBI has detained the leader of a terrorist cell plotting a suicide bombing in New York City. Confronted with evidence that news of the detention may provoke the remaining members of the cell into immediately executing the plot, the president orders the terrorist to be placed in solitary confinement without informing anyone else.[5] Now imagine that one of the supervisors at the solitary confinement facility discovers the undocumented prisoner. Will this supervisor be justified in thinking that the president has abused his authority? The answer here, surely, must be—it depends. As in the case of the secret surveillance program discussed above, the supervisor at the solitary confinement facility will have to take a number of variables into account before she decides whether the president has abused his authority. For instance, she will need to examine whether the Supreme Court and Congress have declared that precautionary detention is never permissible (or have they granted the president some discretion in such matters)? Is there reason to believe that the prisoner really is a terrorist leader (rather than an innocent)? Is there evidence that the prisoner is being mistreated (rather than merely being detained incommunicado)? Is there a time line for the covert detention (or does it seem open-ended)? Crucially, does the president seem prepared to be held accountable for his decision ex post (or are records being destroyed in order to conceal the entire matter)?

The point, in short, is that since adventurous exercises of executive power usually take place in the midst of complicated and fast-moving events, an official cannot rely on a rigid definition of what constitutes wrongdoing. In determining whether a prima facie violation of the law constitutes a genuine abuse of authority, she will need to take account of the broader context within which the violation has occurred. In other words, she will need to evaluate whether the president is behaving in a manner consonant with the authority that has been allocated to him—that is, whether he is following the spirit, if not the letter, of the law.

This procedure for ascertaining whether wrongdoing has occurred has its drawbacks. Since secret intelligence is typically compartmentalized, a subordinate official may find herself lacking the detailed contextual information required to ascertain whether the president is in fact abusing his authority. As a result, she will be left in limbo—aware of an apparent violation of the law, but unable to determine whether the president has actually abused his authority. This may lead her to obey orders that she would actually be justified in disobeying. There are, however, some ways around this obstacle. If there is a clear mismatch between the president's actions and the law (for instance, the president claims that the secret detention is justified by necessity, but he is in fact destroying records that would evidence such a necessity), then a subordinate will have good reason to believe that something profoundly wrong is happening. Furthermore, a subordinate who lacks the information required to ascertain whether wrongdoing has occurred need not be rendered mute; instead, her position obliges her to approach those officials who are likely to have the information she lacks.

The absence of contextual information is not the only barrier to ascertaining whether prima facie wrongdoing constitutes a genuine abuse of authority. There is also the possibility that moral and political disagreements will lead to differences over the rightful bounds of public authority. For instance, suppose our hypothetical supervisor decides that the president's decision to confine the terrorist leader violates a law passed by Congress. Whether the supervisor sees this violation of the law as an abuse of authority will depend on whether she thinks that the president has the right to violate the law during an emergency. It hardly needs to be pointed out that there is little consensus on this question. Yet once we acknowledge that reasonable people can disagree over whether a given violation of the law constitutes an abuse of authority, then it becomes clear that even an unauthorized disclosure that exposes an apparent violation of the law could prove controversial because what one individual sees as wrongdoing will not necessarily be seen as such by others. As we shall see below, this concern does not mean officials must make unauthorized disclosures only when there is likely to be unanimous agreement that an abuse of authority has taken place. Instead, the pervasiveness of disagreement over the rightful bounds of public authority imposes an obligation on the official as to how she ought to proceed when making an unauthorized disclosure—namely, she ought to identify herself so that the public (and potentially, jurors) can examine her motives.

So far I have argued that an official will be justified in making an unauthorized disclosure only if she encounters wrongdoing—understood as the abuse of public authority. This is just one of three threshold conditions that must be met (and only one of the five conditions in sum). A second threshold condition is that an unauthorized disclosure must be based not on hearsay or fragmentary evidence but on clear and convincing evidence. Evidence can be described as clear and convincing when disinterested observers are likely to draw the same inference from it. The explanation for this condition is straightforward: since an official who makes an unauthorized disclosure potentially endangers her fellow citizens, she will not be justified in putting them in harm's way unless she can point to evidence that they are bound to accept. Now, for the reasons outlined above, there may be disagreement over whether the prima facie wrongdoing she has exposed really is an instance of the abuse of authority. Nonetheless, the evidence itself should be clear and convincing. To return to an earlier example, an official must have evidence that the secret surveillance program is *in fact* being used to spy on a political rival before she discloses the existence of the program. Whether the president's decision to spy on his political rival actually constitutes an abuse of authority will depend on contextual variables that citizens and lawmakers will subsequently have to analyze (for instance, an inquiry might reveal that the president had good reason to believe his rival was conspiring with a foreign power and that informing Congress would have alerted his rival, who is a member of the Senate). But evidence that the political rival has in fact been spied upon should be clear and convincing—for instance, there must be logs, physical evidence, or the testimony of credible witnesses.

A third threshold condition is that the unauthorized disclosure should not impose an undue or disproportionate burden on national security. That is, an official ought not to make an unauthorized disclosure with a view to exposing the truth at any cost. Under certain circumstances it will be inadvisable to make an unauthorized disclosure *even when* this will reveal clear and convincing evidence of violations of the law. These circumstances are most likely to arise when the country is at war or in the midst of negotiations leading up to the establishment of rules that will have lasting effects. In this context, embarrassing or incriminating revelations may endanger the country's strategic or diplomatic interests in ways that are significant enough to outweigh the public's otherwise profound interest in uncovering wrongdoing. Hence, before making an unauthorized disclosure, an official must account for the harm that might result from her actions. She ought to look out for grave threats that are specific and imminent rather than vague and remote, because only threats of the former sort can trump the public's interest in being informed of grave wrongdoing. For example, suppose an official discovers that terrorists held at a military prison have been tortured for information. If there is reason to believe that the revelation of this information poses a grave threat that is specific and imminent—the terrorists' compatriots are highly likely to retaliate by torturing American civilians they have captured—then the official ought to refrain from making a public disclosure until after the civilians have been freed. But her final decision will have to depend on the facts of the case. If the wrongdoing itself is likely to have grave consequences that are specific and imminent—perhaps Congress is about to declare war on the basis of false intelligence that the terrorists have provided in order to avoid being tortured—then she will be justified in making the unauthorized disclosure on grounds of proportionality.

These, then, are the three threshold conditions that must be met before an official is justified in making an unauthorized disclosure—the disclosure must (a) concern an abuse of public authority; (b) be based on clear and convincing evidence; and (c) not pose a disproportionate threat to public safety. There remain two further conditions that must be satisfied before an official will be justified in disobeying laws prohibiting unauthorized disclosures. These conditions concern *to whom* and *how* such disclosures should be made.

The former of these conditions asks that the official utilize the *least drastic means* of disclosure. Since the disclosure of classified information is likely to endanger national security, an official is obligated to minimize harm by limiting the scope and scale of disclosures as far as is possible (subject of course to the need to alert others to prima facie wrongdoing). As a first step in this direction, an official must examine whether it is possible to make an unauthorized disclosure within the confines of the executive branch, as this will prevent the disclosure of classified information to unauthorized persons.[6] This kind of disclosure involves circumventing standard reporting procedures in order to bring unlawful conduct directly to the attention of the head of the organization (or to officials he has nominated for this purpose, such as an inspector general). This requirement is especially important where low-ranking officials are concerned because, as noted earlier, they may lack the contextual information necessary to determine whether there really has been an abuse of authority. By approaching senior officials, a subordinate can obtain, if not a more nuanced insight into the broader interests at stake, then at least the assurance that higher-ups in the organization are aware of the activity in question and do not see it as clearly wrongful.[7]

But must officials *always* direct their disclosures toward senior officials? A number of lawmakers and scholars seem to believe so. Gabriel Schoenfeld, for instance, has written that "officials who uncover illegal conduct in the government are by no means bound to . . . permit violations of law to continue." But they must, he argues, sound the alarm only in the manner prescribed by the law. In particular, they must abide by whistleblower statutes "that offer clear and workable procedures for civil servants to report misdeeds and ensure that their complaints will be duly and properly considered." These procedures, he emphasizes, "do not include blowing vital secrets by disclosing them . . . [to] the rest of the world via the front pages of the *New York Times*."[8]

Is this requirement completely defensible? There are reasons to think otherwise. Most immediately, senior officials may ignore or suppress a whistleblower's complaint in order to hide their complicity or to avoid a scandal.[9] Constraining a whistleblower to utilize only official channels would in such cases allow wrongdoing to go unaddressed. Further, reporting wrongdoing internally could leave a whistleblower lacking external support in the event that her colleagues and managers retaliate against her. As a result, limiting whistleblowers to internal channels might deter officials from reporting wrongdoing altogether. Finally, sounding the alarm within the organization could provide wrongdoers with the opportunity to destroy incriminating evidence.[10] Hence limiting whistleblowers in this way could also undermine law enforcement.

Thus it seems that officials cannot be obliged to *only* blow the whistle internally. Certainly, an official must always examine whether she can blow the whistle internally. This will require evaluating the concerns outlined above. Will her complaint be heard? Is there a prospect that she will be severely punished? Could the evidence be destroyed? If these concerns turn out to be minor, then she ought to utilize official channels. And even if these concerns turn out to be more compelling, she will still be obliged to investigate all reasonable alternatives short of public disclosure. For instance, if there is a genuine threat of retaliation, she might examine whether it is possible to file an anonymous complaint.

But what if an official has exhausted all reasonable alternatives? To return to the earlier example, suppose the official who is involved in the secret surveillance program learns that internal complaints provoke a harsh response from higher-ups (for example, a colleague who complains that the president ought not to spy on his political rivals is summarily dismissed). In light of this event, the official decides that she is justified in bringing the matter to the attention of outsiders. But does this mean she is now justified in disclosing classified information to reporters and publishers? Some lawmakers have argued that when internal whistleblowing is likely to prove ineffectual or even counterproductive, an official must approach lawmakers rather than reporters and publishers, as the former could utilize discreet oversight procedures (such as closed-door hearings or investigations) that will prevent the widespread dissemination of classified information. Is this limitation any more reasonable?

I would argue otherwise, because lawmakers too could fail to investigate evidence of wrongdoing. This is most likely to happen when a majority in Congress comes from the same party as the president. In this case lawmakers will have a clear incentive to ignore or downplay evidence of wrongdoing. But the same result may follow even when a majority of law-makers are *not* from the president's party. The president's ostensible adversaries could end up remaining silent for contingent political reasons—for instance, they may decide not to publicize embarrassing or incriminating information lest they be attacked as unpatriotic. They may also choose to be silent because they have been "captured" by the leadership of the agencies they are meant to oversee.[11] And even if they are willing or motivated to challenge the president, their investigation may end up being stalled by the president's privilege to withhold information from Congress. Worse yet, they may disclose classified information selectively in order to deflect blame or obscure their own complicity or neglect, thereby distorting the public's understanding of the president's policies and decisions.

Thus it seems that an official is obliged only to investigate whether disclosing classified information to Congress is likely to lead to a good faith inquiry into the appropriateness of the president's activities. If her disclosure has been suppressed for contingent political reasons or rendered ineffectual by the president's refusal to share further information with Congress, then she will be justified in directing her unauthorized disclosure toward reporters and publishers in order to alert citizens to the wrongdoing as well as to Congress's regulatory failure. Indeed, she will be justified in bypassing Congress altogether if there is good reason to believe that lawmakers are likely to collude with senior officials in a cover-up or to selectively disclose evidence in order to hide their own failures. The broader obligation to use the least drastic means necessary will always remain in place, though. The whistleblower must divulge only so much classified information as is necessary to convince citizens that there has been an abuse of authority.

We have now established that the objection to unauthorized disclosures cited in chapter 1 is not entirely correct. Under certain conditions—in particular, when there is good reason to believe that lawmakers will not subject the president's unlawful or extralegal actions to good faith scrutiny—an official will be justified in directing unauthorized disclosures toward reporters and publishers. However, we have not completed the list of conditions that an official must satisfy before making an unauthorized disclosure. As we shall now see, the fifth and final condition will greatly complicate this picture.

The final condition an official must meet is that she must be willing to disclose her identity. Of the various conditions discussed here, the reasoning behind this one is perhaps the least obvious. As Gene James asks, why do we need to know the identity of a whistleblower when "all that matters is whether wrongdoing has taken place"?[12] Sissela Bok has offered three explanations. First, public disclosures are fairer to those accused of wrongdoing, who would otherwise "be hard put to defend themselves against nameless adversaries."[13] Second, public disclosures are more likely to be effective in revealing wrongdoing because "what is openly stated can be more easily checked."[14] And third, public disclosures allow observers to study a whistleblower's motives.[15]

Bok's first two claims are not entirely persuasive. As Frederick Elliston has pointed out, it is the duty of investigators to conduct a fair and thorough investigation into allegations of wrongdoing. So long as they do their duty, concerns about fairness and efficacy become less pressing, and so it becomes less important to know the identity of the whistleblower.[16] There would of course be a case for revealing the identity of the whistleblower should the accusations turn out to be baseless, but we have guarded against this scenario by requiring the whistleblower to provide clear and convincing evidence of prima facie wrongdoing. A whistleblower who fails to present such evidence would obviously have a strong incentive to hide her identity, but investigators would be justified in discounting her allegations, and indeed in attempting to uncover her identity (and should her identity be uncovered, she would have no moral defense against the law).

So why, then, must a whistleblower who has disclosed clear and convincing evidence of wrongdoing be willing to reveal her identity? Arguably, a whistleblower ought to be willing to reveal her identity for the third reason identified by Bok—namely, that this allows the public (and, potentially, jurors) to examine her motives. This explanation has not gone unchallenged. A number of scholars have argued that a whistleblower's motives are of secondary importance; what really matters is whether the whistleblower has revealed wrongdoing. James, for instance, objects that "it is not necessary for the whistle blower's motive to be praiseworthy for the action to be justified in terms of the public interest."[17] James's objection makes more sense in the context of "ordinary" whistleblowing than in the present context, which is distinct for two reasons. First, unlike an ordinary whistleblower, who typically violates a confidentiality contract, a "national security whistleblower" violates both a confidentiality contract and criminal law. It is widely accepted that an individual who disobeys the law on moral grounds ought to act publicly so as to allow fellow citizens to verify that her disobedience is well-intentioned.[18]

Second, since there is widespread disagreement over the rightful bounds of public authority, there will often be dispute over whether a given instance of prima facie wrongdoing actually constitutes an abuse of authority. For instance, if the hypothetical supervisor we discussed earlier is an advocate of executive power, she will perhaps judge that the president's decision to secretly detain the terrorist leader is not an abuse of authority, but if she is a civil libertarian, she will likely reach the opposite conclusion. Since there can be disagreement on whether prima facie wrongdoing actually constitutes an abuse of authority, how can we be sure that the supervisor is not merely *claiming* to be justified in making an unauthorized disclosure on the grounds that the president has committed "a grave wrongdoing" when her real intention is to defeat a policy she dislikes for sectional or personal reasons? Given this possibility, it is essential that we be able to investigate whether a whistleblower has acted in good faith. In particular, we need to be able to examine whether a whistleblower's view of what constitutes the wrongful exercise of executive power is a disinterested one—the objective here being to weed out the partisan or the zealot who, under the guise of blowing the whistle, will covertly disclose classified information with a view to furthering sectional interests or personal values.

An example will make this point clearer. Suppose, for instance, that the president believes it to be in the interest of the United States to invade a country that is on the verge of developing a fearsome biological weapon. He cannot communicate the urgency of the situation to citizens because doing so would reveal how much the United States knows about that country's biological weapons program, which in turn would allow that country to secure its facilities against bombardment. Nor can he share this secret intelligence with Congress, as it contains a bloc of radical democrats who will disclose the intelligence in an effort to foster "a full and free public discussion." Yet if the president does not communicate the urgency of the situation to citizens and lawmakers, they are unlikely to approve the invasion, as they have little appetite for military action. Faced with this quandary, the president decides to utilize deception. When making the case for invasion, he assures citizens and lawmakers that the casualties will be minimal. He acts this way in the belief that once the invasion is complete, he will be able to safely reveal the existence of the biological weapon, and at that point citizens and lawmakers will agree that his use of deception was justified. But shortly after the president makes his case, an anonymous disclosure reveals that some of his advisers have counseled against an invasion, citing the possibility of heavy casualties. The official responsible for the anonymous disclosure claims that he has disobeyed the law in the belief that the president has gravely abused his authority by deceiving citizens and lawmakers about the likelihood of casualties. The disclosure causes enormous controversy and the invasion plan is scrapped.

Now imagine that an investigation reveals the source of the disclosure to be a cabinet officer who has received campaign contributions from corporations that stand to lose their investments in the target country in the event of war. What interest might citizens and lawmakers (and, potentially, jurors) have in knowing this fact? If they know this, they will be in a position to investigate the basis of the official's judgment that the president has abused his authority: whether it is grounded in a good faith interpretation of the rightful bounds of public authority or in fact motivated by the desire to scuttle the proposed invasion in order to benefit her campaign contributors.

A disclosure made with the latter sort of intention is problematic for a number of reasons. Most immediately, it endangers national security because it compels officials who are in favor of military action to disclose classified information in order to reaffirm the merit of their claims. Further, a disclosure of this variety constitutes a breach of trust because we expect officials to prioritize the public interest rather than sectional or corporate interests, especially when they have been provided with privileged access to classified information. It is also deceptive because the policy it aims to support—preserving the wealth of campaign contributors—would be unlikely to be supported if it were made public (unlike the president's policy of deception, which would probably withstand such a test were the existence of the biological weapon revealed). If the cabinet officer believes that his policy would receive public support—perhaps he believes that the interests of his campaign contributors are indistinguishable from the public interest ("what is good for General Motors is good for America")—then he ought to publicly oppose the war on these grounds rather than by feigning concern about the president's use of deception.

So a covert disclosure is troubling because anonymity makes it difficult for the public to discern whose interests the disclosure is serving, and to take appropriate steps to counter the possibility of manipulation (compare this with the way other sources of influence can be monitored: e.g., electoral contributions are registered, allowing the public to trace the influence of money in policymaking).[19] But do we *always* need to know the motive behind an unauthorized disclosure? Surely we do not. Here we ought to distinguish between *gross* or *obvious* wrongdoing and *suspected* or *prima facie* wrongdoing. The former involves blatant abuses of authority—that is, actions that cannot possibly be justified in terms of the public interest. This includes gross negligence, corruption, and the abuse of police power. In the latter form of wrongdoing, by contrast, the president violates the law in the public interest, and the costs and benefits of his actions are likely be more closely matched; here there will usually be disagreement over whether the violation of the law really amounts to an abuse of authority. Only a whistleblower who reveals suspected wrongdoing must be willing to reveal her motive for the reasons outlined immediately above—namely, so that we can ensure that her unauthorized disclosures are not actually aimed at covertly promoting a sectional or partisan interest. A whistleblower who reveals gross wrongdoing, by contrast, will not be obliged to disclose her identity, as the significance of her motives will pale in comparison to the public interest in confronting a serious misuse of public authority. Moreover, a whistleblower who reveals gross wrongdoing may have a strong reason to avoid disclosing her identity because a president capable of such conduct might also be willing to do whatever it takes to silence her.

From a practical perspective, though, this distinction turns out not to be very meaningful, because national security whistleblowers tend to expose suspected rather than gross wrongdoing. There are two reasons for this. First, gross wrongdoing is a relatively rare occurrence in an advanced industrial democracy such as the United States (Watergate being the prime example). Second, when it comes to matters of national security, presidents can—and do—cite the public interest as the justification for any violation of the law. This implies that most unauthorized disclosures will reveal suspected wrongdoing and that therefore we will typically want national security whistleblowers to be willing to reveal their identity. But this expectation creates a serious quandary. Requiring a whistleblower to be willing to disclose her identity makes it less likely that even those officials who have good intentions will blow the whistle. This is because by disclosing her identity, an official exposes herself to retaliation, not so much from the law (since prosecutors may choose not to prosecute her or else a jury may nullify the prosecution), but from her colleagues and managers, who are likely to take a dim view of the negative publicity resulting from her disclosures. The record on this front is certainly disheartening. As Mike Martin has put it, "sad and tragic stories about whistleblowers are not the exception; they are the rule."[20] The more credible the threat of retaliation, the weaker an official's obligation to blow the whistle becomes, especially when she is a witness to, rather than an active participant in, the wrongdoing in question. For, as Martin argues, although an official is obliged to serve the public, she is not obliged to do so without regard for the adverse effect this may have on her career and personal life.[21]

Now, to be sure, an official cannot care only about her own interests, since she has *chosen* to be a public *servant*. Therefore her obligations to the public do not simply drop away at the first sign of trouble. In particular, she will be obliged to blow the whistle—even at great personal cost—when she comes across grave wrongdoing. But, as noted above, an official is unlikely to actually confront such tragic circumstances, because she is not obliged to reveal her identity when disclosing grave wrongdoing. The real difficulty arises when an official comes across suspected wrongdoing—a prima facie violation of the law, which, as we have seen, is the more common occurrence. In this case, we have seen, the official is obliged to reveal her identity should she decide to blow the whistle. But is she obliged to blow the whistle under the conditions we have imposed on her? Arguably, she is not, since the extent of the wrongdoing, and hence the public's interest in knowing about it, is unclear, whereas for her personally the consequences are likely to be quite negative. As a result, this official will be justified in blowing the whistle, but she will not be obliged to do so.[22]

The Problem of Retaliation

We have now examined the conditions under which an official can be justified in making an unauthorized disclosure. But this exercise has left us facing a predicament: if we take the view that an official is justified in making such a disclosure only when she is willing to disclose her identity, then we run the risk that the ensuing threat of retaliation will justify her "swallowing the whistle," thereby making it less likely that citizens will become aware of abuses of authority. But if we take the view that an official is justified in making such a disclosure anonymously so that she may avoid retaliation, then we run the risk that she will make disclosures in order to covertly further sectional interests or to impose her own values on the public. It is clear that we cannot evade this predicament by requiring officials to direct unauthorized disclosures toward Congress alone, because lawmakers could fail to act in the absence of public pressure. Nor can we hope to evade this predicament by allowing officials to approach reporters and publishers *only* when gross wrongdoing has occurred. This restrictive permission misses the point because whistleblowing in the national security domain will typically expose suspected rather than gross wrongdoing. How, then, to overcome this predicament?

The most obvious answer is to find a way to shield the whistleblower against retaliation. This would make it safe for her to disclose her identity, which in turn would make it safe for the public to trust her disclosures. But where are we to find such a shield? One alternative is to rely on the force of public opinion. This is another way of saying that an official ought to blow the whistle only when she is certain that by doing so she is likely to garner widespread public support, as this would make it difficult for her colleagues or managers to retaliate against her. But this solution is unsatisfactory for a number of reasons. An official will not always be able to confidently predict what the public's response to her disclosure will be. Consider the sorts of questions that she will have to grapple with. Will her disclosures raise a hue and cry in Congress? Will the news media launch follow-up investigations? Will the president's media managers succeed in deflecting public attention? These are questions to which even the most seasoned political observer will not have clear answers. Now, to be sure, an official will have reason to expect public support when her disclosure exposes gross wrongdoing. But a whistleblower who exposes wrongdoing of this sort is under no obligation to reveal her identity in the first place (remember, we are interested in knowing the identity, and thereby the motive, of a whistleblower only when it is unclear whether the activity or policy she has exposed actually constitutes an abuse of authority).

An alternative way to protect a whistleblower against retaliation is to rely on the law. But this is easier said than done. Although lawmakers have long sought to counter retaliation against whistleblowers, the statutes they have enacted have proven less than satisfactory from the perspective of national security whistleblowers.[23] The more far-reaching of these initiatives, the Civil Service Reform Act of 1978, the Whistleblower Protection Act of 1989, and the Whistleblower Protection Enhancement Act of 2012 have declared retaliation against whistleblowers to be a "prohibited personnel practice" and have established institutional mechanisms by which aggrieved officials can seek redress.[24] However, these statutes specifically exclude from their purview any government agency whose "principal function" is the "conduct of foreign intelligence."[25] In addition, the protections established by these statutes do not apply in cases where an unauthorized disclosure is "specifically prohibited by law" and contains information "specifically required by Executive Order to be kept secret in the interest of national defense or the conduct of foreign affairs."[26] In other words, these statutes effectively protect only ordinary whistleblowers: officials who have disclosed information that may be closely held but is not officially classified.

This is not to say that national security whistleblowers enjoy no statutory protections whatsoever against retaliation. They receive a degree of protection under the Inspectors General Act (IGA) of 1978 and the Intelligence Community Whistleblower Protection Act (ICWPA) of 1998. The IGA establishes inspectors general to whom federal employees can report potential wrongdoing;[27] it confronts the threat of retaliation by making it unlawful for supervisors to take "any action against any employee as a reprisal for making a complaint or disclosing information to an Inspector General."[28] The ICWPA establishes mechanisms through which a member of the intelligence community can report wrongdoing to Congress. Though the ICWPA does not directly protect a national security whistleblower against retaliation, it does allow her to lodge a complaint with Congress in the event that her disclosure provokes reprisals.[29]

These provisions certainly constitute an acknowledgment of the threat of retaliation that confronts national security whistleblowers. But as sources of protection against retaliation, they are less than satisfactory in two key respects. First, the protections they offer apply only if an official reports wrongdoing to her managers—that is, if she blows the whistle internally. This qualification means that an official who has lost faith in the willingness or ability of her managers to correct wrongdoing is hobbled.[30] Since she is not legally protected against retaliation in the event that she decides to make the wrongdoing public, she is effectively forced to choose between being protected and being effective. This is another way of saying that current whistleblower protections favor an official who wants to report wrongdoing committed by a renegade employee rather than by senior officials. It is also far from clear that an official who intends to blow the whistle on senior officials can truly count on the protections offered by the IGA. On the contrary, the evidence suggests that in such cases would-be whistleblowers ought to pay heed to William O'Connor, the former special counsel of the Merit Systems Protection Board, who famously advised officials to refrain from blowing the whistle "unless you're in a position to retire or are independently wealthy." In O'Connor's words: "don't put your head up, because it will get blown off."[31]

Consider here the case of Richard Barlow. Between 1985 and 1989, Barlow worked at the CIA, where he participated in intelligence activities aimed at detecting nuclear proliferation by Pakistan. During this time Barlow had the first of a series of run-ins with policymakers from the Reagan administration who were misleading Congress (then controlled by the Democrats) about the extent of Pakistani nuclear proliferation in order to prevent Congress from cutting the military and financial aid needed to ensure Pakistan's assistance against the Soviet Union in Afghanistan.[32] In 1989 Barlow moved to the Office of the Secretary of Defense. Around this time the United States announced its intention to sell Pakistan a large number of F-16s. Barlow's response was to prepare a study showing that the planned sale violated laws controlling military exports because the Pakistanis had learned how to modify the F-16s to deliver nuclear weapons. His efforts to disseminate this study attracted the wrath of policymakers who wanted to keep relations with Pakistan on an even keel. Barlow was ordered to cease investigating the sale, and not long thereafter policymakers testified before Congress that the F-16s could *not* be used to deliver nuclear weapons.[33] Outraged, Barlow complained to his managers that Congress had been misled. Almost immediately he was issued a notice of termination and his security clearance was revoked.[34] He was then given a series of temporary, menial assignments and had to face a nine-month-long investigation into accusations of mental instability leveled against him by managers at the Defense Department. Following an investigation by the inspectors general of the Defense Department, the State Department, and the CIA, these accusations were eventually disproved and Barlow's security clearance was restored. However, he was unable to regain a permanent position in the government.[35] Barlow then brought a claim of relief before the United States Court of Federal Claims, but the suit was dismissed after the Justice Department declared that the case could not proceed without disclosing state secrets.[36]

Barlow's case is not unusual.[37] Consider as well the case of Sibel Edmonds, a linguist who was hired by the FBI shortly after 9/11. Edmonds was tasked with translating phone calls that had been intercepted as part of an FBI investigation into Turkish espionage within the United States. Edmonds soon found herself in an awkward situation when she discovered that a Turkish colleague was associated with the organizations targeted by the wiretaps, and was trying to prevent other linguists, including Edmonds, from translating the intercepts related to those organizations. In December 2002, Edmonds brought her concerns about this conflict of interest to the attention of her supervisor, who told her "not to worry."[38] A month later, though, an FBI agent informed Edmonds that he suspected that their mutual colleague was deliberately misreporting the content of some of the phone calls in order to shield the targets of the wiretaps, a claim that Edmonds reportedly verified by revisiting some of her colleague's translations. Following this discovery, Edmonds requested that her colleague be investigated. Edmonds's supervisor, however, rejected her request, prompting her to approach senior officials at the FBI. After the ensuing investigation vindicated her colleague, Edmonds began alleging that these officials and her supervisor were shielding her colleague, and threatened to go public with her concerns. Shortly thereafter she was fired for being a "disruptive" presence.[39] Edmonds then filed a lawsuit charging wrongful termination, but her suit was dismissed after the Justice Department invoked the state secrets privilege.[40] It was then that Edmonds went public with her concerns.[41] Following public outcry, the Justice Department's inspector general was asked to investigate the matter. His report concluded that while "Edmonds was not an easy employee to manage," many of her allegations "had bases in fact and should have been more thoroughly investigated by the FBI."[42] Instead of investigating Edmonds's colleague, the report concluded, FBI managers treated Edmonds's "aggressive pursuit of her allegations of misconduct" as the problem.[43] Following this development, Edmonds appealed to the Supreme Court, asking it to review the Justice Department's invocation of the state secrets privilege. The court, however, declined to do so.[44]

What these cases make clear is that subordinates can pay a heavy price for voicing their disagreement with the policies and positions championed by senior officials. This is not to presume that Barlow and Edmonds were in the right—I cannot enter into the details of those cases here.[45] Rather, the point is that what happened to Barlow and Edmonds shows that national security whistleblowers are vulnerable to administrative action that is shielded from external scrutiny by the state secrets privilege—and hence that what happened to Barlow and Edmonds could happen to others too. Now, before we address the question of what more can be done to protect national security whistleblowers against retaliation, there is a potential objection to the relevance of these cases that we ought to address. The worry is this: are Barlow's and Edmonds's cases representative of the experience that most national security whistleblowers have had? In other words, is there a possibility that, statistically speaking, these cases are outliers, and that most national security whistleblowers do not routinely experience severe retaliation? Consider the conclusions reached by Marcia Miceli, Janet Near, and Terry Dworkin in their analysis of retaliation against ordinary whistleblowers. They observe that the "cases presented in the media may involve much more serious or unusual retaliation" than is typically experienced by whistleblowers, as surveys based on random samples of federal employees suggest that retaliation is "not an inevitable consequence for federal whistle-blowers"; the percentage of whistleblowers reporting retaliation ranged from 17 percent in 1980 to 38 percent in 1992 to 44 percent in 2003.[46] Although the trend in the data is discouraging, it remains the case, as Miceli, Near, and Dworkin point out, that so far fewer than half of the individuals who have identified themselves as whistleblowers have reported suffering retaliation.

The evidence studied by Miceli, Near, and Dworkin also suggests that even if retaliation against ordinary whistleblowers is as widespread as "common wisdom" has it, the prospect of suffering retaliation is not certain to deter officials from blowing the whistle.[47] At least one survey, they note, has shown that the willingness of ordinary whistleblowers to take the same action again appears to be "uncorrelated with their experience of retaliation."[48] They also cite studies showing that officials take a variety of factors into account when considering whether to blow the whistle, including the likelihood that blowing the whistle will "result in the desired change in managerial behavior."[49] For instance, in a large-scale survey of federal employees, 80 percent of respondents chose efficacy as one of the two most important factors that would motivate them to blow the whistle, while only 40 percent chose protection from retaliation.[50]

Is the evidence cited above cause for optimism as far as national security whistleblowers are concerned? There are reasons to be skeptical about any such parallel. Arguably, national security whistleblowers are more vulnerable to retaliation because the secrecy associated with their work means that, unlike ordinary whistleblowers, they cannot easily report or publicize the retaliation they have experienced. Furthermore, as advocates on behalf of national security whistleblowers point out, the "animus" usually directed against whistleblowers turns into "obsessive hostility" when the whistleblower belongs to an intelligence agency, because organizations of this variety place a premium on loyalty and discretion.[51] Given this, we really need to examine surveys of national security whistleblowers before we can say whether concerns about retaliation against them are overblown. Unfortunately, the secretive nature of the intelligence community means that such surveys are hard to come by. But suppose we are able to show that cases such as Barlow's and Edmonds's are outliers. Would this alleviate concerns about retaliation? There is reason to believe that it would not: such cases might be statistically rare owing to officials' unwillingness to blow the whistle in the first place. After all, surveys have indicated that only a fifth to a third of all federal employees who witness wrongdoing actually report it.[52] It is not unreasonable to assume that this proportion may be significantly lower in the intelligence community, where the presence of secrecy constitutes a further inhibiting factor. Moreover, even if Barlow's and Edmonds's cases can be shown to be atypical, they are still relevant because, as noted above, they demonstrate what can happen to whistleblowers who fall foul of senior officials.

Can We Prevent Retaliation?

We have seen that though we want officials who make unauthorized disclosures to be willing to identify themselves, fulfilling this requirement is likely to expose them to retaliation from managers and colleagues. Given this quandary, let us consider whether the protection currently offered to national security whistleblowers can be enhanced. This development, we will see, is neither likely nor desirable.

In recent years, groups such as the Government Accountability Project (GAP) and the Project on Government Oversight (POGO) that advocate on behalf of national security whistleblowers have argued in favor of bringing employees of the intelligence community under the umbrella of the Whistleblower Protection Act (WPA), as this would allow prospective national security whistleblowers to have their complaints heard by the Merit Systems Protection Board (MSPB) and the Federal Circuit Court of Appeals rather than the various inspectors general, who have, they allege, proven ineffective at protecting officials against retaliation.[53] This is not to say that advocacy groups express complete confidence in the MSPB or the court of appeals. On the contrary, they draw attention to statistics suggesting that these institutions have been less than sympathetic to cases brought before them. For example, between 1999 and 2005, only 2 out of 30 whistleblower claims prevailed before the MSPB, and between 1995 and 2005, only 1 out of 96 claims prevailed before the court of appeals.[54] Although it has been argued that these statistics could simply mean that "many whistleblowers present weak cases," advocacy groups insist that the findings indicate pervasive hostility toward whistleblowers on the part of the MSPB and the court of appeals.[55] At the same time, they also strongly criticize the performance of the Office of Special Counsel (OSC), the federal agency responsible for assisting whistleblowers in combating retaliation. For instance, they cite a report showing that 81 percent of federal employees who sought the OSC's help in cases involving retaliation gave it a "low" to "very low" rating for overall effectiveness.[56] Such statistics, they argue, indicate that the current system needs to be reformed in order to make it more responsive to the concerns of whistleblowers.

The list of reforms that advocates for national security whistleblowers wish to introduce is lengthy. The more prominent include lessening the burden of proof to establish that retaliation has occurred, allowing appeals involving retaliation against whistleblowers to be heard by district courts, and expanding the definition of what constitutes retaliation.[57] With respect to the last of these items, advocacy groups have argued that Congress should authorize the MSPB and the court of appeals to review the revocation of security clearances. Thus far the MSPB and the court of appeals have declined to take on this task because the Supreme Court has ruled in *Department of the Navy v. Egan* (1988) that the Constitution vests the authority to grant security clearances in the hands of the executive branch.[58] According to critics, *Egan* has made the revocation of security clearances the "weapon of choice" for managers who want to punish a national security whistleblower, because an official who cannot access the classified information she needs to perform her job is "effectively fired."[59]

Although there can be no doubt that the institutional features described above contribute greatly to the sense of vulnerability that national security whistleblowers feel, there is reason to doubt the soundness and the likely effectiveness of the reforms proposed by the aforementioned advocacy groups. An immediate obstacle to these reforms is that lawsuits brought by members of the national security community typically involve evidence that is classified. As noted in chapter 2 (and as we have just seen in the cases involving Barlow and Edmonds), federal judges have been averse to challenging the Justice Department's invocations of the state secrets privilege, including in cases where employees belonging to intelligence agencies have complained of discriminatory or abusive treatment. We have already seen why courts are unlikely to take a more active role on this front; let us now focus on a different shortcoming of the proposed reforms—namely, that they are predicated on the idea that determining what sorts of activities constitute wrongdoing is a straightforward business. This assumption seems reasonable in the context of professions such as medicine and engineering. For instance, those constructing a house must follow a code, and a violation of the relevant technical rules by an architect or engineer can be objectively discerned by the concerned employee and by an external auditor. In the national security domain, by contrast, there will typically be disagreement over whether a violation of the law actually constitutes wrongdoing, and therefore whether the violation of the law justifies an unauthorized disclosure. As a result, if we establish laws that prevent the president from dismissing officials who disclose classified information about what *they* see as wrongdoing, we would effectively force *him* to calibrate his policies to meet the objections of his subordinates. This arrangement is undesirable for two reasons. First, we want decisions to be made by the president, whom we have selected and whose judgment and character we have had an opportunity to gauge. Second, the president's subordinates are highly likely to have conflicting views on what constitutes wrongdoing. This means that the president will not be able to make hard decisions without someone in the chain of command concluding that wrongdoing has been committed, and that she is therefore justified in making an unauthorized disclosure. The end result is that it would become impossible for the president to maintain secrecy regardless of what he decides.

It may be objected that robust whistleblower protection will not prevent the president from disciplining his subordinates. Instead, it will only make the president's right to discipline his subordinates hinge upon a judge's concurring that the subordinate was unjustified in thinking that the president had acted wrongfully. Now, there may well be some merit to having such a check in place. It is quite possible that managers will wait for public attention to fade before striking at an employee responsible for blowing the whistle on activities that *are* widely seen as wrongful. In such cases, the presence of an external reviewer could provide a whistleblower with some degree of security against vengeful colleagues. Nonetheless, there are at least two reasons why we should temper our expectations as to what external review can accomplish. Recall here that there often will be no objective answer to the question of what the rightful bounds of public authority really are. Consider, for instance, the hypothetical supervisor who discloses to the *New York Times* that the president has secretly detained a terrorist leader. Whether a judge agrees with the supervisor that the president's action constituted wrongdoing will depend in no small measure on whether he shares the president's interpretation of the Constitution. Therefore, whether the president is allowed to go ahead and discipline the supervisor will not necessarily rely on some sort of objective or foreseeable standard. Rather, the outcome will likely be influenced by the judge's interpretation of the Constitution. Now, if judges are charged with deciding what sorts of national security information could rightfully be disclosed by government employees, then presidents and Congress would begin to take particularly keen interest in appointments to the relevant benches. What are the chances that the views of the relevant district court judges, who will be nominated by the president and confirmed by the Senate, will turn out to be remarkably different from those of existing inspectors general, who are nominated by the president and confirmed by the Senate?

Suppose we are not convinced by the objections outlined above. Perhaps we ought to be persuaded that district courts can in fact be compelled to protect national security whistleblowers against retaliation by their employers (in spite of their long-standing aversion to cases involving state secrets), or that even a limited judicial check on administrative discretion is better than none. Will the introduction of external review put an end to the problem of retaliation? I would argue that the utility of the reforms proposed by the aforementioned advocacy groups is still brought into question by how pervasive and mutable the means of retaliation can be. Note the wide array of administrative and social sanctions that can be brought to bear on the individual in the context of everyday life within any organization. These sanctions range from the mundane (e.g., ostracizing her in the office cafeteria) to the subtle (e.g., giving her assignments that will cause her career to stagnate) to the devious (e.g., assigning her complex tasks and then penalizing her for incompetence when she fails).[60] Needless to say, it can prove extremely difficult for outsiders to detect and counter such retaliatory actions.

Consider in this regard the case of Specialist Joseph Darby, the now-famous whistleblower in the Abu Ghraib prison abuse scandal. Darby, an army reservist, was assigned to Abu Ghraib prison in October 2003. Shortly after his arrival, Darby stumbled across photographic evidence of his fellow military police officers abusing Iraqi detainees. Troubled by what he saw, Darby filed an anonymous complaint with the army's Criminal Investigation Division in January 2004. The ensuing military investigation led to the indictment and conviction of Darby's fellow soldiers and helped reveal that Secretary of Defense Donald Rumsfeld had condoned the practices used at Abu Ghraib.[61] Although investigators had promised to keep Darby's identity secret lest he suffer retribution from fellow soldiers,

Secretary Rumsfeld exposed his role in the affair by commending him by name during a televised press conference.[62] Darby then had to be "bundled out of Iraq" and provided with "armed protection."[63] In the months that followed, Darby received awards and commendations from civil society groups, but he also received death threats and had property vandalized by those who saw him as having put "American soldiers in prison over Iraqis."[64] As one military veteran in Darby's hometown told the *Washington Post*, "they can call him what they want. I call him a rat."[65] In the end Darby and his wife were compelled to do "everything but change their identities," including moving to a new town and changing jobs.[66]

Consider as well the case of Coleen Rowley, a former FBI official who shot to prominence in 2002 after lawmakers disclosed to the press a memo she had written to Robert Muller, the director of the FBI, outlining how officials at the FBI headquarters in Washington had prevented her field office in Minneapolis from aggressively investigating the Al-Qaeda operative Zacarias Moussaoui, and thereby from potentially disrupting the 9/11 attacks. Rowley's memo was praised by lawmakers and the press corps, who saw her candid analysis as offering an "unprecedented indictment" of the FBI's management.[67] The public criticism provoked by her memo cast a shadow over the FBI, forcing Director Muller to initiate an inquiry into the organization's shortcomings.[68] It was not long before Rowley had to pay a price. Although she optimistically declared before Congress in June 2002 that she had been promised that she would suffer no retaliation for her actions, subsequent events soon "cut into her faith."[69] Shortly before being declared *Time*'s "Person of the Year" in December 2002, Rowley admitted to having been "stung by a nasty backlash" from current and retired FBI agents. The retaliation included whispers of impending criminal charges, public criticism of her "disloyalty," and informal pressure to resign.[70] A little under two years later, Rowley retired from the FBI.

The conclusion to be drawn from cases like those of Darby and Rowley is that even if we institute the reforms proposed by advocacy groups such as GAP and POGO, we will not be able to shield national security whistleblowers from a great deal of pain and hardship. There is a very real limit to what the law can accomplish when it comes to deterring informal retaliation. Indeed, scholars who have examined the prospects of ordinary whistleblowers have drawn much the same conclusion. This point was first made nearly three decades ago by Robert Vaughn, who warned after the passage of the Civil Service Reform Act that the greatest difficulty we face in expanding the legal protection afforded to whistleblowers "is that such protection is extraordinarily difficult to provide within a bureaucracy," because so many ways of "penalizing a whistleblower are either not the subject of protection or extremely difficult to prove."[71] This observation has since been reiterated by Mark Bovens, who has argued that experience with whistleblower protections in the United States has highlighted just how difficult it is for outsiders to "straighten out completely the fundamental differences in power that exist within hierarchical organizations."[72] The efforts of reformers, he writes, have "come up against the limits of the law."[73]

If scholars are pessimistic about using the law to shield ordinary whistleblowers from informal retaliation, then there can be little hope for national security whistleblowers working within the recesses of secretive intelligence agencies. Admittedly, it is hard to know the frequency with which national security whistleblowers are subjected to informal retaliation. However, in one survey of ordinary whistleblowers, 66 percent of respondents claimed to have experienced informal retaliation, while another study has shown that 87 percent of ordinary whistleblowers who have experienced formal retaliation have also experienced informal retaliation.[74] It seems fair to assume that the incidence of this sort of retaliation is likely to be even higher in the national security domain, as a whistleblower's colleagues and managers are likely to be emboldened by the knowledge that their actions will be shrouded in secrecy.[75]

Courage or Anonymity?

We have now established how difficult it is to protect whistleblowers against retaliation, especially when the retaliation is informal in nature. This finding implies that though unauthorized disclosures of classified information *can* be justified under certain conditions, officials will have little incentive to fulfill the required conditions, especially the requirement that they be willing to identify themselves. To be sure, officials will not always be obliged to identify themselves. If an unauthorized disclosure reveals gross wrongdoing, then the source of that disclosure need not reveal her identity. However, for the reasons discussed earlier, national security whistleblowers are more likely to expose cases of suspected wrongdoing, which in turn makes it important that we know their identities so that we can scrutinize their motives. But if officials have little incentive to reveal their identity, then would-be national security whistleblowers are likely either to "swallow the whistle" or to make disclosures anonymously. Or are they? Is there reason to think that officials will actually be willing to make unauthorized disclosures in the prescribed manner *in spite of* the risk of retaliation?

There is some reason for hope. As we have seen, at least a small proportion of officials *do* blow the whistle in spite of the threat of retaliation.

If we are able to pinpoint and support the factors that prompt officials to act this way, then perhaps we will be able to increase over time the proportion of public servants willing to openly sound the alarm whenever they come across wrongdoing. To this end, scholars including Myron Glazer and Penina Glazer, Philip Jos, and Peter Robinson have emphasized the importance of fostering a "social climate" that "supports and defends" whistleblowers, citing in particular the need for more and better-funded professional support groups that can provide advice, fund appeals, and rally public support on behalf of individuals who have hazarded their careers in order to expose wrongdoing.[76]

But how far really can we count on such measures to increase the proportion of officials willing to blow the whistle? Although such measures may reduce the suffering experienced by officials *after* they have blown the whistle, it is hard to believe that these measures could substantially affect the calculus that officials confront *before* they do so. After all, this calculus really is quite grim. An official who is contemplating blowing the whistle must envision trading her peace of mind for the uncertain and remote possibility that she will have the desired effect on policy and be accorded due recognition. Under these circumstances, the prospect of having one's legal costs covered must surely add little to the balance. Indeed, little could compensate for the loss of one's accumulated expertise and professional networks and status, especially since individuals who work in the field of national security are not likely to easily find equivalent work in the private sector. One cannot help doubting the assumption, implicit in most proposals intended to bolster whistleblowing, that the actions of the average whistleblower are the product of a rational cost-benefit analysis. No doubt the provision of financial incentives or rewards for whistleblowing could—on the margin—encourage officials to blow the whistle. But if we want to bolster whistleblowing more generally, then it seems we need to understand and build upon the psychological processes that grant an individual the fortitude to challenge senior officials even when it is effectively irrational for her to do so.

What might this psychological process be? It has been argued, quite plausibly, that since the act of whistleblowing pits "a relatively powerless and isolated individual against a powerful company or institution," an individual's willingness to blow the whistle must ultimately hinge on her courageousness.[77] As Geoffrey Scarre has observed, whistleblowing "always calls for the moral courage to risk ostracism, unpopularity with colleagues, bosses and other superiors, and the setting of an invisible ceiling to one's career prospects."[78] Can we cultivate courage in our public servants? The challenge we face is made clear when we meditate on research into the psychic motives that propel whistleblowers to risk their own well-being. There are two accounts on offer. The first is that whistleblowers are driven by a deep commitment to particular religious or moral values. This claim has been borne out in one large survey of former whistleblowers wherein 58 percent of the respondents "not only expressed support for universal moral rules but responded that such rules ought to apply without exception."[79] The other claim is that whistleblowers are ultimately motivated by "moral narcissism." This is the view put forward by Fred Alford, who has persuasively argued that empathy or altruism alone cannot really explain a whistleblower's willingness to "put one's life, or livelihood, on the line for the sake of others."[80] His carefully drawn case studies suggest that it is "narcissism moralized"—a whistleblower's conviction that her actions embody morality—that "provides a quite literally selfish motive for people to sacrifice the apparently objective interests of the self."[81]

If it is true that whistleblowers are motivated by moral conviction or moral narcissism, then, ironically, it may actually be inadvisable to increase the proportion of government employees who have either of these characteristics. Individuals who are enamored of abstract moral ideas or see their own choices as embodying morality itself are going to be prone to "situational blindness"—that is, they are unlikely to appreciate the compromises and concessions that are often required to further the cause of morality in politics, particularly in the international domain. Such individuals may simply refuse to give up operating "according to the rules."[82] Alternatively, when there is disagreement over the rules that ought to be followed, they may decide too readily that their interpretation of the rules is the better one. This charge has been leveled against Rowley, one of the whistleblowers we discussed earlier. Rowley, it will be recalled, complained to Congress about bungling at the FBI after senior officials declined to act on her request for a warrant to search the properties of the individuals who would go on to launch the 9/11 attacks. Critics, however, have since faulted her for failing to appreciate legal complexities: FBI lawyers, they contend, declined to issue the warrants she requested because the evidence she provided them did not satisfy the Fourth Amendment's probable cause standard.[83]

This is not to say that individuals with strong moral convictions are undesirable. Arguably, such "difficult people" (as they are sometimes termed) constitute a vital backstop within the national security apparatus because they are the ones likeliest to refuse to tolerate the sorts of great wrongs that their more "flexible" (i.e., careerist and self-interested) colleagues and managers may readily sweep under the carpet. Nevertheless, it is not clear that we would want to greatly increase the presence of such "difficult people" in the national security apparatus, because what this domain calls for is not only the courage to risk one's career and peace of mind on behalf of the public, but also the prudence to ensure that courage is employed in the service of wisdom rather than dogmatism. Besides, it is not clear that we could increase the numbers of such people even if we wanted to. For if whistleblowing is ultimately driven by moral conviction or moral narcissism, then we will be hard-pressed to systematically cultivate either of these dispositions, as they are likely to take shape long before individuals enter public service. As a result, it seems sensible to assume that whistleblowers are, as the saying goes, "born, not made."[84]

If we cannot rely on courage—that is, if we cannot count on officials to put themselves in the firing line by openly declaring their concerns about potentially wrongful secret policies and activities—then where does that leave us? Must we conclude that unauthorized disclosures will continue to be—as they are now—primarily anonymous and therefore suspect? Or can we point to the pervasiveness of retaliation, and to the limits of our right and ability to cultivate courage, as reasons to relax the requirement that officials be willing to identify themselves? That is to say, can we justify the practice of leaking? If so, then the challenge is to explain how we might prevent self-interested or overzealous officials from exploiting anonymity. We also need to explain what reason there is to believe that well-intentioned officials will be able to leak classified information without being detected. These are the questions we will examine next. If we are able to answer these questions in the affirmative, we will have solved the dilemma posed in chapter 1, because then we will not only be able to count on officials' raising the alarm; we will also be able to distinguish between true and false alarms.

Chapter 6

. . . .

Should We Trust Leakers?

Anonymous Sources and the Problem of Regulation

In chapter 5 I argued that though an official can be justified in making an unauthorized disclosure when she encounters an abuse of state secrecy, she is not obliged to make such a disclosure if doing so will expose her to significant retaliation, and that even when an official is obliged to make such a disclosure, it will take great courage for her to voice her concerns in spite of the prospect of retaliation. The implication of this analysis is that we should expect officials to continue to raise the alarm by leaking classified information rather than by blowing the whistle. This state of affairs is troubling because, as we have seeen, an official can take advantage of anonymity to make selective disclosures that favor sectional interests or partisan causes. Consequently, we need to examine whether the practice of leaking can be justified, and if so, how we might prevent its misuse. But first we must investigate whether it really is possible for leakers to evade detection.

Why Leaks Persist

Given the threat of retaliation, officials who wish to disclose classified information are often advised to leak the incriminating information rather than lodge a formal complaint. In the words of *The Art of Anonymous Activism*, a prominent how-to guide, anonymous disclosures provide a means of "serving the public while surviving public service."[1] But why should an official who discloses classified information anonymously be more confident of evading retaliation? One might reasonably assume that a president could use the powers granted by the laws that prohibit unauthorized disclosures to hunt down and punish the source of an embarrassing disclosure, and that anonymity can therefore provide officials with little more than temporary cover. But the evidence belies this assumption, as only a handful of officials have ever been prosecuted for leaking classified information. Why have successive administrations allowed leaks of classified information to go unpunished even as they have come down hard on whistleblowers like Richard Barlow, Sibel Edmonds, and Coleen Rowley (whom we met in chapter 5)?

The dearth of prosecutions for leaking is typically attributed to the absence of a blanket statutory prohibition against unauthorized disclosures akin to the United Kingdom's Official Secrets Act.[2] The Espionage Act requires the prosecution to show that an official responsible for "willfully" disclosing "information relating to the national defense" to a person who is "not entitled to receive it" had "reason to believe" that such information "could be used to the injury of the United States or to the advantage of any foreign nation."[3] It is widely accepted that this so-called bad faith requirement of the Espionage Act works to the advantage of defendants because often it is difficult for prosecutors to establish that an official had "reason to believe" that the information revealed by his anonymous disclosure could be used "to the injury of the United States."[4] This is especially true when an unauthorized disclosure reveals a prima facie violation of the law. In such cases, prosecutors are confronted with the very real possibility that a jury will decline to convict an official who contends that the violation gave her "reason to believe" that its disclosure would be in the public interest.

Prosecutors are also hindered by the notoriously imprecise language of the Espionage Act. For example, what does it mean to "willfully" communicate information? How do we determine who is a "person not entitled to receive" information relating to the national defense when the classification system does not "entitle" anyone? And what about diplomatic and intelligence secrets that cannot be easily subsumed under the heading of "information relating to the national defense?"[5] Although the courts have made attempts to pin down the meaning of these phrases (or at least to narrow the range of possible interpretations), the absence of settled guidelines has prompted prosecutors to tread carefully, lest an unfavorable interpretation or decision weaken the deterrent effect of the Espionage Act.

The executive has not stood idly by in the face of challenges to its authority over classified information. On the contrary, presidents have periodically urged Congress to revise the Espionage Act and to revisit the Classified Information Procedures Act, a statute that is meant to prevent defendants from engaging in the practice of "graymail" (that is, requesting access to classified information on the grounds that this information is needed to mount a defense).[6] However, these calls have had little effect because lawmakers have long been divided over whether and how to address the practice of leaking. These divisions can be traced to differences among lawmakers over the wisdom of strengthening the president's control over the national security apparatus. Thus, for the foreseeable future at least, the threat of criminal prosecution is likely to remain—in the words of the widely cited report of the Interdepartmental Group on Unauthorized Disclosures of Classified Information (commonly referred to as the Willard Report)—"so illusory as to constitute no real deterrent to the prospective leaker."[7]

Besides, even if the president is able to convince Congress to revise the Espionage Act, it is unlikely that this step alone will turn the tide. Consider that successive administrations have failed to enforce a statute like §798(a), which clearly prohibits the disclosure of classified information relating to communications intelligence.[8] It is notable that the United States has thus far secured only a single conviction under this statute; in that case, moreover, the official in question, Shamai Leibowitz, an FBI linguist who had disclosed the transcripts of a counterintelligence wiretap to an Internet blogger, conceded his guilt as part of a plea bargain.[9] This record suggests that the dearth of prosecutions for leaking owes to factors that extend beyond the shortcomings of the Espionage Act.

What might these factors be? Political constraints constitute one such factor. It can often prove embarrassing or divisive to prosecute public officials, particularly members of Congress. For example, in 2004 the FBI identified Senator Richard Shelby as the person who disclosed to the media that the NSA had intercepted two Arabic-language messages on the eve of September 11, 2001: "The match is about to begin" and "Tomorrow is zero hour."[10] But Senator Shelby was never charged under §798(a) even though his disclosure revealed what President Bush described as "alarmingly specific" information.[11]

Another important factor contributing to the dearth of prosecutions is, paradoxically, a concern for national security. On numerous occasions the government has chosen not to prosecute an official responsible for leaking classified information for fear that such a move would be perceived as confirming the validity of what has been leaked and might even lead to the revelation of additional sensitive information. A recent example is the case of the CIA official Mary McCarthy, who reportedly disclosed to the *Washington Post* highly classified information pertaining to the CIA's use of so-called black sites (or secret prisons) during the war on terror. Although the CIA reportedly uncovered McCarthy's role after she failed a lie-detector test conducted as part of an effort to trace the source of the *Post* story, it chose to fire her rather than press criminal charges, because a trial would likely "wind up airing sensitive information as well as policy dissents" over its handling of detainees in the war on terror.[12]

Of course presidents do not have to rely on criminal laws alone in order to punish disobedient employees. The "more promising approach," the Willard Report notes, is to utilize administrative sanctions, because "for most government employees, a realistic prospect of being demoted or fired for leaking classified information would serve as a deterrent."[13] These sanctions should certainly not be taken lightly, since presidents *have* shown a willingness to use them—as seen in the McCarthy case. Nonetheless, the fact that leaks continue to appear on the front pages of the *New York Times* and the *Washington Post* suggests that a sizable number of officials are no more deterred by the specter of administrative sanctions than they are by the threat of criminal charges. This outcome can be attributed to two factors. The first is sheer defiance. Officials who decide to leak classified information are sometimes so troubled by the wrongdoing they have discovered that they feel they must share it with the public— even at the risk of being discovered and punished.[14] This sort of defiance is most likely to make an appearance when the relevant official is already on the verge of retirement or has a viable career alternative (as was the case with McCarthy, who was identified and then dismissed a few days before she was due to retire to start a new career as a public interest lawyer).

The other, more deep-seated, explanation for the limited deterrent effect of administrative sanctions lies in the fact that investigators are frequently unable to identify the source of an anonymous disclosure. This difficulty was publicly acknowledged by the Willard Report, which observed in 1982 that the FBI had so far "rarely been successful in identifying the sources of such disclosures."[15] Though the Willard Report urged the president to make "better efforts to identify leakers," little seems to have changed in the intervening decades: the Commission on the Intelligence Capabilities of the United States Regarding Weapons of Mass Destruction concluded in 2005 that "the greatest barrier" the president faces in punishing leaks still lies "in identifying the leaker."[16]

What explains this continuing inability to hunt down the officials responsible for leaking classified information? In part, the answer lies in the size and complexity of the national security bureaucracy, where even highly classified information is often accessed by dozens and sometimes hundreds of individuals.[17] This makes it impractical for the FBI to repeatedly undertake the exhaustive investigations needed to identify the individual responsible for a leak of classified information. Indeed, this obstacle is now thought to be so substantial that it has become de rigueur to conclude that "it is generally fruitless to try to discover the source of a leak."[18] The available statistics certainly support this conclusion. For instance, between 2005 and 2009 nearly 200 leaks were referred to the FBI, but "investigators opened only 26 of these cases, identified 14 suspects, and prosecuted none of them."[19]

Although such statistics speak volumes about the obstacles that the Justice Department faces in identifying the officials responsible for leaking classified information, we should not assume that these obstacles are wholly insurmountable. It is important to remember that the Justice Department's poor track record in tracing leakers owes substantially to internal guidelines directing prosecutors to avoid compelling reporters to reveal their sources. Should a future administration discard these guidelines, the odds would almost certainly shift in favor of prosecutors. Nor is the cooperation of reporters always essential to prosecutors. The widely reported successes that the Bush and Obama administrations have recently had in investigating a number of high-profile leaks, including those by McCarthy, Leibowitz, Thomas Tamm, Jeffrey Sterling, Thomas Drake, Bradley Manning, Stephen Kim, and John Kiriakou, provide a sobering reminder that it is not impossible for determined investigators to hunt down the source of a leak even in the absence of cooperation from reporters.[20] And, as the Justice Department informed Congress in 2002, there is reason to think that improvements in information technology, especially in the areas of digital content management and forensics, will further improve the FBI's chances of detecting the officials responsible for leaks.[21]

These possibilities notwithstanding, there is little reason to believe that future administrations will be able to clamp down on leaks in a comprehensive manner. The evidence suggests that stubbornness and shrewdness greatly constrain how far any administration can police its employees. Consider, for example, the aftermath of Dana Priest's report in the *Washington Post* identifying the locations and operations of the CIA's secret prisons, and revealing dissent within the CIA over the legality and morality of utilizing extreme interrogation methods.[22] Priest's report attracted strong criticism from Porter Goss, then director of the CIA, who testified before Congress that it had caused "very severe" damage to relations with the foreign intelligence agencies that had helped the CIA establish these prisons.[23] Yet, in spite of Goss's assurances, the CIA's efforts to track down Priest's sources met with only limited success. While the CIA was able to ascertain that McCarthy had had "unauthorized conversations" with Priest, both McCarthy and the CIA have since claimed that her contact with Priest was not related to the *Post* story.[24] Meanwhile Priest has attributed her report to "multiple current and former intelligence officials on three continents," a claim suggesting that even if McCarthy was in fact a source, she was only one of a number of sources, the bulk of whom have apparently gone undetected.[25]

Questionable Uses of Anonymity

We have now established that an official who wants to make an unauthorized disclosure can take refuge in anonymity. We should not, however, be too quick to celebrate this fact, since anonymity can also be utilized to make disclosures that further sectional interests or partisan causes. But how realistic is the threat that leaks will be misused? Is there really a danger that an official will leak classified information—and thereby risk her peace of mind—in order to covertly impose her own values or beliefs on the public? Many commentators presume otherwise; they believe that leakers are invariably motivated by high principles. Bruce Ackerman, for instance, has described leakers as "patriotic" on the grounds that their disclosures "don't endanger our national security. They promote it, by preserving our constitutional integrity."[26] A closer inspection of the facts, though, shows such enthusiasm to be misplaced, as there appear to be numerous cases where officials have disclosed classified information for reasons unrelated to the merits of the relevant policy. Consider two such instances.

The first concerns the disclosure of the Terrorist Surveillance Program (TSP), a Bush administration initiative that allowed the NSA to eavesdrop on electronic communications without obtaining a warrant from the Foreign Intelligence Surveillance Court (FISC). This program was made public in December 2005 by James Risen and Eric Lichtblau of the *New York Times*. In their report, Risen and Lichtblau claimed that, "nearly a dozen current and former officials" discussed the program with them "because of their concerns about the operation's legality and oversight."[27] Though the reporters have never identified their sources, subsequent developments have allowed us to learn a little about two of them.

One source whom Risen and Lichtblau relied upon was Thomas Tamm, a former Justice Department employee. Tamm joined the Justice Department in 1998 and was initially assigned to a unit evaluating death penalty cases. He reportedly became "disaffected" in 2001 when John Ashcroft took over as attorney general, because unlike his predecessor, Janet Reno, Ashcroft began to encourage prosecutors to seek the death penalty in "as many cases as possible."[28] Subsequently, in 2003, Tamm requested a transfer to the Office of Intelligence Policy and Review, the unit charged with securing wiretap warrants.[29] It was here that Tamm "stumbled upon" the fact that certain wiretap requests were being sent directly by Attorney General Ash-croft to the chief judge of the Foreign Intelligence Surveillance Court, Col-leen Kollar-Kotelly.[30] Although Tamm was not involved in this process and was therefore unaware of the details, including the various (albeit uncon-ventional) safeguards that were in place, he decided on the basis of second-hand information that the whole affair did not "smell right" and therefore contacted Lichtblau, thereby kick-starting the *Times*'s investigation into the NSA program.[31] Note that Risen and Lichtblau's report contained none of these contextual details, least of all that Tamm was motivated in part by his "anger" at unrelated Bush administration policies.[32] These details became public knowledge only after Tamm was declared a target of the FBI inves-tigation into the disclosure, which in turn led him to discuss his case with *Newsweek* in an effort to defend his actions as well-intentioned.[33]

Another source whom Risen and Lichtblau relied on was Russell Tice, a former NSA employee, who disclosed his involvement to ABC News shortly after the *Times* report was published.[34] Tice told ABC News that he was concerned about inadequate oversight at the NSA and hinted at the existence of surveillance programs even more extensive than what the *Times*'s report described. But when reporters subsequently reached out to the congressional intelligence committees about these allegations, congressional staffers reacted cautiously, claiming that Tice "comes with baggage."[35] What this meant became clearer after Tice appeared before Congress in February 2006. His testimony revealed that he had been fired from the NSA in May 2005 following a run-in with administrators over his allegations that a colleague might be engaged in espionage.[36] Though an internal investigation had dismissed Tice's claim, he appar-ently suggested that the colleague be reinvestigated, which in turn led administrators to demand that he undergo psychiatric evaluation.[37] After this evaluation concluded that Tice suffered from paranoia, his security clearance was revoked and he was assigned to a low-level position. When Tice subsequently wrote to 132 members of Congress complaining of mis-treatment, the NSA fired him.[38] Now, it is important not to assume that Tice's allegations against the NSA were influenced by his treatment at the hands of administrators. Tice has stated that he had raised concerns about "suspected illegal activity" at the NSA before 2005, and that the NSA had him diagnosed as paranoid in order to get rid of him.[39] Since the secrecy surrounding the case makes it difficult to ascertain the actual sequence of events, this claim certainly deserves the benefit of the doubt. What *is* remarkable, though, is that the report in the *Times* offered not the slightest hint of this background. Had Tice not come forward of his own accord, we would likely never have had the chance to factor his complicated circum-stances into our assessment of Risen and Lichtblau's account.

The second case involves the disclosure of Operation Merlin, a covert CIA operation to route flawed nuclear technology to Iran, which reportedly went awry after the Russian intermediary had an attack of nerves and tipped off the Iranians, thereby potentially allowing them to make good use of the technology. The public became aware of this operation following the publication of James Risen's *State of War* in 2006, which discusses Operation Merlin as part of a broader story focused on the mismanagement of the CIA's operations inside Iran.[40] Risen's source, it now appears, was Jeffrey Sterling, a former employee of the CIA. A little by way of background: after joining the CIA in 1993 and completing training in Farsi, Sterling was sent to Germany in 1995 to recruit spies who could undertake espionage in Iran. In 1997 Sterling reportedly learned from his supervisor that he was not being given leads to develop because a "big black man speaking Farsi" would "draw too much attention" to Iranian agents working for the CIA.[41] Sterling then elected to move to the CIA office in New York in 1999. However, following "several disagreements" with managers about his performance, Sterling was eventually fired in 2002.[42] He then filed a racial discrimination lawsuit against the CIA, but the case was dismissed in 2005 after the Fourth Circuit accepted the CIA's invocation of the state secrets privilege.[43] Meanwhile the CIA also refused to approve a draft of a memoir that Sterling wanted to publish, on the grounds that it contained classified information. It is now alleged by the government that Sterling, frustrated by these setbacks, decided to retaliate against the CIA by disclosing to Risen what he knew about Operation Merlin.[44] Risen's story, it should be noted, hints at none of this; none of the details outlined above would have become public knowledge had the Justice Department not indicted Sterling for leaking classified information to Risen.

Why should we be troubled by leaks of classified information like the ones made by Tamm, Tice, and Sterling? There are at least two causes for concern. The first is that disclosures made with a view to embarrass decision-makers may well be selective. Bias is especially problematic in the present context because it can prove difficult for decision-makers to correct the public record, as they will usually not want to reveal additional information about the activities that have been disclosed. As a result, the public may end up with a false impression about the motives of elected officials and the efficacy of public institutions.[45] This may have happened in the cases at hand. As more detailed accounts of the inner workings of the Justice Department have emerged, it has become clear that Attorney General Ashcroft and his subordinates actually extracted from President Bush modifications to the NSA program that they saw as necessary to ensure its legality.[46] Meanwhile the CIA has claimed that Sterling's account has "falsely characterized certain facts and circumstances" surrounding Operation Merlin, though it has declined to elaborate further in public.[47]

These leaks are also troubling because the accompanying anonymity makes it very difficult for citizens and lawmakers to guard against being misled. If citizens and lawmakers are aware that the source of an unauthorized disclosure may be a disgruntled employee, then they are put in a position to treat the disclosure with due caution, even when decision-makers are unable to defend themselves. This problem could of course be mitigated if reporters and publishers were to offer their readers some guidance about the motives and circumstances of their sources, but such candor is rare in practice. It may be objected that offering details about the motives and circumstances of a source could make it easier for investigators to identify and punish the official responsible. This is a reasonable concern, but it is not self-evident that *every* piece of information about the motives and circumstances of a source will tend to expose her identity. Note also that reporters, editors, and publishers do not have obligations to their sources alone—they also have obligations to citizens and lawmakers, whom they ought not to mislead. This is all the more true when journalists cite the public's right to know as a justification for publishing classified information, since an insufficient degree of candor on their part actually *prevents* the public from knowing that a given report provides only a partial perspective.[48] This is what seems to have happened in the cases described above, where the reporters involved appear to have made little effort to strike a balance between their obligations to their sources and to the public. For example, after the *Times* published the NSA story (and before Tamm's interview with *Newsweek* was published), Lichtblau claimed that while sources can have an "axe to grind," the original source for the story had "checked out on all counts," and his "angst seemed sincere."[49] However, we now know from Tamm himself that he was motivated in part least by his anger at Bush administration policies that had nothing to do with the NSA surveillance program.

The Sterling case is even more troubling on this count. What could Risen have hoped to achieve, one might wonder, by his silence with regard to Sterling's motives? After all, his silence could hardly have thrown investigators off the scent. Consider the circumstances: Sterling was reportedly the only person who had access to some of the details cited in Risen's account; the memoir that Sterling had submitted to the CIA's Publications Review Board apparently contained a description of Operation Merlin; and Risen had previously chronicled Sterling's employment woes in the *Times*.[50] The persons most affected by Risen's complete silence, it seems, were not investigators from the FBI, but rather citizens and lawmakers, whom he claimed he wanted to educate about the "recklessness" of the Bush administration, but whom he denied the opportunity to evaluate Sterling's claims in context.[51]

Can We Justify Anonymity?

We have seen that though the practice of leaking allows officials to raise the alarm without being easily detected, it can also hinder citizens' and lawmakers' ability to guard against misleading disclosures. This complication raises the question of whether it is possible to regulate the practice of leaking: that is, can we prevent officials from disclosing classified information with a view to covertly furthering sectional or personal agendas? If we cannot regulate the practice of leaking in this way, then we will have reason to worry that leaks actually *increase* rather then reduce the ability of officials to abuse their privileged access to state secrets.

In order to regulate the practice of leaking, we need to outline the conditions under which an official can be justified in making an anonymous disclosure and then identify the means that will allow us to ascertain whether a particular disclosure meets these conditions. The former of these tasks poses the less significant challenge. In order for an official to be justified in leaking classified information, the disclosure must (a) concern an abuse of public authority; (b) be based on clear and convincing evidence; (c) not pose a disproportionate threat to public safety; and (d) be limited in scope and scale as far as is possible. If this formulation sounds familiar, it should. Since an official who leaks classified information does much the same thing as an official who blows the whistle—they both disobey laws prohibiting unauthorized disclosures—it is only to be expected that the conditions under which these practices can be justified should be broadly similar. The crucial difference, of course, is that unlike a national security whistleblower, an official who is justified in leaking classified information is *not* required to disclose her identity. How can this divergence be justified?

Two justifications can be offered. As noted in chapter 5, an official can be justified in making an anonymous disclosure when doing so exposes activities that are so obviously wrongful that her motives, and therefore her identity, are rendered unimportant. This explains why, for example, we should not be troubled by our ignorance of the identity of the official who disclosed to Seymour Hersh details about the military investigation into the mistreatment of detainees at Abu Ghraib prison.[52] This disclosure revealed violations so depraved that the government's response was not to challenge the motives of the source or the appropriateness of the disclosure but rather to take corrective action—to terminate the offending programs and penalize the officers responsible.

Recall, however, that unauthorized disclosures typically expose suspected rather than gross wrongdoing: violations of the law where the costs and benefits are somewhat more evenly matched. Such disclosures usually prove controversial owing to disagreements over the rightful bounds of public authority. For example, rather than provoking formal apologies or corrective action, the disclosures that revealed the NSA's warrantless surveillance program and the CIA's secret prison system were greeted by strong criticism from lawmakers—in the former case Congress responded to the disclosures by enhancing the president's authority to conduct wiretaps without a warrant; in the latter it enacted legislation allowing the CIA to withhold the pensions of employees dismissed for leaking classified information. Needless to say, when a disclosure is formally condemned in this way, the source of a disclosure cannot claim to have unveiled gross wrongdoing. She will have to avail herself of a different justification for maintaining her anonymity in the face of criticism that she ought to submit to the law since she has thrust her values upon an unwilling public. Arguably, such a justification can be derived from the *intention* rather than the *substance* of her disclosure.

As discussed in chapter 5, conflicts over the rightful bounds of public authority invariably lead to differences over whether prima facie wrongdoing actually amounts to an abuse of authority. Unfortunately, these differences can be exploited by officials looking to provide a veneer of respectability to unauthorized disclosures that are actually intended to further a narrow or personal agenda. For instance, an official can cite the public's right to know as her motivation for disclosing a classified study into the pollution caused by the use of depleted uranium in military ordnance, when her real agenda is to embarrass the president into purchasing ordnance from another supplier. I argued in chapter 5 that in order to be able to guard against such self-interested or manipulative disclosures, officials responsible for disclosing evidence about suspected wrongdoing must be willing to identify themselves so that we can investigate their motives.

However, this demand for self-identification has a major drawback. It can be difficult for an official to know *ex ante* whether citizens and lawmakers will agree that the violation of the law she has discovered actually constitutes an abuse of authority. For instance, suppose an official discloses information about a violation of the law that she believes will be viewed as wrongdoing, and her disclosure actually ends up being condemned by Congress, which believes that the president is acting rightfully (as in the secret prisons case). Evidently, this official has misjudged what citizens and lawmakers consider wrongful activity. She genuinely believed the president has exceeded his brief, but her suspicion has turned out to be unfounded, as citizens and lawmakers either support or at least do not formally condemn the president's actions. According to the criteria outlined in chapter 5, this official is now obliged to forgo anonymity. This requirement may not initially seem all that troubling. What does an official who has acted in good faith have to fear from publicity, we might wonder? The answer of course is—*informal* retaliation. As we saw in chapter 5, even an official whose decision to disclose classified information is pardoned by a jury must still contend with colleagues and managers who may not be as forgiving. It seems reasonable to argue, then, that if the official has acted in good faith—if she has exposed activities that she disinterestedly believes constitute wrongdoing—then she should not have to come forward and identify herself when doing so will likely subject her to forms and degrees of retribution, especially harassment and public humiliation that are not commensurate with her actions, but which the law is powerless to curb.[53]

So, to summarize, it is problematic to require an official who makes an unauthorized disclosure about a prima facie violation of the law to identify herself, because this can lead to the penalization of disclosures based on honest errors of judgment about the severity of the wrongdoing. This outcome is undesirable because we do not want to inhibit officials from making disclosures about violations of law that seem to amount to an abuse of authority, especially when we cannot rely on lawmakers or judges to provide oversight or review for the reasons discussed in chapters 2–3. Remember, we demand self-identification only because we want to know if the source of the disclosure is less than disinterested. Since the requirement of self-identification is likely to deter both bad faith *and* good faith disclosures, a more reasonable way to address the threat of distortion or manipulation is to devise a more precise means by which we can *filter out* disclosures made in bad faith.

Having clarified the conditions under which an official can be justified in making an anonymous disclosure, we need to identify the means by which we can ensure that these conditions have been met. It is not difficult to ascertain whether an official is justified in making an anonymous disclosure that reveals gross wrongdoing. If the activity exposed by an anonymous disclosure is formally condemned by lawmakers or judges, then we can conclude that the official responsible for the disclosure is not obliged to reveal her identity. This is why, for example, it was permissible for Deep Throat—Bob Woodward and Carl Bernstein's legendary Watergate source—to keep his role secret. But how do we ascertain whether the source of a disclosure faces the prospect of suffering unwarranted retaliation when we do not know her identity and therefore lack the most important clue to her motives? It would clearly be unwise to allow officials to be judges in their own cases, but, fortunately, this is not the only alternative. Since leaks of classified information are typically routed via reporters, editors, and publishers, we could potentially requisition the assistance of these intermediaries, as they are the likeliest to know the identity of the source of an anonymous disclosure and are therefore best situated to ascertain her motives. But are reporters, editors, and publishers *willing* and *able* to take on the responsibility of acting as filters in the public interest?

There are two reasons to be concerned on this front. First, they themselves may not always know the identity of their sources; these sources may be anonymous "tipsters." Though officials have so far had relatively little need to act as anonymous tipsters, this method of disclosing classified information will surely become more prevalent if reporters are routinely compelled to disclose the identity of their sources. The practice of anonymously tipping off reporters also appears likely to become more widespread owing to technological advances. Consider the profusion of WikiLeaks-inspired websites like the *Wall Street Journal*'s "Safe House" and *Al-Jazeera*'s "Transparency Unit," both of which allow officials to anonymously upload evidence of wrongdoing.

Troubling though these developments may be, they do not rule out the possibility that making dutiful inquiries will allow journalists to learn at least something about the motives of an anonymous informant. For example, in investigating the claim that Iraq was attempting to purchase uranium from Niger, journalists were able to discover, albeit somewhat belatedly, that Rocco Martino, the mysterious individual who provided reporters with forged documents attesting to a sales agreement between Iraq and Niger, was actually a front man for one or more intelligence agencies.[54] There is no reason to think that similar investigative efforts could not be made in other cases involving anonymous informants. Of course this does not mean that journalists will always be able to ascertain the provenance of an anonymous tip. But in such cases their duty is clear: if they take the public's right to know seriously, then they are obliged either to withhold the relevant information or, if the information can be independently verified and is troubling enough to outweigh concerns about the informant's motives, then they ought to publish it alongside an account of the reasons to be concerned about her motives.

The second reason to doubt that reporters, editors, and publishers have the ability to act as filters in the public interest draws on the discussion in chapter 4 where I noted that journalists, who do not have access to the big picture, cannot readily claim to know how far the disclosure of a piece of classified information will harm national security. Even if they are able to verify that a source is acting in good faith, they may still end up publishing information that is deeply harmful to national security. But this challenge too is not insurmountable. The fact that reporters, editors, and publishers do not have access to the big picture should be seen as obliging them to approach the executive branch prior to publication in order to allow the president the opportunity to offer reasons against disclosing classified information.[55] In addition, it seems reasonable to think that reporters who have built careers on reporting national security affairs can acquire a network of trusted contacts whom they can use to vet the sensitivity of the information that they intend to disclose. These contacts could also help them gauge the cautionary advice offered by the president. There is of course the risk that "old hands" will come to see the world through the lens of the officials whom they are meant to subject to critical scrutiny. We must remain alert to this danger. But the existence of this danger does not preclude journalists from drawing upon the expertise of senior officials in order to act as filters in the public interest.

So reporters, editors, and publishers can serve as filters in the public interest, but are they *willing* to assume this responsibility? The challenge lies in the prevalence of the belief that "the presumptive duty of the press is to publish, not to guard security or to be concerned with the morals of its sources."[56] This belief has grown out of Alexander Bickel's epochal observation in his *Morality of Consent* that the existence of the First Amendment effectively establishes a "contest" between the press and the government, because the freedom afforded to the press by the First Amendment means that though the government is allowed to "guard mightily" against leaks, it is forced to "suffer them if they occur."[57] Bickel commended this "contest" because—writing in the wake of the Pentagon Papers episode—he saw it as one of the only means by which citizens could get a handle on the president's vast national security apparatus. Hence, not surprisingly, he took the view that "the chief responsibility of the press is to play its role in that contest": to publish everything "newsworthy" that it can get its hands on.[58] And the need to satisfy this "chief responsibility" in turn meant, Bickel argued, that the press ought to behave—and ought to be allowed to behave—as a "morally neutral, even an unconcerned, agent as regards the provenance of newsworthy material that comes to hand."[59]

To be clear, Bickel did not believe that the press has no responsibilities other than to publish. On the contrary, he warned that "not everything is fit to print."[60] There ought to be, he wrote, due regard for "probable factual accuracy, for danger to innocent lives, for human decencies, and even, if cautiously, for nonpartisan considerations of the national interest."[61] However—and this is the key point—Bickel insisted that the enforcement of these norms must depend on "self-discipline and self-restraint, and on public opinion, not on law."[62] He disfavored using the law to regulate this "unruly contest" between the executive and the press for the simple reason that "if we should let the government censor as well as withhold, that would be too much dangerous power."[63] This was equally true, Bickel argued, when it came to the use of anonymous sources, because any legal regulation "forcing reporters to divulge such confidences would dam the flow to the press, and through it to the people, of the most valuable sort of information."[64]

The fact that Bickel's view has garnered widespread support among members of the media establishment has meant that the standard-bearers of the profession have been willing to accept that they ought to act as filters in the public interest. For example, when the *New York Times* was heavily criticized for revealing the existence of the Treasury Department's Terrorist Financing Tracking Program, the deans of some of America's leading schools of journalism issued a statement, entitled "When in Doubt, Publish," defending the *New York Times* on the grounds that it "is the business—and the responsibility—of the press to reveal secrets."[65] But the same statement also rapped the *Washington Post* on the knuckles for having allowed Robert Novak to disclose Valerie Plame's identity, warning that "the public wants the press to keep a sharp lookout, but wants the job performed responsibly."[66] Bill Keller and Dean Baquet, former editors of the *New York Times* and the *Los Angeles Times*, respectively, have expressed similar sentiments. They have argued that while the decision on whether or not to publish classified information "is not one we can surrender to the government," it is also "not a responsibility we take lightly."[67]

These Bickelian affirmations of the need to respect "self-disciplined limits" have extended to the use of anonymous sources as well. For instance, following a series of scandals involving the misuse of anonymous sources, the *New York Times* issued a revised "Confidential News Sources Policy" in 2004 warning its reporters that "when we use such sources, we accept an obligation not only to convince a reader of their reliability but also to convey what we can learn of their motivation," adding for good measure that "we do not grant anonymity to people who use it as cover for a personal or partisan attack."[68] The *Washington Post* offered its readers similar assurances. Its editor, Leonard Downie, pledged in 2004 that his reporters were aware that the *Post*'s reporting guidelines contain the exhortation that "we must strive to tell our readers as much as we can about why our unnamed sources deserve our confidence."[69]

Heartening though these proclamations may be, they seem not to have had great effect. If the troubling cases outlined earlier are not proof enough, consider how extensively the public editors and ombudsmen of the *Times* and the *Post* have criticized their employers on this count. Since 2004 the *Times*'s public editors, Daniel Okrent, Byron Calame, and Clark Hoyt, have altogether written nearly a dozen articles about the "integrity issues" raised by the paper's use of anonymous sources.[70] Hoyt, for example, has pointed out that the *Times*'s use of anonymous sources "to air opinion, not fact" actually increased after it revised its "Confidential News Sources Policy" in 2004, even though "the policy would seem to discourage that," adding that nearly 80 percent of the anonymous sources used "were not adequately described to readers."[71] The *Post* has not been far behind on this count. Writing more than five years after Downie's pledge, the *Post*'s ombudsman, Andrew Alexander, observed in 2009 that many of the newspaper's "lofty standards" on the use of anonymous sources are "routinely ignored," while others "are unevenly applied." "The Post's sourcing rules are fine," he added, "the problem is compliance."[72]

Why have the *Times* and the *Post* failed to abide by the standards that they themselves have publicly endorsed? If their public editors and ombudsmen are to be believed, the indiscriminate use of anonymous sources should be attributed to laxness. For instance, Alexander, the *Post*'s ombudsman, has written that "the solution must come in the form of unrelenting enforcement by editors, starting with those at the top."[73] Similarly, Calame, the *Times*'s public editor, has recommended "commitment to top-level oversight, and to providing sufficient editing attention."[74] But in spite of all the policies and memos that have been drafted and circulated by the editors of the *Times* and the *Post*, the indiscriminate use of anonymous sources largely continues unabated. The editors of the *Times*, for instance, have themselves admitted that they continue to "stray" from their "own guidelines" regarding the use of anonymous sources.[75] The *Post* has been equally helpless. As Alexander has admitted, ombudsmen, himself among them, have complained "for decades" about the *Post*'s "unwillingness to follow its own lofty standards" concerning the use of anonymous sources—all to little effect.[76]

The continuing inability of the *Times* and the *Post* to abide by their own declared standards indicates that there is something fundamentally wrong with the diagnosis offered by their public editors and ombudsmen. It may be that this diagnosis rests on a false assumption. The belief that we can prevent the indiscriminate use of anonymous sources simply by demanding that editors make more of an effort to police reporters assumes that editors themselves (and the publishers who hire them) have no incentive to permit the indiscriminate use of anonymous sources. This assumption can be traced directly back to Bickel's view—and it is demonstrably false. Bickel assumed that the reporter's interest is *inevitably* aligned with the public interest, because the former's desire to profit by reporting the news would have the effect of serving the latter's desire to know. The "professional interest of the reporter," he declared, serves as a "sentinel over the public rights."[77] Bickel saw little reason to be concerned about the use of anonymous sources. "The reporter's access *is* the public's access," he wrote.[78] But what about the possibility that instead of treating anonymous sources in a "morally neutral" or "unconcerned" manner, reporters (and the editors who supervise them and the publishers who hire them) will use their privileged access to sources to further their careers or their favored causes? It is certainly not difficult to imagine how the parochial interests (the desire for prizes, promotions, and readers) and political affiliations of reporters, editors, and publishers could end up influencing decisions on this count, especially when their use of anonymous sources is, by definition, not open to public scrutiny.[79]

Indeed, how else, if not by invoking the narrow interests of reporters, editors, and publishers, can one explain some of the most sensational disclosures of the past decade? Consider, for instance, the *Times*'s decision to disclose the NSA's warrantless surveillance program. As is now well known, the *Times* had initially agreed to withhold Risen and Lichtblau's report after being warned by President Bush that its publication could jeopardize national security. So what prompted the *Times*'s editors and publisher to change their minds? Though Risen and Lichtblau's report cited "concerns" about "the operation's legality and oversight," this claim is undercut by their own acknowledgment that the NSA program was neither obviously unlawful (as the chief judge of the Foreign Intelligence Surveillance Court had agreed to cooperate on Article II grounds) nor without oversight (as the Bush administration had briefed the congressional leadership). These safeguards were unconventional, but they placed officials from all three branches of government in the position of being able to raise the alarm in the event that they felt that the NSA program was wholly unconstitutional. So why, then, did the *Times* suddenly feel the need in late 2005 to give precedence to the concerns of officials like Tice and Tamm? Lichtblau has indicated that the editors at the *Times* revisited their decision to put the report on hold after being confronted with the prospect of being "scooped" by Risen, who, frustrated by the *Times*'s willingness to defer publication, had decided to publish the report in his forthcoming book, *State of War*.[80]

Consider as well the *Times*'s decision to disclose the Department of the Treasury's efforts to monitor international money transfers in spite of the pleas of numerous officials, including two Democrats, Lee Hamilton, cochair of the 9/11 Commission, and Representative John Murtha, an otherwise fierce critic of the Bush administration. This report's publication was met with an outpouring of criticism; among the critics was the

Times's own public editor, Calame, who argued that the disclosure was unwarranted in view of the "apparent legality of the program in the United States, and the absence of any evidence that anyone's private data had actually been misused." Keller, the *Times*'s editor, responded to critics by defending the story as "newsworthy" on the grounds that "some officials who have been involved in these programs have spoken to the *Times* about their discomfort over the legality of the government's actions and over the adequacy of oversight."[81] Who were these officials and what were their motives? This Keller did not say. His silence notwithstanding, it is hard to impute disinterested motives to the *Times*'s sources, for, as the *Wall Street Journal* observed at the time, "since the Treasury story broke . . . no one but . . . a few cranks have even objected to the program, much less claimed illegality."[82] One is hard-pressed here to discount the *Journal*'s suspicion that the *Times*'s decision to run the story owed less to its concern for the "newsworthy" and more to its desire to revive its "watchdog" credentials, which had been tarnished by its evident subservience to the White House in the run-up to the Iraq War.

To be clear, the cases highlighted above should not be seen as implying that reporters, editors, and publishers are *bound* to use anonymous sources without due care. Happily, there have been instances where members of the press have exercised admirable self-restraint in exposing classified information.[83] There have reportedly also been numerous instances where members of the press have refused to grant anonymity to sources with questionable motives (albeit unbeknownst to the public, who cannot witness the confabulations that take place within the newsroom, much less between a reporter and his source). But the above cases do show that it would be unwise to assume that reporters, editors, and publishers will *always* filter out rash or malicious disclosures; on the contrary, there is always the danger that their parochial interests could warp their judgment.

Can Leaks Be Regulated?

If the interests of reporters, editors, and publishers do not always align with those of the public, then arguably we should disregard Bickel's view and take recourse to the law in the hope that the threat of punishment will prompt journalists to filter out rash or malicious disclosures. Consider what such a law might look like. The misuse of anonymous sources, as we have seen, can occur either when reporters, editors, and publishers *neglect* to investigate whether the source of a controversial disclosure has acted in good faith, or when they *fail* to disclose that the source of a controversial disclosure has less than disinterested motives. The law could track the former kind of wrongdoing by establishing procedural tests or criteria, such as "due diligence" requirements that reporters, editors, and publishers must satisfy before publishing a leak of classified information.[84] For instance, the law could require them to obtain from sources an explicit declaration of any potential conflict of interest on the condition that if a source misleads the reporter, then the reporter is no longer obliged to protect the source's identity. The law could also require reporters, editors, and publishers to sign a statement confirming that they have ascertained that a source does not have a conflict of interest (a step that would help fix individual and corporate responsibility and thus preempt pleas of ignorance or efforts to shift blame).

The law could track the latter kind of wrongdoing by subjecting reporters, editors, and publishers to a "bad faith test," which would examine whether a failure to disclose a source's conflict of interest could be reasonably attributed to recklessness, malice, or self-interest. It is difficult to exhaustively specify in advance the sorts of actions that would indicate the presence of bad faith, but the law would be interested in ascertaining whether, for example, a member of the press made a reasonable effort to describe a source's conflict of interest, or if he misrepresented or even obscured a source's interests in order to reduce the appearance of conflict and thereby enhance the credibility of a given news report.

Finally, in the event that wrongdoing is proven on either of the counts described above, the law could impose a fine and require the publication of a correction where appropriate. The former penalty, which could extend to the confiscation of profits, would bring home the costs of irresponsible behavior, while the latter penalty would correct the public record. Let me stress that under such a law members of the press would be obliged to disclose a source's identity *only* to a judge, and *only* in the event that her disclosure is formally condemned by Congress or becomes the subject of a criminal investigation. This means that the proposed law could never warrant an injunction (since a disclosure has to be published before it can prove controversial).

In light of our concerns about the misuse of anonymity, such a law seems quite attractive. But would it be feasible? One major obstacle is a cluster of legal challenges emanating from the First Amendment. The most immediate of these challenges comes from the protection afforded to speech under the First Amendment. Under prevailing First Amendment doctrine, "content-based regulations" that restrict "high-value speech" are "presumed unconstitutional."[85] The Supreme Court has made clear that "uninhibited, robust, and wide-open" debate on political issues, and "criticism of official conduct" in particular, constitute speech of the highest value; thus any law attempting to regulate disclosures that allege wrongdoing by public officials is likely to run afoul of the First Amendment.[86]

There may be an escape route, though. The court has accepted that a law that burdens "political speech" can be upheld "if it is narrowly tailored to serve an overriding state interest."[87] The proposed law satisfies both these requirements. It is narrowly tailored, because it targets only leaks by officials with undisclosed conflicts of interest. Furthermore, it serves a compelling interest because it makes it harder for officials to obscure their efforts to manipulate public opinion. What makes this interest particularly compelling is that the interest that the First Amendment would otherwise protect—vigorous public discussion—is less likely to be realized in the present context. The First Amendment, as Judge Learned Hand famously put it, "presupposes that right conclusions are more likely to be gathered out of a multitude of tongues than through any kind of authoritative selection."[88] But how can the "right conclusions" be drawn when a multitude of tongues are rendered silent or discredited by the lack of an equivalent access to classified information? How can the "marketplace of ideas" serve as a "test of truth" when few, if any, competing voices can warn listeners against being hoodwinked?[89] Some might respond that the First Amendment calls for forbearance on the grounds that an "uninhibited, robust, and wide-open" public debate will occur as and when contrary evidence forces its way into public sight. But then again, do we want to extend the protections afforded by the First Amendment to anonymous disclosures made by officials with undisclosed conflicts of interest in the hope that subsequent, and possibly quite belated, disclosures will confirm that their claims and motives were prudent and decent?

Unfortunately, there are few, if any, precedents that can help us gauge how the Supreme Court might react to this sort of argument. There have been, to be sure, strong defenses of anonymous political speech, most notably in *McIntyre v. Ohio Elections Commission* (1995) where the court, having spoken warmly of a "respected tradition of anonymity in the advocacy of political causes," struck down an Ohio regulation banning the distribution of anonymous leaflets during an election on the grounds that an "interest in providing voters with additional relevant information does not justify a state requirement that a writer make statements or disclosures she would otherwise omit."[90] But the circumstances the court confronted in *McIntyre* differed markedly from those envisioned by the law proposed here. The Ohio regulation scrutinized in *McIntyre* preempted publication, did not discriminate between misleading and valuable anonymous speech, and demanded up-front disclosure of the identity of the speaker, whereas the law proposed here does not prevent publication, targets only anonymous speech that is misleading, and requires only the disclosure of conflicts of interest. Furthermore, *McIntyre* involved the use of anonymity by an author (rather than a source), who was a private citizen (rather than an official), and whose claims were not misleading. It is hardly surprising, then, that the court concluded in *McIntyre* that knowing "the name and address of the author [would] add little, if anything, to the reader's ability to evaluate the document's message."[91]

Equally inconclusive are cases where the court *has* upheld limitations on anonymous political speech in the face of First Amendment challenges. For instance, in *Buckley v. Valeo* (1976) and *McConnell v. Federal Election Commission* (2003) the court accepted the claim that laws requiring campaign contributors to disclose their identity aided "voters in evaluating those who seek federal office," and it reminded those who objected to such disclosure requirements on First Amendment grounds that they must not overlook "the competing First Amendment interests of individual citizens seeking to make informed choices in the political marketplace."[92] But the court also emphasized here that such disclosure requirements might constitute an "unconstitutional burden" if those whose identities were disclosed were thereby rendered vulnerable to retaliation.[93] This qualification creates uncertainty as to whether a court influenced by *Buckley* and *McConnell* would support the proposed law, as the disclosure of a source's conflict of interest *could* lead to the revelation of her identity and thereby expose her to retaliation. Its decision could ultimately turn on whether it thinks the First Amendment permits the chilling of a particular class of political speech, namely, leaks by unnamed officials with undisclosed conflicts of interest.

There is one case that gives some reason for optimism on this count: *Cohen v. Cowles* (1991). This case arose after Dan Cohen, a member of a gubernatorial campaign, provided reporters from the Minneapolis *Star Tribune* and the St. Paul *Pioneer Press* court records pertaining to a rival candidate. Although the reporters had promised Cohen anonymity, their editors decided to disclose his role. This led to Cohen's losing his job, prompting him to sue the newspapers for breach of confidentiality. The newspapers responded to Cohen's action by arguing that allowing him to sue for damages would burden speech "because news organizations will have legal incentives not to disclose a confidential source's identity even when that person's identity is itself newsworthy."[94] The court, however, disagreed with this logic. A five-member majority led by Justice White argued that no First Amendment interests were at stake because the burden on publication was "self-imposed": the reporters had voluntarily offered and promised confidentiality.[95] However, the four-member minority responded that this view relied on "a conception of First Amendment rights as those of the speaker alone, with a value that may be measured without reference to the importance of the information to public discourse."[96] If we were to take the *audience*, rather than the *speaker*, as the bearer of First Amendment rights, Justice Souter argued, then we would conclude that, on balance, Cohen's claim for damages ought to be denied, because knowing about "Cohen's identity expanded the universe of information relevant to the choice faced by Minnesota voters," as it revealed something about "the character of the candidate who had retained him as an adviser."[97] Although the majority was not convinced by this argument, it remains to be seen whether the court might warm to this view in cases involving classified information leaks where *both* the public interest in the motive of the source and the threat of retaliation faced by the source are greater.

A second legal challenge to the proposed law comes from the protections afforded to the press under the First Amendment. In particular, the provision requiring a news organization to correct the public record would appear to run afoul of the court's stance in *Miami Herald Publishing Company v. Tornillo* (1974) that compelling editors or publishers "to publish that which " 'reason' tells them should not be published" is unconstitutional.[98] It is difficult to see how we could overcome this challenge. An answer, insofar as it exists, lies in emphasizing the fact that the court's remarks in *Tornillo* were addressed to a candidate for office who was seeking a right to reply to critical remarks published by the *Miami Herald*, whereas the proposed law seeks to correct news reports featuring misleading content. The success of this line of reasoning depends on whether the court can be persuaded that misleading content is at least as troubling as false content (which the press *can* be ordered to retract under current First Amendment doctrine). Misleading content, at least of the sort envisioned by the proposed law, *is* deeply troubling, because its flaws cannot be easily discerned or corrected through careful reading and public debate. But the court may respond here with the argument that it is still up to readers to exercise due caution when digesting anonymous disclosures.[99] As the court stated in *Tornillo*, "a responsible press is an undoubtedly desirable goal, but press responsibility is not mandated by the Constitution and like many other virtues it cannot be legislated."[100] If this view holds, it suggests that even if the court were otherwise amenable to the proposed law, it would uphold only a more modest version of it, one that does not require the press to correct the public record.

A further challenge to the proposed law comes in the form of the so-called reporter's privilege, a legal privilege granting reporters the right to refuse to disclose information about confidential sources. The proposed law potentially conflicts with the reporter's privilege because it requires members of the press to disclose before a court information pertaining to the conflicts of interests of their confidential sources. It may seem that this conflict does not raise any significant constitutional issue because (as we saw in chapter 4) the court has stated in *Branzburg v. Hayes* (1972) that reporter's privilege cannot be used to thwart the administration of justice. Note, however, that the *Branzburg* court saw itself as addressing the "sole issue" of whether reporters can be compelled to testify in instances where "news sources themselves are implicated in crime or possess information" relevant to a criminal investigation.[101] Its opinion emphasized that "no penalty, civil or criminal, related to the content of published material is at issue here," adding that "use of confidential sources by the press is not forbidden or restricted . . . [n]o attempt is made to require the press to publish its sources of information or indiscriminately to disclose them on request."[102] This disclaimer leaves open the question of whether the proposed law, which compels news reporters to testify about their confidential sources in order to ascertain whether *they* themselves should be punished, is compatible with the First Amendment's guarantee of the freedom of the press.[103]

Although there are few, if any, precedents that could shed clear light on this question, the case can be made that the proposed law does not undermine what the First Amendment finds valuable in a reporter's privilege. The reporter's privilege is founded on the notion that while the First Amendment "guarantees a free press primarily because of the important role it can play as a vital source of public information," the "newsgathering and reporting activities of the press are inhibited when a reporter cannot assure a confidential source of confidentiality."[104] Now, does the proposed law really challenge this line of reasoning? It is not self-evident that requiring members of the press to provide a court with details pertaining to their confidential sources would make it harder to obtain the cooperation of sources willing to act in good faith, namely, officials willing to leak classified information that they disinterestedly believe constitutes wrongdoing. The confidentiality of such a source would be preserved since the court would have no reason to compel reporters, editors, or publishers to publicly reveal any additional details that might expose such a source to retaliation. Hence it is not clear what *valuable* news-gathering interest would be put at risk by legislation making the reporter's privilege dependent on the willingness of reporters, editors, and publishers to faithfully investigate and disclose conflicts of interest.

This argument may be confronted with a point made earlier. It can prove difficult for an official to gauge how a leak of classified information will be received, and this could mean that sources with merely an *appearance* of a conflict of interest may not come forward with valuable information. These sources might well fear that should their disclosures prove controversial enough to spark a criminal investigation into the leak, a court could demand that further information about their interests be disclosed, at which point their cover might be blown, exposing them to retaliation, even though their decision to leak classified information was not actually motivated by self-interest.

Admittedly, this danger exists. But it is not clear that it will be easily realized in practice. Under the proposed law, it would be up to a judge to decide if and what corrections to the public record are warranted, and such corrections could, presumably, be tailored to forestall retaliation. It is possible that a judge could, after having balanced the relevant interests, still demand corrections that have a tendency to reveal the identity of the source. Hence an element of risk would always remain for sources who are not willing to have their conflicts of interests disclosed in the event that their disclosures result in a criminal investigation. But it is not clear how much this element of risk would actually impinge on the willingness of such sources to cooperate with reporters. There is little empirical evidence to show causation, and so we are, as Lillian BeVier has pointed out, "simply awash in indeterminacy about the impact that recognizing or not recognizing a reporter's privilege would actually have."[105]

But what if it could be proven that the risk of exposure would cause the aforementioned sources to clam up? In that case, the court would need to consider whether the news-gathering exercise that the First Amendment seeks to protect is better or worse off when sources of this kind—who refuse to disclose potential or apparent conflicts of interest—decline to cooperate with reporters. In light of the cases discussed earlier in this chapter, it seems probable that weeding out sources of this kind would actually *increase* the likelihood of the press's furthering what Alexander Meiklejohn and Vincent Blasi have respectively described as the self-governing and checking value of the First Amendment.[106]

We have so far been discussing challenges to the constitutionality of the proposed law. Let us now consider a juridical challenge relating to whether such a law can be applied fairly. Recall that the proposed law would use two different tests to determine whether anonymous sources have been misused. The first would examine whether a member of the press has followed established due diligence standards, while the second would examine whether there is evidence indicating bad faith on the part of the concerned reporter, editor, or publisher. The former of these tests should not raise serious concerns about fairness, since the criteria will be objective (e.g., did the reporter warn government officials about the impending disclosure and allow them the opportunity to explain or at least mitigate the likely harm?). The same cannot be said about the latter test, though. Here we have reason to be concerned about fairness because the basis of this subjective assessment will not be open to review. Requiring a member of the press to disclose before an open court the details needed to assess whether he has acted in bad faith would almost certainly reveal the identity of his source, an outcome that would defeat the purpose of the trial, which is to determine whether the motive (much less the identity) of the source ought to have been disclosed. Consequently, the judges tasked with applying the proposed law will have to utilize in camera, ex parte hearings, and they will also have to issue redacted or truncated opinions. These arrangements will require them to make the substantive assessments called for by the law without the benefit of adversarial proceedings, while also impeding the public's ability to understand the reasoning behind their decisions. Under these conditions there will be substantial scope for judicial discretion, and it will not be easy to determine whether the law is being applied consistently—that is, whether like cases are being treated alike.

Troubling as the challenge outlined above may be, it is not without an answer. While we cannot alter the fact that closed proceedings will be necessary, we can lessen the possibility that such proceedings will lead to unfair judgments by raising the standard of proof required to establish wrongdoing. Of course raising the standard of proof comes at a cost—it makes it more likely that only the grossest misuses of anonymous sources are likely to be punished. But there is little alternative here; it makes sense to err on the side of caution when asking judges far removed from the hurly-burly of politics to decode the motives of officials, reporters, editors, and publishers whose activities may at times have more to them than meets the eye.

We have seen that a law intended to punish the misuse of anonymous sources confronts significant legal challenges, and that the concessions required to overcome these challenges are likely to diminish the force and the reach, and therefore the utility, of this law. Let us now consider a final cause of concern: the practical challenge of enforcing such a law. As we saw in chapter 4, no reporter, editor, or publisher has ever been prosecuted for publishing classified information, not even when they have violated a statute like §798, which clearly prohibits the publication of classified information relating to communications intelligence. If presidents do not have an incentive to enforce a statute like §798, it is difficult to see why they will have an incentive to enforce the law under discussion here, since the factors that make it unappealing to enforce the law in the former context are operative in the present context as well. One such factor, as we have seen, is the concern that a trial would draw attention to the classified information revealed by an unauthorized disclosure (and might even demand the disclosure of additional classified information). Another factor is that presidents have a strong incentive to avoid confrontations with reporters and publishers, who can easily retaliate by publicizing the political and personal foibles of the president and his aides. The adage that one should never pick a fight with a man who buys ink by the barrel is only too well known in Washington.

This analysis may provoke the response that the business of law enforcement could be made easier if the authority to initiate and adjudicate cases were vested in the hands of an agency or commission designed to withstand the political power of the press and to use ex parte, in camera procedures. Such a move might solve the reverse problem as well—that is, it would also lessen the possibility that the proposed law would be used to harass reporters, editors, and publishers, especially if this agency or commission were composed of distinguished individuals drawn from civil society, including retired members of the media establishment. But even assuming such an arrangement were feasible, it could do little to overcome a separate obstacle to enforcement, namely, the ease with which reporters, editors, and publishers can evade law enforcement.

It has, of course, long been possible to evade legal constraints on the publication of classified information by operating beyond national boundaries. Take, for example, the publication in 1975 of *Inside the Company* by Philip Agee, a disaffected former CIA official. Agee avoided legal challenges in America by publishing his book, which revealed the identities of covert CIA officers, in England. Consider as well the 1987 publication of *Spycatcher*, an exposé penned by Peter Wright, a former member of the British secret service. Wright got around a court order banning his book by having it published in Scotland and Australia (from where it was reportedly smuggled into England in large numbers). The emergence of new media, particularly Internet-based communication channels, has, of course, dramatically increased the ease with which reporters, editors, and publishers can evade laws or regulations pertaining to the publication of classified information. We live in a world where leaks of classified information can be instantly transmitted to "information clearinghouses" like WikiLeaks and OpenLeaks and mirrored on websites based around the world. It is not unreasonable, then, to wonder whether there is any point in enacting the law under discussion here.

It is important not to overstate the challenge. The existence of websites like WikiLeaks and OpenLeaks should not blind us to the fact that the American media establishment continues to exercise enormous influence owing to its subscriber base, editorial independence, and professional standards. Indeed, the recent disclosure of diplomatic cables can be viewed as having reaffirmed the importance of the American media establishment, because it is unlikely that WikiLeaks's "data dump" would have had the public impact that it did, had the *New York Times* not "curated" the disclosures, drawing the attention of readers to particular facts, providing context, and commissioning supporting editorials.[107] We also must not overlook the fact that the vast majority of leaks pertaining to the United States continue to be published by American news organizations. There is a simple reason for this: the protections offered to the press under the First Amendment have thus far made it unnecessary for officials to take recourse to reporters, editors, and publishers based overseas. Thus, at present, a leak of classified information that is published on the Internet is likely to be—and perhaps ought to be—treated with suspicion: one must wonder why the official responsible for the disclosure could not find an American outlet willing to report her story.

The fact that the ongoing media revolution has failed to undermine the American news establishment's role in channeling leaks of classified information might lead one to conclude that it is not too late to enact a law regulating the use of anonymous sources. How difficult could it be to enforce such a law so long as the *New York Times* and the *Washington Post* continue to serve as the primary channels by which leaks of classified information are disseminated? However, this line of thought overlooks an important point. If the law actually began demanding that the *Times* and the *Post* justify their use of anonymous sources, then officials who are fearful of being "outed" by the ensuing investigations will in fact develop a strong incentive to channel their disclosures via the Internet (as noted previously, it is not only officials with bad motives who have reason to fear being outed by investigations). This development would then naturally lead the American public to begin according greater credibility to anonymous disclosures made via the Internet. In short, the problem that the emergence of websites like WikiLeaks and OpenLeaks poses for law enforcement is not that these outlets have *already* displaced (or are about to displace) the American media establishment as the primary channel by which leaks of classified information are made public, but that they *could* do so if the American media establishment were to come under stricter scrutiny.[108]

Making the Best of It

It seems unlikely, then, that we can rely on the law to compel reporters, editors, and publishers to filter anonymous disclosures on behalf of the public. For even if the proposed law is able to overcome the First Amendment challenges discussed above, the executive is unlikely to be able to enforce its provisions in the age of the Internet. Thus we have little choice but to rely on the good faith of reporters, editors, and publishers—and perhaps the skepticism of readers. This is not a cause for outright alarm, since there certainly *have* been cases where reporters, editors, and publishers have chosen to act responsibly. But the evidence on this count is not exactly overwhelming. As a result, we must learn to make our way in a political universe in which leaks of classified information will continue to be used not only to sound the alarm but also to further sectional interests and partisan causes. Let us now consider what we can do to make the best of a difficult situation.

Conclusion

· ·

Bitter Medicine

Our investigation is now at a close. Before I offer some concluding observations, let me briefly retrace our steps. Recall that we began by drawing attention to the deep sense of anxiety that pervades contemporary discussions on state secrecy. This anxiety, we observed, is felt less at the level of principle and more at the level of practice. It stems not from the concern that state secrecy is contrary to democracy but rather from the concern that the government can use state secrecy to conceal wrongdoing. What, I asked, explains the lack of confidence in the institutions that have been established to monitor state secrecy?

Chapter 1 traced the lack of confidence to a dilemma. The institutions charged with regulating the use of state secrecy, namely, Congress and the courts, have struggled to detect wrongdoing owing to constraints of information and expertise. Meanwhile, the institutions that have succeeded in uncovering wrongdoing—whistleblowing and leaking—have been criticized and indeed penalized for violating laws and regulations prohibiting the unauthorized disclosure of classified information. This dilemma, we argued, implies that if we wish to resolve lingering anxieties over state secrecy, we must either bolster the effectiveness of judicial review and legislative oversight or defend the legitimacy of whistleblowing and leaking.

Chapters 2–3 revealed that in order to make judicial review and legislative oversight more effective, we need to transfer the final say over the classification of information to a bench or committee that can marshal expertise and maintain due discretion. But this move, I argued, begs the question as to why we should feel confident that the members of this bench or committee will behave any more responsibly than the president. After all, there will rarely be objective answers to the question of what information should be made public. Given this, what is to prevent the members of this bench or committee from publishing or withholding information as best suits their own narrow or partisan agendas, especially when they know that outsiders cannot scrutinize their decisions? Why, in particular, should we assume that the members of this bench or committee will be able to resist capture by the organized interests that otherwise pervade contemporary politics?

Chapters 4–6 examined whether whistleblowing and leaking constitute legitimate means of regulating state secrecy. There I argued that, for two reasons, officials, reporters, and publishers should not be granted a legal right to make unauthorized disclosures: first, because they typically lack the information necessary to balance the public's interests in secrecy and in disclosure; and second, because they cannot be easily held accountable for rash or malicious disclosures. We saw, however, that officials, reporters, and publishers can be morally justified in disobeying the law so long as the resulting disclosure (a) reveals an abuse of public authority; (b) is based on clear and convincing evidence; (c) does not pose a disproportionate threat to public safety; (d) is limited in scope and scale as far as is possible; and (e) is made publicly. Nonetheless, we concluded that officials will usually not be willing to abide by the last of these conditions because doing so exposes them to retaliation. This predicament, we argued, justifies relaxing the last condition, but only when we can ascertain that an unauthorized disclosure has been made in good faith. Unfortunately, it turns out that we cannot compel reporters, editors, and publishers to consistently weed out self-interested or manipulative disclosures on our behalf, because legal, political, and practical constraints make it difficult to enact, much less administer, such a norm.

It should be clear from this summary that there is little hope of finding a neat answer to the dilemma identified in chapter 1. Simply transferring the final say on classification from the executive to another branch revives rather than resolves the problem of credibility because we cannot tell whether the appointed regulators are acting dutifully. Yet dispersing regulatory authority by allowing officials, reporters, and publishers to take matters into their own hands is not entirely satisfactory either, as it can lead to too few or too many disclosures—the former when they lack courage, the latter when they are overzealous or manipulative. That we have been unable to find a satisfactory answer to the dilemma at hand does *not* mean, however, that we have provided no answer whatsoever. Arguably, we have cause for cheer on two fronts.

In Chapter 1 we acknowledged the concern that should the right to make unauthorized disclosures not be acknowledged by the law, the specter of legal action might deter officials from making such disclosures. We have now seen that the president cannot hope to stifle unauthorized disclosures:

officials whose moral sensibilities are gravely offended by violations of the law will blow the whistle in spite of the threat of retaliation; those who lack the courage to speak up publicly can leak information, confident in the knowledge that law enforcement will often find it difficult to identify, much less prosecute, them. As a result, the concern that the prohibition of unauthorized disclosures will deter officials from making such disclosures now appears overblown. Indeed the evidence suggest that decision-makers already think twice before they authorize a potentially unlawful policy, as they cannot be confident that their decision will remain secret.

We have also rejected the view that unauthorized disclosures are *always* illegitimate. Under certain conditions officials *will* be justified in making an unauthorized disclosure. Crucially, we have established that not every such disclosure need be made publicly. Anonymous disclosures are justified when they reveal gross wrongdoing. They may also be justified when they reveal suspected wrongdoing, so long as reporters, editors, and publishers credibly verify and signal to the public that the source of the disclosure has acted in good faith. Importantly, these conditions do not appear to be unrealistic. We have examined anonymous disclosures—for instance, revelations about the use of inhumane interrogation practices at Abu Ghraib and the existence of secret CIA prisons—that have satisfied these conditions.

So, to summarize, we have established that there *are* means for effectively, credibly, and legitimately alerting citizens and lawmakers to wrongdoing. Nonetheless, our celebrations must be muted, because these regulatory means can misfire: overzealous officials may blow the whistle without good cause, and reporters, editors, and publishers may fail to weed out manipulative or self-interested leaks. This unruliness has two adverse consequences. The first concerns the exercise of executive power. Chapter 1 characterized the office of president as a product of hard-nosed thinking about the nature of international politics. In particular, the Framers emphasized the need for "energy" on the grounds that speed and secrecy are essential to mastering international politics. It is not difficult to see that energy is imperiled when little prevents a disgruntled or overzealous subordinate from exposing the delicate schemes that the president is within his rights to pursue in complete secrecy. The long-term effect of such unruliness is especially worrying. The more commonplace it becomes for covert actions or intelligence operations to be disrupted at inopportune moments, the more likely a president is to base his decision to undertake such actions or operations not on whether his decision will be approved retrospectively, once the relevant information can be shared with the public, but rather on whether his decision can withstand being made public at any moment.

A second adverse consequence concerns the quality of public deliberation. As we have seen, it can prove difficult for the public to discern whether an official responsible for making an unauthorized disclosure has acted in good faith. All too often this worry is countered by a recitation of various occasions on which reporters, editors, and publishers have refrained from publicizing rash or manipulative disclosures. These examples indicate, the argument goes, that many journalists do serve as trustworthy intermediaries. But this response misses the point. In the absence of a credible assurance that reporters, editors, and publishers will reliably filter out partisan or manipulative disclosures, the public will often be left to wonder—indeed it *ought* to wonder—whether the disclosures that have found their way into the public sphere should be believed. Thus, when we rely on unauthorized disclosures to combat the abuse of state secrecy, we inevitably degrade the quality of public deliberation, because the public can never be entirely certain as to which disclosures are reliable. The end result is intrigue, conspiracy, and indeed paranoia, as we see public opinion being shaped via a battle of leaks and counterleaks.

These consequences are disconcerting, but it should be clear by now why we must learn to live with them. For even if we could somehow clamp down on unauthorized disclosures, this is *not* something we ought to do, because such disclosures are the principal means by which citizens and lawmakers can be alerted to concealed wrongdoing. It would be preferable of course if we could ensure that only "deserving" leaks are in fact made public. But this degree of control, we have seen, is out of our reach. The result is a painful paradox. By relying on unauthorized disclosures to deter the president from doing ill, we make it harder for him to do good, and harder still for the public to tell the difference between the two. This is bitter medicine indeed! We have little choice, though, but to follow this regimen, because we have been brought to this point by facts that we cannot easily alter—the steady increase in the scope and scale of state secrecy since the turn of the twentieth century, the limited utility of having judges and lawmakers challenge the president's control over classified information, and the difficulties associated with regulating unauthorized disclosures.

This is not, however, a counsel of despair. Certainly, the analysis presented here implies that it would be a mistake to assume, as so many First Amendment scholars do, that officials, reporters, editors, and publishers will always act in the public interest. But this does not mean that we must quietly suffer the unruliness of these regulatory mechanisms. Now that we understand why we must tolerate whistleblowing and leaking—because they can provide an effective, credible, and legitimate means to combat the abuse of state secrecy—we ought to focus on fashioning norms and practices that will help lessen the chance that these regulatory mechanisms will be used improperly. Let me now discuss some of the ways by which this might be done. While limitations of space preclude detailed analysis here, the following discussion will highlight the direction that further research on this topic might take.

A Credible Executive

In chapters 5–6, I argued that an official is justified in disclosing classified information only if doing so reveals an abuse of authority. However, because there can be disagreement over the rightful bounds of public authority, an official may be unsure as to whether a prima facie violation of the law really constitutes an abuse of authority. Now, ideally, an official who comes across suspected wrongdoing ought to approach senior managers who have the information necessary to assess whether an abuse of authority has in fact occurred. In practice, however, the fear of retaliation is likely to deter her from taking this step. How, then, can a president convince this official (and the reporters and publishers she contacts) that his decision to violate the law in secret is worthy of deference? The president will not be able to cite the law, since the rightful bounds of his authority will themselves be in dispute. Nor will he be able to share classified information that could convince officials, reporters, and publishers that his policies are justified. How, then, can the president convince officials as well as reporters, editors, and publishers that they ought to trust his judgment? The answer is—by possessing *credibility*.[1] The president must convey to observers the sense that his decisions are well-founded and disinterested. Consider three ways in which this can be done.

The first is by signaling that his private interest tracks the public interest. For instance, the president might say, "Trust me, I will do only what is best for the country, because this is my homeland too." Or he might say, "Rest assured, I will do what is best because I am mindful of my legacy." Such claims have a distinguished lineage. In 1782 Congress recommended that the states impose a 5 percent duty on imports in order to rescue the finances of the United States—a recommendation that met with popular resistance. Called upon to defend the policy, Thomas Paine wrote in the *Pennsylvania Gazette* that Americans had no reason to suspect their delegates' intentions because though "their situation enables them to know the more secret circumstances of things, and that such or such revenues are necessary for the security and defence of their constituents," beyond this "the distinction ends" as their "estates and property are subject to the same taxation with those they represent."[2]

Claims of this kind suffer from an obvious weakness, though. No doubt there are scenarios where the president's interests will closely track those of the public. The president will, for instance, have no incentive to allow the country to be destroyed in nuclear war. But in less extreme scenarios, the president's interests may be obscure and prone to change, making it difficult for observers to ascertain whether a secret policy (or a policy founded on secret information) impinges on the president's interests in quite the same way as it impinges on the public. For instance, a president who authorizes covert action that risks igniting a war may have neither children liable to conscription nor financial interests that are likely to be harmed by the ensuing spike in taxation. Indeed, a war might well suit his interests should corporations that stand to profit from military conflict offer to support him. This is a concern that the Constitutional Convention seems to have taken quite seriously. The argument was put forward there that the power of making treaties be vested in the president alone because "from his situation he was more interested in making a good treaty than any other man in the United States." But this view, Charles Cotesworth Pinckney reports, was rejected on the grounds that the president might "show an improper partiality for the state to which he particularly belonged."[3] The fear of corruption or partiality, Pinckney states, was the key reason the convention divided the treaty-making power between the president and the Senate.

It might seem that once we concede that the interests of elected officials can diverge from those of the public, then the only way to bolster the credibility of decisions made in secret is to expand the number and variety of interests represented in the decision-making process. This "safety in numbers" approach is one that a number of Anti-Federalists espoused when they argued that the House of Representatives ought to also be included in the treaty-making process, lest the president and two-thirds of a quorum of the Senate betray the country behind closed doors.[4] Since the Framers were averse to granting the House a share in the treaty-making process, they sought instead to bolster trust in the president and Senate by reviving the kind of argument cited earlier by Paine. The president and Senate, John Jay argued in *The Federalist* No. 64, would have "no interests distinct from that of the nation," because it would not be in their power "to make any treaties by which they and their families and estates will not be equally bound and affected with the rest of the community." But aware no doubt that this claim had limited appeal, Jay crucially added that the Constitution's provisions would ensure that only public-spirited individuals would fill public offices. As the Constitution had "taken the utmost care" to ensure that the president and Senators "shall be men of talents and integrity," he wrote, "we have reason to be persuaded that the treaties they make will be as advantageous as, all circumstances considered, could be made."[5]

The notion that we can design public institutions so as to ensure that the men and women who become our representatives are virtuous, and are therefore intrinsically trustworthy, must not be treated lightly. But which institutions can we rely on to produce this outcome? It is not clear that electoral politics, which the Framers saw as the foremost mechanism for the selection of a "natural aristocracy," invariably leads to the selection of virtuous individuals.[6] The influence of money, "spin," and special interests are too well known to bear elaboration. With good reason we have come to fear that our leaders will pursue not what the common good demands, but rather the agenda of the interest groups that have propelled them into office. The problem, to be clear, is not that presidents *have* been or undoubtedly *will be* corrupted by special interests. Rather, it is that the need for discretion can make it difficult for them to prove that they have *not* been corrupted, in turn making it easy for skeptics to raise doubts about their "talents and integrity" (recall here the aspersions cast upon Vice President Cheney owing to his links to corporations that profited from the Iraq War).[7]

Consequently, if presidents are to be able to signal their freedom from corrupting influences, we will have to reform how they are chosen. In particular, we will have to make it possible for them to be elected without needing the assistance of sectional interests, because it is only by minimizing apparent conflicts of interest that one can minimize the suspicions that breed unauthorized disclosures. But this is a Sisyphean challenge, surely. And even if we could make some headway on this front, it is not clear that even a well-insulated president will enjoy lasting credibility, for trust founded on character is also vulnerable to suspicions about corruption other than that of the material kind. Arguably, the Framers underestimated the degree to which even individuals of "talents and integrity" can come under suspicion when observers are left unable to determine whether they have utilized secrecy to quietly impose their own values on an unsuspecting citizenry. Could there be a more poignant example of this phenomenon than the brouhaha over the Jay Treaty? "What its contents are, the Executive alone as yet know," Representative M adison wrote to James Monroe in March 1795, owing to the "most impenetrable secrecy being observed." Nonetheless, the suspicions of observers sympathetic to France had been repressed, Madison affirmed, "by the confidence that some adequate reasons exist for the precaution."[8] This confidence was not to last, though. Once the Federalist-dominated Senate decided to ratify the treaty in secret, the fears of the Democratic-Republicans boiled over. The resulting political upheaval proved so great that Senator Stevens Mason felt justified in disclosing his copy of the treaty to the provocateurs at the *Philadelphia Aurora*. Now, if the Democratic-Republicans could not find it in themselves to trust President Washington to make a treaty in secret, what hope is there that uprightness can quiet the suspicions generated by ideological conflict in our time?

A second way for the president to signal credibility is to cultivate a "reputation for restraint and commitment to the rule of law."[9] Few have emphasized this point more than Jack Goldsmith, who writes that in order to foster credibility, an administration "should be as open as possible, and when secrecy is truly necessary it must organize and conduct itself in a way that is beyond reproach, even in a time of danger."[10] What exactly does this mean? At the level of conduct, this means that the president must make a concerted effort to calm the public's nerves by adopting the rhetoric of moderation. One example Goldsmith offers is the almost "apologetic" language that the Obama administration has employed when exercising the state secrets privilege.[11] It also means that the president and his senior advisers must refrain from making self-serving disclosures, lest they set a bad example. An "open defiance and manipulation of the secrecy system at the top," Goldsmith asserts, "indicates a lack of seriousness about secrecy that invariably corrodes the respect that lower-level officials give it in their discussions with journalists."[12]

Goldsmith also recommends that at an organizational level presidents adopt decision-making procedures that convey to observers that policies and decisions have accounted for important objections and interests. An especially important step, in his view, is to have policies subjected to critical review by executive branch lawyers charged with ensuring that the administration's actions are in compliance with the law. A president who establishes and abides by such internal checks and balances, Goldsmith argues, will give observers less cause for concern than one who relies on the concurrence of a few, handpicked lawyers and advisers known to espouse positions favorable to his own cause.[13] The decision-making process that President Obama has established for authorizing covert drone strikes seems to follow this standard. Recent disclosures, no doubt intended to underscore the president's reputation for "restraint and law-abidingness," have emphasized the "contentious discussions" that precede the selection of targets, the "moral rectitude" of the participants in the decision-making process, and procedural safeguards that have been employed to minimize collateral damage, the most notable of these being that the president must "personally" approve every strike.[14]

Few would deny that Goldsmith's advice is valuable. A reputation for "restraint and law-abidingness" may well give overzealous subordinates pause and thereby stem at least some mistaken disclosures. However, we must be realistic about what this advice can accomplish. There are two reasons to believe that conducting and organizing an administration "in a way that is beyond reproach" is unlikely to prevent many troubling disclosures. First, a president's good reputation will not prevent subordinates who are politically opposed to him from making malicious disclosures intended to hurt his political standing. Goldsmith arguably underplays the harsh reality of political life, which is better captured by Stephen Hess's observation that "the people who are most likely to come to Washington with each political administration bring with them a high talent and tolerance for intrigue."[15] Second, it is not clear that the president can consistently behave in a manner that is "beyond reproach." A central challenge that the president confronts as a leader is the pervasiveness of moral and political disagreement, which can produce irreconcilable differences among his subordinates over the rightness of a particular course of action. When such disputes arise (and they are likeliest to arise during crises that call for bold and decisive action), it will often not be possible for the president to take everyone along. There can be qualifications and compromises, but in the end the president cannot always proceed by halves when confronted with subordinates pulling strongly in either direction. In other words, sometimes the president cannot help but disappoint a subset of his subordinates.

Now, when the president knows that a morally and politically charged decision will generate opposition from some subset of his subordinates, we should not be surprised to find him cutting these subordinates out of the decision-making process (or riding roughshod over their objections).[16] As Hess notes, presidents who wish to conceal important matters typically "turn inward": they "involve the absolute minimum number of advisers" and "compartmentalize" information.[17] Goldsmith recognizes of course that this tendency exists, and he warns—quite rightly—that tightening rather than loosening "the normal circle of secrecy" can prove counterproductive over the long run, because it often provokes the kind of suspicions that lead to unauthorized disclosures.[18] Nonetheless, it is unrealistic to expect the president to share information liberally when this would merely increase and strengthen the number of dissenting voices that he has to silence or overcome in the short run. If anything, this setting encourages him to value loyalty over competence when it comes to appointing advisers and lawyers.

The third way in which the president can bolster his credibility is by adopting decision-making arrangements that convey to observers that grave and respectable political actors agree with his decisions and policies. In a groundbreaking essay Eric Posner and Adrian Vermeule have identified a number of mechanisms that can be employed to this end, including bilateralism in cabinet appointments and multilateralism in foreign policy.[19] The former of these proposals—that the president appoint to the cabinet political heavyweights whose interests, inclinations, and experiences are different from his own—is especially interesting. This proposal is attractive because it creates the equivalent of the canary in a coal mine—so long as the president is able to retain the support of these heavyweights, observers have reason to believe that his secret decisions and policies have the concurrence of men and women of experience. Conversely, should these heavyweights make what Albert Hirschman has termed a "clamorous exit," then would-be whistleblowers and leakers as well as reporters and editors will have more reason to disclose and publish what they know about suspected wrongdoing.[20]

Posner and Vermeule depict their proposal as a response to the increased opacity of the presidency following 9/11. In fact, the underlying concept is as old as democracy itself. In the *Library of History* Diodorus Siculus recounts that Themistocles, the leading politician of early fifth-century Athens, once wanted to launch a covert operation against the Spartans. In order to dispel fears that he might actually be plotting a coup, Themistocles offered to disclose his plan to two men chosen by the Assembly who could then advise the Athenians on whether the plan ought to be executed. According to Diodorus, the Athenians accepted Themistocles's advice and appointed Aristides and Xanthippus, not only because they were "upright characters," but also because they were in "active rivalry" with Themistocles "for glory and leadership." Themistocles then disclosed his plan to these men, and after they (and subsequently the Council) concurred that the plan was "advantageous" and "feasible," the Athenians allowed Themistocles to proceed.[21]

This Athenian episode captures both what is desirable and what is troubling about Posner and Vermeule's proposal. By allowing Themistocles to share his plan with rivals who had the authority to veto the plan but not to disclose its contents, the Athenians were able to take advantage of adversarialism without jeopardizing secrecy. Yet, by allowing Aristides and Xanthippus to veto Themistocles's plan, the Athenians also opened themselves up to the risk that these intermediaries might reject Themistocles's plan for reasons that the Athenians might not endorse were they aware of the plan's details. Perhaps this is what actually happened. According to another version of the story, when Themistocles shared his plan with Aristides, the latter informed the Athenians that the plan was "extremely beneficial, but not at all honorable," whereupon the Athenians, Plutarch writes, "commanded Themistocles to think no farther of it."[22]

To be sure, Posner and Vermeule's proposal does not leave the president vulnerable to an Aristides-type figure who assumes that deception is always contrary to honor. Since the heavyweights invited into the cabinet will not have the right to veto the president's decisions, they will not be able to prevent him from exercising secrecy as he sees fit. Nonetheless, if the president is to retain the support of these heavyweights, he will have to be mindful of the limits to which they can be pushed. Hence, as Posner and Vermeule admit, from the president's perspective, credibility will sometimes have to be "gained at the expense of control."[23] Not every such loss need be troubling. The threat by Justice Department officials, including Attorney General John Ashcroft, to resign en masse in 2004 reportedly compelled President Bush to make modifications to the NSA's surveillance program that addressed their concerns about its legality.[24] In this case the objections to the president's program appear to have been narrowly tailored and well informed. But it is not difficult to imagine instances where cabinet appointees might have more dogmatic objections—consider, for example, Secretary of State William Jennings Bryan's pacifism in the run-up to World War I.[25]

Posner and Vermeule acknowledge that this problem exists. The proposed mechanisms, they write, are not "good for all times and places."[26] But the problem might be deeper than they admit. Should it become a norm for presidents to act multilaterally or to make bilateral appointments, a decision to forgo these arrangements may end up arousing unwarranted skepticism on the part of observers. Suppose, for instance, a president orders a covert strike after determining that America's allies lack the requisite capabilities. A subordinate official who has grown accustomed to multilateral action might incorrectly interpret the president's unilateralism as evidence of adventurism. Consider as well the problem that political heavyweights in the cabinet will face in signaling *their* independence to critics on the hunt for signs of co-optation. The critics will want reassurance that these heavyweights are not being silent out of a misplaced sense of loyalty to their colleagues or an inflated sense of their contribution as a counterbalance to the administration's excesses.[27] They will also want reassurance that these heavyweights have not succumbed to the lure of office and thereby become complicit in wrongdoing. What issues will these heavyweights fix upon to burnish their credentials in the eyes of outsiders? And at what cost to the president's effectiveness? These unknowns are likely to make bilateral appointments quite tricky to handle in practice.

A Responsible Press

The president can stem unauthorized disclosures, then, by signaling that his decisions or policies are well-founded and disinterested rather than arbitrary or self-interested. He can do so, we have seen, by showing that these decisions either (a) adversely affect his own interests; or (b) have not been made without due consideration of widely shared interests and objections; or (c) have the support of grave and respected political actors. Of course would-be whistleblowers and leakers, and the reporters, editors, and publishers they contact, will care about these signals only if they are themselves well-intentioned. If their objective is to malign the president, then they will care not one whit for his credibility. Instead, they will make selective disclosures in order to further their own particular agendas. Hence if we wish to stem not only mistaken but also malicious disclosures, we need a responsible press. But how can we encourage the press to behave responsibly when we cannot rely on legal sanctions?

There appear to be two alternatives. The first is to persuade the press to exercise self-censorship. This is not a new idea. As early as 1917 lawmakers rejected the Espionage Act's censorship provision on the grounds that America could rely on the "patriotism" and the "active and self-imposed censorship" of the press.[28] On two occasions—during World Wars I and II—pressure was brought to bear on the press in a systematic manner through the offices of the Committee on Public Information and the Office of Censorship, respectively. Subsequently, during the early decades of the Cold War, there were calls for a peacetime equivalent of the Office of Censorship. For instance, in 1963 Allen Dulles, the former director of the Central Intelligence Agency, drew attention to the British Defense Advisory Notice System (commonly referred to as the DA-Notice System) whereby the British government provides media organizations with "general guidance" about the implications of publishing national security information, which they are free to accept or reject.[29] The success of this system, Dulles wrote, ought to inspire "quiet discussions" between "selected government officials" and "leaders of the press" in the United States about the extent to which "there can be mutual agreement for setting up machinery to keep the press confidentially advised as to the matters in which secrecy is essential to our security."[30] But Dulles's advice found few supporters at the time, and it is unlikely to do better for the foreseeable future. In the press's view, the censorship systems established during World Wars I and II were tolerable only because the censor's mandate was limited both substantively (to matters relating directly to the war effort) and temporally (to the duration of the war).[31]

The absence of an American equivalent to the DA-Notice System has not, however, precluded officials from *informally* pressuring reporters, editors, and publishers to refrain from publishing harmful or malicious disclosures. Anecdotal evidence suggests that these efforts have met with a fair degree of cooperation when officials have asked journalists to withhold classified information that is only incidental to a news report.[32] For example, in 2005 the Bush administration was able to convince the *Washington Post* to withhold the names of countries that helped the CIA establish its secret prison system. But such interventions have met with far less success when officials have asked journalists to withhold news reports whose very subject matter concerns a state secret, be this CIA Director William Colby's attempt to keep the *Glomar Explorer* project under wraps (see chapter 4) or the Bush administration's request that the *New York Times* withhold the story on the Terrorist Financing Tracking Program (see chapter 6).

So what more can be done to foster self-censorship in cases of the latter sort, i.e., disclosures that do not expose serious wrongdoing? The first challenge that any initiative to foster responsibility must overcome is resistance from reporters, editors, and publishers, who take the Bickelian view that the First Amendment demands an adversarial press. This view is summarized by Ted Galen Carpenter's assertion that the "media play a questionable role when they become accomplices in preserving government secrecy," because such action "maximizes the ability of officials to conceal information about unwise or disreputable actions."[33] Perhaps the most cogent defense for this position is the one offered by Ted Gup. He argues that refraining from cooperation serves two important interests. The first is deterrence. "The dread of exposure," he writes, "is a stern corrective that should always weigh upon government's deliberations." However, the force of this corrective, Gup asserts, is weakened if the government feels that it can appeal to the press to "delay publication to a more propitious time." Hence it is "only by being a predictable force for holding government accountable," he writes, that the press can "play its most vital role."[34] Gup does not favor blind adversarialism, though. "The press," he writes, "is still entirely free to entertain government's appeals for special consideration if sought on behalf of programs and efforts that would not . . . compromise commonly held views of decency and law." But to consider self-censorship in cases that lie beyond this point, he argues, hurts the press's credibility. Criticizing, for instance, the *Post*'s willingness to withhold the names of the countries that hosted the CIA's secret prisons, he writes that "accommodating government's appeals regarding suspect, unscrupulous, or inhumane actions creates a kind of toxic partnership," because the press's silence can be "misconstrued" by citizens and lawmakers as an "implicit endorsement" of the government's actions. Moreover, cooperation may discourage "potential sources from taking the risk of coming forward," because it leaves them uncertain as to "whether the press will have the courage to publish their story."[35]

These are powerful arguments, but they are not entirely convincing. For one thing, the claim that journalists should refuse to even consider censoring themselves once they become aware of activity that violates "commonly held views of decency and law" seems too strong. This criterion rules out nearly every interesting case, i.e., unauthorized disclosures concerning prima facie violations of the law. The reason we want the press to consider self-censorship in such cases is precisely because it is not always clear whether a violation of the law amounts to an abuse of authority, much less whether a given source might not be exploiting the appearance of wrongdoing in order to further a narrow or partisan agenda. Furthermore, the claim that officials will be deterred from wrongdoing only if they believe that the press can never be convinced to withhold unauthorized disclosures seems overly pessimistic. Arguably, the likelihood that information about wrongful decisions will be disclosed to outsiders should be enough to give most decision-makers pause, since they cannot know who the recipient of the disclosure might turn out to be (and therefore how amenable the recipient might be to pleas to withhold the disclosure). Finally, an official who summons the courage to make an unauthorized disclosure is not without alternatives should a reporter (or his editor or publisher) withhold the disclosure in response to a plea from the president. Nothing prevents this official from approaching other reporters or indeed blowing the whistle in the event that she believes the press has failed to comprehend the importance of her disclosure.

There appears, then, to be no compelling reason for the press to adopt a stubbornly adversarial stance, publishing *every* disclosure concerning suspected wrongdoing that comes its way. But even if the bulk of reporters, editors, and publishers accept the need to exercise judicious self-censorship (as many of them claim they do), an insurmountable practical problem remains: we lack the means by which to rein in the black sheep in the journalistic community, who delight in and profit from sensation.[36] This pessimistic statement is not a knee-jerk reaction to recent events, such as WikiLeaks's indiscriminate disclosure of the United States' diplomatic communications. In fact few officials or lawmakers have ever been optimistic about the prospects of self-censorship.[37] The Coolidge Committee's remarks on the issue neatly capture the problem. "We have run across instances," the committee observed in 1956, "where information of high news value has been voluntarily withheld, only to have it 'scooped' by someone less scrupulous." Such instances show, it declared, that the "competitive element in news gathering is too strong" for any attempt at voluntary censorship "to be successful."[38]

The Coolidge Committee's conclusion might be challenged on the grounds that peer pressure could deter journalists from "scooping each other." But the problem with such a strategy, as Dulles pointed out long before WikiLeaks arrived on the scene, is that the pluralism of the American media establishment limits the efficacy of peer pressure. Unlike England, he wrote, the United States features "no comparable center of authority in the matter of press and publicity, and it would be harder here to find any relatively restricted group of men in the field of news media whose judgment would be accepted by the press in all parts of the country."[39] This is precisely why Dulles called for the American equivalent of an Official Secrets Act, which, he believed, would scare the press into taking official requests to withhold publication more seriously. However, this proposal is something of a red herring. For one thing, it is founded on a conceptual error, since legal sanctions against unauthorized disclosures deter publication rather than promote self-censorship (the latter referring to the decision to withhold information even when there is no legal obstacle or consequence to publication). Furthermore, Dulles's approach is unlikely to pass constitutional muster. An Official Secrets Act that punishes publication without concern for the nature and intent of an unauthorized disclosure is certain to be struck down as an overbroad violation of the First Amendment. Such a statute is also likely to join the list of statutes against unauthorized disclosures that officials have declined to enforce on the grounds that prosecuting the press only draws further attention to revelations that are better forgotten.

Thus even though we are justified in calling upon the press to censor rash or malicious disclosures, there is little reason to think that every member of the press will cooperate. It makes sense, then, to approach the problem from another direction. If it is unrealistic to expect every member of the press to display due caution before publishing sensational disclosures, perhaps we ought to punish (and thereby hopefully deter) irresponsibility by criticizing the offenders and undermining their credibility with the public. But who should do the criticizing?

One possibility is for the president and Congress to take the lead. They can, for instance, try to persuade the public to boycott the relevant media organizations. This is what happened in the WikiLeaks case, where the United States was able to prevail on American corporations to cut off support services to the website.[40] But this method of enforcing accountability is both dangerous and unreliable. It is dangerous because the president and Congress may turn public opinion against media organizations that have actually published a disclosure made in good faith.[41] In theory, such organizations ought to be able to defend themselves by making further disclosures to back up their claims. In practice, however, government-led pressure might lead weakhearted and financially vulnerable publishers to fold. On the other side of the table, the president and Congress can prove unreliable critics because, as discussed in chapter 4, it will often make more sense for them to ignore rather than engage with unauthorized disclosures lest this prolong the controversy and lead to the disclosure of even more information. Furthermore, as discussed in chapter 6, they may choose not to criticize influential media organizations out of the fear that these organizations will retaliate against them by splashing their (unrelated) errors and follies all over the front page.

A second possibility is to rely on self-criticism, that is, on the ombudsman. This idea is appealing because at first glance the ombudsman appears to have a desirable mix of incentives. Because she is employed by the media organization she evaluates, she is unlikely to be biased in the way that critics from officialdom might be. Furthermore, because ombudsmen tend to be experienced journalists, there is reason to think that they will be realistic about the degree to which ethical guidelines can be followed in practice. And finally, because the ombudsman is typically protected against direct interference by management, there is reason to believe that her judgments will be relatively independent.

But why, when the office embodies such desirable incentives, have ombudsmen had so little effect? As we saw in chapter 6, the ombudsmen of the *New York Times* and the *Washington Post* openly admit that their criticism of the undiscriminating use of anonymous sources has had no discernible effect on their organizations.[42] Some scholars have attributed this outcome to flaws in the design of the ombudsman's office. For instance, it has been argued that the tendency to recruit the ombudsman from within the ranks of a media organization serves to limit the effectiveness of the occupant, since the occupant then may not only lack critical distance but may also be fearful of stepping on her colleagues' toes lest this hurt her future prospects within the organization.[43] This is an important observation, certainly. But arguably the more fundamental problem is their lack of enforcement power. As we saw in chapter 6, the ombudsmen of the *Times* and the *Post* have been only too aware of the misuse of anonymous sources, and their fairness, sensitivity, and independence in addressing the matter has been admirable. The problem is that the very reporters, editors, and publishers who have hired them have either rebuked them or, worse still, simply ignored their advice and criticism.[44] Consider what happened when Byron Calame, the *Times*'s public editor, sought to determine how far the *Times*'s decision to publish James Risen and Eric Lichtblau's report on the NSA warrantless surveillance program had been influenced by Risen's threat to publish the report in his *State of War*. Writing soon after the publication of the NSA story, Calame noted that in spite of the *Times*'s editor's claims to the contrary, Risen's publisher had informed Calame that he had spoken about the book with the *Times*'s

Washington bureau chief twice in the month preceding the publication of the NSA report. "So it seems to me," Calame observed, that "the paper was quite aware that it faced the possibility of being scooped by its own reporter's book." The "key question" then, Calame concluded, was "to what extent did the book cause top editors to shrug off the concerns that had kept them from publishing the eavesdropping article for months?" But when he sought an answer to this question from the *Times*'s management, Calame drew a blank. As he informed the *Times*'s readers: "For the first time since I became public editor, the executive editor and the publisher have declined to respond to my requests for information about news-related decision-making."[45]

Calame's experience supports media critics' assertions that grand claims notwithstanding, media organizations actually want ombudsmen to serve more as a mechanism for addressing readers complaints and less as a fount of professional criticism.[46] This realization has prompted some to demand that ombudsmen be empowered to enforce the codes of conduct drafted by media organizations themselves.[47] But this seems exactly the wrong way to proceed. If these organizations cannot be relied upon to voluntarily abide by codes of ethics that they themselves have drafted, then they cannot be trusted to appoint ombudsmen who will compel them to follow these codes. The premise defeats the conclusion. Indeed demanding that ombudsmen be granted powers to punish bad behavior makes it *less* likely that they will be able to serve the role that they do play now, which, as in the *Times* example cited above, is to reveal the moment at which reporters, editors, and publishers seem to suddenly lose their much-professed regard for the public's right to know. Should we demand more from the office, it is inevitable that only a "safe" sort of person will be appointed to fill the position. Hence if we want to retain the function of the ombudsman as a critic, the punishment for unethical behavior must come from outside the organization.

Who else can we rely on to challenge the press? Another possibility is to foster the sort of media environment in which the misuse of anonymous sources is likely to be subject to public rebuke by rival media organizations. This idea is far from new: it lies at the heart of the much-discussed 1947 Report of the Commission on the Freedom of the Press (commonly referred to as the Hutchins Commission). Citing evidence showing that professional associations such as the American Society of Newspaper Editors had quietly "passed over" the "frauds and crimes" committed by their members, the commission recommended that the press "engage in vigorous mutual criticism."[48] But what incentive did the commission think reporters, editors, and publishers have to undertake this backbreaking labor? The commission's simple reply: self-preservation. Members of the press must criticize each other, the commission argued, because it is only by showing that are willing to hold each other accountable that the press can forestall the calls for legal regulation that will inevitably follow in the wake of malpractice. Otherwise, "not even the First Amendment will protect their freedom," the commission warned, for the "amendment will be amended."[49]

Thus far, the Hutchins Commission's threat has turned out to be hollow. Note that its report was written shortly after World War II, a time when the idea of formal press censorship seemed a realistic threat. Following the Pentagon Papers case we now know that the executive can do very little to censor the press in the absence of explicit congressional authorization. Since Congress has wisely refrained from arming the executive with a censorial power, and since the executive has been loath to prosecute the press following publication, lest this draw unwanted attention to the relevant disclosure and make a martyr out of the journalist responsible, the press currently has little reason to fear that its failure to hold itself accountable for how it uses anonymous sources will lead to its being subjected to formal regulation.

Is there any other way to stimulate the "vigorous mutual criticism" that the Hutchins Commission called for? There may be an economic incentive. For more than two decades now, scholars and practitioners have argued that the use of anonymous sources "hurts the credibility of media organization because it makes audiences "suspicious . . . about the motives of both reporter and source."[50] This dynamic, they emphasize, can impact a media organization's bottom line. "It's a matter of trust," according to Fred Brown of the Society of Professional Journalists, "and if the media can't be trusted, they can't compete in an environment where there are innumerable sources of information."[51] As it turns out, though, the evidence on this point is not entirely clear. Certainly, there is some support for the notion that any use of anonymous sources, regardless of purpose, hurts a media organization's credibility. For example, a recent survey by the Annenberg Public Policy Center has shown that 89 percent of readers agree that "news stories relying on anonymous sources should be questioned for accuracy, while 53% said such stories should not be published at all."[52] But this evidence is contested, and it does not distinguish the effect that the misuse—as distinct from the general use—of anonymous sources has on credibility.[53]

In spite of the absence of clear evidence, media organizations seem convinced that the use of anonymous sources weakens the credibility of their product in the marketplace.[54] Assuming that this belief has some foundation, can we hope that it will foster responsible behavior? Presumably, if editors and publishers really believe that the use of anonymous sources harms their product, then they ought to see it as being in their own interest to punish their employees' disreputable conduct (in order to forestall a loss of credibility and thereby market share) and to expose such conduct on the part of their rivals (in order to undermine their rivals' credibility and market share).

There is some reason to be optimistic on this count when we consider the fate of Judith Miller, the *New York Times* reporter responsible for conveying manipulative disclosures in the run-up to the Iraq War. Following the controversy over its reporting on Iraq's purported weapons of mass destruction program, the *Times* disclosed in 2004 that the Iraqi defectors who had been quoted anonymously in a number of Miller's news reports had been "groomed" by Ahmed Chalabi, a founder of the Iraqi National Congress, an organization dedicated to the overthrow of Saddam Hussein.[55] Although the *Times* failed to criticize either Miller or her editors, a few media critics, most notably Jack Shafer and Michael Massing, took Miller to task for having failed to disclose her sources' conflict of interest. Initially, the *Times* defended Miller. Its editor, Bill Keller, showered disdain on Miller's critics, saying that "it's a little galling to watch her pursued by some of these armchair media ethicists who have never ventured into a war zone or earned the right to carry Judy's laptop."[56] But the critics had succeeded in drawing blood—Miller's credibility had been damaged. And so when the next controversy involving her use of anonymous sources arose (when it was revealed that she had been willing to misleadingly cite Vice President Cheney's aide, Lewis Libby, as a "former Hill staffer," so as to obscure his role in an organized smear campaign against a critic of the Bush administration), the stage was set for her downfall. The final blows were delivered by two of her colleagues: Calame, the public editor, who publicly questioned whether she ought to continue at the *Times*; and Maureen Dowd, the prominent columnist, who published a scathing indictment of Miller's reporting techniques.[57] Shortly thereafter, Miller resigned from the *Times*.

Although the outcome in the Miller case provides an indication of how a competitive media environment can help guard against the misuse of anonymous sources, the fact is that members of the so-called mainstream media usually shy away from turning their firepower on each other. This point is underscored by the *Times*'s reaction to the *Post*'s decision to publish an internal *Times* email exchange in which Miller confirmed that Chalabi was the source for a number of her reports. When asked for his comment on the report, Andrew Rosenthal, an editor at the *Times*, rapped the *Post*'s media critic, Howard Kurtz, on the knuckles; in Rosenthal's view, it is "a pretty slippery slope" to publish reporters' private communications and "reveal whatever confidential sources they may or may not have."[58] Notably, this reaction produced no response from the *Post*, and there were no follow-up stories on the *Times*'s conduct.

What explains the media's lack of interest in probing the questionable use of sources? Is there something of a market failure here? Has the oligopolistic nature of the media market with its high barriers to entry made it difficult for new entrants to challenge the unscrupulous practices of the established players, all of whom, being equally complicit in the loose and easy use of anonymous sources, have no incentive to cast the first stone? This is not an implausible idea, especially in view of the growing concentration of media ownership, which dampens competition.[59] Nonetheless, what the exchange between the *Times* and the *Post* cited above indicates is that when it comes to anonymous sources, the more immediate obstacle to media regulation through media criticism is the esprit de corps of the American media establishment, whose practitioners have gladly taken to heart Justice Hugo Black's claim in the Pentagon Papers case that "the press was protected so that it could bare the secrets of government and inform the people."[60] This claim, we have seen, cannot stand. It ignores both the Framers' deep concern for energy and the fact that reporters, editors, and publishers have interests of their own. Nonetheless, as this doctrine has been trumpeted far and wide, members of the press have come to believe (or so they claim) that they really are serving the Constitution when they disclose classified information without shedding light on the motives of their sources.

Can we hope that the analysis presented here will alter the esprit de corps of the journalistic profession? There is little room for optimism. What incentive do media organizations have to hold themselves or each other accountable when the public's appetite for propriety pales in comparison to its appetite for controversy, especially when matters pertaining to the mysterious world of secret intelligence are at stake? Consider the fact that Risen's reporting in the Sterling case was originally meant to appear in the *Times*. When the CIA learned of Risen's intention to disclose the existence of Operation Merlin, it convinced the *Times* that his report ought to be withheld owing to the harm that might be caused to national security.[61] But then Risen simply went ahead and published the report in his *State of War*, which quickly ascended the best-seller lists, reportedly earning him royalties in the "low six figures."[62] This example suggests that there are simply too many ways in which irresponsibility on the part of journalists can prove profitable. Readers, book reviewers, and Pulitzer Prize committee members are only too willing to lap up and praise every embarrassing revelation that makes its way into print without sufficient regard for the broader principles that ought to govern how anonymous sources are used. And so long as journalists who make questionable decisions find themselves rewarded in this way, there is little reason to be optimistic that criticism from "armchair media ethicists" will give them sleepless nights.[63]

The foregoing analysis suggests that if we want a more responsible press, we ultimately need more discerning consumers. Yet there is little reason to believe that American consumers have an appetite for media criticism.[64] For this reason we must turn to civil society. In particular, we must hope that enterprising citizens will establish an independent and well-funded organization dedicated to scrutinizing media performance, which could name and shame reporters and editors who misuse anonymous sources, and the publishers who condone such behavior. This is not a new proposal, to be sure. It echoes what the Hutchins Commission had to say more than half a century ago.[65] Well aware that the media establishment might lack the wisdom to do what is in its own long-term interest, the commission's report recommended that civil society endow an "independent agency to appraise and report . . . upon the performance of the press."[66] Since this proposal proved unpopular with the media establishment, it has been allowed to fade from public consciousness. Now that we have understood why this proposal is so important—because there are so few viable means of regulating the press—let us hope that it will be revived.

But we must be more realistic than the Hutchins Commission was about the challenges that such an organization is likely to face. Since the press's ability to get away with irresponsible behavior stems from a lack of discernment on the part of consumers, presumably even a well-funded and independent body dedicated to media oversight will be hard-pressed to influence the public, and to thereby threaten the bottom line of irresponsible media organizations. Looking back, it is impossible not to be astonished by the optimism of the Hutchins Commission, which took the view that "a chain of educational FM stations could put before the public the best thought of America and could make many present radio programs look as silly as they are."[67] Today, this claim appears laughably naive. It is entertainment that the people want, and so the way forward lies in combating sensation with sensation.[68] We must also not forget that there will always be partisans willing to shelter, praise, and promote the reporters, editors, and publishers who serve their cause regardless (or perhaps because) of how they employ anonymous sources. Indeed these partisans will spare little effort in attacking media critics who expose how they benefit from the misuse of anonymous sources.[69] These dynamics will no doubt greatly blunt the effect of and interest in what media critics have to say. This does not mean, however, that we ought not to persevere. Politics is, after all, "a strong and slow boring of hard boards."[70]

The Dilemma of State Secrecy

We have identified two measures that, if adopted, might lessen the chance that rash or malicious disclosures of classified information will find their way into print. The president can make commitments that signal the credibility of his decisions and policies, and media critics can subject anonymously sourced reports to critical review. But these measures, we have seen, can go only so far. The president will not always be able to take everyone along when hard decisions need to be made, and even the threat of public censure will not always deter journalists from publishing rash or manipulative disclosures. But these outcomes are not certain. Constructive behavior will be more feasible in certain times and places: not every political season will feature frenzied partisanship. Therefore, scholars ought to examine, more thoroughly than we have done here, the conditions under which such constructive behavior might become feasible.

Still, there is a good chance that what Bickel called the "unruly contest" between the executive and the press will remain the norm for much of the time—with all the attendant disadvantages. In that case, the single most important step that can be taken to prevent this contest from becoming even more unruly is for the referees—namely, lawmakers and judges—to refrain from picking sides. This caution becomes necessary because the press and the executive will each occasionally try to knock out the other side. Should an unauthorized disclosure reveal a terrifying abuse of power, lawmakers and judges will be urged to make it easier for officials and journalists to expose classified information. Conversely, should an unauthorized disclosure cause a terrible loss of life and property, lawmakers and judges will be urged to make it easier for the president to clamp down on his subordinates and the press. What will make these cries especially powerful is that they will both call on the Constitution for support. The former will claim that only the First Amendment can save the United States from the transformation of the executive into an "imperial presidency," whereas the latter will voice outrage at the interlopers who have endangered the nation by trespassing on the president's prerogative under Article II. We should be under no illusion about what will follow should we succumb to these pleas. The harder we make it for the executive to keep secrets, the likelier the president is to retreat into the "black world" and to surround himself with an ever-smaller circle of advisers in the hope of thwarting leaks. Equally, the harder we make it for officials to voice their discontent, the likelier it becomes that they will route their disclosures via foreign media organizations, a practice that will make the problem of indiscriminate publication even more widespread than it already is.

Consequently, when crises occur, lawmakers and judges, to whom the executive and the press will turn for aid, must remember that we are safest when we allow the existing cat-and-mouse game to continue.[71] This is not, to be sure, a call for neutrality. Lawmakers and judges ought to revisit the rules when this is necessary to allow this "unruly contest" to continue. In particular, they ought to ensure that neither the press nor the executive is able to prevent the other from carrying out its core function. Should the government begin to hemorrhage state secrets, or should we witness a near cessation of unauthorized disclosures—circumstances that seem quite unlikely at present—then lawmakers and judges should consider intervening. What they must not do is fall into the trap of rewriting the rules under the assumption that one or the other side deserves to win the game. It ought to be clear to them by now, I hope, that the "unruly contest" between the press and the president is the product of historical, institutional, and political factors that cannot be easily swept aside, and that there is, at present, no better way to regulate the exercise of state secrecy.

The dilemma that state secrecy poses for democracy is here to stay then. To be clear, the dilemma we are left confronting is *not* the one we started out with. The original dilemma was the appearance of a mismatch between who *should* regulate state secrecy (lawmakers and judges) and who actually *does* (whistleblowers and leakers). To solve this dilemma, we said, we would need to show that lawmakers and judges could in fact oversee the executive, or we would need to prove that whistleblowers and leakers could be justified in disobeying the laws and regulations enacted to ensure secrecy.

This dilemma, we have seen, is not unsolvable. Admittedly, giving the final say over classification to lawmakers or judges does not grant confidence that state secrecy will not be used to conceal wrongdoing. This is because the secrecy that these regulators must operate under makes it difficult to ascertain whether they have been able to resist vested interests who have every incentive to corrupt them. But we have made progress here by showing that unauthorized disclosures need not *always* be illegitimate. Under certain circumstances, such disclosures will be compatible with democracy, namely, when they genuinely expose wrongdoing. As disclosures of this kind, and leaks in particular, are not easily suppressed, we have every reason to believe that democracies have available a legitimate *and* effective means of combating the abuse of state secrecy.

The true dilemma of state secrecy grows out of this success. Ironically, the irrepressibility of unauthorized disclosures also means that there is no easy way to distinguish between true and false alarms. Because of this, we must greet unauthorized disclosures with bated breath, aware that they may actually serve to *harm* democracy by weakening an elected president, by undercutting policies we might support if we knew the bigger picture, by fouling public deliberation with aspersions and half-truths, and by evading democratic accountability through the cunning use of anonymity. That we must rely on a regulatory weapon that has the tendency to backfire at least as often as it finds its target—*this* is the dilemma that state secrecy creates for democracy.

Perhaps it will be argued that this dilemma is not especially worrying. After all, contemporary democracies fall short in so many respects, suffused as they are with inequalities of income, opportunity, and capability. So why, then, should we be particularly troubled by the asymmetries of information embodied in and furthered by secrets and leaks? These asymmetries, it will be argued, ought to be placed on the reformer's to-do list and treated as another inequality that should be minimized as far as possible. But this stance fails to realize the depth of the dilemma. The analysis presented here does not encourage democratic reform; instead, it reveals the limits or even the futility of such reform. As such, it invites democracies—and democratic theory—to adopt a more realistic stance. It bids them to forgo platitudinous calls for "transparency" and quixotic endeavors to "tame the prince," and invites them to study instead how we can best ensure that executives and those who watch over them—the many princes of our secretive republics—will utilize responsibly the discretion they are bound to enjoy.

Notes

. . . .

Introduction
Who Watches the Watchers?

1. "Gonzales Defends NSA, Rejects Call for Prosecutor," *CNN*, January 17, 2005, online at http://tinyurl.com/9z2kq.

2. Dunn, *Democracy*, 185–86. Also see Russett, *Controlling the Sword*, 148; Manin, *The Principles of Representative Government*, 167–68; Dahl, *A Preface to Democratic Theory*, 73. Emerson, "Legal Foundations of the Right to Know," 14; Meiklejohn, *Free Speech*, 88–89; Meiklejohn, "The First Amendment Is an Absolute," 257; Emerson, "National Security and Civil Liberties," 80.

3. Thompson, "Democratic Secrecy," 192.

4. Schlesinger, *Imperial Presidency*, 447–49, emphasis added.

5. For an overview see Olmstead, *Challenging the Secret Government*, chap. 1.

6. For examples see Chambers, "Behind Closed Doors"; Elster, "Deliberation and Constitution Making"; Schepple, *Legal Secrets*; Bok, *Secrets*, chaps. 9–10.

7. Scholars often blur this distinction. For example, they often cite the secrecy of the Constitutional Convention as evidence of the Framers' acceptance of the need for state secrecy (see Hoffman, *Governmental Secrecy*, 20–24; Kitrosser, "Secrecy and Separated Powers," 526–27; Schoenfeld, *Necessary Secrets*, 60–62). Unfortunately, this reference clouds the issue because the convention's secrecy was intended to ensure candor rather than national security. Notice the conceptual difference in these cases. In the former information is meant to be kept from citizens, whereas in the latter information is kept from citizens only incidentally, i.e., in order to keep it from foreigners. This conceptual difference has normative and practical implications. Since the need for state secrecy depends on the scope and scale of national security threats, there can be no fixed rule about when declassification will occur. Civil secrecy, by contrast, is more accommodating of fixed rules, as in the case of the Federal Reserve, for example, which discloses minutes of its deliberations on a prescheduled basis.

8. Consider, for example, the oft-cited story about the "man-size" safe that Vice President Cheney reportedly used to store his documents (Barton Gellman and Jo Becker, "A Different Understanding with the President," *Washington Post*, June 24, 2007). Also see Savage, *Takeover*, chaps. 5 and 7.

9. For instance, see John Schwartz, "Obama Backs Off a Reversal on Secrets," *New York Times*, February 9, 2009; Karen De Young, "Secrecy Defines Obama's Drone War," *Washington Post*, December 19, 2011; Shane Harris, "Plugging the Leaks," *Washingtonian*, July 21, 2010.

10. Chris Buckley, "China Warns U.S. to Be Careful in Military Refocus," *Reuters*, January 9, 2012. Also see Friedberg, *A Contest for Supremacy*.

11. Scott Pelley, "Panetta: Iran Will Not Be Allowed Nukes," *CBS News*, December 19, 2011. Also see Sanger, *Confront and Conceal*, chaps. 6–9.

Chapter 1
The Problem

1. Schlesinger, *Imperial Presidency*, 317, 329.

2. Ibid., 326, 329.

3. Ibid., 326.

4. Ibid., 318; Commager, *The Defeat of America*, 87; Berger, *Executive Privilege*, 203–4; Hoffman, *Governmental Secrecy*, 12–13.

5. Kitrosser, "Secrecy and Separated Powers," 520–21; Pozen, "Deep Secrecy," 298; Stone, *Top Secret*, 1; Pallitto and Weaver, *Presidential Secrecy and the Law*, 1. Compare with Michael Doyle, "Misquoting Madison," *Legal Affairs*, July/August 2002.

6. For example, see Sofaer and Cox, *War, Foreign Affairs, and Constitutional Power*; Schoenfeld, *Necessary Secrets*; Rozell, *Executive Privilege*, chaps. 1–2; Knott, *Secret and Sanctioned*, chaps. 1–2. Also see *Halperin v. CIA*, 629 F. 2d 144, 154–62 (D.C. Cir. 1980); Casper, "Government Secrecy and the Constitution," 924–26; Hamilton and Inouye, *Report*, chap. 13.

7. On Greece see Starr, *Political Intelligence in Classical Greece*; Gerolymatos, *Espionage and Treason*; Russell, *Information Gathering in Classical Greece*. On Rome see Austin and Rankov, *Exploratio*; Sheldon, *Intelligence Activities in Ancient Rome*. On the Framers' sources see McDonald, *The American Presidency*, 74–89.

8. Evans, *The Principal Secretary of State*, 10–12.

9. Hutchinson, *Elizabeth's Spy Master*, appendix 1; Evans, *The Principal Secretary of State*, 8. Also see Beale, "A Treatise," 428; Hughes, "Nicholas Faunt's Discourse," 502.

10. Firth, "Thomas Scot's Account"; Evans, *The Principal Secretary of State*, 113.

11. Firth, "Thurloe and the Post Office," 532; Peacey, *Politicians and Pamphleteers*, 227.

12. Maffeo, *Most Secret and Confidential*, 4.

13. Knott, *Secret and Sanctioned*, 29, 35–37.

14. Hoffman, for instance, has written that republican movements of the seventeenth and eighteenth centuries "tended to brand governmental secrecy as an

outmoded relic of absolutist, aristocratical regimes" and thus saw it as "intrinsically wrong" (Hoffman, *Governmental Secrecy*, 12–13). Also see Kitrosser, "Secrecy and Separated Powers," 520–21.

15. Mattingly, *Renaissance Diplomacy*, 52–53, 57–58, 96–97. Also see Machiavelli, "Confidential Instructions," 422, 425.

16. Guicciardini, *Dialogue on the Government of Florence*, 61. This concern had also been raised in Bruni, *History of the Florentine People*, 3:247.

17. Harrington, *The Commonwealth of Oceana*, 126, 129–30.

18. Nedham, *The Excellencie of a Free State*, 100–102.

19. Milton, *The Ready and Easy Way to Establish a Free Commonwealth*, 22.

20. Hutcheson, *A Short Introduction to Moral Philosophy*, 248.

21. Hume, "Idea of a Perfect Commonwealth," 229.

22. Price, *Political Writings*, 79–80.

23. Paley, *The Principles of Moral and Political Philosophy*, 209.

24. Donaldson, *Machiavelli and the Mystery of State*, 132–39. For examples from the Renaissance see Guicciardini, *Maxims and Reflections*, 108; Botero, *The Reason of State*, 47.

25. Theodorus Verax [Clement Walker], *Relations and Observations*, 4–5, 118, 181–82. Also see Lewalski, *The Life of John Milton*, 275.

26. Milton, "A Defence of the People of England," 61; Nedham, *The Excellencie of a Free State*, 102–3. For precursors see Bodin, *On Sovereignty*, 60; Guicciardini, *The History of Italy*, 2:255.

27. Sidney, *Discourses Concerning Government*, 12–13, and chap. 2, sec. 23. Sidney was responding to Filmer, *Patriarcha and Other Writings*, 3–4.

28. Jeremy Bentham, "A Plan for an Universal and Perpetual Peace," in Bentham, *The Works*, 2:559.

29. Ibid., 560. Bentham is better known today for his later, more pragmatic, view of state secrecy, which is that publicity ought to be "suspended" where it is calculated to "favor the projects of an enemy" (Bentham, *Political Tactics*, 39. Also see Bentham, *Constitutional Code*, 1:165). More generally see Conway, "Bentham on Peace and War." For a wider survey of the literature see Hinsley, *Power and the Pursuit of Peace*, chaps. 1–5; Howard, *War and the Liberal Conscience*, chap. 1.

30. Hamilton, Madison, and Jay, *The Federalist*, 68 (hereafter cited as *The Federalist*); James Madison, "Universal Peace," in Madison, *The Writings*, 6:88.

31. Commager, for instance, has claimed that "the generation that made the nation thought secrecy in government one of the instruments of Old World tyranny and committed itself to the principle that a democracy cannot function unless the people are permitted to know what their government is up to" (*The Defeat of America*, 87). Also see Berger, *Executive Privilege*, 207.

32. Adams, "Thoughts on Government," 404.

33. Demophilus [George Bryan?], "The Genuine Principles of the Ancient Saxon or English Constitution," 353.

34. Parsons, "The Essex Result," 489.

35. Ford, *Journals of the Continental Congress*, 2:22, 3:342–43; Committee of Secret Correspondence to Arthur Lee, December 12, 1775, in Wharton, *Diplomatic Correspondence*, 2:63; Robarge, *Intelligence in the War of Independence*, 12.

36. In May 1784, Congress overwhelmingly approved a resolution moved by Thomas Jefferson declaring all diplomatic correspondence be "considered, at all times, as under an injunction of secrecy, except as to such parts of them as Congress shall, by special permission, allow to be published or communicated" (Ford, *Journals of the Continental Congress*, 26:331–32). For a critical view see Samuel Adams to Arthur Lee, April 21, 1783, in Adams, *The Writings*, 4:281–82.

37. *Articles of Confederation*, Article IX.

38. George Washington to James Madison, March 31, 1787, in Washington, *The Writings*, 11:132–33.

39. George Washington to Henry Knox, February 3, 1787, in Washington, *The Writings*, 11:111. For a broader survey see Wood, *The Creation of the American Republic*, chaps. 12–13.

40. *The Federalist*, 12–13. More generally see Tarcov, "The Federalists and Anti-Federalists on Foreign Affairs."

41. *The Federalist*, 68.

42. Ibid., 196.

43. Ibid., 342.

44. Parsons, "The Essex Result," 489–90.

45. Ibid., 501. This observation did not, however, lead Parsons to recommend eliminating secrecy. The preservation of society, he emphasized, required an executive capable of "secrecy and expedition." Instead, he advised that the "respective excellencies be united"—that a powerful executive be balanced by a wise and public-spirited legislative body (490–91).

46. Adams, "Election Sermon," 549.

47. *United States Constitution*, Article I, §5, Cl. 3.

48. Elliot, *Debates*, 2:469.

49. Ibid., 4:72.

50. Ibid., 2:76.

51. Ibid., 3:61.

52. Ibid., 84.

53. Ibid., 170.

54. Ibid., 233.

55. Ibid., 315–16.

56. Ibid., 331. Evidently the latter view carried the day, as none of the amendments proposed by the state conventions challenged Congress's right to employ secrecy as it saw fit. See, for example, ibid., 1:330, 336; 4:245.

57. Ibid., 3:409.

58. Ibid., 34. Also see Randolph, "Letter on the Federal Constitution," 267–68.

59. Jay, *The Correspondence*, 3:223, 226.

60. Farrand, *Records*, 1:70. However, Madison's *Notes* and William Pierce's *Notes* do not report Wilson mentioning secrecy (Farrand, *Records*, 1:65, 73–74).

61. According to King's *Notes*, John Dickinson argued on June 6 that "secrecy, vigour, and dispatch, are *not* the properties of [republics]—we cannot have them in that form." However, Madison's *Notes* report Dickinson saying that "secrecy, vigor, and dispatch are not *the principal properties* [required] in the executive," but that they are "important" nonetheless (Farrand, *Records*, 1:140, 144, emphases added).

62. Ibid., 112. Mason appears not to have delivered the speech he prepared on this subject, but others at the convention were doubtless aware of his views on the subject.

63. Ibid., 113.

64. Ibid., 66.

65. Ibid., 2:541–42.

66. Ellsworth, "The Landholder, VI," 163. For Wilson's views see Farrand, *Records*, 1:70. Also see Ramsay, *The History of the American Revolution*, 1:448.

67. Elliot, *Debates*, 4:104. Davie was echoing here arguments that Dickinson had made in the convention (Farrand, *Records*, 1:140, 144).

68. Farrand, *Records*, 3:269; 1:140, 144; *The Federalist*, 346.

69. *The Federalist*, 252.

70. Ibid., 123.

71. For an overview see Ford, *Journals of the Continental Congress*, 23:769–70, 792–93, 814–19, 863–65; David Howell to John Carter, October 16, 1782, in Smith, *Letters of Delegates to Congress*, 19:268.

72. Ford, *Journals of the Continental Congress*, 23:814–16.

73. Ibid., 868. For another sharp critique see Samuel Osgood to John Lowell, January 6, 1783, in Smith, *Letters of Delegates to Congress*, 19:545–46. But also see Jonathan Arnold to William Greene, December 8, 1782, in Smith, *Letters of Delegates to Congress*, 19:458–59, 492.

74. Ford, *Journals of the Continental Congress*, 23:812, 818.

75. Jonathan Arnold to William Greene, December 6, 1782, in Smith, *Letters of Delegates to Congress*, 19:458–59; David Howell to John Carter, January 6, 1783, in Smith, *Letters of Delegates to Congress*, 19:538; Jonathan Arnold to William Greene, January 8, 1783, in Smith, *Letters of Delegates to Congress*, 19:562. For the wider context see Polishook, *Rhode Island and the Union*, 88–92.

76. *The Federalist*, 263.

77. Ibid., 366–67.

78. Farrand, *Records*, 2:260.

79. Ibid., 538.

80. Ibid.

81. Ibid., 613. A similar proposal put forward on August 11 by Madison and John Rutledge had also been defeated by a large margin (ibid., 259–60).

82. Elliot, *Debates*, 3:509. Also see 4:263.

83. Ibid., 4:280. His colleague David Ramsay concurred. Should the House, he asked, be trusted with the power of making treaties? "When sixty-five men can keep a secret, they may" (Ramsay, "An Address," 376).

84. Elliot, *Debates*, 2:469. Also see Ramsay, "An Address," 376.

85. Elliot, *Debates*, 4:281, 265.

86. *The Federalist*, 314. Jay was not alone in making this point. See the views expressed by William Davie and John Pringle of North Carolina (Elliot, *Debates*, 4:119–20, 269).

87. *The Federalist*, 315.

88. Richardson, *Compilation*, 1:148–49, 446–47; 4:2530.

89. Rawle, *A View of the Constitution*, 160.

90. Story, *Commentaries on the Constitution,* 2:377.

91. For important examples see Hoffman, *Governmental Secrecy,* 152–58, 184–96.

92. *Annals of Congress,* 4th Cong., 1st Sess., 1796, 435–36.

93. Tucker, *View of the Constitution,* 111.

94. Kerr, *The Origin and Development of the United States Senate,* 40. Also see *Annals of Congress,* 3rd Cong., 1st Sess., 1794, 34, 47.

95. Richardson, *Compilation,* 1:152.

96. Ibid., 194–95.

97. For an exhaustive list see Department of Justice, "Is a Congressional Committee Entitled to Demand and Receive Information?" reprinted in *Hearing Before the Subcommittee on Constitutional Rights of the Committee of the Judiciary,* 85th Congress, 2nd Sess., 1958, Appendix No. 11, pt. 1; Ramsey and Daniels, "Selected Cases," appendix 17, pt. 1. For a magisterial analysis of these disputes see the two-volume Sofaer and Cox, *War, Foreign Affairs, and Constitutional Power;* and Rozell, *Executive Privilege.*

98. Kent, *Commentaries on American Law,* 1:285.

99. *Annals of Congress,* 4th Cong., 1st Sess., 1796, 773.

100. *Congressional Debates,* 19th Cong., 1st Sess., 1826, 174.

101. *Congressional Globe,* 28th Cong., 1st Sess., 1844, 98.

102. Ibid., 100.

103. *Annals of Congress,* 4th Cong., 1st Sess., 1796, 438, 773.

104. Von Holst, *The Constitutional and Political History of the United States,* 3:56.

105. *Congressional Debates,* 19th Cong., 1st Sess., 1826, 1265.

106. Ibid., 1270.

107. Ibid., 1282, 1272.

108. *Register of Debates in Congress* (Washington, DC: Gales and Seaton, 1825), vol. 7, 2nd Sess., 21st Cong., 233–34, 293–94. On the disclosure of the Jay Treaty see Dennis, "Stolen Treaties and the Press," 6–8. Also see Haynes, *The Senate of the United States,* 2:665.

109. *Register of Debates,* vol. 7, 2nd Sess., 21st Cong., 294.

110. Richardson, *Compilation,* 4:2416–17.

111. Von Holst, *The Constitutional and Political History of the United States,* 3:56. Another prominent scholar would write soon after that contests between Congress and the president "as to the right of the former to compel the furnishing to it of information as to specific matters" had "practically established that the President may exercise a full discretion as to what information he will furnish, and what he will withhold" (Willoughby, *The Constitutional Law of the United States,* 3:1167).

112. Consider here Alexis de Tocqueville's observation that the United States "has no enemies, and its interests are only rarely in contact with those of other nations." These conditions, he wrote, left the United States with relatively little need for the vigorous exercise of executive power. Though "the laws permit him to

be strong," Tocqueville famously wrote of the president, "circumstances keep him weak" (*Democracy in America*, 118–19, 123).

113. Lieber, *On Civil Liberty and Self-Government*, 130.

114. Ibid.

115. For an overview see McNeil, "The Evolution of the U.S. Intelligence Community," 5; Relyea, "The Evolution," 15.

116. O'Toole, *Honorable Treachery*, 106. Also see Sayle, "Historical Underpinnings of the U.S. Intelligence Community," 13–16. For a concise survey of the "secret agents" utilized during this period see Writson, *Executive Agents in American Foreign Relations*, 692–744. For an in-depth study of covert action during this period see Knott, *Secret and Sanctioned*.

117. O'Toole, *Honorable Treachery*, 106.

118. Relyea, "The Evolution," 2–3.

119. Sofaer, "Executive Power," 48.

120. Richardson, *Compilation*, 4:434. The statute establishing the Contingent Fund, which was used to finance intelligence activities, permitted the president to withhold details of an expenditure by issuing a certificate in lieu of receipts.

121. Sofaer, "Executive Power," 48. Polk, for example, had great difficulty conducting secret diplomacy with Mexico because the press kept exposing his initiatives. On this see Nelson, "Secret Agents and Security Leaks."

122. Silbey, *Storm over Texas*, 40–41, 45–46.

123. For an overview these battles see Smith, *War and Press Freedom*, chap. 5.

124. "The Philippine Murder Will Out," *Nation* 69, no. 1787 (1899): 236. For the cable see Pettigrew, *The Course of Empire*, 676–84. Also see Harold Martin, "The Manila Censorship," *Forum* 31 (1901).

125. Schlesinger, *Imperial Presidency*, 333.

126. *Senate Executive Journal*, 6:273.

127. According to one recent study, Congress asked more than two hundred journalists to reveal their sources, and incarcerated at least ten of them for failing to cooperate (see Kielbowicz, "The Role of News Leaks," 441). Those incarcerated included John Nugent of the *New York Herald* in 1848 and Zebulon White of the *New York Tribune* in 1871 (*Senate Executive Journal*, 7:372–73; *Congressional Globe*, 42nd Cong., 1st Sess., 1871, 885). Nugent's incarceration served only to reveal the depth of the problem after the *Herald* retaliated by publishing a list of "leaky Senators" who, it claimed, had served as sources for rival publications (on this see Marbut, *News from the Capital*, 92). The House had earlier used the same tactic against Nathaniel Rounsavell of the *Alexandria Herald* after President Madison's communiqué regarding an embargo prior to the War of 1812 found its way into that newspaper (*Annals of Congress*, 12th Cong., 1st Sess., 1812, 1255–74). On these episodes see Byrd, Hall, and Wolff, *The Senate*, 438–40; Dennis, "Stolen Treaties and the Press," 9–11.

128. Ritchie, *Press Gallery*, 166–69

129. Bryce, *The American Commonwealth*, 1:48.

130. Wilson, *Congressional Government*, xi. Also see Van Dyke, *The American Birthright and the Philippine Pottage*, 10.

131. Wilson, *Congressional Government*, xi–xii. For the original forecast see *Federalist* No. 8.

132. *Congressional Record*, 59th Cong., 1st Sess., 1906, 2130.

133. Ibid.

134. Ibid., 2142.

135. Ibid., 2143.

136. Mazzini, "On Publicity in Foreign Affairs," 169–76; Kossuth, "Speech before the Corporation of London," 40–41; Kossuth, *Select Speeches of Kossuth*, 16; Constant, "Principles of Politics," 232; Guizot, *General History of Civilization in Europe*, 1:238; Guizot, *The History of the Origins of Representative Government in Europe*, 63, 69, 80–81, 296. More generally see Hinsley, *Power and the Pursuit of Peace*, chap. 6; Howard, *War and the Liberal Conscience*, 30–38. Perhaps the most revered importer of these ideas was Alexis de Tocqueville, who famously observed that should the United States immerse itself in international affairs, there would be some major complications to contend with, because a democracy "is hardly capable of combining measures in secret and of patiently awaiting their result" (*Democracy in America*, 219).

137. Root, *The Effect of Democracy on International Law*, 8–9. Root was hardly alone in taking this view. For example, see Moore, *The Principles of American Diplomacy*, 426–27; Straus, "Democracy and Open Diplomacy," 157, 349; Van Dyke, *Fighting for Peace*, 3–4.

138. Wilson, "Address to the League to Enforce Peace," 118–19; Wilson, "Fourteen Points," 404. Also see Lippmann, *The Stakes of Diplomacy*, 195; Dewey, *Lectures in China*, 170; Dickinson, *The Choice before Us*, chap. 13; Alexander, *Liberty and Democracy*, 39; Reinsch, *Secret Diplomacy*, 178. For a broader discussion of the coalition in favor of this view see Lippmann, *The Political Scene*, 43.

139. Reinsch, *Secret Diplomacy*, 173–74.

140. Bryce, *Modern Democracies*, 371.

141. Ibid., 382.

142. Ibid. Also see Root, "A Requisite for the Success of Popular Democracy," 12.

143. Corwin, *The President's Control of Foreign Relations*, 205; Wright, *The Control of American Foreign Relations*, 368; Friedrich, *Constitutional Government and Politics*, 39, 418–19; Laski, *The American Presidency*, 177.

144. Lippmann, *Liberty and the News*, 59–60.

145. Ibid., 60.

146. Wright, *The Control of American Foreign Relations*, 371–72. Also see Sutherland, *Constitutional Power and World Affairs*, 125–28.

147. Poole, *The Conduct of Foreign Relations under Modern Democratic Conditions*, 160–68.

148. Lippmann, *Liberty and the News*, 64.

149. Lippmann, *Public Opinion*, 248–49, 398–402.

150. Ibid., 392.

151. Graves, "The Value of a Free Press," 175; Martin, "A Plea for an Uncensored Press," 364.

152. *Congressional Record*, 65th Cong., 1st Sess., 1917, 831–37, 1592, 1594, 1602–3, 1698–99, 1705–6, 1716, 1719, 1764, 1769, 1773–74, 1808, 2119–20, 3133, 3140. Also see Blasi, "The Checking Value."

153. *Congressional Record*, 65th Cong., 1st Sess., 1917, 833–34, 881, 1603, 1751, 1754, 1762, 2011, 2339, 3080, 3135. As Representative Charles B. Smith informed Representative Edwin Webb, the sponsor of the Espionage Act, it was wrong to assume that critics of the act were "opposed to restraining newspapers"; they were only "opposed to this particular way"—namely, using prior restraint (ibid., 1812).

154. Andrew, *For the President's Eyes Only*, 29; Relyea, "The Evolution," 75–119.

155. Godfrey, "Intelligence in the United States," 446–47. Also see O'Toole, *Honorable Treachery*, 345; Andrew, *For the President's Eyes Only*, 83–84.

156. Andrew, *For the President's Eyes Only*, 29, 133; Ransom, *Central Intelligence and National Security*, 52.

157. Stuart, *Creating the National Security State*, 7. "In contrast to our custom in the past of letting the intelligence function die when the war was over," Allen Dulles would later write, it was "allowed to grow to meet the ever-widening and more complex responsibilities of the time" (*Craft of Intelligence*, 46).

158. Morrissey, *Disclosure and Secrecy*, 8–19; Mayer, *With the Stroke of a Pen*, 142–48.

159. *Hearings Before the Subcommittee on Constitutional Rights of the Committee on the Judiciary*, United States Senate, 85th Cong., 2nd Sess., 1958, 271. Brownell was drawing here on Wolkinson, "Demands of Congressional Committees for Executive Papers."

160. For an overview see Chesney, "State Secrets," 1270–83.

161. *United States v. Reynolds*, 345 U.S. 1, 10–11 (1953).

162. Lasswell, *National Security and Individual Freedom*, 40.

163. Parks, "Secrecy and the Public Interest in Military Affairs," 36.

164. Dahl, *A Preface to Democratic Theory*, 70, 73; Coser, "Government by Secrecy," 59.

165. Chafee, *Government and Mass Communications*, 1:13–14.

166. Lasswell, *National Security and Individual Freedom*, 92.

167. Chafee, *Government and Mass Communications*, 14. Also see Goldschmidt, "Publicity, Privacy, and Secrecy," 414.

168. Rourke, *Secrecy and Publicity*, 6.

169. Gerth and Mills, *From Max Weber*, 233. Also see Coser, "Government by Secrecy," 58.

170. Defense Department Committee on Classified Information, *Report to the Secretary of Defense*, 7, 16

171. Commission on Government Security, *Report of the Commission on Government Security*, 688.

172. Chafee, *Government and Mass Communications*, 14.

173. Rourke, *Secrecy and Publicity*, 79.

174. Cross, *The People's Right to Know*; Wiggins, *Freedom or Secrecy*. For an overview of this history see Archibald, "The Early Years of the Freedom of Information Act."

175. Wiggins, "Government Operations and the Public's Right to Know," 188.

176. Moss, "Introduction," 101.

177. Hennings, "The Executive Privilege and the People's Right to Know," 116.

178. The Freedom of Information Act, Pub. L. 89-487, July 4, 1966, 80 Stat. 250 (codified as amended at 5 USC §552(6)(b)(1)).

179. Senate Committee on the Judiciary, *Clarifying and Protecting the Right of the Public to Information and for Other Purposes*, S. Rep 88-1219 (Washington, DC: GPO, 1964), 8.

180. *Hearings Before the Subcommittee on Constitutional Rights of the Committee on the Judiciary*, United States Senate, 85th Cong., 2nd Sess., 1958, Part 1, 455.

181. *McGrain v. Daugherty*, 272 U.S. 135, 175 (1927).

182. Smist, *Congress Oversees*, 5. Also see Ransom, "Congress and the Intelligence Agencies," 160; Johnson, "The CIA and the Question of Accountability," 180. David Barrett has argued that oversight during this period was informal rather than absent, but he concurs in the assessment that the "barons" in charge of oversight favored granting the president wide leeway on intelligence matters (Barrett, "An Early 'Year of Intelligence,'" 497–98. Also see Barrett, *The CIA and Congress*, 458–61; Snider, *The Agency and the Hill*, 6–11, 17–20).

183. R. W. Apple, "Lessons from the Pentagon Papers," *New York Times*, June 23, 1996. Also see Daniel Ellsberg, "Lying about Vietnam," *New York Times*, June 29, 2001. For a contrary view see Leslie H. Gelb, "Misreading the Pentagon Papers," *New York Times*, June 29, 2001.

184. Ely, *War and Responsibility*, 102.

185. Kutler, *The Wars of Watergate*, 218–22.

186. Seymour Hersh, "Huge C.I.A. Operation Reported in U.S. against Antiwar Forces, Other Dissidents in Nixon Years," *New York Times*, December 22, 1974.

187. Schlesinger, *Imperial Presidency*, 317, 329.

188. Bickel, *Morality of Consent*, 80–81.

189. Henkin, "The Right to Know and the Duty to Withhold," 280.

190. Schlesinger, *Imperial Presidency*, 344.

191. Ibid., 353, 349. Also see Halperin and Hoffman, "Secrecy and the Right to Know," 134.

192. Schlesinger, *Imperial Presidency*, 343, 357.

193. Kaiser, "Congress and the Intelligence Community," 282–84.

194. Ibid., 296–97.

195. Treverton, "Intelligence," 89.

196. Deyling, "Judicial Deference," 67.

197. Koh, *The National Security Constitution*, 167–69, 171–73.

198. Bok, *Secrets*, 174, 180.

199. Commission on Protecting and Reducing Government Secrecy, *Report of the Commission on Protecting and Reducing Government Secrecy*, S. Rep 105-2, 103rd Cong., xxii–xxiii.

200. Ibid., xxii.

201. Senate Select Committee on Intelligence, *Report of the Select Committee on Intelligence on the U.S. Intelligence Community's Prewar Intelligence Assessments on Iraq*, S. Rep. 108-301, 108th Cong., 485.

202. Ibid., 481.

203. Sheryl Gay Stolberg, "Senators Left Out of Loop Make Their Pique Known," *New York Times*, May 19, 2006.

204. Pallitto and Weaver, *Presidential Secrecy and the Law*, 16–17.

205. Chesney, "State Secrets," 1271. Also see Herman, *Taking Liberties*, 204–6.

206. Phil Mattingly and Hans Nichols, "Obama Pursuing Leakers Sends Warning to Whistle-Blowers," *Business Week*, October 17, 2012, online at http://tinyurl.com/d8hmyjf.

207. Stone, "Government Secrecy vs. Freedom of the Press," 195.

208. Schoenfeld, *Necessary Secrets*, 267; BeVier, "The Journalist's Privilege," 472.

Chapter 2
Should We Rely on Judges?

1. Aftergood, "Reducing Government Secrecy," 407–9; Wells, "State Secrets and Executive Accountability," 642; Pozen, "Deep Secrecy," 324.

2. Pozen, "Deep Secrecy," 270.

3. Wells, "State Secrets and Executive Accountability," 642–43.

4. Clark, "Architecture of Accountability," 395–96. Consider as well Lawrence Walsh's complaint that Attorney General Richard Thornburgh's support for the CIA's refusal to acknowledge the existence of intelligence facilities in Latin America—facilities that were already known to the public—thwarted the independent counsel's prosecution of a CIA official who had tried to cover up the Iran-Contra affair ("Secrecy and the Rule of Law," 587).

5. Thompson, *Political Ethics*, 23–24.

6. Luban, "Publicity Principle," 157. Also see Wells, "State Secrets and Executive Accountability," 646. For a discussion on the consequences of dissent see Shane, *Madison's Nightmare*, 106–7.

7. Thompson, *Political Ethics*, 24–26.

8. Ibid., 24.

9. "Declaration of Steven Aftergood," July 20, 2004, located online at http://tinyurl.com/8uyprjr.

10. *Aftergood v. Central Intelligence Agency*, 355 F. Supp. 2d 557, 563 (D.D.C. 2005). Also see *Wolf v. CIA*, 473 F. 3d 370, 375–76 (D.C. Cir. 2007); *Larson v. Department of State*, 565 F. 3d 857, 864–65 (D.C. Cir. 2009).

11. Armstrong, "The War over Secrecy." Also see *Armstrong v. Bush*, 924 F. 2d 282, 294–95 (D.C. Cir. 1991); *Kissinger v. Reporters Committee*, 445 U.S. 136, 167–68 (1980).

12. Stanley I. Kutler, "Bush's Secrecy Fetish," *Chicago Tribune*, January 2, 2002.

13. *EPA v. Mink*, 410 US 73, 80 (1973).

14. 5 U.S.C. § 552(b)(1); 5 U.S.C. § 552(b)(3).

15. For an overview see Department of Justice, "Statutes Found to Qualify under Exemption 3 of the FOIA," located online at http://www.justice.gov/oip/exemption3.pdf.

16. *EPA v. Mink*, 94–95.

17. *Freedom of Information Act Amendments*, H. Rep. No. 93-1380, 93rd Cong., 2nd Sess., 1974, 226, 229, emphases added.

18. *Weissman v. CIA*, 565 F.2d 692, 697 (D.C. Cir. 1977).

19. *Halperin v. CIA*, 148–50.

20. Ibid., 150.

21. *CIA v. Sims*, 471 US 159, 179 (1985), emphasis added.

22. *Fitzgibbon v. CIA*, 578 F.Supp. 704, 710–11 (D.D.C. 1983).

23. *Fitzgibbon v. CIA*, 911 F.2d 755, 762 (D.C. Cir. 1990).

24. Ibid., 766.

25. For an overview see Department of Justice, *Guide to the FOIA*, 141–58. Also see *Center for National Security Studies v. DOJ*, 331 F.3d 918, 927–28 (D.C. Cir. 2003).

26. *Ellsberg v. Mitchell*, 709 F.2d 51, 56 (D.C. Cir.1983).

27. *United States v. Reynolds*, 11, emphasis added.

28. Ibid., 8–9.

29. Ibid., 10.

30. Ibid.

31. Ibid.

32. Chesney, "State Secrets," 1287–88; Fisher, "The State Secrets Privilege," 397.

33. *Jabara v. Kelley*, 75 F.R.D. 475, 10 (E.D. Mich. 1977).

34. Ibid., 8.

35. Ibid., 11.

36. *Halkin v. Helms*, 598 F. 2d 1, 8 (D.C. Cir. 1978).

37. Ibid., 5.

38. Ibid., 8.

39. Ibid., 9, internal citations omitted, emphasis added. Here the *Halkin* court was drawing on *United States v. Nixon*, 418 US 683, 710 (1974).

40. *Kasza v. Browner*, 133 F. 3d 1159, 1163 (9th Cir. 1998).

41. Ibid., 1165.

42. Ibid., 1168.

43. Ibid., 1170.

44. *Mohamed v. Jeppesen Dataplan, Inc.*, 563 F. 3d 992, 1000 (9th Cir. 2009).

45. Ibid., 1003.

46. Ibid., 1003–4. Also see *In re United States*, 872 F. 2d 472, 478 (D.C. Cir. 1989).

47. *Mohamed v. Jeppesen Dataplan, Inc.*, 1006–7.

48. Ibid., 1007. A faint precedent can be discerned in *Spock v. United States*, 464 F. Supp. 510, 519–20 (S.D.N.Y. 1978).

49. *Mohamed v. Jeppesen Dataplan, Inc.*, 614 F. 3d 1070, 1090 (9th Cir. 2010).

50. Ibid.

51. Ibid., 1088.

52. Ibid., 1089.

53. Fisher, "The State Secrets Privilege," 408. Also see Weaver and Pallitto, "State Secrets and Executive Power," 90.

54. Chesney, "National Security Fact Deference," 1435.

55. *United States v. United States Dist. Court*, 407 US 297, 320–21 (1972). Also see Zagel, "The State Secrets Privilege," 886; Weaver and Pallitto, "State Secrets and Executive Power," 98; Berger, *Executive Privilege*, 370.

56. *Ellsberg v. Mitchell*, 58, fn. 31. Also see *United States v. United States Dist. Court*, 321.

57. *Sterling v. Tenet*, 416 F. 3d 338, 343–44 (4th Cir. 2005).

58. *Mohamed v. Jeppesen Dataplan, Inc.*, 1089.

59. *El-Masri v. United States*, 479 F. 3d 296, 305 (4th Cir. 2007). Also see *Ellsberg v. Mitchell*, 58, fn. 31.

60. Samaha, "Government Secrets," 958.

61. On this see Chesney, "National Security Fact Deference," 1410; Wald, "Two Unsolved Constitutional Problems," 760.

62. Yoo, "Courts at War," 597.

63. *Hepting v. AT&T Corp.*, 439 F. Supp. 2d 974, 996–97 (N.D. Cal. 2006); *ACLU v. NSA*, 438 F. Supp. 2d 754, 765–66 (E.D. Mich. 2006). Both the decisions were overturned on appeal.

64. Fuchs and Webb, "Greasing the Wheels of Justice," 3–5.

65. Fuchs, "Judging Secrets," 175; Pozen, "The Mosaic Theory," 677–78.

66. Chesney, "State Secrets," 1313–14. Also see Halstuk, "Holding the Spymasters Accountable," 131; "The Military and State Secrets Privilege," 580–81.

67. Fuchs and Webb, "Greasing the Wheels," 5.

68. Ibid.

69. Ibid.; Pozen, "The Mosaic Theory," 678.

70. "The Cost of Doing Your Duty," *New York Times*, October 11, 2006.

71. *Department of Navy v. Egan*, 484 US 518, 529–30 (1988). Also see Berkowitz and Goodman, *Best Truth*, xi.

72. *Weatherhead v. United States*, 157 F. 3d 735, 740 (9th Cir. 1998).

73. Ibid., 737.

74. Ibid., 742.

75. Ibid., 743.

76. Ibid.

77. *Weatherhead v. United States*, 112 F. Supp. 2d 1058, 1062–63 (E.D. Wash. 2000).

78. *Chicago & Southern Air Lines, Inc. v. Waterman SS Corp.*, 333 US 103, 111 (1948).

79. Electronic Privacy Information Center, "Foreign Intelligence Surveillance Act Court Orders 1979–2011," online at http://epic.org/privacy/wiretap/stats/fisa_stats.html. Also see Minnow, "The Lesser Evil," 2153–54; Telman, "Our Very Privileged Executive," 509–10.

80. "Justice in the Shadows," *New York Times*, September 12, 2002.

81. Ballou and McSlarrow, "Plugging the Leak"; Fenster, "The Opacity of Transparency," 947.

82. Yoo, "Courts at War," 598.

83. Ibid., 597–98

84. Frost, "The State Secrets Privilege"; Chesney, "State Secrets," 1311–12.

85. Wells, "Questioning Deference," 947–48; Telman, "Our Very Privileged Executive," 516–17; Frost, "The State Secrets Privilege," 1953.

86. Frost, "The State Secrets Privilege," 1960–61.

87. Gutmann and Thompson, *Democracy and Disagreement*, 103. The concepts of shallow and deep secrecy originated with Scheppele, *Legal Secrets*, 21–22.

88. Gutmann and Thompson, *Democracy and Disagreement*, 103. Also see Bok, *Secrets*, 202–3.

89. Gutmann and Thompson, *Democracy and Disagreement*, 121.

90. Ibid.

91. *Phillippi v. CIA*, 546 F. 2d 1009, 1013 (D.C. Cir. 1976).

92. *Cozen O'Connor v. U.S. Dep't of Treasury*, 570 F. Supp. 2d 749, 765 (E.D. Pa. 2008); *Vaughn v. Rosen*, 484 F. 2d 820, 826–27 (D.C. Cir. 1973).

93. *Phillippi v. CIA*, 1013.

94. *Vaughn v. Rosen*, 826–27.

95. *Phillippi v. CIA*, 1012.

96. Ibid., 1013. The D.C. Circuit eventually went on to clarify in *Hayden v. NSA* (1979) that judges have the authority to disclose "nonsensitive portions" of a classified affidavit. Note, however, that if judges believe they are not qualified to assess the potential harm stemming from the disclosure of classified *records*, then presumably they are unlikely to consider themselves qualified to assess the harm that may ensue from the disclosure of classified *affidavits* either.

97. Ibid.

98. *Hayden v. NSA*, 608 F.2d 1384-85 (D.C.Cir.1979). For recent examples see *Edmonds v. FBI*, 272 F. Supp. 2d 35, 46–47 (D.C. Dir. 2003); *Bassiouni v. CIA*, 392 F. 3d 244, 245 (7th Cir. 2004).

99. *Gardels v. CIA*, 689 F. 2d 1100, 1104 (D.C. Cir. 1982). Also see *Miller v. Casey*, 730 F.2d 773, 776 & 778 (D.C. Cir. 1984); *Hunt v. CIA*, 981 F. 2d 1116, 1119–20 (9th Cir. 1992); *Wolf v. CIA*, 473 F. 3d 370, 375–77 (D.C. Cir. 2007).

100. *Gardels v. CIA*, 1106.

101. *Halkin v. Helms*, 690 F. 2d 977, 992 (D.C. Cir. 1982).

102. Ibid., 992, emphasis added.

103. Ibid., 993.

104. *Ellsberg v. Mitchell*, 60–61.

105. Ibid., 63–64.

106. Ibid., 58.

107. Chesney, "National Security Fact Deference," 1411, 1419.

108. Pozen, "The Mosaic Theory," 679.

109. *United States v. United States Dist. Court*, 320.

110. Department of Justice, *Guide to the FOIA*, 147.

111. *Horn v. Huddle*, Civil Action No. 94–1756 (RCL) (D.D.C. 2009). Also see Del Quentin Wilber, "U.S. District Court Judge Rules Withheld CIA Info in Suit Was Fraud," *Washington Post*, July 21, 2009.

112. *Horn v. Huddle*, 2, fn. 2.

113. Kreimer, "The Freedom of Information Act and the Ecology of Transparency"; Kreimer, "Rays of Sunlight in a Shadow War." For a broader analysis see Rosenblum, "Constitutional Reason of State," 162–63; Herman, *Taking Liberties*, 211–14.

114. Kreimer, "The Freedom of Information Act and the Ecology of Transparency," 1077.

Chapter 3
Should We Rely on Congress?

1. Clark, "Architecture of Accountability," 404; Ransom, "A Half Century of Spy Watching," 188; Shane Harris, "The CIA Briefing Game," *National Journal*, June 6, 2009.

2. Snider, *Sharing Secrets*, 53–54.

3. Snider, *The Agency and the Hill*, chaps. 7–9. Also see Aberbach, *Keeping a Watchful Eye*, 40–41.

4. Johnson, "The CIA and the Question of Accountability," 190–91. Also see Commission on the Roles and Capabilities of the United States Intelligence Community, *Preparing for the 21st Century: An Appraisal of U.S. Intelligence* (Washington, DC: GPO: 1996).

5. Treverton, "Intelligence," 93.

6. Johnson, "Congress, the Iraq War, and the Failures of Intelligence Oversight," 188.

7. Johnson, "The Church Committee Investigation of 1975," 198.

8. *Final Report of the National Commission on Terrorist Attacks upon the United States*, 420–21; *Commission on the Roles and Capabilities of the United States Intelligence Community*, 144. Also see Posner, *Uncertain Shield*, 174–76.

9. Smist, *Congress Oversees*, 91–93. Also see Ott, "Partisanship and the Decline of Intelligence Oversight," 87.

10. Devins, "Congressional-Executive Information Access Disputes," 108–9, 121–22. Also see Schmitt, "Executive Privilege," 178; Rozell, *Executive Privilege*, 160–64.

11. Crockett, "Executive Privilege," 227. Also see Fisher, *Congressional Access to Executive Branch Information*.

12. Thompson, *Political Ethics*, 26.

13. Department of Justice, *Legal Authorities Supporting the Activities of the National Security Agency Described by the President* (Washington, DC, January 19, 2006), 2, online at http://www.justice.gov/opa/whitepaperonnsalegalauthorities.pdf.

14. Thompson, *Political Ethics*, 29.

15. Devins, "Congressional-Executive Information Access Disputes," 109–16.

16. Bishop, "The Executive's Right to Privacy," 485. Also see Patterson, *To Serve the President*, 80.

17. Holt, *Secret Intelligence and Public Policy*, 226, 234; Sofaer, "Executive Privilege," 293–94.

18. Cited in Halperin and Hoffman, *Top Secret*, 99.

19. Banks and Raven-Hansen, *National Security Law and the Power of the Purse*, 178.

20. *Hearings Before the Subcommittee on Intergovernmental Relations of the Committee on Government Operations*, 94th Cong., 1st Sess., 1975, 122–23 (Statement of Antonin Scalia).

21. Koh, *The National Security Constitution*, 59–60; Smist, *Congress Oversees*, 122–23.

22. Johnson, "A Shock Theory," 345.

23. Kean and Hamilton, *Without Precedent*, chap. 4.

24. Ibid., 90.

25. Aberbach, *Keeping a Watchful Eye*, 87–88.

26. Snider, *Sharing Secrets*, 17, 35–36.

27. The term "executive privilege" refers to the right of the president to withhold certain kinds of official information from the other branches of government. This includes information pertaining to internal deliberations (increasingly referred to as a "deliberative process privilege"), which may be withheld from both of the other branches, and information concerning national security, which may be withheld from Congress alone (national security information is withheld from the courts under a different title—the "state secrets privilege"). I focus here solely on the latter aspect of executive privilege, i.e., the president's right to withhold national security information from Congress. For an overview of the different aspects of the privilege see Breckenridge, *The Executive Privilege*, 12; Sagar, "Executive Privilege."

28. On precedent see Brownell, "Memorandum," appendix 13, 272; Rozell, *Executive Privilege*, 28. For a rebuttal see Schwartz, "A Reply to Mr. Rogers," 468; Prakash, "A Critical Comment," 1180. On original intent see Rozell, *Executive Privilege*, 19–28; Schmitt, "Executive Privilege," 173–77. For a rebuttal see Prakash, "A Critical Comment," 1173–77; Berger, *Executive Privilege*, chap. 6; Kitrosser, "Secrecy and Separated Powers," 510–22. On implied powers see Crockett, "Executive Privilege," 217; Rozell, *Executive Privilege*, 23–26; Dixon, "Congress, Shared Administration and Executive Privilege," 130–34. For a rebuttal see Fisher, *The Politics of Executive Privilege*, 233; Prakash, "A Critical Comment," 1151–69.

29. *United States v. A.T&T*, 567 F.2d 121 (D.C. Cir. 1977); *United States v. A.T&T*, 551 F.2d 384 (D.C. Cir. 1976). Also see Fein, "Access to Classified Information," 835–43; Rozell, *Executive Privilege*, 81–82; Fisher, *The Politics of Executive Privilege*, 246–47. There is some support for the executive privilege in two cases. In the Pentagon Papers case Justice Potter Stewart opined that "it is the constitutional duty of the Executive—as a matter of sovereign prerogative and not as a matter of law as the courts know law—through the promulgation and enforcement of executive regulations, to protect the confidentiality necessary to

carry out its responsibilities in the fields of international relations and national defense" (*New York Times Co. v. United States*, 403 U.S. 713, 729–30 (1971)). And in *Department of Navy v. Egan* the court declared that the president's authority to control information bearing on national security flows primarily from his role as commander-in-chief, "and exists quite apart from any explicit congressional grant" (484 U.S. 518, 527 (1988)). However, these declarations are far from conclusive. As Louis Fisher has pointed out, neither case explicitly addresses the question of whether the Constitution precludes Congress from seeking unrestricted access to national security information. Moreover, opinions in both cases indicate that Congress is entitled to make laws regulating the classification system. Such laws could presumably include provisions granting members of Congress unrestricted access to national security information (Fisher, *The Politics of Executive Privilege*, 242–43. Also see Brooks, *The Protection of Classified Information*, 2).

30. Rogers, "Constitutional Law," 1011; *Kilbourne v. Thompson*, 103 U.S. 191 (1880).

31. Rogers, "Constitutional Law," 1011–12. Also see *Hearings Before the Subcommittee on Intergovernmental Relations of the Committee on Government Operations*, 108–10 (Statement of Antonin Scalia).

32. Schwartz, "A Reply to Mr. Rogers," 526.

33. Crockett, "Executive Privilege," 217. Also see Rozell, *Executive Privilege*, 23–26; Schmitt, "Executive Privilege," 162–76.

34. Crockett, "Executive Privilege," 211.

35. *The Federalist*, 342. Also see *The Federalist*, 314.

36. Wharton, *Diplomatic Correspondence*, 2:151–52. Franklin and Morris had just discovered that word of Congress's plan to send Franklin and others to negotiate a treaty of alliance with France had begun to circulate, less than a week after Congress had specifically enjoined its members from discussing the particulars of the mission lest the British take measures to intercept the delegation (Ford, *Journals of the Continental Congress*, 5:827. Also see Committee of Secret Correspondence to Silas Deane, October 2, 1776, in Smith, *Letters of Delegates to Congress*, 5:288–89). For additional examples see John Jay to Robert Morris, October 6, 1776, in Wharton, *Diplomatic Correspondence*, 2:165; George Washington to James Duane, May 14, 1780, in Washington, *The Writings*, 8:265–66.

37. *Hearings Before the Subcommittee on Separation of Powers of the Committee on the Judiciary*, 92nd Cong., 1st Sess., 1971, 424 (Statement of William Rehnquist).

38. Posner and Vermeule, "The Credible Executive," 885; Pozen, *Deep Secrecy*, 331.

39. Wilson, *The Works*, 1:294.

40. For an overview see Kaiser, *Protection of Classified Information by Congress*.

41. *Gravel v. United States*, 408 U.S. 606, 626 (1972). In 1975 Senator Gravel read out excerpts from a classified memorandum on the floor of the Senate before a closed session could reach a decision on whether he ought to be allowed to do so (Hamilton and Inouye, *Report*, 577).

42. Smist, *Congress Oversees*, 136. There are numerous examples of this variety. See Barrett, "An Early 'Year of Intelligence,'" 476 (disclosure of intelligence on Soviet space capabilities); Crabb and Holt, *Invitation to Struggle*, 171 (disclosure of covert operations in the Congo); Jake Tapper, "Bush Scolds Congress," *Salon*, October 9, 2001, online at http://tinyurl.com/96h5pu9 (disclosure of plans for the invasion of Afghanistan).

43. As Jeremy Bentham observes, in a parliamentary setting, "whatever the conduct of an individual may be, he will almost always be secure in the suffrages of one party, in opposition to the other" (*Political Tactics*, 30).

44. "Congressman Avoids Inquiry into U.S.-Iraq Disclosures," *New York Times*, September 20, 1992; Clark, "Congress's Right to Counsel in Intelligence Oversight," 945; Martin Tolchin, "Inquiry into U.S. Aid to Iraq Urged," *New York Times*, May 18, 1992. The first censure issued in the Senate's history is instructive on this front. In 1811 Senator Timothy Pickering introduced during an open session a letter that President Jefferson had previously communicated to the Senate in confidence. Pickering introduced the letter (which argued that West Florida was not included in the Louisiana Purchase) with the intention of embarrassing President Madison, who had recently proclaimed West Florida a part of the Louisiana Purchase. The Democratic-Republicans retaliated by seizing on Pickering's use of confidential material and subsequently moved to censure him on the grounds that "if the President could not have some degree of security that documents confidentially communicated to the Congress. . . . would not be disclosed; must not all reliance on the Senate be lost?" To this Pickering's Federalist colleagues replied that he was "not the first" to use confidential documents to make a point in a Senate debate. "What we have acquiesced in when done by others, should be tolerated in him," said Senator Samuel Dana (*Annals of Congress*, 11th Cong., 3rd Sess., 1811, 67). The Democratic-Republicans piously voiced horror at this line of reasoning. "If it is a common practice to divulge secret proceedings," Senator Richard Brent declared, "it is necessary to put a stop to a course so disgraceful and ruinous to the country" (ibid., 72). For an overview of this episode see Hoffman, *Governmental Secrecy*, 247–48.

45. Cited in Greenstein, *The Hidden-Hand Presidency*, 205.

46. Kitrosser, "Congressional Oversight of National Security Activities," 1075; Pozen, "Deep Secrecy," 331. In fact Congress has struggled with unauthorized disclosures from its earliest days. Following disclosures by Senators Steven Mason in 1795, Thomas Pickering in 1811, and Benjamin Tappan in 1844, the Senate resolved that members who divulged confidential documents were liable to "suffer expulsion" (*Senate Executive Journal*, 6:273). But this threat was soon shown to be utterly ineffective. In 1848 and 1854, two treaties with Mexico under consideration in the Senate were leaked. Then again in 1869 and 1871, the confidential correspondence of John Hale, the United States' minister in Spain, and the Treaty of Washington with Great Britain were disclosed (McClendon, "Violations of Secrecy," 38–40, 43–44; *Congressional Globe*, 41st Cong., Special Sess., 1869, 30–31). The Senate responded to these violations of its "honor" by attempting to trace the perpetrators, but to little avail. In 1884, for example, no fewer than five

confidential treaties found their way into the press (McClendon, "Violations of Secrecy," 45–46. Also see Haynes, *The Senate of the United States*, 2:667–68). Not surprisingly, then, by the close of the nineteenth century observers were writing that "whatever the [Founding] Fathers may have intended, the executive sessions of the Senate have come to be mere farces," as they are "always reported, and even more fully than the open debates" (Reinsch, *Readings on American Federal Government*, 179).

47. Koh, *The National Security Constitution*, 173; Fisher, *The Politics of Executive Privilege*, 250. Also see Berger, *Executive Privilege*, 288–89.

48. Hyde, "Leaks and Congressional Oversight," 147.

49. Knott, *Secret and Sanctioned*, 178.

50. Johnson, "Intelligence and the Challenge of Collaborative Government," 180.

51. Knott, *Secret and Sanctioned*, 178.

52. Bishop, "The Executive's Right to Privacy," 486.

53. Ibid.

54. Wheeler and Healy, *Yankee from the West*, 387–88.

55. Smist, *Congress Oversees*, 134.

56. Woodward, *Veil*, 136–38.

57. Ibid., 138.

58. Smist, *Congress Oversees*, 316–17; "Loose Lips Sink Trust in Congress," *Chicago Tribune*, July 16, 1987.

59. Smist, *Congress Oversees*, 316; Dorothy Collin, "Aspin, Michael Trade Barbs on Gulf-Escort Disclosures," *Chicago Tribune*, July 16, 1987.

60. Calhoun, "Confidentiality and Executive Privilege," 178. For additional examples see Hamilton and Inouye, *Report*, chap. 13; Clark, "Congress's Right to Counsel in Intelligence Oversight," 941–49.

61. Colton, "Speaking Truth to Power," 599–600.

62. "Keeping Secrets," 906.

63. Koh, *The National Security Constitution*, 167–69, 171–73; Kitrosser, "Congressional Oversight of National Security Activities," 1071–72. Also see Berger, *Executive Privilege*, 291–93.

64. Allan Lengel and Dana Priest, "Investigators Conclude Shelby Leaked Message," *Washington Post*, August 5, 2004.

65. Graham and Nussbaum, *Intelligence Matters*, 140.

66. Letter from Senator Jay Rockefeller to Vice President Richard Cheney, July 17, 2003, online at http://www.fas.org/irp/news/2005/12/rock121905.pdf. Also see Nancy Pelosi, "The Gap in Intelligence Oversight," *Washington Post*, January 15, 2006; Clark, "'A New Era of Openness?'" 319; Pfiffner, *Power Play*, 176.

67. Halperin and Hoffman, *Top Secret*, 98–100.

68. Kitrosser, "Congressional Oversight of National Security Activities," 1072.

69. "About That Rebellion," *New York Times*, March 11, 2006.

70. Ackerman, "The Emergency Constitution," 1051.

71. Ibid., 1052. Also see Levinson and Pildes, "Separation of Parties, Not Powers," 2374–75.

72. Scheppele, "We Are All Post-9/11 Now," 619. Also see Katyal, "The Internal Separation of Powers," 2341–42.

73. Scheppele, "We Are All Post-9/11 Now," 618–19.

74. Minnow, "The Constitution as Black Box during Emergencies," 597–98. Also see Chanley, "Trust in Government in the Aftermath of 9/11," 469–83.

75. For an overview of the difficulties that can arise see Blechman and Ellis, *The Politics of National Security*, 151; Johnson, *Secret Agencies*, 136.

76. Crabb and Holt, *Invitation to Struggle*, 172–73.

77. Smist, *Congress Oversees*, 265–66.

78. Quoted in Blechman and Ellis, *The Politics of National Security*, 156.

79. Scott Shane, "Democrats Say C.I.A. Deceived Congress," *New York Times*, July 8, 2009; Scott Shane, "News of Surveillance Is Awkward for Agency," *New York Times*, December 22, 2005.

80. For example, see David Gordon Smith and Kristen Allen, "Electronic Surveillance Scandal Hits Germany," *Der Spiegel*, October 10, 2011; Matthias Gebauer, "Interior Ministry Ordered Destruction of Intelligence Files," *Der Spiegel*, July 19, 2012.

81. Smist, *Congress Oversees*, 176–86; Knott, *Secret and Sanctioned*, 176–77; Block and Rivkin, "The Battle to Control the Conduct of Foreign Intelligence and Covert Operations," 327, 344. Also see Smist, *Congress Oversees*, 110.

82. For example, see Helms, *Empire for Liberty*, 69–70.

83. Commission to Assess the Ballistic Missile Threat to the United States, *Report*; Eric Schmitt, "Panel Says U.S. Faces Risk of a Surprise Missile Attack," *New York Times*, July 16, 1998.

84. Michael Dobbs, "How Politics Helped Redefine Threat," *Washington Post*, January 14, 2002; Diamond, *The CIA and the Culture of Failure*, 251–60; Graham, *Hit to Kill*, 47–51; Hartung, *Prophets of War*, 200–202.

85. Orman, *Presidential Secrecy and Deception*, 207.

86. Pallitto and Weaver, *Presidential Secrecy*, 215–16; Berger, *Executive Privilege*, 381–82; Dorsen and Shattuck, "Executive Privilege, the Congress and the Courts," 174–75.

87. *United States v. A.T&T*, 551 F.2d 384, 385 (D.C. Cir. 1976); *United States v. AT&T*, 567 F.2d 121, 123 (D.C. Cir. 1977).

88. *United States v. AT&T*, 123.

89. Smist, *Congress Oversees*, 319–20.

90. Schmitt, "Executive Privilege," 181–82.

91. *United States v. AT&T*, 123.

92. See the discussion in Cox, *The Myths of National Security*, 161–65.

93. Snider, "Congressional Oversight of Intelligence after September 11," 242–46.

94. I owe this formulation to Dennis Thompson.

95. Minnow, "The Constitution as Black Box during Emergencies," 604–5.

96. Kitrosser, "Congressional Oversight of National Security Activities," 1085–86.

97. Clark, "Congress's Right to Counsel in Intelligence Oversight," 958–59.

98. McCubbins and Schwartz, "Congressional Oversight Overlooked." Also see Johnson, "A Shock Theory," 345.

Chapter 4
Should the Law Condone Unauthorized Disclosures?

1. Information Security Oversight Office, *Briefing Booklet: Classified Information Nondisclosure Agreement* (Washington, DC: NARA, 2001), 5. Also see 32 C.F.R. 2003.

2. *National Federation of Federal Employees v. United States*, 695 F. Supp. 1196, 13 (D.D.C. 1988).

3. Ibid., 14.

4. 50 U.S.C. § 403(d)(3). Also see Headley, "Secrets, Free Speech, and Fig Leaves," 75.

5. Marchetti and Marks, *The CIA and the Cult of Intelligence*.

6. *United States v. Marchetti*, 466 F.2d 1309, 32 (4th Cir. 1972).

7. Ibid., 31. Also see *Knopf v. Colby*, 509 F. 2d 1362, 1370 (4th Cir. 1975).

8. Snepp, *Decent Interval*.

9. *Snepp v. United States*, 444 U.S. 507, 516, fn. 3 (1980). Also see *McGehee v. Casey*, 718 F.2d 1137 (D.C. Cir. 1983); *Stillman v. CIA*, 517 F. Supp. 2d 32 (D.D.C. 2007); *Berntsen v. CIA*, 05-1482 (D.D.C. 2009).

10. 18 U.S.C. § 952; 18 U.S.C. § 798(a); 50 U.S.C. § 421(a); 42 U.S.C. § 2274(b), 2014.

11. 18 U.S.C. §641; 18 U.S.C. § 793. In particular, §793(d) of the Espionage Act threatens up to ten years imprisonment for any person who, being "lawfully" entrusted with documents or information "relating to the national defense . . . willfully communicates . . . the same to any person not entitled to receive it."

12. *United States v. Morison*, 844 F. 2d 1057, 61 (4th Cir. 1988).

13. Ibid., 31, 61. More generally see Dmitrieva, "Stealing Information."

14. 18 U.S.C. § 793(g). For an overview see Vladeck, "Inchoate Liability and the Espionage Act," 231–32; Lee, "Probing Secrets." In a recent leak investigation, a Fox News reporter was described as a "co-conspirator," but he was not actually charged as such. On this see "Another Chilling Leak Investigation," *New York Times*, May 21, 2013.

15. 18 U.S.C. § 793(e).

16. Recently in *United States v. Rosen*, 445 F. Supp. 2d 629 (E.D. Va. 2006), two lobbyists were prosecuted under the Espionage Act after they sought and received classified information from a Defense Department employee. When the lobbyists sought cover under the First Amendment, Judge Thomas Ellis responded that while "the collection and discussion of information about the conduct of government by defendants and others in the body politic is indispensable to the healthy functioning of a representative government," it remains the case that "both common sense and the relevant precedent point persuasively to the

conclusion that the government can punish those outside of the government for the unauthorized receipt and deliberate retransmission of information relating to the national defense." As this case involved neither reporters nor information that revealed wrongdoing, its implication for the kind of case we are interested in here is unclear. But see Lee, "Probing Secrets," 171–72; Epstein, "Balancing National Security and Free-Speech Rights," 504–5; "Prosecuting the Press," 1013–15.

17. *Branzburg v. Hayes*, 408 U.S. 665, 24 (1972).

18. Siegel, "Trampling on the Fourth Estate," 507. Also see 28 C.F.R. § 50.10.

19. Lee, "Probing Secrets," 162. Prosecutors can also utilize secret subpoenas, as they did in a recent investigation into a leak to the Associated Press. On this see Charlie Savage and Leslie Kaufman, "Phone Records of Journalists Seized by U.S.," *New York Times*, May 13, 2013.

20. *In Re Special Counsel Investigation*, 332 F. Supp. 2d 26 (D.D.C. 2004); *In Re Special Counsel Investigation*, 338 F. Supp. 2d 16 (D.D.C. 2004).

21. Pearlstine, *Off the Record*, chap. 6.

22. *In Re Grand Jury Subpoena*, 397 F.3d 964, 968–72 (D.C. Cir. 2005). In *New York Times Company v. Gonzales*, 459 F.3d 160, 38–40, 48 (2nd Cir. 2007), and *United States v. Sterling*, No. 1:10cr485, 2011 WL 4852226 at 13–15 (E.D. Va. 2011), support has been voiced for the idea that there is a qualified reporter's privilege based in common law. But even in these cases it has been affirmed that a qualified privilege will be overcome when the information sought from reporters is vital to the prosecution's case and is not obtainable from other sources.

23. *Near v. Minnesota* 283 U.S. 697, 29 (1931).

24. *New York Times Co. v. United States*, 714.

25. Ibid., 720.

26. Ibid., 730, 732.

27. *United States v. Progressive*, 486 F. Supp. 5, 7 (W.D. Wis. 1979).

28. 42 U.S.C. § 2280.

29. *United States v. Progressive*, 467 F. Supp. 990, 994 (W.D. Wis. 1979).

30. Ibid., 1000.

31. See the discussion in *New York Times Co. v. United States*, 721, 730, 734–38, 745, 752, 754. Also see 18 U.S.C. § 794(b); 18 U.S.C. § 797.

32. Ibid., 738–39. For a recent affirmation of Justice White's position see *United States v. Rosen*, 638–39.

33. For example, see *New York Times Co. v. United States*, 730, 745, 751, 759.

34. Ibid., 721.

35. The scholarly literature has reproduced this dispute. For instance, Harold Edgar and Benno Schmidt have argued that the Espionage Act was never intended to be applied to publishers and that appearances to the contrary are the result of poor draftsmanship, whereas Richard Posner has argued that publication is "obviously" a form of communication, and that therefore the publication of damaging leaks ought to be treated as a violation of the Espionage Act (see Edgar and Schmidt, "The Espionage Statutes and the Publication of Defense Information," 1033; Posner, *Not a Suicide Pact*, 109).

36. On this see Interdepartmental Group on Unauthorized Disclosures of Classified Information, *Report*; Hurt, "Leaking National Security Secrets," 9–18.

37. Bruce, "How Leaks of Classified Intelligence Help U.S. Adversaries," 400; Commission on the Intelligence Capabilities of the United States Regarding Weapons of Mass Destruction, *Report*, 381. Also see Hamilton and Inouye, *Report*, 578.

38. Stanley Johnston, "Navy Had Word of Jap Plan to Strike at Sea," *Chicago Tribune*, June 7, 1942.

39. Frank, "The United States v. the *Chicago Tribune*." Also see Schoenfeld, *Necessary Secrets*, 135–39.

40. Aid, *The Secret Sentry*, 152–53; Andrew, *For the President's Eyes Only*, 359.

41. Katherine Graham, "Safeguarding Our Freedoms As We Cover Terrorist Acts," *Washington Post*, April 19, 1986. For additional examples see David Ignatius, "When Does Blowing Secrets Cross the Line?" *Washington Post*, July 2, 2002; Cater, "News and the Nation's Security," 26–27; Xanders, "A Handyman's Guide to Fixing National Security Leaks," 783; Abel, *Leaking*, 36.

42. Bovens, *The Quest for Responsibility*, 150–51, 195.

43. Dallek, *Nixon and Kissinger*, 350–52; Isaacson, *Kissinger*, 380–90. For another episode see Feldstein, *Poisoning the Press*, chap. 8.

44. Kitrosser, "Classified Information Leaks," 885; Cheh, "Judicial Supervision of Executive Secrecy," 731; Ballou and McSlarrow, "Plugging the Leak," 885.

45. Stone, "Free Speech and National Security," 961; Coliver, "Commentary on the Johannesburg Principles," 63–68.

46. Katz, "Government Information Leaks," 121.

47. Kitrosser, "Classified Information Leaks," 896; Ballou and McSlarrow, "Plugging the Leak," 885; Stone, "Free Speech and National Security," 961.

48. Borjesson, *Feet to the Fire*, 211.

49. Nelson, *U.S. Government Secrecy*, 23. Also see Greg Miller, "CIA Looks to Los Angeles for Would-Be Iranian Spies," *Los Angeles Times*, January 15, 2002.

50. Nelson, *U.S. Government Secrecy*, 23. For another example see Aldrich, "Regulation by Revelation," 31–32.

51. *Knopf v. Colby*, 1368.

52. Katz, "Government Information Leaks," 145; Stone, *War and Liberty*, 154.

53. As Charles Fried has recently observed, "We would have left the rule of law far behind if any individual could take it upon himself to break the law in defense of his personal view of what the Constitution demands" (Charles Fried, "Why Leakers Should Be Punished," *New York Times* June 18, 2012). Also see Bovens, *The Quest for Responsibility*, 167–68.

54. BeVier, "The Journalist's Privilege," 475.

55. Nelson, *U.S. Government Secrecy*, 25. Also see Tim Weiner, "CIA Reexamines Hiring of Ex-Terrorist as Agent," *New York Times*, August 21, 1995.

56. As the media critic Renata Adler has observed, in recent decades the role played by anonymous disclosures has come to be "precisely reversed." Where once the purpose of providing sources with confidentiality was to allow the powerless to speak up without fearing retaliation from the powerful, she writes, more recently

"almost every 'anonymous source' in the press . . . has been an official of some kind, or a person in the course of a vendetta speaking from a position of power" (*Canaries in the Mineshaft*, 27). Also see Overholser, "The Seduction of Secrecy," 35–36; Klaidman and Beauchamp, *The Virtuous Journalist*, 197–99; Abel, *Leaking*, 61.

57. On the Lee case see Matthew Purdy and James Sterngold, "The Prosecution Unravels: The Case of Wen Ho Lee," *New York Times*, February 5, 2001. On the Hatfill case see Eric Lichtblau, "Scientist Officially Exonerated in Anthrax Attacks," *New York Times*, August 8, 2008; Nicholas D. Kristof, "Media's Balancing Act," *New York Times*, August 28, 2008. On the Plame case see Barton Gellman and Dafna Linzer, "A 'Concerted Effort' to Discredit Bush Critic," *Washington Post*, April 9, 2006; Maureen Dowd, "Woman of Mass Destruction," *New York Times*, November 10, 2005.

58. Eric Boehlert, "How the New York Times Helped Railroad Wen Ho Lee," *Salon*, September 21, 2000, online at http://tinyurl.com/8urxu6x. The relevant cases are *Lee v. Department of Justice*, 413 F.3d 53 (D.C. Cir. 2005); *Hatfill v. Ashcroft*, 404 F. Supp. 2d 104 (D.D.C. 2005); *In Re Special Counsel Investigation*, 332 F. Supp. 2d 26 (D.D.C. 2004).

59. Michael Gordon and Judith Miller, "U.S. Says Hussein Intensifies Quest for A-Bomb Parts," *New York Times*, September 8, 2002. For other cases see Finnegan, *No Questions Asked*, chap. 4; Hoyle, *Going to War*, chap. 16. More generally see Isikoff and Corn, *Hubris*.

60. Massing, "Now They Tell Us."

61. *Supporting Intelligence and Law Enforcement Programs*, H. Res. 895, 109th Cong., 2006.

62. For one such proposal see Morse, "Honor or Betrayal?" 445–46.

63. Department of Justice, "Access to Classified Information," November 26, 1996; *Department of the Navy v. Egan*, 527. Also see *New York Times Co. v. United States*, 729–30.

64. House Permanent Select Committee on Intelligence, *Intelligence Community Whistleblower Protection Act of 1998*, H. Rep. 105747, 105th Cong., 2nd Sess., 1998. Also see Senate Permanent Select Committee on Intelligence, *The Disclosure to Congress Act of 1998*, S. Rep. 105-165, 105th Cong., 2nd Sess., May 20, 1998 (Statement of Randolph D. Moss).

65. "S. 372, The Whistleblower Protection Enhancement Act of 2009," *Hearing Before the Senate Homeland Security and Governmental Affairs Committee*, 111th Cong., 1st Sess., 2009, 52–54 (Statement of Danielle Brian).

66. Wheeler and Healy, *Yankee from the West*, 33–34; "Media Incentives and National Security Secrets," 2242, fn. 102. Also see Ritchie, *Reporting from Washington*, 22.

67. Knott, "Executive Power and the Control of American Intelligence," 174.

68. Levinson, *Outspoken*, chap. 1; Tim Weiner, "Guatemalan Agent of CIA Tied to Killing of American," *New York Times*, March 23, 1995.

69. Jason DeParle, "Bob and Bianca to the Rescue," *New York Times*, June 4, 1995.

70. Katz, "Government Information Leaks," 110–11, fn. 5.

71. *Prewar Intelligence Assessments on Iraq*, 484–85 (Additional views of Senator Dianne Feinstein).

72. Sunstein, "Government Control of Information," 904. Also see Kitrosser, "Classified Information Leaks," 905–16; Posner, *Not a Suicide Pact*, 110.

73. Henkin, "The Right to Know and the Duty to Withhold," 278–79. Also see BeVier, "An Informed Public," 512–14.

74. Stone, "Free Speech and National Security," 961.

75. Kitrosser, "Classified Information Leaks," 913–15.

76. *New York Times Co. v. United States*, 722–23, fn. 3, 762–63,

77. Kitrosser, "Classified Information Leaks," 913.

78. *United States v. Progressive*, 996.

79. Ibid., 998.

80. "Press: Letter Bomb," *Time*, October 1, 1979. The outcome in *Progressive* also gives courts a strong prudential reason to refrain from adjudicating unauthorized disclosures, as they have increasingly few means in the Internet Age to compel publishers to obey their orders.

81. *Report of the Commission on the Intelligence Capabilities of the United States*, 381.

82. Bruce, "How Leaks of Classified Intelligence Help U.S. Adversaries," 402; Ballou and McSlarrow, "Plugging the Leak," 801–2.

83. Olmstead, *Challenging the Secret Government*, 73.

84. For an overview of the complexity see the discussion in *Military Audit Project v. Casey*, 656 F. 2d 724 (D.C. Cir. 1981) and *Phillippi v. Central Intelligence Agency*, 655 F. 2d 1325 (D.C. Cir. 1981).

85. Olmstead, *Challenging the Secret Government*, 73.

86. Ibid., 70.

87. "The Great Submarine Snatch," *Time*, March 31, 1975; Schwartz, *Atomic Audit*, 248.

88. Colby, *Honorable Men*, 418.

89. This is not a hypothetical. During World War II legal action against the *Chicago Tribune* was dropped out of concern that a high-profile prosecution would lead the Japanese to change codes that the navy had recently cracked (Schoenfeld, *Necessary Secrets*, 137–38). Similarly, in 1975 the Ford administration decided not to press charges against Seymour Hersh for revealing Operation Holystone, a secret submarine-based surveillance program, lest this alert the Soviets (Olmstead, *Challenging the Secret Government*, 75–76).

90. Betts, *Enemies of Intelligence*, 181.

91. Martin Sieff, "Terrorist Is Driven by Hatred for U.S., Israel," *Washington Times*, August 21, 1998.

92. Benjamin and Simon, *The Age of Sacred Terror*, 261.

93. *Final Report of the National Commission on Terrorist Attacks upon the United States*, 127.

94. Keefe, "The Challenge of Global Intelligence Listening," 25, fn. 9.

95. Hoekstra, *Secrets and Leaks*, 2; David E. Rosenbaum, "Bush Account of a Leak's Impact Has Support," *New York Times*, December 20, 2005.

96. Jack Shafer, "Don't Blame the Washington Times," *Slate*, December 21, 2005, online at http://tinyurl.com/chdkdnt.

97. Glenn Kessler, "File the Bin Laden Phone Leak under 'Urban Myths,'" *Washington Post*, December 22, 2005; Glenn Kessler, "On Leaks, Relying on a Faulty Case Study," *Washington Post*, December 23, 2005.

98. Bergen, *The Osama Bin Laden I Know*, 397.

99. Bill Gertz and Rowan Scarborough, "Inside the Ring," *Washington Times*, December 23, 2005.

100. Kessler, "File the Bin Laden Phone Leak Under 'Urban Myths.'"

101. Gertz and Scarborough, "Inside the Ring."

102. Porter Goss, "Loose Lips Sink Spies," *Washington Post*, February 10, 2006.

Chapter 5
Should We Rely on Whistleblowers?

1. As Frederick Elliston has pointed out, the Code of Ethics for United States Government Service states that a government employee should "put loyalty to the highest moral principles and to country above loyalty to persons, party or Government department" (Elliston, "Civil Disobedience and Whistleblowing," 25). Note also that the rules governing the classification system instruct that information shall not be classified in order to "conceal violations of law, inefficiency, or administrative error" or to "prevent embarrassment to a person, organization, or agency" (President Barack H. Obama, "Executive Order 13526, Classified National Security Information," *Federal Register*, vol. 75 (January 5, 2010), 707).

2. Bickel, *Morality of Consent*, 115. Also see Gutmann and Thompson, *Ethics and Politics*, 93.

3. As Arthur Applbaum has argued, there is "one circumstance under which appeal to the legitimate authority of the elected politician is not sufficient to demand of a public servant obedience to role, and that is when the elected politician . . . acts without legitimate authority" ("The Remains of the Role," 554). Also see Applbaum, *Ethics for Adversaries*, 228–29. Or as Mark Bovens has contended, "indiscretion and disloyalty are justifiable only when the rule of law is thereby served" (Bovens, *The Quest for Responsibility*, 169).

4. Stone, "Government Secrecy vs. Freedom of the Press," 195–96. Also see Bruce Ackerman, "Protect, Don't Prosecute, Patriotic Leakers," *New York Times*, June 12, 2012.

5. For the reasons discussed in chapter 3 the president would not be obligated to make lawmakers aware of these circumstances if he believes a renegade lawmaker might disclose this information, disregarding not only the president's wishes but also those of his fellow lawmakers.

6. De George, "Whistleblowing," 137–38.

7. Because dissenters "act against the judgments of the many," Applbaum writes, they "must practice a special sort of humility, seek whatever wisdom is

available, and safeguard against overconfidence or special pleading in their own judgments by taking cooler counsel" (Applbaum, *Ethics for Adversaries*, 238).

8. Schoenfeld, *Necessary Secrets*, 262–63. Also see BeVier, "The Journalist's Privilege," 483.

9. Johnson, *Whistleblowing*, 107. Also see Morse, "Honor or Betrayal?" 449.

10. James, "In Defense of Whistleblowing," 318.

11. Thompson, *Political Ethics*, 30; Morse, "Honor or Betrayal?" 446.

12. James, "In Defense of Whistleblowing," 318. Also see Elliston, "Anonymous Whistleblowing," 50.

13. Bok, "Whistleblowing and Professional Responsibilities," 336.

14. Ibid. Also see McConnell, "Whistleblowing," 572–73.

15. Bok, "Whistleblowing and Professional Responsibilities," 336; Scharf, "On Terrorism and Whistleblowing," 579–80.

16. Elliston, "Anonymous Whistleblowing," 52; James, "In Defense of Whistleblowing," 318.

17. James, "In Defense of Whistleblowing," 319. Also see Elliston, "Anonymous Whistleblowing," 50; Callahan, Dworkin, and Lewis, "Whistleblowing," 907.

18. Rawls, *A Theory of Justice*, 366; Walzer, *Obligations*, 20–21; Gutmann and Thompson, *Ethics and Politics*, 93. Kent Greenawalt emphasizes the importance of openness not necessarily during the act, but subsequently, as a step toward submitting to legal processes (Greenawalt, *Conflicts of Law and Morality*, 238–40).

19. Bovens, *The Quest for Responsibility*, 195.

20. Martin, *Meaningful Work*, 141. Also see Bok, *Secrets*, 212–13.

21. Martin, *Meaningful Work*, 144.

22. De George, "Whistleblowing," 139–40; McConnell, "Whistleblowing," 578. As the latter summarizes, "the greater the sacrifice, the more likely it is that blowing the whistle is supererogatory."

23. Glazer and Glazer, *The Whistleblowers*, 11–12. For an overview of the legal context see Moberly, "Whistleblowers and the Obama Presidency," 89–111.

24. Begg, "Whistleblower Law and Ethics," 192–93.

25. 5 U.S.C. § 2302(a)(2)(C)(ii). Also see Sasser, "Silenced Citizens," 780–81.

26. 5 U.S.C. § 2302(b)(8)(A)(ii). Also see Vaughn, "Statutory Protection of Whistleblowers," 630–31.

27. 5 App. U.S.C § 7(a).

28. 5 App. U.S.C § 7(c). 50 U.S.C. § 403(q) extends similar protection to employees of the CIA. More generally see Fisher, *National Security Whistleblowers*, 9–12.

29. 5 App. U.S.C § 8H(h)(C).

30. Vladeck, "The Espionage Act and National Security Whistleblowing after Garcetti," 1546. Also see Bowman, "Whistle-Blowing in the Public Service," 273–75.

31. Johnson, *Whistleblowing*, 100. For a number of pertinent examples see Foerstel, *Free Expression and Censorship in America*, 232–36.

32. Levy and Scott-Clark, *Deception*, 160–63; Seymour M. Hersh, "On the Nuclear Edge," *New Yorker*, March 29, 1993.

33. Levy and Scott-Clark, *Deception*, 202–3.

34. Ibid.

35. Adrian Levy and Cathy Scott-Clark, "The Man Who Knew Too Much," *Guardian*, October 13, 2007; Fisher, *In the Name of National Security*, 246–48.

36. Lyndsey Layton, "Whistleblower's Fight for Pension Drags On," *Washington Post*, July 7, 2007.

37. A number of similar cases are discussed in "National Security Whistleblowers in the Post–September 11th Era: Lost in a Labyrinth and Facing Subtle Retaliation," *Hearing Before the Subcommittee on National Security, Emerging Threats, and International Relations of the House Committee on Government Reform*, 109th Cong., 2nd Sess., February 14, 2006.

38. David Rose, "An Inconvenient Patriot," *Vanity Fair*, August 15, 2005; David Kohn, "Lost in Translation," *CBS News*, September 10, 2009, online at http://tinyurl.com/d2etd6z.

39. "A Review of the FBI's Actions in Connection with Allegations Raised by Contract Linguist Sibel Edmonds," *Report of the Department of Justice Inspector General* (Washington, DC: Department of Justice, July 1, 2004), 31.

40. *Edmonds v. Department of Justice*, 323 F. Supp. 2d 65 (D.D.C. 2004).

41. James V. Grimaldi, "2 FBI Whistle-Blowers Allege Lax Security, Possible Espionage," *Washington Post*, June 19, 2002; Chris Gourlay, Jonathan Calvert, and Joe Lauria, "For Sale: West's Deadly Nuclear Secrets," *Sunday Times*, January 6, 2008.

42. "A Review of the FBI's Actions," 31. Also see Eric Lichtblau, "Inspector General Rebukes F.B.I. over Espionage Case and Firing of Whistle-Blower," *New York Times*, January 15, 2004.

43. "A Review of the FBI's Actions," 31.

44. *Edmonds v. Department of Justice*, 546 U.S. 1031 (2005).

45. Given that the evidence in these cases is classified, we cannot be certain that either Barlow or Edmonds actually identified abuses of authority. Barlow, for instance, may have failed to sufficiently weigh the strategic constraints that the Reagan administration faced, i.e., the need to placate Pakistan. Similarly, in Edmonds's case, it is conceivable that the FBI allowed suspected Turkish spying to continue in order to fully ascertain the nature and extent of the enterprise. In the absence of evidence, it would be unwise to presume either guilt or innocence.

46. Miceli, Near, and Dworkin, *Whistleblowing in Organizations*, 23–24, 28; U.S. Merit Systems Protection Board, *The Federal Workforce for the 21st Century*, 35.

47. Near and Miceli, "Organizational Dissidence," 13.

48. Ibid.

49. Ibid., 8.

50. Ibid., 6. Also see Bovens, *The Quest for Responsibility*, 198, 206.

51. "S. 372, The Whistleblower Protection Enhancement Act of 2009," 83 (Statement of Thomas Devine).

52. Jos, Tompkins, and Hays, "In Praise of Difficult People," 557; Miceli, Near, and Dworkin, *Whistleblowing in Organizations*, 22.

53. Government Accountability Project, *The Art of Anonymous Activism*, 20; Truelson, "Whistleblowers and Their Protection," 294.

54. Project on Government Oversight, *Homeland and National Security Whistleblower Protections*, 8.

55. Fisher, *National Security Whistleblowers*, 21; Project on Government Oversight, *Homeland and National Security Whistleblower Protections*, 25; Truelson, "Whistleblowers and Their Protection," 295–97.

56. Fisher, *National Security Whistleblowers*, 21.

57. "S. 372, The Whistleblower Protection Enhancement Act of 2009," 86–87 (Statement of Thomas Devine).

58. *Department of the Navy v. Egan*, 484 U.S. 527 (1988).

59. Project on Government Oversight, *Homeland and National Security Whistleblower Protections*, 26; "National Security Whistleblowers," 240–41 (Statement of Mark Zaid). President Obama recently issued a directive prohibiting retaliation that allows a national security whistleblower to request review by a multi-agency inspector general panel of the revocation of her security clearance (Barack Obama, "Protecting Whistleblowers with Access to Classified Information," *Presidential Policy Directive/PPD-19*, Washington, DC: The White House, October 10, 2012, online at http://tinyurl.com/awl8tz9). The directive has not been received enthusiastically because, as critics point out, external review depends on the approval of the agency's inspector general, and the panel's report goes to the head of the agency, the person responsible for revoking the whistleblower's security clearance in the first place (on this see "National Security Whistleblowers Not Effectively Protected by New White House Directive," Washington, DC: National Whistleblowers Center, October 11, 2012 online at http://tinyurl.com/ae9cz7p).

60. Truelson, "Whistleblowers and Their Protection," 285–86; Ellsberg, "Secrecy and National Security Whistleblowing," 781.

61. Hersh, *Chain of Command*, chap. 2; Daniel Schorn, "Exposing the Truth of Abu Ghraib," *CBS News*, December 10, 2006, online at http://tinyurl.com/aexrhqd; Cockburn, *Rumsfeld*, 193–95.

62. Dawn Bryan, "Abu Ghraib Whistleblower's Ordeal," *BBC News*, August 5, 2007, online at http://tinyurl.com/c76h984; Joe Darby, "Why I Had to Tell the World What They'd Done," *Sunday Times*, August 5, 2007.

63. Bryan, "Abu Ghraib Whistleblower's Ordeal"; Randi Kaye, "Abu Ghraib Whistleblower: 'I Lived in Fear,'" *CNN*, August 15, 2006, online at http://tinyurl.com/d7om58c.

64. Bryan, "Abu Ghraib Whistleblower's Ordeal."

65. Hanna Rosin, "When Joseph Comes Marching Home," *Washington Post*, May 17, 2004.

66. Dawn Bryan, "Abu Ghraib Whistleblower's Ordeal."

67. For example, see William Safire, "The Crowley Memo," *New York Times*, May 27, 2002.

68. James Risen and David Johnston, "Agent Complaints Lead F.B.I. Director to Ask for Inquiry," *New York Times*, May 24, 2002.

69. Amanda Ripley and Maggie Sieger, "Coleen Rowley: The Special Agent," *Time*, December 30, 2002, 40; Michael Kilian, "Ashcroft: Whistle-Blower's Job Is Safe," *Chicago Tribune*, June 3, 2002. Also see Coleen Rowley, "The Wrong Side of 'Us vs. Them,'" *Minneapolis Star Tribune*, October 12, 2003.

70. Ripley and Sieger, "Coleen Rowley," 37.

71. Vaughn, "Statutory Protection of Whistleblowers," 663.

72. Bovens, *The Quest for Responsibility*, 213.

73. Ibid.

74. Miceli, Near, and Dworkin, *Whistleblowing in Organizations*, 15.

75. The difficulties involved in challenging adverse personnel decisions are discussed in Brookner, *Piercing the Veil*. Also see Peter Carlson, "Counter Intelligence," *Washington Post*, March 10, 2004.

76. Glazer and Glazer, *The Whistleblowers*, 255. Also see Robinson, *Deceit, Delusion, and Detection*, 284–87; Jos, Tompkins, and Hays, "In Praise of Difficult People," 554.

77. Scarre, *On Courage*, 146.

78. Ibid.

79. Jos, Tompkins, and Hays, "In Praise of Difficult People," 556. Also see Dozier and Miceli, "Potential Predictors of Whistle-Blowing," 828–29.

80. Alford, *Whistleblowers*, 95.

81. Ibid., 93.

82. On moral absolutism see Beth Hawkins, "The Purity of Coleen Rowley," *Mother Jones*, March 1, 2006).

83. Thompson, *Restoring Responsibility*, 255; "H.R. 1507, The Whistleblower Protection Enhancement Act of 2009," *Hearing Before the House Committee on Oversight and Government Reform*, 111th Cong., 1st Sess., May 14, 2009, 24–25 (Statement of Robert F. Turner).

84. Jos, Tompkins, and Hays, "In Praise of Difficult People," 557.

Chapter 6
Should We Trust Leakers?

1. Government Accountability Project, *The Art of Anonymous Activism*, 2. Also see Svara, *The Ethics Primer for Public Administrators*, 118–19.

2. Interdepartmental Group on Unauthorized Disclosures of Classified Information, *Report*, 2; Bruce, "How Leaks of Classified Intelligence Help U.S. Adversaries," 406–7.

3. 18 U.S.C. § 793(d).

4. Ibid.

5. Ballou and McSlarrow, "Plugging the Leak," 805–11.

6. For example, see "The Espionage Statutes: A Look Back and a Look Forward," *Hearing Before the Subcommittee on Terrorism and Homeland Security of the Senate Committee on the Judiciary*, 111th Cong., 2nd Sess., May 12, 2010 (Statement of Kenneth L. Wainstein).

7. Interdepartmental Group on Unauthorized Disclosures of Classified Information, *Report*, 20.

8. Bazan, *Intelligence Identities Protection Act*, 5; Croner, "A Snake in the Grass?" 773–74.

9. *United States v. Leibowitz*, No: AW-09-0632 (D. Md. 2009).

10. Allan Lengel and Dana Priest, "Investigators Conclude Shelby Leaked Message," *Washington Post*, August 5, 2004. Also see White, "The Need for Governmental Secrecy," 1080.

11. "Justice May Probe Leaked Pre-9/11 Intercepts," *CNN*, June 20, 2002, online at http://tinyurl.com/cjjcero.

12. David Johnston and Scott Shane, "C.I.A. Fires Senior Officer over Leaks," *New York Times*, April 22, 2006; R. Jeffrey Smith and Dafna Linzer, "CIA Officer's Job Made Any Leaks More Delicate," *Washington Post*, April 23, 2006; Dan Eggen, "Little Is Clear in Law on Leaks," *Washington Post*, April 28, 2006.

13. Interdepartmental Group on Unauthorized Disclosures of Classified Information, *Report*, 20.

14. Note that even an Official Secrets Act has not prevented a steady trickle of headline-grabbing leaks of classified information in England, including those by Clive Ponting, Cathy Massiter, Sarah Tisdall, Peter Wright, Richard Tomlinson, David Shayler, Katherine Gun, David Keogh, and Derek Pasquill, with the most recent example being the so far still-anonymous disclosure of the so-called Downing Street Memo. On this see "The Downing Street Memo," *Sunday Times*, May 1, 2005. For the other cases see Maer and Oonagh Gay, *Official Secrecy*, 11–19; Article 19 and Liberty, *Secrets, Spies, and Whistleblowers* (London: Guardian, 2000).

15. Interdepartmental Group on Unauthorized Disclosures of Classified Information, *Report*, 16. Also see Dulles, *Craft of Intelligence*, 244–45.

16. Commission on the Intelligence Capabilities of the United States Regarding Weapons of Mass Destruction, *Report*, 383; Interdepartmental Group on Unauthorized Disclosures of Classified Information, *Report*, 20.

17. Dulles, *Craft of Intelligence*, 244–45.

18. Edwards and Wayne, *Presidential Leadership*, 158

19. Shane Harris, "Plugging the Leaks," *Washingtonian*, August 2010, 36. Also see Hurt, "Leaking National Security Secrets," 20.

20. Josh Gerstein, "Justice Dept. Cracks Down on Leaks," *Politico*, May 25, 2010, online at http://tinyurl.com/23olzaq; Moberly, "Whistleblowers and the Obama Presidency," 75–80.

21. Letter from Attorney General John Ashcroft to Representative J. Dennis Hastert, October 15, 2002, 4, online at http://tinyurl.com/9l9zax2. Also see Adam Liptak, "A High Tech War on Leaks," *New York Times*, February 11, 2012.

22. Dana Priest, "CIA Holds Terror Suspects in Secret Prisons," *Washington Post*, November 2, 2005.

23. "Current and Projected National Security Threats to the United States," *Hearing Before the Senate Select Committee on Intelligence*, United States Senate, 109th Cong., 2nd Sess., February 2, 2006, 51–52.

24. R. Jeffrey Smith and Dafna Linzer, "Dismissed CIA Officer Denies Leak Role," *Washington Post*, April 25, 2006.

25. R. Jeffrey Smith, "Fired Officer Believed CIA Lied to Congress," *Washington Post*, May 14, 2006; Robert G. Kaiser, "Public Secrets," *Washington Post*, June 11, 2006. For another striking example see Feldstein, *Poisoning the Press*, 147–48.

26. Ackerman, "Protect, Don't Prosecute, Patriotic Leakers."

27. James Risen and Eric Lichtblau, "Bush Lets U.S. Spy on Callers without Courts," *New York Times*, December 16, 2005.

28. Michael Isikoff, "The Fed Who Blew the Whistle," *Newsweek*, December 12, 2008.

29. Ibid.

30. Ibid.

31. Lichtblau, *Bush's Law*, 188–89.

32. Isikoff, "The Fed Who Blew the Whistle."

33. Michael Isikoff, "Looking for a Leaker," *Newsweek*, August 12, 2007.

34. Brian Ross, "NSA Whistleblower Alleges Illegal Spying," *ABC News*, January 10, 2006, online at http://tinyurl.com/c6jy5h3.

35. Chris Strohm, "Ex-NSA Official Seeks Avenue for Sharing New Allegations," *Government Executive*, January 19, 2006.

36. "National Security Whistleblowers," 109th Cong., 2nd Sess., February 14, 2006, 169–70 (Statement of Russell D. Tice).

37. Ibid., 173.

38. Ibid., 174.

39. Chris Strohm, "Former NSA Officer Alleges Illegal Activities under Hayden," *Government Executive*, May 12, 2006

40. Risen, *State of War*, chap. 9.

41. James Risen, "Fired by the C.I.A., He Says Agency Practiced Bias," *New York Times*, March 2, 2002.

42. Todd C. Frankel, "Life Away from CIA Still Tangled, Lonely for Indicted Ex-Spy," *St. Louis Post-Dispatch*, January 23, 2011.

43. *Sterling v. Tenet*, 416 F.3d 338 (4th Cir. August 3, 2005).

44. *United States v. Sterling*, No. 1:10cr485 (E.D. Va. 2010) [Indictment, 7–14].

45. This concern is widely acknowledged in the media ethics literature. For example, see Carlson, "Whither Anonymity?"; Boeynik, "Anonymous Sources," 238, 240. Also see Smith, *Ethics in Journalism*, 176–77; Sanders, *Ethics and Journalism*, 114; Flynn, "Covert Disclosures," 261.

46. Goldsmith, *The Terror Presidency*, 38–48.

47. *United States v. Sterling*, No. 1:10cr485 (E.D. Va. 2010) [Indictment, 13].

48. This concern too is widely acknowledged in the media ethics literature. For example, see Carlson, "Whither Anonymity?" 42–43; Boeynik, "Anonymous Sources," 242–44; Jacquette, *Journalistic Ethics*, 169; Wasserman, "A Critique of Source Confidentiality," 563.

49. Lichtblau, *Bush's Law*, 187.

50. *United States v. Sterling*, No. 1:10-cr485 (E.D. Va. 2011) [Indictment, 7–18].

51. Risen, *State of War*, chap. 9.

52. Seymour M. Hersh, "Torture at Abu Ghraib," *New Yorker*, May 10, 2004.

53. Bovens, *The Quest for Responsibility*, 209; Elliston, "Anonymous Whistle-blowing," 47.

54. For instance see Sophie Arie, "Crude Niger Forgeries Surface in Italian Paper," *Guardian*, July 17, 2003; Seymour M. Hersh, "The Stovepipe," *New Yorker*, October 27, 2003; Unger, *American Armageddon*, chap. 14; Hoyle, *Going to War*, chap. 9.

55. For an excellent analysis of prepublication procedures that the media ought to follow in order to mitigate national security harm, see "Media Incentives and National Security Secrets." This article proposes that procedural safeguards be enforced through law, but it provides little reason to believe that such a law could survive a First Amendment challenge, not to mention be enforced against foreign media organizations, including online publications. Arguably, the more plausible strategy is to rely on media criticism, which, as discussed in this book's conclusion, can direct public attention and condemnation toward publications that fail to abide by the recommended procedural safeguards.

56. Bickel, *Morality of Consent*, 81.

57. Ibid., 80.

58. Ibid., 81. Here Bickel was building on Justice Black's observation in the Pentagon Papers case that "the press was protected so that it could bare the secrets of government and inform the people" (*New York Times Co. v. United States*, 717).

59. Bickel, *Morality of Consent*, 81.

60. Ibid.

61. Ibid.

62. Ibid.

63. Ibid., 80.

64. Ibid., 84.

65. "When in Doubt, Publish," *Washington Post*, July 9, 2006. Also see Bill Keller and Dean Baquet, "When Do We Publish a Secret?" *New York Times*, July 1, 2006; "An Alert Press," *Washington Post*, June 29, 2006.

66. "When in Doubt, Publish."

67. Keller and Baquet, "When Do We Publish a Secret?"

68. "Confidential News Sources Policy" (New York Times Company, March 1, 2004), online at http://www.nytco.com/company/business_units/sources.html.

69. Leonard Downie Jr., "The Guidelines We Use to Report the News," *Washington Post*, March 7, 2004; Andrew Alexander, "Ignoring the Rules on Anonymous Sources," *Washington Post*, August 16, 2009. For a wider survey see Son, "Leaks." Son notes that few codes of ethics currently in use discuss the problem of malicious disclosures. This deficiency has been addressed in Duffy and Freeman, "Unnamed Sources," 310–11. Unfortunately, Duffy and Freeman do not discuss how the code of ethics they propose might be enforced, especially when leaks are channeled via websites like WikiLeaks. The same shortcoming can be seen in Kielbowicz, "The Role of News Leaks," 489.

70. For example, see Daniel Okrent, "An Electrician from the Ukrainian Town of Lutsk," *New York Times*, June 13, 2004; Daniel Okrent, "Briefers and Leakers

and the Newspapers Who Enable Them," *New York Times*, May 8, 2005; Byron Calame, "Anonymity: Who Deserves It?" *New York Times*, November 20, 2005; Byron Calame, "More Flexibility and Reality in Explaining Anonymity," *New York Times*, June 30, 2006; Clark Hoyt, "Culling the Anonymous Sources," *New York Times*, June 8, 2008; Clark Hoyt, "Those Persistent Anonymous Sources," *New York Times*, March 21, 2009; Clark Hoyt, "No Comment. But You Didn't Hear It From Me," *New York Times*, March 28, 2009; Clark Hoyt, "Cloaked Identities, Even with Names," *New York Times*, August 15, 2009; Clark Hoyt, "Squandered Trust," *New York Times*, April 17, 2010; Clark Hoyt, "Anonymous Sources Postscript," *New York Times*, April 17, 2010.

71. Hoyt, "Culling the Anonymous Sources."

72. Andrew Alexander, "Ignoring the Rules on Anonymous Sources," *Washington Post*, August 16, 2009.

73. Andrew Alexander, "For The Post, Anonymous Sources Remain a Problem," *Washington Post*, June 13, 2010.

74. Calame, "Anonymity: Who Deserves It?"

75. Phil Corbett, "A Reminder on Anonymous Sources," *New York Times*, August 31, 2010. Also see Bill Keller, "Assuring Our Credibility," *New York Times*, June 23, 2005, 4–6; Calame, "More Flexibility and Reality in Explaining Anonymity."

76. Alexander, "Ignoring the Rules on Anonymous Sources." For additional evidence and excellent analysis see Glenn Greenwald, "The Casual, Corrupting Use of Anonymity for Political Officials," *Slate*, March 6, 2009, online at http://tinyurl.com/bfczjku; Glenn Greenwald, "The Ongoing Journalistic Scandal at the New York Times," *Slate*, July 9, 2007, online at http://tinyurl.com/8zurd8h. There is some debate about the extent to which editors and publishers have been able to rein in the use of anonymous sources over the past decade. For example, see Duffy and Williams, "Use of Unnamed Sources Drops"; Martin-Kratzer and Thorson, "Use of Anonymous Sources Declines." Note, however, that this data is not disaggregated by subject area. Therefore, we do not know whether national security reporting has actually seen a decline in the use of anonymous sources (for an earlier study see Hallin, Manoff, and Weddle, "Sourcing Patterns of National Security Reporters"). Note also that our concern here is to prevent the *misuse* of anonymous sources—not to eliminate their use altogether. Hence, from our perspective, the overall number of anonymous disclosures is less relevant. It is the quality, not the quantity, of anonymous disclosures that matters.

77. Bickel, *Morality of Consent*, 83.

78. Ibid., 85, emphasis in original.

79. For a sophisticated analysis of the relationship between reporters and sources see Levi, "Dangerous Liaisons," 690–706. Another insightful study is Carlson, *On Condition of Anonymity*, chap. 1.

80. Lichtblau, *Bush's Law*, 202. Also see Goldsmith, "Secrecy and Safety"; Schoenfeld, *Necessary Secrets*, 47–48.

81. Byron Calame, "Can 'Magazines' of The Times Subsidize News Coverage?" *New York Times*, October 22, 2006; Byron Calame, "Bill Keller Responds to Column on Swift Mea Culpa," *New York Times*, November 6, 2006; "Letter from

Bill Keller on The Times's Banking Records Report," *New York Times*, June 25, 2006.

82. "Fit and Unfit to Print," *Wall Street Journal*, June 30, 2006.

83. Scott Shane, "A History of Publishing, and Not Publishing, Secrets," *New York Times*, July 2, 2006; Smolkin, "Judgment Calls"; Keller, "The Boy Who Kicked the Hornet's Nest," 8, 13.

84. David Abramowicz notes that these procedural norms can be patterned on the norms that have already been fleshed out in the various codes of ethics developed by the journalism industry ("Calculating the Public Interest in Protecting Journalists' Confidential Sources," 1971–74). He does not discuss, however, the constitutional and practical challenges associated with enforcing these norms, which, as we shall see, are quite severe. The same drawback arises in Carlson's *On Condition of Anonymity*, which puts forward sourcing principles that reporters, editors, and publishers ought to follow, but provides no enforcement mechanism (154–61).

85. Strauss, "Freedom of Speech and the Common-Law Constitution," 38.

86. *New York Times Co. v. Sullivan*, 376 U.S. 254, 270–71 (1964).

87. *McIntyre v. Ohio Elections Commission*, 514 U.S. 334, 347 (1995).

88. *United States v. Associated Press*, 52 F. Supp. 362, 372 (S.D.N.Y. 1943).

89. *Abrams v. United States*, 250 U.S. 616, 630 (1919).

90. *McIntyre v. Ohio Elections Commission*, 348–49, and fn. 11.

91. Ibid., 349–51.

92. *Buckley v. Valeo*, 424 U.S. 1, 67 (1976); *McConnell v. Federal Election Commission*, 540 U.S. 93, 197 (2003). Also see *First National Bank of Boston v. Bellotti*, 435 U.S. 765, fn. 32 (1978), where the court cited the "prophylactic effect" of such disclosures.

93. *Buckley v. Valeo*, 68; *McConnell v. Federal Election Commission*, 198.

94. *Cohen v. Cowles Media Co.*, 501 U.S. 663, 671–72 (1991).

95. Ibid., 671.

96. Ibid., 677–78.

97. Ibid., 678.

98. *Miami Herald Publishing Co. v. Tornillo*, 418 US 241, 256–58 (1974). Also see *Associated Press v. United States*, 326 U.S. 1 (1945), fn. 18.

99. *McIntyre v. Ohio Elections Commission*, fn. 11.

100. *Miami Herald Publishing Co. v. Tornillo*, 256.

101. *Branzburg v. Hayes*, 682, 691.

102. Ibid.

103. Note, however, that the D.C. Circuit Court has observed that in cases "when the journalist is a party, and successful assertion of the privilege will effectively shield him from liability, the equities weigh somewhat more heavily in favor of disclosure" (*Zerilli v. Smith*, 656 F.2d 705, 714 (D.C. Cir. 1981)).

104. Ibid., 711; *McKevitt v. Pallasch*, 339 F. 3d 530, 532 (7th Cir. 2003). For a broader defense of the reporter's privilege see Blasi, "The Checking Value," 602–7; Emerson, "Legal Foundations of the Right to Know," 19–20; Stone, "Why We Need a Federal Reporter's Privilege"; Werhan, "Rethinking Freedom of the Press

after 9/11," 1603–5. Regrettably, none of these scholars gives sustained attention to the prospect that unauthorized disclosures might themselves be misused. One exception on this front is Fargo, "The Year of Leaking Dangerously," 1008–10, 1119. Because Fargo takes the view that sources will not come forward if there is a risk that a reporter cannot guarantee confidentiality, he ultimately recommends self-regulation. For reasons discussed earlier, this proposal lacks credibility.

105. BeVier, "The Journalist's Privilege," 475. Some proponents of a reporter's privilege argue that even having to answer government subpoenas imposes a significant legal and administrative burden on news organizations that limits their ability to exercise their First Amendment rights (see, for example, Dalglish, *Agents of Discovery*, 4, 12). However, the evidence Dalglish offers is anecdotal. More recent research shows that a reported decline in the use of anonymous sources is "tied more closely to journalism-industry norms than to legal environment" (Jones, "Avalanche or Undue Alarm?" 651). But even if the evidence supports Dalglish's view, this would not itself be conclusive. We would still need to ask whether, and if so how far, we want reporters, editors, and publishers to be protected from scrutiny when they collect and publish disclosures from sources unwilling to disclose potential conflicts of interest.

106. Blasi, "The Checking Value," 538, 607; Meiklejohn, *Free Speech*, 88–89. It is worth recalling Meiklejohn's critical remarks about the tendency of commercial pressure to make the news media cater to sensationalism. The radio, he writes, "is not entitled to the protection of the First Amendment," because it is "engaged in making money." The "First Amendment," he adds, "does not intend to guarantee men freedom to say what some private interest pays them to say for its own advantage." Arguably, Meiklejohn's criticism of commercial radio for corrupting the "reasoned judgment . . . upon which the enterprise of self-government depends" implies that he would also frown upon anonymity when it is used to covertly serve partisan ends (*Free Speech*, 104–5).

107. Keller, "The Boy Who Kicked the Hornet's Nest," 14, 21.

108. A recent warning is provided by the case of Edward Snowden, the former NSA employee who made unauthorized disclosures via the *Guardian* in England. Snowden reportedly chose this route because he did not trust either the *Washington Post* (since it wanted to obtain the government's input on the harm likely to be caused by the publication of his disclosure) or the *New York Times* (as it had previously acceded to President Bush's request to temporarily withhold Risen's and Lichtblau's story on warrantless wiretapping). On this see Howard Kurtz, "Leakers Seek Out Advocacy Journalists," *CNN*, June 12, 2013, online at http://tinyurl.com/lnmovx7.

Conclusion
Bitter Medicine

1. As Justice Potter Stewart famously warned in the Pentagon Papers case, "secrecy can best be preserved only when credibility is truly maintained" (*New York Times Co. v. United States*, 729).

2. Paine, "The Necessity of Taxation," 310. At the time he wrote this essay, Paine was being paid by Robert Livingston, Congress's secretary of foreign affairs, as part of a highly secret plan drawn up by Robert Morris, and seconded by George Washington, to "prepare the minds of the people for such restraints and such taxes and imposts, as are absolutely necessary for their own welfare" (Morris, *The Papers of Robert Morris*, 328). Compare with Paine, "The Rights of Man, Part II," 183, 225, 227. For a trusting contemporaneous voice see A Moderate Whig, "A Short Receipt for a Continental Disease," 769.

3. Elliot, *Debates*, 4:264–65.

4. See for example, Hampden [William Findley], "A Note Protesting the Treaty-Making Provisions of the Constitution," *Pittsburgh Gazette*, February 16, 1788; An Old Whig, "Essay III," 26–27.

5. *The Federalist*, 316. For a valuable discussion on the Framers' expectation that the design of the presidency would "strengthen existing virtues . . . or generate them where they did not already exist," see Fatovic, *Outside the Law*, chap. 6, esp. 210–11.

6. Manin, *The Principles of Representative Government*, 115–20.

7. For example, see David E. Rosenbaum, "A Closer Look at Cheney and Halliburton," *New York Times*, September 28, 2004.

8. James Madison to James Monroe, March 11, 1795, in Madison, *Letters and Other Writings*, 2:37.

9. Goldsmith, *Power and Constraint*, 42.

10. Goldsmith, "Secrecy and Safety," 36.

11. Goldsmith, *Power and Constraint*, 42. For a skeptical view see Herman, *Taking Liberties*, 8–9.

12. Goldsmith, *Power and Constraint*, 71.

13. For a recent critique along these lines see Bruff, *Bad Advice*.

14. Jo Becker and Scott Shane, "Secret 'Kill List' Proves a Test of Obama's Principles and Will," *New York Times*, May 29, 2012.

15. Hess, *The Government/Press Connection*, 93.

16. This is what happened during Iran-Contra where President Reagan overruled the objections raised by Secretary of State George Schultz. On this see Alterman, *When Presidents Lie*, 278.

17. Hess, *The Government/Press Connection*, 93.

18. Goldsmith, "Secrecy and Safety," 35–36.

19. Posner and Vermeule, "The Credible Executive," 897–910.

20. Hirschman, *Exit, Voice, and Loyalty*, 117. I am grateful to Sanford Levinson for emphasizing this point in our discussion.

21. Diodorus Siculus, *Library of History*, 11.42.

22. Plutarch, "Themistocles"; Cicero, *On Duties*, 118. According to Diodorus, Themistocles's secret plan was to fortify the Piraeus, whereas Plutarch and Cicero depict him as scheming to burn the Spartan navy.

23. Posner and Vermeule, "The Credible Executive," 911.

24. Dan Eggen and Paul Kane, "Gonzales Hospital Episode Detailed," *Washington Post*, May 16, 2007; David Stout, "Gonzales Pressed Ailing Ashcroft on Spy

Plan, Aide Says," *New York Times*, May 15, 2007. Also see Goldsmith, *The Terror Presidency*, 38–48.

25. Kazin, *A Godly Hero*, 232–39.

26. Posner and Vermeule, "The Credible Executive," 912.

27. Weisband and Franck, *Resignation in Protest*, 122; Dobel, "Doing Good by Staying In?" 191. For an interesting recent example see Paul Starobin, "A Moral Flip-Flop? Defining a War," *New York Times*, August 6, 2011.

28. *Congressional Record*, 65th Cong., 1st Sess., 1917, 837.

29. "The DA-Notice System," online at http://www.dnotice.org.uk/.

30. Dulles, *Craft of Intelligence*, 245–46. Secretary of Defense James Forrestal proposed a similar arrangement (see Carpenter, *The Captive Press*, 121).

31. Cater, *The Fourth Branch of Government*, 126–27; *Report to the Secretary of Defense*, 21.

32. For example, see Kaiser, "Public Secrets"; Keller and Baquet, "When Do We Publish A Secret?"; Smolkin, "Judgment Calls"; Shane, "A History of Publishing, and Not Publishing, Secrets."

33. Carpenter, *The Captive Press*, 89. For similar critiques of cooperation see Olmstead, *Challenging the Secret Government*, 60–62, 73–74, 183–85; Cox, *The Myths of National Security*, 119–29.

34. Gup, *Nation of Secrets*, 167.

35. Ibid., 167–68.

36. See, for example, the views expressed in Smolkin, "Judgment Calls." On the role of sensationalism in intelligence reporting see Omand, "Intelligence Secrets and Media Spotlights," 47–48.

37. It is often forgotten that the unreliability of self-censorship was the key justification offered on behalf of the Espionage Act's censorship provision. For instance see *Congressional Record*, 65th Cong., 1st Sess., 1917, 1606, 1721, 1717, 1810–12.

38. *Report to the Secretary of Defense*, 21. Consider one well-known example: in 1985 the *Washington Post* delayed publishing a story on the "Ivy Bells" program, following a personal request from President Reagan. The *Post* was then scooped by *NBC*, which disregarded requests as well as threats of prosecution from CIA Director William Casey (on this see Kaiser, "Public Secrets").

39. Dulles, *Craft of Intelligence*, 246. Also see Cater, "News and the Nation's Security," 26.

40. For example, see Paul Sonne, "WikiLeaks Says It Could Close," *Wall Street Journal*, October 25, 2011.

41. For troubling accounts of press intimidation see Smith, *War and Press Freedom*, chaps. 5–6.

42. Nemeth, *News Ombudsman*, 57.

43. Ibid., 50.

44. For example, see Calame, "Bill Keller Responds to Column on Swift Mea Culpa." For a broader analysis of the "irrelevance" of ombudsmen see Bunton, "Media Criticism as Self-Regulation," 79.

45. Byron Calame, "Behind the Eavesdropping Story, a Loud Silence," *New York Times*, January 1, 2006.

46. Nemeth, *News Ombudsmen*, 143–49. The foundational study here is Ettema and Glasser, "Public Accountability or Public Relations?"

47. See, for example, Meyers, "Creating an Effective Newspaper Ombudsman Position," 249–52.

48. The Commission on Freedom of the Press, *A Free and Responsible Press*, 74–75, 94.

49. Ibid., 80.

50. Brown, "Anonymous Sources," 56; Brown, "Anonymity Hurts Reporters and Politicians," 38–39.

51. Brown, "Anonymous Sources," 56.

52. Joe Strupp, "Losing Confidence," *Editor and Publisher*, July 1, 2005, 36.

53. Sternadori and Thorson, "Anonymous Sources Harm Credibility of All Stories." Contrast with Smith, "Impact of Unnamed Sources on Credibility Not Certain."

54. Shepard, "Anonymous Sources," 22. Also see Strupp, "Losing Confidence," 34; Jones, "Avalanche or Undue Alarm?" 651.

55. "The Times and Iraq," *New York Times*, May 26, 2004.

56. Franklin Foer, "The Source of the Trouble," *New York Magazine*, May 21, 2005. Also see Jack Shafer, "Reassessing Judith Miller," *Slate*, May 29, 2003, online at http://tinyurl.com/chpey20; Jack Shafer, "The Times Scoops That Melted," *Slate*, July 25, 2003, online at http://tinyurl.com/8yj6pqt; Jack Shafer, "Miller Time (Again)," *Slate*, February 12, 2004, online at http://tinyurl.com/crh723r; Massing, *Now They Tell Us*. For a survey of the critical coverage see Carlson, *On Condition of Anonymity*, 34–39.

57. Byron Calame, "The Miller Mess: Lingering Issues among the Answers," *New York Times*, October 23, 2005; Maureen Dowd, "Woman of Mass Destruction."

58. Howard Kurtz, "Intra-Times Battle over Iraqi Weapons," *New York Times*, May 26, 2003.

59. See, for example, Curran, *Media and Power*, 219–21, 226–29. The foundational text here is Bagdikian, *The New Media Monopoly*.

60. *New York Times Co. v. United States*, 717. Consider, for example, the uncritical treatment in Thomas, *Watchdogs of Democracy?*, chap. 6. The chapter's title is "Hail to the Heroic Leakers and Whistle-Blowers—And the Journalists Who Protect Them."

61. *United States v. Sterling*, No. 1:10-cr485 (E.D. Va. 2011) [Memorandum Opinion, 6–7].

62. Schoenfeld, *Necessary Secrets*, 50.

63. According to one survey, fewer than one in four editors consider media critics to be "well qualified . . . to make criticisms of daily newspapers" (Lambeth, *Committed Journalism*, 119).

64. There is little new to be said here. Scholars of media ethics have been criticizing sensationalism for well over a century now—to little effect. For a brief overview see Ferré, "A Short History of Media Ethics," 17–18; Norris, *A Virtuous Circle*, 4–8. For recent critiques of sensationalism see Flink, *Sentinel under Siege*, 11–14; Rosen, *What Are Journalists For?*, 286, 296; Schultz, *Reviving the Fourth Estate*, 95–99, 115–16.

65. *A Free and Responsible Press*, 100–103. For a recent iteration see Scheuer, *The Big Picture*, 158–63.

66. *A Free and Responsible Press*, 100–101. On the short-lived National News Council created in the wake of the Hutchins Commission report see Lambeth, *Committed Journalism*, 109–11.

67. *A Free and Responsible Press*, 98.

68. For a key example, namely, *The Daily Show*'s role as a media critic, see Hayes, *Press Critics Are the Fifth Estate*, chap. 9.

69. For an analysis of the "hard-nosed political tactics" that can be used to "silence or short-circuit" critics of the presidency, see Bennet, Lawrence, and Livingston, *When the Press Fails*, chap. 5, 136.

70. Weber, *Essays in Sociology*, 128.

71. As Justice Stewart put it, as far as the Constitution goes, the press "is free to do battle against secrecy and deception in government," but it "cannot expect from the Constitution any guarantee that it will succeed." This is because the Constitution "establishes the contest, not its resolution." For the resolution we must rely "on the tug and pull of the political forces in American society" (Stewart, "Or of the Press," 635–36.

Selected Bibliography

Abel, Elie. *Leaking: Who Does It? Who Benefits? At What Cost?* New York: Priority Press, 1987.

Aberbach, Joel. *Keeping a Watchful Eye: The Politics of Congressional Oversight.* Washington, DC: Brookings Institution Press, 1990.

Abramowicz, David. "Calculating the Public Interest in Protecting Journalists' Confidential Sources." *Columbia Law Review* 108 (2008).

Ackerman, Bruce. "The Emergency Constitution." *Yale Law Journal* 113 (2004).

Adams, John. "Thoughts on Government." In *American Political Writing during the Founding Era*, ed. Charles S. Hyneman and Donald Lutz, vol. 1. Indianapolis: Liberty Fund, 1983.

Adams, Samuel. *The Writings of Samuel Adams 1778–1802.* Ed. Harry A. Cushing. New York: G. P. Putnam's Sons, 1908.

Adams, Zabdiel. "Election Sermon." In *American Political Writing during the Founding Era*, ed. Charles S. Hyneman and Donald Lutz, vol. 1. Indianapolis: Liberty Fund, 1983.

Adcock, F. E., and Derek J. Mosley. *Diplomacy in Ancient Greece.* London: Thames and Hudson, 1975.

Adler, Renata. *Canaries in the Mineshaft: Essays on Politics and Media.* New York: St. Martin's Press, 2001.

Aftergood, Steven. "Reducing Government Secrecy: Finding What Works." *Yale Law and Policy Review* 27, no. 2 (2009).

Aid, Matthew M. *The Secret Sentry: The Untold History of the National Security Agency.* New York: Bloomsbury, 2010.

Aldrich, Richard J. "Regulation by Revelation: Intelligence, Media, and Transparency." In *Spinning Intelligence: Why Intelligence Needs the Media, Why the Media Needs Intelligence*, ed. Robert Dover and Michael S. Goodman. New York: Columbia University Press, 2009.

Alexander, Hartley B. *Liberty and Democracy: And Other Essays in War-Time*, Boston: Marshall Jones, 1918.

Alford, Fred C. *Whistleblowers: Broken Lives and Organizational Power*. Ithaca, NY: Cornell University Press, 2001.

Alterman, Eric. *When Presidents Lie: A History of Official Deception and Its Consequences*. New York: Viking, 2004.

A Moderate Whig. "A Short Receipt for a Continental Disease." In *Political Sermons of the Founding Era: 1730–1805*, ed. Ellis Sandoz, vol. 1. Indianapolis: Liberty Fund, 1991.

Andrew, Christopher. *For the President's Eyes Only: Secret Intelligence and the American Presidency from Washington to Bush*. New York: Harper Collins, 1995.

An Old Whig. "Essay III." In *The Complete Anti-Federalist*, ed. Herbert J. Storing and Murray Dry, vol. 1. Chicago: University of Chicago Press, 1981.

Applbaum, Arthur I. *Ethics for Adversaries*. Princeton, NJ: Princeton University Press, 2000.

———. "The Remains of the Role." *Governance* 6, no. 4 (1993).

Archibald, Sam. "The Early Years of the Freedom of Information Act: 1955 to 1974," *PS: Political Science and Politics* 26, no. 4 (1993).

Armstrong, Scott. "The War over Secrecy: Democracy's Most Important Low-Intensity Conflict." In *A Culture of Secrecy*, ed. Robert Dover and Michael S. Goodman. Lawrence: University Press of Kansas, 1998.

Austin, Norman, and Boris Rankov. *Exploratio: Military and Political Intelligence in the Roman World*. Routledge: New York, 1995.

Bagdikian, Ben H. *The New Media Monopoly*. Boston: Beacon Press, 2004.

Ballou, Eric E., and Kyle E. McSlarrow. "Plugging the Leak: A Case for Legislative Resolution of the Conflict between Demands of Secrecy and the Need for an Open Government." *Virginia Law Review* 71, no. 5 (1985).

Banks, William C., and Peter Raven-Hansen. *National Security Law and the Power of the Purse*. New York: Oxford University Press, 1994.

Barrett, David M. "An Early 'Year of Intelligence': The CIA and Congress, 1958." *International Journal of Intelligence and Counterintelligence* 17, no. 3 (2004).

———. *The CIA and Congress: The Untold Story from Truman to Kennedy*. Wichita: University Press of Kansas, 2004.

Elizabeth B. Bazan. *Intelligence Identities Protection Act*. Washington, DC: Congressional Research Service, 2003.

Beale, Robert. "A Treatise of the Office of a Councellor and Principall Secretarie to her Majestie." In Conyers Read, *Mr. Secretary Walsingham and the Policy of Queen Elizabeth*. Cambridge, MA: Harvard University Press, 1925.

Begg, Robert T. "Whistleblower Law and Ethics." In *Ethical Standards in the Public Sector*, ed. Patricia E. Salkin. Chicago: American Bar Association, 2009.

Benjamin, Daniel, and Steven Simon. *The Age of Sacred Terror*. New York: Random House, 2002.

Bennet, W. Lance, Regina G. Lawrence, and Steven Livingston. *When the Press Fails: Political Power and the News Media from Iraq to Katrina*. Chicago: University of Chicago Press, 2007.

Bentham, Jeremy. *Constitutional Code.* Ed. F. Rosen and J. H. Burns. New York: Oxford University Press, 1983.

———. *Political Tactics.* Ed. Michael James, Cyprian Blamires, and Catherine Pease-Watkin. New York: Oxford University Press, 1999.

———. *The Works of Jeremy Bentham.* Ed. John Bowring. Edinburgh: William Tait, 1843.

Bergen, Peter L. *The Osama Bin Laden I Know.* New York: Free Press, 2006.

Berger, Raoul. *Executive Privilege: A Constitutional Myth.* Cambridge, MA: Harvard University Press, 1974.

Berkowitz, Bruce D., and Allan E. Goodman. *Best Truth: Intelligence in the Information Age.* New Haven, CT: Yale University Press, 2000.

Betts, Richard K. *Enemies of Intelligence: Knowledge and Power in American National Security.* New York: Columbia University Press, 2007.

BeVier, Lillian R. "An Informed Public, an Informing Press: The Search for a Constitutional Principle." *California Law Review* 68 (1980).

———. "The Journalist's Privilege—A Skeptic's View." *Ohio Northern University Law Review* 32, no. 3 (2006).

Bickel, Alexander M. *Morality of Consent.* New Haven, CT: Yale University Press, 1975.

Bishop, Joseph W., Jr. "The Executive's Right to Privacy: An Unresolved Constitutional Question." *Yale Law Journal* 66, no. 4 (1957).

Blasi, Vincent. "The Checking Value in First Amendment Theory." *American Bar Foundation Research Journal* 2, no. 3 (1977).

Blechman, Barry M., and W. Philip Ellis. *The Politics of National Security: Congress and U.S. Defense Policy.* New York: Oxford University Press, 1990.

Block, Lawrence J., and David B. Rivkin. "The Battle to Control the Conduct of Foreign Intelligence and Covert Operations: The Ultra-Whig Counterrevolution Revisited." *Harvard Journal of Law & Public Policy* 12, no. 2 (1989).

Bodin, Jean. *On Sovereignty: Four Chapters from the Six Books of the Commonwealth.* Trans. Julian H. Franklin. New York: Cambridge University Press, 1992.

Boeynik, David E. "Anonymous Sources in News Stories: Justifying Exceptions and Limiting Abuses." *Journal of Mass Media Ethics* 5, no. 4 (1990).

Bok, Sissela. *Secrets: On the Ethics of Concealment and Revelation.* New York: Vintage Books, 1989.

———. "Whistleblowing and Professional Responsibilities." In *Ethical Issues in Professional Life,* ed. Joan C. Callahan. New York: Oxford University Press, 1988.

Borjesson, Kristina. *Feet to the Fire: The Media after 9/11.* New York: Prometheus, 2005.

Botero, Giovanni. *The Reason of State.* Trans. P. J. Waley and D. P. Waley. New Haven, CT: Yale University Press, 1956.

Bovens, Mark. *The Quest for Responsibility: Accountability and Citizenship in Complex Organizations.* Cambridge: Cambridge University Press, 1998.

Bowman, James S. "Whistle-Blowing in the Public Service." In *Classics of Administrative Ethics,* ed. Willa M. Bruce. Boulder, CO: Westview Press, 2001.

Breckenridge, Adam. *The Executive Privilege: Presidential Control over Information.* Lincoln: University of Nebraska Press, 1974.

Brookner, Janine. *Piercing the Veil: Litigation against U.S. Intelligence.* Durham, NC: Carolina Academic Press, 2003.

Brooks, Nathan. *The Protection of Classified Information: The Legal Framework.* Washington, DC: Congressional Research Service, 2004.

Brown, Fred. "Anonymity Hurts Reporters and Politicians." *Quill,* December, 2003.

———. "Anonymous Sources Needed, But Must Be Used With Care," *Quill,* June/July, 2005.

Brownell, Herbert. "Memorandum." Reprinted in *Hearing Before the Subcommittee on Constitutional Rights of the Committee of the Judiciary,* 85th Congress, 2nd Sess., 1958, appendix 13.

Bruce, James B. "How Leaks of Classified Intelligence Help U.S. Adversaries: Implications for Laws and Secrecy." In *Intelligence and the National Security Strategist: Enduring Challenges and Issues,* ed. Roger Z. George and Robert D. Kline. New York: Rowan and Littlefield, 2006.

Bruff, Harold H. *Bad Advice: Bush's Lawyers in the War on Terror.* Lawrence: University of Kansas Press, 2009.

Bruni, Leonardo. *History of the Florentine People.* Trans. James Hankins, Cambridge, MA: Harvard University Press, 2007.

Bryce, James. *The American Commonwealth.* Indianapolis: Liberty Fund, 1995.

———. *Modern Democracies.* New York: Macmillan, 1921.

Bunton, Kristie. "Media Criticism as Self-Regulation." In *Holding the Media Accountable: Citizens, Ethics, and the Law,* ed. David Pritchard. Bloomington: Indiana University Press, 2000.

Byrd, Robert C., Mary Sharon Hall, and Wendy Wolff. *The Senate: 1789–1989.* Washington, DC: GPO, 1988.

Calhoun, George W. "Confidentiality and Executive Privilege." In *The Tethered Presidency,* ed. Thomas Franck. New York: New York University Press, 1981.

Callahan, Elletta S., Terry M. Dworkin, and David Lewis. "Whistleblowing: Australian, U.K., and U.S. Approaches to Disclosure in the Public Interest." *Virginia Journal of International Law* 44, no. 3 (2003).

Carlson, Matt. *On Condition of Anonymity: Unnamed Sources and the Battle for Journalism.* Urbana: University of Illinois Press, 2011.

———. "Whither Anonymity? Journalism and Unnamed Sources in a Changing Media Environment." In *Journalists, Sources, and Credibility,* ed. Bob Franklin and Matt Carlson. New York: Routledge, 2011.

Carpenter, Ted Galen. *The Captive Press: Foreign Policy Crises and the First Amendment.* Washington, DC: Cato Institute, 1995.

Casper, Gerhard. "Government Secrecy and the Constitution." *California Law Review* 74, no. 3 (1986).

Cater, Douglass. *The Fourth Branch of Government.* Boston: Houghton Mifflin, 1959.

———. "News and the Nation's Security." *Reporter,* July 6, 1961.

Chafee, Zechariah, Jr. *Government and Mass Communications*. Chicago: University of Chicago Press, 1947.

Chambers, Simone. "Behind Closed Doors: Publicity, Secrecy and the Quality of Deliberation." *Journal of Political Philosophy*. 12, no. 4 (2004).

Chanley, Virginia A. "Trust in Government in the Aftermath of 9/11: Determinants and Consequences." *Political Psychology* 23, no. 3 (2002).

Cheh, Mary. "Judicial Supervision of Executive Secrecy: Rethinking Freedom of Expression for Government Employees and the Public Right of Access to Government Information." *Cornell Law Review* 69 (1983).

Chesney, Robert M. "National Security Fact Deference." *Virginia Law Review* 95, no. 6 (2009).

———. "State Secrets and the Limits of National Security Litigation." *George Washington Law Review* 75, nos. 5–6 (2007).

Cicero. *On Duties*. Trans., M. T. Griffin and E. M. Atkins. Cambridge: Cambridge University Press, 2003.

Clark, Kathleen. "The Architecture of Accountability: A Case Study of the Warrantless Surveillance Program." *Brigham Young University Law Review* 2010, no. 2 (2010).

———. "Congress's Right to Counsel in Intelligence Oversight." *University of Illinois Law Review* 2011 no. 3 (2011).

———. " 'A New Era of Openness?' Disclosing Intelligence to Congress under Obama." *Constitutional Commentary* 26. no. 3 (2010).

Cockburn, Andrew. *Rumsfeld: His Rise, Fall, and Catastrophic Legacy*. New York: Simon & Schuster, 2007.

Colby, William. *Honorable Men: My Life in the CIA*. New York: Simon and Schuster, 1978.

———. "Intelligence Secrecy and Security in a Free Society." *International Security* 1, no. 2 (1976).

Coliver, Sandra. "Commentary on the Johannesburg Principles." In *Secrecy and Liberty: National Security, Freedom of Expression and Access to Information*, ed. Sandra Coliver et al. Cambridge, MA: Kluwer Law, 1999.

Colton, David E. "Speaking Truth to Power: Intelligence Oversight in an Imperfect World." *University of Pennsylvania Law Review* 137, no. 2 (1988).

Commager, Henry Steele. *The Defeat of America: Presidential Power and the National Character*. New York: Simon and Schuster, 1974.

Commission on Freedom of the Press. *A Free and Responsible Press: A General Report on Mass Communication*. Chicago: University of Chicago Press, 1947.

Commission on Government Security. *Report of the Commission on Government Security*. Washington, DC: GPO, 1957.

Commission on Protecting and Reducing Government Secrecy. *Report of the Commission on Protecting and Reducing Government Secrecy*. Washington, DC: GPO, 1997.

Commission on the Intelligence Capabilities of the United States Regarding Weapons of Mass Destruction. *Report of the Commission on the Intelligence*

Capabilities of the United States Regarding Weapons of Mass Destruction. Washington, DC: GPO, 2005.

Commission to Assess the Ballistic Missile Threat to the United States. *Report of the Commission to Assess the Ballistic Missile Threat to the United States.* Washington, DC: GPO, July 15, 1998.

Constant, Benjamin. "Principles of Politics." In *Political Writings*, trans. Biancamaria Fontana. New York: Cambridge University Press, 1988.

Conway, Stephen. "Bentham on Peace and War." *Utilitas* 1, no. l (1989).

Corwin, Edward S. *The President's Control of Foreign Relations.* Princeton, NJ: Princeton University Press, 1917.

Coser, Lewis. "Government by Secrecy." *Dissent* 1 (1954).

Cox, Arthur M. *The Myths of National Security: The Peril of Secret Government.* Boston: Beacon Press, 1975.

Crabb, Cecil V., and Pat M. Holt. *Invitation to Struggle: Congress, the President, and Foreign Policy.* Washington, DC: Congressional Quarterly Press, 1984.

Crockett, David. "Executive Privilege." In *The Constitutional Presidency*, ed. Joseph Bessette and Jeffrey K. Tulis. Baltimore: Johns Hopkins University Press, 2009.

Croner, Andrew. "A Snake in the Grass? Section 798 of the Espionage Act and Its Constitutionality As Applied to the Press." *George Washington Law Review* 77, no. 3 (2009).

Cross, Harold L. *The People's Right to Know: Legal Access to Public Recordings and Proceedings.* New York: Columbia University Press, 1953.

Curran, James. *Media and Power.* London: Routledge, 2002.

Dahl, Robert A. *A Preface to Democratic Theory.* Chicago: University of Chicago Press, 1956.

Dalglish, Lucy, ed. *Agents of Discovery: A Report on the Incidence of Subpoenas Served on the News Media in 2001.* Arlington, VA: The Reporters Committee for Freedom of the Press, 2003.

Dallek, Robert. *Nixon and Kissinger.* New York: Harper Collins, 2007.

Defense Department Committee on Classified Information. *Report to the Secretary of Defense.* Washington, DC: Department of Defense, 1956.

De George, Richard T. "Whistleblowing." In *Applied Ethics: Critical Concepts in Philosophy*, ed. Ruth F. Chadwick and Doris Schroeder, vol. 5. London: Routledge, 2002.

Demophilus. "The Genuine Principles of the Ancient Saxon or English Constitution." In *American Political Writing during the Founding Era*, ed. Charles S. Hyneman and Donald Lutz, vol. 1. Indianapolis: Liberty Fund, 1983.

Dennis, Everette E. "Stolen Treaties and the Press: Two Case Studies." *Journalism History* 2, no. 1 (1975).

Department of Justice. *Guide to the FOIA.* Washington, DC: Department of Justice, 2009.

Devins, Neal. "Congressional-Executive Information Access Disputes: A Modest Proposal—Do Nothing." *Administrative Law Review* 48, no. 1 (1996).

Dewey, John. *Lectures in China, 1919–1920.* Trans. Robert W. Clopton and Tsuin-Chen Ou. Honolulu: University Press of Hawaii, 1973.

Deyling, Robert P. "Judicial Deference and De Novo Review in Litigation over National Security Information under the Freedom of Information Act." *Villanova Law Review* 37 (1992).

Diamond, John M. *The CIA and the Culture of Failure.* Stanford, CA: Stanford University Press, 2008.

Dickinson, G. Lowes. *The Choice before Us.* New York: Dodd, Mead & Co., 1917.

Diodorus Siculus. *Library of History.* Trans. C. H. Oldfather. Cambridge: Loeb Classical Library, 1989.

Dixon, Robert G. "Congress, Shared Administration and Executive Privilege." In *Congress against the President,* ed. Harvey C. Mansfield, Sr. New York: Praeger, 1975.

Dmitrieva, Irina Y. "Stealing Information: Application of a Criminal Anti-Theft Statute to Leaks of Confidential Government Information." *Florida Law Review* 55, no. 4 (2003).

Dobel, J. Patrick. "Doing Good by Staying In?" In *Combating Corruption, Encouraging Ethics: A Sourcebook for Public Service Ethics,* ed. William L. Richter et al. Washington, DC: ASPA, 1990.

Donaldson, Peter S. *Machiavelli and the Mystery of State.* New York: Cambridge University Press, 1988.

Dorsen, Norman, and John H. F. Shattuck, "Executive Privilege, the Congress and the Courts." *Ohio State Law Journal* 35 (1974).

Dozier, Janelle Brinker, and Marcia P. Miceli. "Potential Predictors of Whistle-Blowing: A Prosocial Behavior Perspective." *Academy of Management* 10, no. 4 (1985).

Duffy, Matt J., and Carrie P. Freeman. "Unnamed Sources: A Utilitarian Exploration of Their Justification and Guidelines for Limited Use." *Journal of Mass Media Ethics* 26, no. 4 (2011).

Duffy, Matt J., and Ann E. Williams. "Use of Unnamed Sources Drops from Peaks in 1960s and 1970s." *Newspaper Research Journal* 32, no. 4 (2011).

Dulles, Allen W. *Craft of Intelligence.* New York: Harper & Row, 1963.

Dunn, John. *Democracy: A History.* New York: Grove/Atlantic, 2005.

Edgar, Harold, and Benno C. Schmidt, Jr. "The Espionage Statutes and the Publication of Defense Information." *Columbia Law Review.* 73 (1973).

Edwards, George C., and Stephen J. Wayne. *Presidential Leadership: Politics and Policy-Making.* New York: St. Martin's Press, 1997.

Elliot, Jonathan. *The Debates in Several State Conventions.* Philadelphia: J. B. Lippincott & Co., 1876.

Elliston, Frederick A. "Anonymous Whistleblowing." *Business and Professional Ethics Journal* 1, no. 2 (1982).

———. "Civil Disobedience and Whistleblowing: A Comparative Appraisal of Two Forms of Dissent." *Journal of Business Ethics* 1, no. 1 (1982).

Ellsberg, Daniel. "Secrecy and National Security Whistleblowing." *Social Research* 77, no. 3 (2010).

———. *Secrets: A Memoir of Vietnam and the Pentagon Papers.* New York: Viking, 2002.

Ellsworth, Oliver. "The Landholder, VI." In *Pamphlets on the Constitution of the United States*, ed. Paul L. Ford. New York: Burt Franklin, 1892.

Elster, Jon. "Deliberation and Constitution Making." In *Deliberative Democracy*, ed. Jon Elster. Cambridge: Cambridge University Press, 1998.

Ely, John Hart. *War and Responsibility: Constitutional Lessons of Vietnam and Its Aftermath*. Princeton, NJ: Princeton University Press, 1995.

Emerson, Thomas I. "Legal Foundations of the Right to Know." *Washington University Law Quarterly* 1976, no. 1 (1976).

———. "National Security and Civil Liberties." *Yale Journal of World Public Order* 9 (1982).

Epstein, Robert D. "Balancing National Security and Free-Speech Rights: Why Congress Should Revise the Espionage Act." *CommLaw Conspectus* 15, no. 2 (2007).

Ericson, Timothy L. "Building Our Own `Iron Curtain': The Emergence of Secrecy in American Government." *American Archivist* 68, no. 1 (2005).

Ettema, James S., and Theodore L. Glasser. "Public Accountability or Public Relations? Newspaper Ombudsmen Define Their Role." *Journalism Quarterly* 64, no. 1 (1987).

Evans, Florence M. G. *The Principal Secretary of State*. London: Longmans Green & Co., 1923.

Fargo, Anthony L. "The Year of Leaking Dangerously: Shadowy Sources, Jailed Journalists, and the Uncertain Future of the Federal Journalist's Privilege." *William and Mary Bill of Rights Journal* 14, no. 4 (2006).

Farrand, Max. *The Records of the Federal Convention of 1787*. New Haven, CT: Yale University Press, 1911.

Fatovic, Clement. *Outside the Law: Emergency and Executive Power*. Baltimore: Johns Hopkins University Press, 2009.

Fein, Bruce E. "Access to Classified Information: Constitutional and Statutory Dimensions." *William and Mary Law Review* 26 (1985).

Feldstein, Mark. *Poisoning the Press*. New York: Farrar, Straus, and Giroux, 2010.

Fenster, Mark. "The Opacity of Transparency." *Iowa Law Review* 91, no. 3 (2006).

Ferré, John P. "A Short History of Media Ethics in the United States." In *The Handbook of Mass Media Ethics*, ed. Lee Wilkins and Clifford G. Christians. New York: Routledge, 2008.

Filmer, Robert. *Patriarcha and Other Writings*. Ed. Johann P. Sommerville. Cambridge: Cambridge University Press, 1991.

Final Report of the National Commission on Terrorist Attacks upon the United States. Washington, DC: GPO, 2004.

Finnegan, Lisa. *No Questions Asked: News Coverage since 9/11*. Westport, CT: Praeger, 2006.

Firth, Charles H. "Thomas Scot's Account of Actions as Intelligencer during the Commonwealth." *English Historical Review* 12 (1897).

———. "Thurloe and the Post Office." *English Historical Review* 13 (1898).

Fisher, Louis. *Congressional Access to Executive Branch Information: Legislative Tools*. Washington, DC: Congressional Research Service, May 17, 2001.

———. *In the Name of National Security: Unchecked Presidential Power and the Reynolds Case.* Lawrence: University Press of Kansas, 2006.

———. *National Security Whistleblowers.* Washington, DC: Congressional Research Service, December 30, 2005.

———. *The Politics of Executive Privilege.* Durham, NC: Carolina Academic Press, 2004.

———. "The State Secrets Privilege: Relying on Reynolds." *Political Science Quarterly* 122, no. 3 (2007).

Flink, Stanley E. *Sentinel under Siege: The Triumphs and Troubles of America's Free Press.* New York: Westview, 1998.

Flynn, Kathryn. "Covert Disclosures: Unauthorized Leaking, Public Officials, and the Public Sphere." *Journalism Studies* 7, no. 2 (2006).

Foerstel, Herbert N. *Free Expression and Censorship in America: An Encyclopedia.* Westport, CT: Greenwood Press, 1997.

Ford, Worthington Chauncey. *Journals of the Continental Congress.* Washington, DC: GPO, 1904.

Franck, Thomas M., and Edward Weisband. *Secrecy and Foreign Policy.* New York: Oxford University Press, 1974.

Frank, Larry J. "The United States v. the *Chicago Tribune.*" *Historian* 42, no. 2 (1980).

Friedberg, Aaron L. *A Contest for Supremacy: China, America, and the Struggle for Mastery in Asia.* New York: W. W. Norton & Company, 2011.

Friedrich, Carl J. *Constitutional Government and Politics: Nature and Development.* New York: Harper & Brothers, 1937.

Frost, Amanda. "The State Secrets Privilege and Separation of Powers." *Fordham Law Review* 75, no. 4 (2007).

Fuchs, Meredith. "Judging Secrets: The Role of the Courts in Preventing Unnecessary Secrecy." *Administrative Law Review* 58, no. 1 (2006).

Fuchs, Meredith, and G. Gregg Webb. "Greasing the Wheels of Justice: Independent Experts in National Security Cases." *American Bar Association National Security Law Report* 28, no. 4 (2006).

Galnoor, Itzhak. *Government Secrecy in Democracies.* New York: New York University Press, 1977.

Gerolymatos, André. *Espionage and Treason: A Study of Proxenia in Political and Military Intelligence Gathering in Classical Greece.* Amsterdam: Gieben, 1986.

Gerth, Hans H., and C. Wright Mills, eds. *From Max Weber: Essays in Sociology.* New York: Oxford University Press, 1946.

Glazer, Myron Peretz, and Penina Migdal Glazer. *The Whistleblowers: Exposing Corruption in Government and Industry.* New York: Basic Books, 1989.

Godfrey, John. "Intelligence in the United States." Reprinted in Bradley F. Smith, "Admiral Godfrey's Mission to America." *Intelligence and National Security* 1, no. 3 (1986).

Goldschmidt, Maure L. "Publicity, Privacy, and Secrecy." *Western Political Quarterly* 7, no. 3 (1954).

Goldsmith, Jack L. *Power and Constraint: The Accountable Presidency after 9/11.* New York: W. W. Norton & Co., 2012.

Goldsmith, Jack L. "Secrecy and Safety." *New Republic*, August 13, 2008.
———.*The Terror Presidency: Law and Judgment inside the Bush Administration*. New York: W. W. Norton, 2009.
Government Accountability Project. *The Art of Anonymous Activism*. Washington, DC: Government Accountability Project, 2002.
Graham, Bob, and Jeff Nussbaum. *Intelligence Matters*. Wichita: University of Kansas Press, 2008.
Graham, Bradley. *Hit to Kill: The New Battle over Shielding America from Missile Attack*. Cambridge, MA: Public Affairs, 2001.
Graves, John T. "The Value of a Free Press." In *The Foreign Relations of the United States*, ed. Henry R. Mussey and Stephen P. Duggan. New York: Academy of Political Science, 1917.
Greenawalt, Kent. *Conflicts of Law and Morality*. New York: Oxford University Press, 1987.
Greenstein, Fred I. *The Hidden-Hand Presidency: Eisenhower as Leader*. Baltimore: Johns Hopkins University Press, 1994.
Guicciardini, Francesco. *Dialogue on the Government of Florence*. Trans. Alison Brown. Cambridge: Cambridge University Press, 2002.
———. *The History of Italy*. Trans. Austin Parke Goddard. London: John Towers, 1755.
———. *Maxims and Reflections*. Trans. Mario Domandi. Philadelphia: University of Pennsylvania Press, 1972.
Guizot, François. *General History of Civilization in Europe*. Ed. C. S. Henry. New York: D. Appleton and Company, 1846.
———. *The History of the Origins of Representative Government in Europe*, Trans. Andrew R. Scoble. London: Henry G. Bohn, 1861.
Gup, Ted. *Nation of Secrets: The Threat to Democracy and the American Way of Life*. New York: Doubleday, 2007.
Gutmann, Amy, and Dennis F. Thompson. *Democracy and Disagreement*. Cambridge, MA: Belknap Press of Harvard University Press, 1996.
———. *Ethics and Politics: Cases and Comments*. Chicago: Nelson-Hall, 1990.
Hallin, Daniel C., Robert K. Manoff, and Judy K. Weddle. "Sourcing Patterns of National Security Reporters." *Journalism Quarterly* 70, no. 4 (1993).
Halperin, Morton, and Daniel Hoffman, "Secrecy and the Right to Know." *Law and Contemporary Problems* 40, no. 3 (1976).
———. *Top Secret: National Security and the Right to Know*. Washington, DC: New Republic Books, 1977.
Halstuk, Martin E. "Holding the Spymasters Accountable after 9/11." *Hastings Communications and Entertainment Law Journal* 27 (2004).
Hamilton, Alexander, James Madison, and John Jay, *The Federalist*. Ed. Terence Ball. New York: Cambridge University Press, 2003.
Hamilton, Lee H., and Daniel K. Inouye, eds. *Report of the Congressional Committees Investigating the Iran-Contra Affair*. Washington, DC: GPO, 1987.
Harrington, James. *The Commonwealth of Oceana*. Ed. J.G.A. Pocock. Cambridge: Cambridge University Press, 1992.

Hartung, William D. *Prophets of War: Lockheed Martin and the Making of the Military-Industrial Complex.* New York: Nation Books, 2011.

Hayes, Arthur S. *Press Critics Are the Fifth Estate: Media Watchdogs in America.* Westport, CT: Praeger, 2008.

Haynes, George. *The Senate of the United States: Its History and Practice.* Boston: Houghton Mifflin Co., 1938.

Headley, John H. "Secrets, Free Speech, and Fig Leaves." *Studies in Intelligence* 41, no. 5 (1998).

Helms, Jesse. *Empire for Liberty: A Sovereign America and Her Moral Mission.* Washington, DC: Regnery, 2001.

Henkin, Louis. "The Right to Know and the Duty to Withhold." *University of Pennsylvania Law Review* 120, no. 2 (1971).

Hennings, Thomas C., Jr. "The Executive Privilege and the People's Right to Know." *Federal Bar Journal* 19, no. 1 (1959).

Herman, Susan N. *Taking Liberties: The War on Terror and the Erosion of American Democracy.* New York: Oxford University Press, 2011.

Hersh, Seymour. *Chain of Command: The Road from 9/11 to Abu Ghraib.* New York: HarperCollins, 2005.

Hess, Stephen. *The Government/Press Connection: Press Officers and Their Offices.* Washington, DC: Brookings Institution, 1984.

Hinsley, F. H. *Power and the Pursuit of Peace.* Cambridge: Cambridge University Press, 1963.

Hirschman, Albert O. *Exit, Voice, and Loyalty: Responses to Decline in Firms, Organizations, and States.* Cambridge, MA: Harvard University Press, 1970.

Hoekstra, Pete. *Secrets and Leaks: The Costs and Consequences for National Security.* Washington, DC: Heritage Foundation, September 6, 2005.

Hoffman, Daniel N. *Governmental Secrecy and the Founding Fathers: A Study in Constitutional Controls.* Westport, CT: Greenwood Press, 1981.

Holt, Pat M. *Secret Intelligence and Public Policy: A Dilemma of Democracy.* Washington, DC: CQ Press, 1995.

Howard, Michael E. *War and the Liberal Conscience.* New York: Columbia University Press, 2008.

Hoyle, Russ. *Going to War: How Misinformation, Disinformation, and Arrogance Led America into Iraq.* New York: St. Martin's Press, 2008.

Hughes, Charles. "Nicholas Faunt's Discourse Touching the Office of Principal Secretary of Estate." *English Historical Review* 20, no. 79 (1905).

Hume, David. "Idea of a Perfect Commonwealth." In David Hume, *Political Essays,* ed. Knud Haakonssen. New York: Cambridge University Press, 1994.

Hurt, Michael. "Leaking National Security Secrets." *National Security Studies Quarterly* 7, no. 4 (2001).

Hutcheson, Francis. *A Short Introduction to Moral Philosophy.* Ed. Luigi Turco. Indianapolis: Liberty Fund, 2007.

Hutchinson, Robert. *Elizabeth's Spy Master.* London: Weidenfeld and Nicolson, 2006.

Hyde, Henry J. "Leaks and Congressional Oversight." *George Mason University Law Review* 11, no. 1 (1988).

Interdepartmental Group on Unauthorized Disclosures of Classified Information. *Report of the Interdepartmental Group on Unauthorized Disclosures of Classified Information.* Washington, DC: GPO, March 31, 1982.

Isaacson, Walter. *Kissinger.* New York: Simon and Schuster, 1992.

Isikoff, Michael, and David Corn. *Hubris: The Inside Story of Spin, Scandal, and the Selling of the Iraq War.* New York: Random House, 2007.

Jacquette, Dale. *Journalistic Ethics: Moral Responsibility in the Media.* Upper Saddle River, NJ: Prentice Hall, 2007.

James, Gene G. "In Defense of Whistleblowing." In *Ethical Issues in Professional Life,* ed. Joan C. Callahan. New York: Oxford University Press, 1988.

Jay, John. *The Correspondence and Public Papers of John Jay.* Ed. Henry P. Johnston. New York: G. P. Putnam's Sons, 1890–93.

Johnson, Loch K. "The Church Committee Investigation of 1975 and the Evolution of Modern Intelligence Accountability." *Intelligence and National Security* 23, no. 2 (2008).

———. "The CIA and the Question of Accountability." *Intelligence and National Security* 12, no. 1 (1997).

———. "Congress, the Iraq War, and the Failures of Intelligence Oversight." In *Intelligence and National Security Policymaking on Iraq: British and American Perspectives,* ed. James P. Pfiffner and Mark Pythian. College Station: Texas A&M University Press, 2008.

———. "Intelligence and the Challenge of Collaborative Government." *Intelligence and National Security* 13, no. 2 (1998).

———. *Secret Agencies: U.S. Intelligence in a Hostile World.* New Haven, CT: Yale University Press, 1996.

———. "A Shock Theory of Congressional Accountability for Intelligence." In *Handbook of Intelligence Studies,* ed. Loch K. Johnson. New York: Routledge, 2007.

Johnson, Roberta A. *Whistleblowing: When It Works—And Why.* Boulder, CO: Lynne Reiner, 2003.

Jones, RonNell Andersen. "Avalanche or Undue Alarm? An Empirical Study of Subpoenas Received by the News Media." *Minnesota Law Review* 93, no. 2 (2008).

Jos, Philip, Mark E. Tompkins, and Steven W. Hays. "In Praise of Difficult People: A Portrait of the Committed Whistleblower." *Public Administration Review* 49, no. 6 (1989).

Kaiser, Frederick M. "Congress and the Intelligence Community: Taking the Road Less Travelled." In *The Postreform Congress,* ed. Roger H. Davidson. New York: St. Martin's Press, 1992.

———. *Protection of Classified Information by Congress: Practices and Proposals.* Washington, DC: Congressional Research Service, 2005.

Katyal, Neal K. "The Internal Separation of Powers." *Yale Law Journal* 115, no. 9 (2006).

Katz, Alan M. "Government Information Leaks and the First Amendment." *California Law Review* 64, no. 1 (1976).

Kazin, Michael. *A Godly Hero: The Life of William Jennings Bryan*. New York: Knopf, 2006.

Kean, Thomas H., and Lee H. Hamilton. *Without Precedent: The Inside Story of the 9/11 Commission*. New York: Alfred A. Knopf, 2006.

Keefe, Patrick K. "The Challenge of Global Intelligence Listening." In *Strategic Intelligence*, ed. Loch K. Johnson, vol. 2. Westport, CT: Praeger, 2007.

"Keeping Secrets: Congress, the Courts, and National Security Information." *Harvard Law Review* 103, no. 4 (1990).

Keller, Bill. "The Boy Who Kicked the Hornet's Nest." In *Open Secrets: WikiLeaks, War and American Diplomacy*, ed. Alexander Star. New York: New York Times, 2011.

Kent, James. *Commentaries on American Law*. Ed. John M. Gould. Boston: Little, Brown, & Co., 1896.

Kerr, Clara H. *The Origin and Development of the United States Senate*. Ithaca, NY: Andrus and Church, 1895.

Kielbowicz, Richard B. "The Role of News Leaks in Governance and the Law of Journalists' Confidentiality, 1795–2005." *San Diego Law Review* 43 (2006).

Kitrosser, Heidi. "Classified Information Leaks and Free Speech." *University of Illinois Law Review* 2008, no. 3 (2008).

———. "Congressional Oversight of National Security Activities: Improving Information Funnels." *Cardozo Law Review* 29, no. 3 (2008).

———. "Secrecy and Separated Powers: Executive Privilege Revisited." *Iowa Law Review* 92, no. 2 (2007).

Klaidman, Stephen, and Tom L. Beauchamp. *The Virtuous Journalist*. New York: Oxford University Press, 1987.

Knott, Stephen F. "Executive Power and the Control of American Intelligence." *Intelligence and National Security* 13, no. 2 (1998).

———. *Secret and Sanctioned: Covert Operations and the American Presidency*. New York: Oxford University Press, 1996.

Koh, Harold H. *The National Security Constitution: Sharing Power after the Iran-Contra Affair*. New Haven, CT: Yale University Press, 1990.

Kossuth, Lajos. *Select Speeches of Kossuth*. Ed. Francis Newman. New York: C. S. Francis & Co., 1854.

———. "Speech before the Corporation of London." Reprinted in Daniel Webster, *Sketch of the Life of Louis Kossuth*. New York: Stringer and Townsend, 1851.

Kreimer, Seth F. "The Freedom of Information Act and the Ecology of Transparency." *University of Pennsylvania Journal of Constitutional Law* 10, no. 5 (2008).

———. "Rays of Sunlight in a Shadow War: FOIA, the Abuses of Anti-Terrorism, and the Strategy of Transparency." *Lewis and Clark Law Review* 11, no. 4 (2010).

Kutler, Stanley I. *The Wars of Watergate: The Last Crisis of Richard Nixon*. New York: W. W. Norton, 1992.

Lambeth, Edmund B. *Committed Journalism: An Ethic for the Profession*. Bloomington: Indiana University Press, 1992.

Laski, Harold J. *The American Presidency: An Interpretation*. London: George, Allen & Unwin, 1940.

Lasswell, Harold D. *National Security and Individual Freedom*. New York: McGraw-Hill, 1950.

Lee, William. "Probing Secrets: The Press and Inchoate Liability for Newsgathering Crimes." *American Journal of Criminal Law* 36, no. 2 (2009).

Levi, Lili. "Dangerous Liaisons: Seduction and Betrayal in Confidential Press-Source Relations." *Rutgers Law Review* 43 (1991).

Levinson, Daryl J., and Richard H. Pildes. "Separation of Parties, Not Powers." *Harvard Law Review* 119, no. 8 (2006).

Levinson, Nan. *Outspoken: Free Speech Stories*. Berkeley: University of California Press, 2003.

Levy, Adrian, and Catherine Scott-Clark. *Deception: Pakistan, the United States, and the Secret Trade in Nuclear Weapons*. New York: Walker & Co., 2007.

Lewalski, Barbara K. *The Life of John Milton*. Oxford: Blackwell, 2003.

Lichtblau, Eric. *Bush's Law: The Remaking of American Justice*. New York: Pantheon, 2008.

Lieber, Francis. *On Civil Liberty and Self-Government*. Ed. Theodore Woolsey, Philadelphia: Lippincott, 1888.

Lippmann, Walter. *Liberty and the News*. New York: Harcourt, Brace, and Howe, 1920.

———. *The Political Scene: An Essay on the Victory of 1918*. New York: Henry Holt, 1919.

———. *Public Opinion*. New York: Harcourt, Brace & Co., 1922.

———. *The Stakes of Diplomacy*. New York: Henry Holt, 1915.

Luban, David. "Publicity Principle." In *The Theory of Institutional Design*, ed. Robert E. Goodin. New York: Cambridge University Press, 1996.

Machiavelli, Niccolò. "Confidential Instructions." In *The Historical, Political and Diplomatic Writings of Niccolò Machiavelli*, vol. 4, trans. Christian E. Detmold. Boston: James R. Osgood & Co., 1882.

Madison, James. *Letters and Other Writings*. Philadelphia: J. B. Lippincott & Co., 1865.

———. *The Writings of James Madison*. Ed. Gaillard Hunt. New York: G. P. Putnam's Sons, 1910.

Maer, Lucinda, and Oonagh Gay. *Official Secrecy*. London: House of Commons Library, Standard Note 02023, December 30, 2008.

Maffeo, Steven E. *Most Secret and Confidential: Intelligence in the Age of Nelson*. Annapolis, MD: Naval Institute Press, 2000.

Manin, Bernard. *The Principles of Representative Government*. Cambridge: Cambridge University Press, 1997.

Mansfield, Harvey C. *Taming the Prince: The Ambivalence of Modern Executive Power*. New York: Free Press, 1993.

Marbut, Frederick B. *News from the Capital: The Story of Washington Reporting*. Carbondale: Southern Illinois University Press, 1971.

Marchetti, Victor L., and John D. Marks. *The CIA and the Cult of Intelligence*. New York: Knopf, 1974.

Martin, Frederick R. "A Plea for an Uncensored Press." In *The Foreign Relations of the United States*, ed. Henry Raymond Mussey and Stephen Pierce Duggan. New York: Academy of Political Science, 1917.

Martin, Mike W. *Meaningful Work: Rethinking Professional Ethics*. New York: Oxford University Press, 2000.

Martin-Kratzer, Renee, and Esther Thorson. "Use of Anonymous Sources Declines in U.S. Newspapers." *Newspaper Research Journal* 28, no. 2 (2007).

Massing, Michael. "Now They Tell Us." *New York Review of Books* 51 (2004).

———. *Now They Tell Us: The American Press and Iraq*. New York: New York Review Books, 2004.

Mattingly, Garret. *Renaissance Diplomacy*. New York: Dover Publications, 1988.

Mayer, Kenneth R. *With the Stroke of a Pen: Executive Orders and Presidential Power*. Princeton, NJ: Princeton University Press, 2001.

Mazzini, Giuseppe. "On Publicity in Foreign Affairs." In *A Cosmopolitanism of Nations: Giuseppe Mazzini's Writings on Democracy, National Building, and International Relations*, ed. Stefano Recchia and Nadia Urbinati. Princeton, NJ: Princeton University Press, 2009.

McClendon, R. Earl. "Violations of Secrecy In Re Senate Executive Sessions, 1789–1929." *American Historical Review* 51, no. 1 (1945).

McConnell, Terence. "Whistleblowing." In *A Companion to Applied Ethics*, ed. R. G. Frey and Christopher H. Wellman. Oxford: Blackwell, 2005.

McCubbins, Mathew D., and Thomas Schwartz. "Congressional Oversight Overlooked: Police Patrols versus Fire Alarms." *American Journal of Political Science* 28, no. 1 (1984).

McDonald, Forrest. *The American Presidency: An Intellectual History*. Lawrence: University Press of Kansas, 1995.

McNeil, Phyllis P. "The Evolution of the U.S. Intelligence Community: An Historical Overview." In *Preparing for the 21st Century: An Appraisal of U.S. Intelligence*. Washington, DC: GPO, 1996.

"Media Incentives and National Security Secrets." *Harvard Law Review* 122, no. 8 (2009).

Meiklejohn, Alexander. "The First Amendment Is an Absolute." *Supreme Court Review* 1961 (1961).

———. *Free Speech and Its Relation to Self-Government*. New York: Harper & Brothers, 1948.

Meyers, Christopher. "Creating an Effective Newspaper Ombudsman Position." *Journal of Mass Media Ethics* 15, no. 4 (2000).

Miceli, Marcia P., Janet P. Near, and Terry M. Dworkin. *Whistleblowing in Organizations*. New York: Routledge, 2008.

"The Military and State Secrets Privilege: Protection for the National Security or Immunity for the Executive?" *Yale Law Journal* 91, no. 3 (1982).

Milton, John. "A Defence of the People of England." In John Milton, *Political Writings*, ed. Martin Dzelzainis and Claire Gruzelier. New York: Cambridge University Press, 2000.

———. *The Ready and Easy Way to Establish a Free Commonwealth*. Ed. Evert M. Clark. New Haven, CT: Yale University Press, 1915.

Minnow, Martha. "The Constitution as Black Box during National Emergencies." *Fordham Law Review* 75 (2006).

———. "The Lesser Evil." *Harvard Law Review* 118, no. 7 (2005).

Moberly, Richard. "Whistleblowers and the Obama Presidency: The National Security Dilemma." *Employee Rights and Employment Policy Journal* 16 (2012).

Moore, John Bassett. *The Principles of American Diplomacy*. New York: Harper & Brothers, 1918.

Morris, Robert. *The Papers of Robert Morris*. Ed. James E. Ferguson and John Catanzariti. Pittsburgh: University of Pittsburgh Press, 1978.

Morrissey, David H. *Disclosure and Secrecy: Security Classification Executive Orders*. Iowa City, IA: AEJMC, 1997.

Morse, Mika C. "Honor or Betrayal? The Ethics of Government Lawyer-Whistleblowers." *Georgetown Journal of Legal Ethics* 23 (2010).

Moss, John E. "Introduction: A Legislator's View." *Federal Bar Journal* 19, no. 1 (1959).

Moynihan, Daniel P. *Secrecy: The American Experience*. New Haven, CT: Yale University Press, 1998.

Near, Janet P., and Marcia P. Miceli. "Organizational Dissidence: The Case of Whistle-Blowing." *Journal of Business Ethics* 4, no. 1 (1985).

Nedham, Marchamont. *The Excellencie of a Free State*. London: Thomas Brewster, 1656.

Nelson, Anna K. "Secret Agents and Security Leaks: President Polk and the Mexican War." *Journalism Quarterly* 52, no. 1 (1975).

Nelson, Jack. *U.S. Government Secrecy and the Current Crackdown on Leaks*. Cambridge, MA: Joan Shorenstein Center, 2002.

Nemeth, Neil. *News Ombudsman in North America: Assessing an Experiment in Social Responsibility* Westport, CT: Praeger, 2003.

Newcomb, Thomas. "In from the Cold: The Intelligence Community Whistleblower Protection Act." *Administrative Law Review* 53 (2001).

Norris, Pippa. *A Virtuous Circle: Political Communication in Postindustrial Societies*. New York: Cambridge University Press, 2000.

Olmstead, Kathryn S. *Challenging the Secret Government: Post-Watergate Investigations of the CIA and FBI*. Durham: North Carolina University Press, 1996.

Omand, David. "Intelligence Secrets and Media Spotlights: Balancing Illumination and Media Spotlights." In *Spinning Intelligence: Why Intelligence Needs the Media, Why the Media Needs Intelligence*, ed. Robert Dover and Michael S. Goodman. New York: Columbia University Press, 2009.

Orman, John M. *Presidential Secrecy and Deception: Beyond the Power to Persuade*. Westport, CT: Greenwood Press, 1980.

O'Toole, George J. A. *Honorable Treachery*. New York: Atlantic Monthly, 1991.

Ott, Marvin C. "Partisanship and the Decline of Intelligence Oversight." *International Journal of Intelligence and Counterintelligence* 16, no. 1 (2003).

Overholser, Geneva. "The Seduction of Secrecy: Toward Better Access to Government Information on the Record." *Nieman Reports*, Summer 2005.

Paine, Thomas. "The Necessity of Taxation." *Pennsylvania Gazette*, April 3, 1782. Reprinted in *Collected Writings*. New York: Library of America, 1955.

———. "The Rights of Man, Part II." In *Political Writings*, ed. Bruce Kuklick. Cambridge: Cambridge University Press, 2000.

Paley, William. *The Principles of Moral and Political Philosophy*. In *The Works of William Paley*. London: Thomas Allman, 1851.

Pallitto, Robert M., and William G. Weaver. *Presidential Secrecy and the Law*. Baltimore: Johns Hopkins University Press, 2007.

Parks, Wallace. "Secrecy and the Public Interest in Military Affairs." *George Washington Law Review* 26 (1957).

Parsons, Theophilus. "The Essex Result." In *American Political Writing during the Founding Era*, ed. Charles S. Hyneman and Donald Lutz, vol. 1. Indianapolis: Liberty Fund, 1983.

Patterson, Bradley H. *To Serve the President: Continuity and Innovation in the White House Staff*. Washington, DC: Brookings Institution Press, 2008.

Peacey, Jason. *Politicians and Pamphleteers: Propaganda during the English Civil Wars and Interregnum*. Aldershot: Ashgate, 2004.

Pearlstine, Norman. *Off the Record: The Press, the Government, and the War over Anonymous Sources*. New York: Farrar, Straus and Giroux, 2007.

Pettigrew, Richard F. *The Course of Empire*. New York: Boni & Liveright, 1920.

Pfiffner, James P. *Power Play: The Bush Presidency and the Constitution*, Washington, DC: Brookings Institution Press, 2009.

Plutarch. "Themistocles." In *Lives II*, trans. Bernadotte Perrin. Cambridge, MA: Loeb Classical Library, 1914.

Polishook, Irwin H. *Rhode Island and the Union 1774–1795*. Evanston, IL: Northwestern University Press, 1969.

Poole, DeWitt. *The Conduct of Foreign Relations under Modern Democratic Conditions*. New Haven, CT: Yale University Press, 1924.

Posner, Eric, and Adrian Vermeule. "The Credible Executive." *Chicago Law Review* 74, no. 3 (2007).

Posner, Richard A. *Not a Suicide Pact: The Constitution in a Time of National Emergency*. New York: Oxford University Press, 2006.

———. *Uncertain Shield: The U.S. Intelligence System in the Throes of Reform*. Lanham, MD: Rowman & Littlefield, 2006.

Pozen, David E. "Deep Secrecy." *Stanford Law Review* 62, no. 2 (2010).

———. "The Mosaic Theory, National Security, and the Freedom of Information Act." *Yale Law Review* 115, no. 3 (2005).

Prakash, Saikrishna B. "A Critical Comment on the Constitutionality of the Executive Privilege." *Minnesota Law Review* 83, no. 5 (1999).

Price, Richard. *Political Writings*. Ed. David Oswald Thomas. New York: Cambridge University Press, 1991.

Project on Government Oversight. *Homeland and National Security Whistleblower Protections: The Unfinished Agenda*. Washington, DC: Project on Government Oversight, April 28, 2005.

"Prosecuting the Press: Criminal Liability for the Act of Publishing." *Harvard Law Review* 120, no. 4 (2007).

Ramsay, David. "An Address to the Freemen of South Carolina" (May 1787). In *Pamphlets on the Constitution of the United States: Published during Its Discussion by the People, 1787–1788*, ed. Paul Leicester Ford. Brooklyn, NY, 1888.

——. *The History of the American Revolution*. Trenton, NJ: James Wilson, 1811.

Ramsey, Mary Louise, and Michael Daniels. "Selected Cases in Which Information Has Been Withheld from Congress by the Executive Division." Reprinted in *Hearing Before the Subcommittee on Constitutional Rights of the Committee of the Judiciary*, 85th Congress, 2nd Sess. Washington, DC: GPO, 1958.

Randolph, Edmund. "Letter on the Federal Constitution." In *Pamphlets on the Constitution of the United States: Published during Its Discussion by the People, 1787–1788*, ed. Paul Leicester Ford. Brooklyn, NY, 1888.

Ransom, Harry H. *Central Intelligence and National Security*. Cambridge, MA: Harvard University Press, 1958.

——. "Congress and the Intelligence Agencies." *Proceedings of the Academy of Political Science* 32, no. 1 (1975).

——. "A Half Century of Spy Watching." In *Strategic Intelligence*, ed. Loch K. Johnson, vol. 5. Westport, CT: Praeger, 2007.

Rawle, William. *A View of the Constitution*. Philadelphia: H. C. Carey, 1825.

Rawls, John. *A Theory of Justice*. Cambridge, MA: Harvard University Press, 1991.

Reinsch, Paul S. *Readings on American Federal Government*. New York: Ginn & Co., 1909.

——. *Secret Diplomacy*. New York: Harcourt, Brace & Co., 1922.

Relyea, Harold C. "The Evolution and Organization of the Federal Intelligence Function: A Brief Overview." Reprinted in *Senate Select Committee to Study Governmental Operations with Respect to Intelligence Activities*. Washington, DC: GPO, 1976.

Richardson, James Daniel. *A Compilation of the Messages and Papers of the Presidents*. Washington, DC: Bureau of National Literature and Art, 1897.

Risen, James. *State of War: The Secret History of the CIA and the Bush Administration*. New York: Free Press, 2006.

Ritchie, Donald A. *Press Gallery: Congress and the Washington Correspondents*. Cambridge, MA: Harvard University Press, 1991.

——. *Reporting from Washington: The History of the Washington Press Corps*. New York: Oxford University Press, 2005.

Robarge, David. *Intelligence in the War of Independence*. Washington, DC: Center for the Study of Intelligence, 1997.

Roberts, Alasdair S. *Blacked Out: Government Secrecy in the Information Age*. Cambridge: Cambridge University Press, 2006.

Robinson, W. Peter. *Deceit, Delusion, and Detection*. London: Sage, 1996.

Rogers, William P. "Constitutional Law: The Papers of the Executive Branch." *American Bar Association Journal* 44 (1958).

Root, Elihu. *The Effect of Democracy on International Law*. Washington, DC: Carnegie Endowment for International Peace, 1917.

———. "A Requisite for the Success of Popular Democracy." In *The American Encounter: The United States and the Making of the Modern World*, ed. James F. Hoge, Jr., and Fareed Zakaria. New York: Basic Books, 1997.

Rosen, Jay. *What Are Journalists For?* New Haven, CT: Yale University Press, 2001.

Rosenblum, Nancy L. "Constitutional Reason of State: The Fear Factor." In *Dissent in Dangerous Times*, ed. Austin Sarat. Ann Arbor: University of Michigan Press, 2005.

Rourke, Francis E. *Secrecy and Publicity: Dilemmas of Democracy*. Baltimore: Johns Hopkins University Press, 1961.

———. "Secrecy in American Bureaucracy." *Political Science Quarterly* 72, no. 4 (1957).

Rowat, Donald C., ed. *Administrative Secrecy in Developed Countries*. New York: Columbia University Press, 1979.

Rozell, Mark J. *Executive Privilege: Presidential Power, Secrecy, and Accountability*. Lawrence: University Press of Kansas, 2002.

Russell, Frank Santi. *Information Gathering in Classical Greece*. Ann Arbor: University of Michigan Press, 1999.

Russett, Bruce M. *Controlling the Sword: The Democratic Governance of National Security*. Cambridge, MA: Harvard University Press, 1990.

Sagar, Rahul. "Executive Privilege." In *The Oxford Companion to American Politics*, ed. David Coates et al. New York: Oxford University Press, 2012.

———. "On Combating the Abuse of State Secrecy," *Journal of Political Philosophy* 15, no. 4 (December 2007).

Samaha, Adam. "Government Secrets, Constitutional Law, and Platforms for Judicial Intervention." *UCLA Law Review* 53, no. 4 (2006).

Sanders, Karen. *Ethics and Journalism*. London: Sage, 2003.

Sanger, David E. *Confront and Conceal: Obama's Secret Wars and Surprising Use of American Power*. New York: Crown, 2012.

Sasser, Jamie. "Silenced Citizens: The Post-Garcetti Landscape for Public Sector Employees Working in National Security." *University of Richmond Law Review* 41, no. 3 (2007).

Savage, Charlie. *Takeover: The Return of the Imperial Presidency and the Subversion of American Democracy*. New York: Little, Brown, 2007.

Sayle, Edward F. "Historical Underpinnings of the U.S. Intelligence Community." *International Journal of Intelligence and Counterintelligence* 1, no. 1 (1986).

Scarre, Geoffrey. *On Courage*. New York: Routledge, 2010.

Scharf, Michael. "On Terrorism and Whistleblowing." *Case Western Journal of International Law* 38 (2006).

Schepple, Kim L. *Legal Secrets: Equality and Efficiency in the Common Law*. Chicago: University of Chicago Press, 1990.

Schepple, Kim L. "We Are All Post-9/11 Now." *Fordham Law Review* 75 (2006).

Scheuer, Jeffrey. *The Big Picture: Why Democracies Need Journalistic Excellence.* New York: Routledge, 2007.

Schlesinger, Arthur M. *The Imperial Presidency.* New York: Mariner Books, 2004.

Schmitt, Gary J. "Executive Privilege: Presidential Power to Withhold Information from Congress." In *The Presidency in the Constitutional Order,* ed. Joseph M. Bessette and Jeffrey Tulis. Baton Rouge: Louisiana State University Press, 1981.

Schoenfeld, Gabriel. *Necessary Secrets: National Security, The Media, and The Rule of Law.* New York: Norton, 2010.

Schultz, Julianne. *Reviving the Fourth Estate: Democracy, Accountability, and the Media.* New York: Cambridge University Press, 1998.

Schwartz, Bernard. "A Reply to Mr. Rogers: The Papers of the Executive Branch." *American Bar Association Journal* 45 (1959).

Schwartz, Stephen I. *Atomic Audit: The Costs and Consequences of U.S. Nuclear Weapons.* Washington, DC: Brookings Institution Press, 1998.

Senate Select Committee on Intelligence. *Report of the Select Committee on Intelligence on the U.S. Intelligence Community's Prewar Intelligence Assessments on Iraq.* Washington, DC: GPO, 2004.

Shane, Peter M. *Madison's Nightmare: How Executive Power Threatens American Democracy.* Chicago: University of Chicago Press, 2009.

Sheldon, Rose Mary. *Intelligence Activities in Ancient Rome: Trust in the Gods but Verify.* London: Frank Cass, 2005.

Shepard, Alicia C. "Anonymous Sources." *American Journalism Review,* December 1994.

Shils, Edward. *The Torment of Secrecy: The Background and Consequences of American Security Policies.* Chicago: Ivan R. Dee, 1996.

Sidney, Algernon. *Discourses Concerning Government.* Ed. Thomas G. West, Indianapolis: Liberty Fund, 1996.

Siegel, Leslie. "Trampling on the Fourth Estate: The Need for a Federal Shield Law." *Ohio State Law Journal* 67, no. 2 (2006).

Silbey, Joel H. *Storm over Texas: The Annexation Controversy and the Road to Civil War.* New York: Oxford University Press, 2005.

Smist, Frank J., Jr. *Congress Oversees the United States Intelligence Community 1947–1994.* Knoxville: University of Tennessee Press, 1994.

Smith, Jeffrey A. *War and Press Freedom: The Problem of Prerogative Power.* New York: Oxford University Press, 1999.

Smith, Paul H. *Letters of Delegates to Congress.* Washington, DC: Library of Congress, 2000.

Smith, Ron F. *Ethics in Journalism.* Oxford: Blackwell, 2008.

———. "Impact of Unnamed Sources on Credibility Not Certain." *Newspaper Research Journal* 28, no. 3 (2007).

Smolkin, Rachel. "Judgment Calls." *American Journalism Review,* October/November 2006.

Snepp, Frank W. *Decent Interval: An Insider's Account of Saigon's Indecent End.* New York: Random House, 1977.

Snider, L. Britt. *The Agency and the Hill: CIA's Relationship with Congress*. Washington, DC: Center for the Study of Intelligence, 2008.

———. "Congressional Oversight of Intelligence after September 11." In *Transforming U.S. Intelligence*, ed. Jennifer E. Sims and Burton Gerber. Washington, DC: Georgetown University Press, 2005.

———. *Sharing Secrets with Lawmakers: Congress as a User of Intelligence*. Washington, DC: Center for the Study of Intelligence, 1997.

Sofaer, Abraham D. "Executive Power and the Control of Information: Practice under the Framers." *Duke Law Journal* 1977, no. 1 (1977).

———. "Executive Privilege." *Harvard Law Review* 88 (1971).

Sofaer, Abraham D., and Henry Bartholomew Cox. *War, Foreign Affairs, and Constitutional Power*. 2 vols. Cambridge, MA: Ballinger, 1976.

Son, Taegyu. "Leaks: How Do Codes of Ethics Address Them?" *Journal of Mass Media Ethics* 17, no. 2 (2002).

Starr, Chester G. *Political Intelligence in Classical Greece*. Mnemosyne Supplement 21, Leiden: Brill, 1974.

Sternadori, Miglena Mantcheva, and Esther Thorson. "Anonymous Sources Harm Credibility of All Stories." *Newspaper Research Journal* 30, no. 4 (2009).

Stewart, Potter. "Or of the Press." *Hastings Law Journal* 26 (1975).

Stone, Geoffrey R. "Free Speech and National Security." *Indiana Law Journal* 84 (2009).

———. "Government Secrecy vs. Freedom of the Press." *Harvard Law and Policy Review* 185 (2007).

———. *Top Secret*. New York: Rowman and Littlefield, 2007.

———. *War and Liberty: An American Dilemma*. New York: W. W. Norton, 2007.

———. "Why We Need a Federal Reporter's Privilege." *Hofstra Law Review* 34, no. 39 (2005).

Story, Joseph. *Commentaries on the Constitution*. Vol. 2. Boston: Little, Brown & Co., 1858.

Straus, Oscar S. "Democracy and Open Diplomacy." In *The Foreign Relations of the United States*, ed. Henry R. Mussey and Stephen P. Duggan. New York: Academy of Political Science, 1917.

Strauss, David A. "Freedom of Speech and the Common-Law Constitution." In *Eternally Vigilant: Free Speech in the Modern Era*, ed. Lee C. Bollinger and Geoffrey R. Stone. Chicago: University of Chicago Press, 2003.

Stuart, Douglas T. *Creating the National Security State: A History of the Law That Transformed America*. Princeton, NJ: Princeton University Press, 2008.

Sunstein, Cass. "Government Control of Information." *California Law Review* 74, no. 3 (1986).

Sutherland, George. *Constitutional Power and World Affairs*. New York: Columbia University Press, 1919.

Svara, James H. *The Ethics Primer for Public Administrators in Government and Nonprofit Organization*. Boston: Jones and Bartlett, 2006.

Tarcov, Nathan. "The Federalists and Anti-Federalists on Foreign Affairs." *Teaching Political Science* 14, no. 1 (1986).

Telman, D. A. Jeremy. "Our Very Privileged Executive: Why the Judiciary Can (and Should) Fix the State Secrets Privilege." *Temple Law Review* 80, no. 2 (2007).

Theoharis, Athan G. *A Culture of Secrecy: The Government versus the People's Right to Know*. Lawrence, Kansas: University Press of Kansas, 1998.

Thomas, Helen. *Watchdogs of Democracy? The Waning Washington Press Corps and How It Failed the Public*. New York: Scribner, 2007.

Thompson, Dennis F. "Democratic Secrecy." *Political Science Quarterly* 114, no. 2 (1999).

———. *Political Ethics and Public Office*. Cambridge, MA: Harvard University Press, 1987.

———. *Restoring Responsibility: Ethics in Government, Business, and Healthcare*. New York: Cambridge University Press, 2004.

Tocqueville, Alexis de. *Democracy in America*. Trans. Harvey C. Mansfield and Delba Winthrop. Chicago: University of Chicago Press, 2000.

Treverton, Gregory F. "Intelligence: Welcome to the American Government." In *A Question of Balance: The President, the Congress, and Foreign Policy*, ed. Thomas E. Mann. Washington, DC: Brookings Institution Press, 1990.

Truelson, Judith A. "Whistleblowers and Their Protection." In *Handbook of Administrative Ethics*, ed. Terry L. Cooper. New York: Marcel Dekker, 1994.

Tuck, Richard. "The Dangers of Natural Rights." *Harvard Journal of Law & Public Policy* 20, no. 3 (1997).

Tucker, St. George. *View of the Constitution*. Ed. Clyde N. Wilson. Indianapolis: Liberty Fund, 1999.

Turner, Stansfield. *Secrecy and Democracy: The CIA in Transition*. Boston: Houghton Mifflin, 1985.

Unger, Craig. *American Armageddon*. New York: Scribner, 2007.

U.S. Merit Systems Protection Board Report. *The Federal Workforce for the 21st Century: Results of the Merit Principles Survey 2000*. Washington, DC: MSPB, 2003.

Van Dyke, Henry. *The American Birthright and the Philippine Pottage*. New York: Charles Scribner's Sons, 1898.

———. *Fighting for Peace*. New York: Scribner's Sons, 1917.

Vaughn, Robert. "Statutory Protection of Whistleblowers in the Federal Executive Branch." *University of Illinois Law Review* 1982, no. 3 (1982).

Verax, Theodorus [Clement Walker]. *Relations and Observations*. London, 1648.

Vladeck, Stephen I. "The Espionage Act and National Security Whistleblowing after Garcetti." *American University Law Review* 57, no. 5 (2008).

———. "Inchoate Liability and the Espionage Act: The Statutory Framework and the Freedom of the Press." *Harvard Law and Policy Review* 1, no. 1 (2007).

Von Holst, Hermann. *The Constitutional and Political History of the United States*. Trans. John J. Lalor and Paul Shorey. Chicago: Callaghan & Co., 1881.

Wald, Patricia M. "Two Unsolved Constitutional Problems." *University of Pittsburgh Law Review* 49 (1988).

Walsh, Lawrence. "Secrecy and the Rule of Law." *Oklahoma Law Review* 43 (1990).

Walzer, Michael. *Obligations: Essays on Disobedience, War, and Citizenship*. Cambridge, MA: Harvard University Press, 1970.

Washington, George. *The Writings of George Washington*. Ed. Chauncey Worthington Ford. New York: G. P. Putnam's Sons, 1891.

Wasserman, Edward. "A Critique of Source Confidentiality." *Notre Dame Journal of Law, Ethics, and Public Policy* 19 (2005).

Weaver, William, and Robert Pallitto. "State Secrets and Executive Power." *Political Science Quarterly* 120, no. 1 (2005).

Weber, Max. *Essays in Sociology*. Trans. C. Wright Mills and H. H. Gerth. New York: Routledge, 2007.

Weisband, Edward, and Thomas M. Franck. *Resignation in Protest*. New York: Viking Press, 1975.

Wells, Christina E. "Questioning Deference." *Missouri Law Review* 69 (2004).

———. "State Secrets and Executive Accountability." *Constitutional Commentary* 26 (2010).

Werhan, Keith. "Rethinking Freedom of the Press after 9/11." *Tulane Law Review* 82 (2008).

Wharton, Francis. *The Revolutionary Diplomatic Correspondence of the United States*. Washington, DC: GPO, 1889.

Wheeler, Burton K., and Paul F. Healy. *Yankee from the West*. New York: Octagon Books, 1977.

White, Laura. "The Need for Governmental Secrecy: Why the U.S. Government Must Be Able to Withhold Information in the Interest of National Security." *Virginia Journal of International Law* 43, no. 4 (2003).

Wiggins, James. *Freedom or Secrecy*. New York: Oxford University Press, 1956.

———. "Government Operations and the Public's Right to Know." *Federal Bar Journal* 19, no. 1 (1959).

Willoughby, Westle W. *The Constitutional Law of the United States*. New York: Baker, Voorhis & Co., 1910.

Wilson, James. *The Works*. Ed. R. G. McCloskey. Cambridge, MA: Harvard University Press, 1967.

Wilson, Woodrow. "Address to the League to Enforce Peace." In *President Wilson's Great Speeches*. Chicago: Stanton and Van Vliet, 1917.

———. *Congressional Government: A Study in American Politics*. Boston: Houghton Mifflin Co., 1901.

———. "Fourteen Points." In *Woodrow Wilson: Essential Writings and Speeches of the Scholar-President*, ed. Mario R. Di Nunzio. New York: New York University Press, 2006.

Wolkinson, Herman. "Demands of Congressional Committees for Executive Papers—Part I." *Federal Bar Journal* 10 (1949).

Wood, Gordon. *The Creation of the American Republic: 1776–1787*. Chapel Hill: University of North Carolina Press, 1998.

Woodward, Bob. *Veil: The Secret Wars of the CIA, 1981–87*. New York: Simon and Schuster, 2005.

Wright, Quincy. *The Control of American Foreign Relations*. New York: Macmillan, 1922.

Writson, Henry M. *Executive Agents in American Foreign Relations*. Baltimore: Johns Hopkins University Press, 1929.

Xanders, Edward L. "A Handyman's Guide to Fixing National Security Leaks: An Analytical Framework for Evaluating Proposals to Curb Unauthorized Publication of Classified Information." *Journal of Law and Politics* 5, no. 4 (1989).

Yoo, John. "Courts at War." *Cornell Law Review* 91, no. 2 (2006).

Zagel, James. "The State Secrets Privilege." *Minnesota Law Review* 50 (1965).

Index